Thomas Jefferson Conant

The Book of Genesis

the common version revised for the American Bible union with explanatory notes

Thomas Jefferson Conant

The Book of Genesis

the common version revised for the American Bible union with explanatory notes

ISBN/EAN: 9783337100094

Printed in Europe, USA, Canada, Australia, Japan

Cover: Foto ©Lupo / pixelio.de

More available books at **www.hansebooks.com**

GENESIS.

REVISED VERSION

WITH

EXPLANATORY NOTES.

THE
BOOK OF GENESIS.

THE COMMON VERSION REVISED

FOR

THE AMERICAN BIBLE UNION,

WITH

EXPLANATORY NOTES.

BY THOMAS J. CONANT.

New York:
AMERICAN BIBLE UNION, No. 32 GREAT JONES STREET.
LONDON: TRÜBNER & CO., 60 PATERNOSTER ROW.

1873.

THOMAS HOLMAN, PRINTER,
Corner Centre and White Streets, New York.

INTRODUCTION.

§ 1.

Object of the Book, and its Relation to the divine Canon.

THE object of the book is to reveal to us the origin of the material universe; man's origin and relation to God the Creator, and the equality of all men before him; the divinely constituted relation of the sexes; the divine institution of the Sabbath; the origin of moral and physical evil; the primæval history of the human race, and the origin of nations;* the selection of one as the depository of the sacred records, and of the divine purpose and method for man's redemption; the history of its ancestral founders, and their relation to its subsequent history.

Of these truths, to the knowledge of which we owe the present advancement in civilization, it is the object of the book to furnish a divinely accredited record. Its value is apparent on the face of the above statement, and is attested by the history of civilization; for without it, no amount of intellectual culture, of refinement in taste, of progress in the sciences and arts, has ever been found sufficient to save a people from moral corruption, and ultimate decay and ruin. In these truths, and the divine attestation of them, lies the only basis of popular progress, and of permanent national prosperity; and on all these we should be in the profoundest ignorance, without the revelations contained in this book.†

From this results its relation to the divine canon. Its teachings are presupposed in all subsequent revelations, and are assumed to be known to the reader. Passing allusions are made to them, in which they are recognized as known; but no formal, full, and connected statement of them is elsewhere made, as though it were not already done and familiar to

---

* Compare the suggestions of one of the most profound of philosophical thinkers, quoted in the third foot-note on p. 49.

† Compare the striking remarks of Auberlen, quoted in the foot-note on p. 50.

the reader. The ground-truths, on which the whole structure of religious teaching rests, are assumed to have been already taught; such, for example, as the relation of the material world to the Supreme Being, who created it out of nothing, and who therefore controls all the forces of its elements, brought into existence by him, and hence subject to his will; the relation of man, in his material and spiritual nature, to the Being who created him, and who therefore has a sovereign right to control the use of the powers which he created; a right paramount to that of the creature himself, who possesses these powers by the gift of Him who brought them into being; the cause of the moral and physical evils that universally prevail, throughout the world and among all races and generations of men; the divine origin and universal obligation of the positive institutions of marriage and the Sabbath; the inviolable sanctity of human life in every individual, until forfeited by his own violation of it in another; the initiatory steps for perpetuating the knowledge of the true God, and for carrying into effect the divine plan for the redemption of the race.

These are the ground-work of all subsequent teachings, and in all of them are assumed as known.

Moreover, the histories of various personages, treated of here in their minutest details, are often referred to as already known; so that no part of subsequent revelation could be understood, without a familiar acquaintance with this book.

Such is its place in the divine canon.

§ 2.

*Divine Authority and Inspiration of the Book.**

THE claim of this book, to be regarded as a part of divine revelation, is established beyond question by the authority of Christ and his apostles. It was a part of that collection of sacred writings, the Oracles of God, which were committed to the care and guardianship of the Jewish people (Rom 3 : 2). Of these writings, collectively, the Savior and his apostles often speak as the word of God; recognizing, and directly asserting, their divine authority and inspiration. See such passages, for example, as Matt. 5 : 17-19; John 5 : 39; Rom. 3 : 2; Matt. 22 : 43, and Mark 12 : 36; 2 Tim. 3 : 16; 1 Pet. 1 : 10-12; 2 Pet. 1 : 21. This book was, therefore, as a part of those divine writings (called in the New Testament the Scrip-

---

* The remarks in this section are repeated here from § 1 of the writer's Introduction to the *Book of Job, Part Second.*

tures, the Holy Scriptures, the Oracles of God) expressly recognized by the Savior and his apostles as of divine authority, and was declared to be "profitable for teaching, for reproof, for correction, for instruction in righteousness" (2 Tim. 3 : 16).

The genuineness of the book (in other words, that it is a DIVINE BOOK; that, in this sense, it is not a spurious production) is thus established by the highest authority. It is a question of less importance by whom the book was written; and this will be considered in § 5. In regard to many books of the Old Testament, this can not be determined with certainty. Nor is this necessary to be known; nor would it by itself prove their inspiration and divine authority, which must rest on other grounds.*

§ 3.

Composition of the Book.

THE attentive reader will observe very marked peculiarities in the composition of the book.

There are striking variations of style and manner, not only in treating of subjects differing in their nature, where it might be expected, but also where the subjects are of the same general character. These variations are observable even in a translation, and still more so in the original text, where words and forms of expression, familiar to some portions, are never found in others. With these variations in the general manner of the writer are connected certain other peculiarities, which mark the transition from one portion to another. In the first subdivision of the book, for example, embracing the first chapter and the first three verses of the second, the name of the Divine Being is uniformly GOD. In the second, extending from the fourth verse of the second chapter to the end of the third, it is uniformly JEHOVAH GOD.† In the third, contained in the fourth chapter, it is uniformly JEHOVAH.‡ In the fourth, contained in the fifth chapter, it is again uniformly GOD.§

---

* The authority of a writing, claimed to be divine, does not in any case rest on the particular writer or human instrumentality, but on the divine attestation given to it; and this attestation can be given, as in many cases it has been, to writings which have come to us anonymously, and of which the particular writer can not be determined with certainty.

† Except in the quoted words of the tempter's address to Eve, and of her reply (ch. 3 : 1-5), which are not the language of the narrator.

‡ Except in the quoted language of Eve, v. 25. Compare the note on v. 26, third paragraph.

§ Except in v. 29, in the words quoted from Lamech. Compare the fourth paragraph of the note on that verse, and the note on ch. 4 : 26, the last paragraph.

In the subsequent portions of the book, the alternations are more frequent and less regular, but no less distinctly marked.

For the object of this section it is not necessary to add further illustrations on this point.* But the careful reader will also observe, that there are portions where the name GOD is chiefly employed, with the occasional use of the name JEHOVAH, in which the sense is complete, and the connection clear, without the passages containing the latter name. Take, for example, chs. 6–10. If the reader will inclose in brackets the passages containing the name JEHOVAH, namely, v. 3 and vv. 6–8 in ch. 6, vv. 1–6 and the last clause of v. 16 in ch. 7, vv. 20–22 in ch. 8, vv. 20–29 in ch. 9, and v. 9 in ch. 10, he will find that the thread of the narrative is unbroken, and the sense complete, when this portion is read without these passages. They make additional statements which are important in themselves, but are not necessary to the coherency of the narrative.

The natural inference is, that the Book of Genesis consists of different revelations, made at different times, anterior to the age of the inspired writer to whom we owe its present form; and that he embodied them in a connected narrative, supplying what was wanting in one from the others and adding himself what was necessary for its completion.†

This conclusion is strengthened by the character of large portions of its contents, consisting of genealogies, or accounts of births and other incidents of family history,‡ long anterior to the age of Moses, the writer of the book (§ 5).

Of the date of the earliest of these divine communications there is no intimation. But it would be unreasonable to suppose that the ancient patriarchs, Enoch and Noah who "walked with God," Abraham the "Friend of God," had no authentic and divinely attested record of these truths, on which their own relation to the Divine Being depended, and without the knowledge of which it could not be understood. We have therefore reason for holding, that these earliest revelations come to us from the inspiration of the remote and unknown past, beyond the date of the writings of Moses himself.§

---

* In *Smith's Bible Dictionary*, article Genesis, C, 3, (1)—(7), the details are fully given. Paragraphs (1)—(3) give all the passages in which these names are severally used, either exclusively, or with occasional exceptions, for the most part readily accounted for.

† This in no degree detracts from the divine authority of the book, which (as already remarked in § 2, second foot-note) depends not on the human writer, or on our knowledge of him, but on the divine attestation; and this is given to the book itself, irrespective of the human instrumentality through which it was communicated.

‡ Compare the note on ch. 2 : 4, second paragraph.

§ Compare the note on ch. 14 : 2, second paragraph, and ch. 36 : 2, 3, note, third paragraph.

§ 4.

Unity of Plan in the Book. Its Divisions and Contents.

THE book first reveals God's relation to the universe, and to its sentient and intelligent occupants, as the Creator and rightful Proprietor and Sovereign of all.

It then records the early history and universal corruption of man, and the interposition of divine justice in the destruction of the guilty race.

It then proceeds with the general history of the new race of man, till it becomes manifest that the signal lesson is without effect, that the tendency to evil is innate and universal, and that there is no power of self-renovation.

It then records the initiatory steps of the divine arrangement for the renovation of man, and for perpetuating the knowledge and worship of the true God.

Thenceforward it is occupied with the personal history of the family, in whom and their descendants this divine purpose was to be carried into effect. In the details of their history, as in the subsequent history of the nation, it is made evident that the wonderful truths of which they were the depository did not originate from themselves, but were divinely communicated.*

In all this there is a manifest unity of design, indicating a special purpose and aim in the composition of the book.

It should be observed of this, as of every other part of the divine volume, that it is not a declaration of abstract principles, or of abstract truths, which convince without moving. It takes hold on the life, through its

---

* If an intellectual and philosophic people, such as the Greeks for example, with a capacity for acute and metaphysical speculation, had been selected as the depository of these truths, it might with more show of reason be maintained, that they originated in the tendencies of the national mind. But how should the pure monotheism of the Hebrew Scriptures, the doctrine of the One Eternal God, have originated with a people ever prone to idolatry? And whence was that light which illumined Palestine, a mere patch on the earth's surface, while all other nations, the world around, were enveloped in darkness? And whence were those conceptions of God and his attributes sung by Psalmists and Prophets, and now the ground-work of the highest civilization to which man has ever attained, while Homer and Hesiod were singing of the gods of Olympus and the mythic fables of the Theogony? He who believes that the unphilosophical and unlearned Hebrews outstripped the most intellectual and wisest nations of antiquity, put to shame their learning and philosophy, and have become the instructors of the most enlightened nations of modern times, believes a greater wonder than the divine inspiration of the Hebrew Scriptures.

details of life, and influences action by showing the power and tendencies of principles in action. The minuteness of its details of every-day life is therefore in harmony with its spirit and purpose, as it is with all other parts of the divine word; and on these depends its power, instrumentally, as an element in progressive civilization.

The general divisions and contents of the book are as follows:

First division, chs. 1-3. Account of the Creation, and of the entrance of moral evil into the world.

Second division, chs. 4-9. Account of sinful man, and of the prevalence of irreligion and immorality, from the fall to the first universal manifestation of divine justice in the destruction of the guilty race.

Third division, chs. 10, 11. Continued development of its history and proof of its alienation from the true God, and of the want of a self-renovating power.

Fourth division, chs. 12-50. Initiation, and progressive steps, of the divine arrangement for the renovation of the race.

The contents of the more minute subdivisions are prefixed to each, in the explanatory notes.

§ 5.

Writer of the Book.

The truths recorded in the Book of Genesis are presupposed as known in the books which follow it in the Pentateuch, and in all the subsequent books of the Hebrew Scriptures. The Book of Exodus takes up and continues the history, from the point where it is left in Genesis, with an express reference to what had been related in that book.* It recognizes incidentally, as known facts, God's "covenant with Abraham, with Isaac, and with Jacob" (ch. 2 : 24), his relation to them as "the God of Abraham, the God of Isaac, and the God of Jacob" (ch. 3 : 6), and their posterity as "his people" (v. 7), styling him "the God of their fathers" (vv. 13, 15, 16), and "Jehovah, God of their fathers, the God of Abraham, the God of Isaac, and the God of Jacob" (ch. 4 : 5); his "appearing to Abraham, to Isaac, and to Jacob," and his "covenant with them to give them the land of Canaan, the land of their sojournings" (ch. 6 : 3-5 and 8); the charge given by Joseph (Gen. 50 : 25) respecting his remains (ch. 13 : 19); the

---

* Compare Exodus, 1 : 1-8.

institution of the Sabbath (ch. 16 : 5, and 22–30*); the six days of creation and the rest on the seventh (ch. 20 : 11).

These are only incidental allusions to things known, and necessarily presuppose the revelations and historical details in this book, to which they refer.

Without these revelations, the Hebrews would have had no knowledge of the God whom they were required to worship and obey, as the Creator and Supreme Lawgiver, or of the guilt of idolatry as a sin against him. Without these historical details, the frequent allusions to their connection with the early patriarchs, and with the promises made to them, would have been an unintelligible enigma.

The Book of Genesis was therefore an integral and necessary part of that divine code, which, under the name Law (Deut. 31 : 9, 24), Law of Jehovah (Ex. 13 : 9), Book of the Law of God (Josh. 24 : 26), Book of the Law of Moses (Josh. 23 : 6), Law of Moses (1 Kings 2 : 3), is ascribed to him as the writer. This is claimed by himself, in the body of the code. It is there said, that "Moses wrote this law" (Deut. 31 : 9), that he "made an end of writing the words of this law in a book, until they were finished" (Deut. 31 : 24).

That the writings which bore this general name, including Genesis, were from the hand of Moses, is thus proved by his own assertion, and by the uniform testimony of the writers nearest to his own age.

The Book of Genesis comes to us, therefore, with the authority of the inspired Lawgiver, having the same divine attestation as the writings first communicated through him.

§ 6.

Account of the Creation.

The book opens with the grandest theme that ever occupied the thoughts of created intelligences; the Work of God, in bringing into being the material universe, and peopling it with organic, conscious, and spiritual life.† The style and manner of treatment are in harmony with the grandeur of the theme. In few and powerful strokes, the progressive stages of

---

* Compare the note on Gen. 2 : 3, third and following paragraphs.

† Compare the sublime allusion to this in Job 38 : 7;
  When the morning-stars sang together,
  And all the sons of God shouted for joy!

the work are pictured to the mind, on a scale of magnificence unparalleled in writings human or divine.

It is much to be regretted that these characteristic traits of the account of the Creation, shadowing forth its impenetrable mysteries in broad and general outlines, should have been overlooked in its interpretation. This sublime Epic of Creation, with its boldly figurative imagery, and poetic grandeur of conception and expression, has been subjected to a style of interpretation, suited only to a plain and literal record of the ordinary occurrences of life. Hence not only its true spirit, but its profound teachings, have been misconceived and misinterpreted; and its exhibition of the mysteries of creative power, which science traces in its own observation of Nature, have been confounded with popular misapprehensions, irreconcilable with the well-known facts of science.

It is now established, beyond question, that the earth we inhabit was brought into existence many ages before man was created. During these ages it was in process of formation, and was gradually prepared, under the divine direction, for its future occupation by man. In those vast periods, succeeding each other in long procession, it was fitted up for his abode by accumulations of mineral wealth within its bosom. These processes required ages for their completion, as represented in the sacred narrative, and recorded by the divine hand in the successive strata enveloping the earth, and marking the progressive stages of its formation.*

The writer has no claim to speak as a geologist, and does not profess to do so. He takes the teachings of geology as given us by eminent masters of the science, entitled to speak on its behalf.† But speaking as an interpreter of God's word, and taking their representation of their own science, he sees no discordance between the two records, which the same divine Author has given us in his word and in his works. The former, when rightly interpreted, is in perfect accord with the latter, when truly exhibited. And geologists themselves assert, that the word of God, so interpreted, is in harmony with the teachings of their science. This alone is sufficient to satisfy the candid and conscientious inquirer. But they assert also, that the divine word explains the divine work, while the divine work

---

* "Every great feature in the structure of the planet corresponds with the order of the events narrated in the sacred history."—*Prof. Silliman, Outline of Geological Lectures*, appended to *Bakewell's Geology*, p. 67, note. "This history furnishes a record important alike to philosophy and religion; and we find in the planet itself the proof that the record is true" (p. 30).

† *Guyot, Lectures on the Concordance of the Mosaic Account of the Creation with that given by Modern Science*, 1852. A full abstract, revised by himself, is given in the *Bibliotheca Sacra* for 1855, vol. xii., pp. 324 and following.

Dana, Manual of Geology, art. Cosmogony, pp. 741–746 (revised edition, 1864).

confirms the divine word. Moreover, no human philosophy could have discovered, or conjectured, what is here revealed.* The divine record was made when science had not yet penetrated the mysteries of Nature ; when the earth's record of its own history was still buried deep in its enveloping strata, and had been read by no human eye. As, therefore, no one witnessed the scenes described, or had read the "testimony of the rocks," the written account if true, as science admits it to be, must have been of superhuman origin.

The successive stages in the account of the Creation are as follows :

1. The act of bringing matter into being. Its condition as "waste and empty," and subjection to the divine influence imparting to it its active properties. Production of light, as the first effect of this imparted action.†

2. Separation of the fluid mass into waters above and waters below.

3. Separation of land and water on the earth. Vegetation, beginning with its lowest orders.

4. Sun, moon, and stars.

5. Animal life, beginning with inhabitants of the waters the lowest in the scale, and winged species on the land.

6. Terrestrial animals, in ascending grades. MAN, and his dominion over all.‡

These periods of creative activity, and the cessation that followed, were presented to the mind of the sacred writer under the familiar symbolism of the six days of labor and the seventh of rest. This was a natural and intelligible application of it ; the word *day*, the simplest and most familiar measure of time, being used in all languages for any period of duration, of greater or less extent ;§ and it is specially appropriate in such a style of

---

* "No human mind was witness of the events; and no such mind in the early age of the world, unless gifted with superhuman intelligence, could have contrived such a scheme;—would have placed the creation of the sun, the source of light to the earth, so long after the creation of light, even on the *fourth* day, and, what is equally singular, between the creation of plants and that of animals, when so important to both; and none could have reached to the depths of philosophy exhibited in the whole plan."—*Dana, Manual of Geology*, art. Cosmogony, p. 743.

† Styled *cosmical* in distinction from *solar* light.

‡ "In this succession," says Prof. Dana (*Manual of Geology*, as above, p. 745), "we observe not merely an order of events, like that deduced from science ; there is a system in the arrangement, and a far-reaching prophecy, to which philosophy could not have attained, however instructed."

§ In the Hebrew Scriptures it is used : 1. For past or future time without limit ; Isaiah 30 : 8, "that it may be for the time (day) to come, forever and ever ;" Prov. 31 : 25, "she shall rejoice in time (day) to come." 2. For a future prophetic period of indefinite length ; Isaiah 2 : 11, 17, "Jehovah alone shall be exalted in that day ;" Ezek. 38 : 14, "in that day, when my people of Israel dwells safely ;" compare Isaiah 11 : 10, 11 ; Hos. 2 : 16, 18, 21 ; Micah 4 : 6 ; Zech. 2 : 11, 3 : 10, 12 : 9. 3. For an epoch, or a period of time, in history ; Judges 18 : 1, "for unto that

representation as we find in this chapter. The word *day* is used in various ways in this brief account of the Creation; in ch. 1 : 5, for *light*, without reference to duration, and also for a period of alternating light and darkness; in v. 14, for a period of light alone (in distinction from *night*), and also for the full natural day including both; and in ch. 2 : 4, it is used for the whole period of time occupied in the work of creation. These various applications result naturally from its primary use; and the examples given in the foot-note show that its use for periods of indefinite duration is common in the Hebrew Scriptures.

The six days of labor, and the seventh of rest, having been adopted as the symbolism under which these sublime mysteries are revealed, whatever properly belongs to it, and is essential to its full expression, is pertinent to the writer's object. Each period being represented by a day, its beginning and end are described in terms proper to represent a day, "there was evening and there was morning." This was necessary, in order to preserve the symbolic representation.*

It should be observed that the sacred writer, throughout this account, represents things under forms of expression most easily apprehended by the common mind. The narrative was given to instruct, and not to perplex and confound the common reader, as it would have done if expressed in scientific forms, adapted to a higher stage of culture than the Bible requires, or could properly presuppose, in its readers.

Such a view of the sacred narrative exalts our conception of the divine Architect, and of his work. He who inhabits eternity has no need to be in a hurry. With him, a thousand years are as one day.† 'It was not till ages of preparation had passed away, that his purposes found their entire fulfillment, and his work its completed unity, in the creation of man. See the writer's remarks on vv. 26-28 of the first chapter.

---

day" (the time referred to in the two preceding clauses, "in those days there was no king," etc.); 20 : 15, "at that time" (day), namely, that period of their history; 1 Sam. 8 : 18, "in that day," namely, the period of his arbitrary rule, and oppressive exactions, described in vv. 11-17; Deut. 31 : 17, 18 (referring to an age of idolatry, v. 16) "my anger shall be kindled against them in that day, . . . and I will surely hide my face in that day." 4. For a season of the year; Prov. 25 : 13, "as the coolness of snow in the time (day) of harvest;" 2 Sam. 23 : 20, "in the time (day) of snow." 5. For a period of life, as of old age; Eccles. 12 : 3, "in the day when the keepers of the house shall tremble." 6. For any specified time of indefinite length; 1 Sam. 3 : 2, "at that time" (day), the time referred to in the preceding verse.

* It is hardly to be supposed, that a practiced exegete would make a mere incident of the figurative costume an objection to the symbolic representation, as though a literal day must be meant, because a literal day is described. Yet this mistake has been made.

† "In the plan of an infinite God, centuries are required for the maturing of some of the plants with which the earth is adorned."—*Dana, Manual of Geology* (as above, p. 744).

According to the distinguished teachers of science referred to in the second foot-note on p. xvi., the account of the creation recognizes two great eras, an *inorganic* and an *organic*, consisting of three days each; each era opening with the appearance of light, that of the first being cosmical, that of the second solar for the special uses of the earth.*

It need not be supposed, that the sacred writer read in these wonderful revelations all the mysteries which they contain, or that they were seen by those to whom the revelations were first addressed. It was not necessary that he or they should be made wise in physical learning beyond the wants of their time; and the symbolism itself conveyed all the instruction they needed. So it was with the prophets of the Jewish people, when they foretold the universal extension of the Divine Kingdom in symbolism familiar to the Jewish mind; as when it is said (Isaiah 2 : 2), that "in the last days the mountain of Jehovah's house shall be established in the top of the mountains, . . . and all the nations shall flow to it." The profound and far-reaching truths, conveyed in these prophetic words, are now clearly understood by us, even though the prophet, and those whom he addressed, may not have looked beyond the instructive and impressive symbolism in which they were vailed.

A reconciliation of the Biblical account with the facts of Geological science has been attempted on another theory; namely, that the several stages in the earth's formation took place in an assumed interval of time between the first and second verses; an interval of vast and indefinite length, unnoticed by the sacred writer. During this interval, the successive processes in the formation of the earth were completed, and the successive orders of vegetable and animal life, the remains of which are found imbedded in its strata, were brought into existence and perished. The account of the present state of things on the earth's surface begins with the description in the second verse, representing the chaotic condition of its surface after the last of its great internal convulsions; and what follows, in vv. 3–31, occurred in six natural days of twenty-four hours.

---

* "I. Inorganic era:
 1st Day.—LIGHT cosmical.
 2d Day.—The earth divided from the fluid around, or individualized.
 3d Day.— { 1. Outlining of the land and water.
            { 2. Creation of vegetation.
 II. Organic era:
 4th Day.—LIGHT from the sun.
 5th Day.—Creation of the lower orders of animals.
 6th Day.— { 1. Creation of Mammals.
            { 2. Creation of Man."—*Dana, Manual of Geology* (as above, p. 745).

The objections to this theory are :

1. There is no foundation for it in the sacred writer's statement. He gives no intimation of such an interval. It is thrust in, where there is no indication that it was present to his mind, and no reason for it in the connection.

2. It assumes that the sacred writer has not given us an account of the Creator's work, but only of a part of it; that for unknown ages the earth was peopled with vegetable and animal life, of which no record is made.

3. It is without support in the facts ascertained by science. Scientific investigation shows that no such convulsion, as is assumed in this theory, occurred at the period preceding the creation of man.

Hence the latest advocates of this theory* are driven to the assumption, that what is revealed in vv. 3–31 has reference only to a small area of western Asia; being nothing more than the reconstruction of that little segment of the earth's surface, broken up and thrown into confusion by an internal convulsion, and the creation there of the new orders of vegetable and animal life that now occupy the globe.

On this supposition, the earth had already enjoyed the full light of the sun for ages, before the work of the first day (v. 3) began. Even then, all around this little tract, the earth was in a blaze of light; but over this tract dense mists shut out the rays of the sun. God said: "Let there be light!" The mists grew thinner, letting in sufficient light for the time, though not enough to disclose the forms of the heavenly orbs, which were not seen there till the fourth day, though visible everywhere else. Then follow, in rapid successions of single days, the formation of continents and seas, the clothing of the earth with vegetation, and the peopling of it with the various classes of irrational animals, and finally with MAN.

The infinite God has not revealed his work of creation on such a scale as this; and its proportions are better suited to the conception of the timid interpreter, stumbling at minute difficulties and seeking to evade them, than to the grand and fearless exposition of his work from God's own hand.

4. It is an unworthy conception of the Creator and of his work. Why was the work of creation extended through six natural days, when a single divine volition would have brought the whole universe into being, with all its apparatus for the support of life, and its myriads of living beings? Its extension through six successive periods, of whatever duration, can be explained only by the operation of those secondary causes, which the structure of the earth itself proves to have been active in its formation, requiring ages for their accomplishment.

---

* J. Pye Smith, *Geology and Scripture*; J. G. Murphy, *Commentary on the Book of Genesis*.

REVISED VERSION

WITH

EXPLANATORY NOTES.

GENESIS.

1 IN the beginning, God created the heavens and the earth.
2 Now the earth was waste and empty; and darkness was

Chap. 1 : 1—2 : 3. First part of the first division: *General account of the Creation; Institution of the Sabbath.*

The first verse declares that divine act of creative power, which brought this material universe into being.

It is a brief declaration of these great truths: 1. That the material universe, and all it contains, had no origin,—were not self-existing from eternity. 2. That they were created by the act of an intelligent and almighty Being,—were not the result of chance, or of the action of elementary principles of matter. 3. That the Being who created them is GOD.

How worthy of its place, at the beginning of a revelation from God! Imagine the book placed in our hands for the first time. On opening it, we read, in the first sentence, "In the beginning, God created the heavens and the earth." What could divine wisdom have suggested that would have been more appropriate? It solves the first and greatest question, on which the thoughtful inquirer seeks information, Whence is this world, of which I am a part? It declares also God's relation to this world and its occupants, as their only rightful proprietor and sovereign. For what he has made from nothing is absolutely his, and at his disposal.

This sentence combines all the elements of sublimity; for nothing can exceed the grandeur of the thought, or the simplicity, conciseness, and majesty of the expression.

V. 1. *In the beginning:* with reference to the universe, of which the writer is speaking. It was the beginning, the origin, of the material universe.

Created. It has been maintained of late, and by devout Christian scholars, that the Hebrew verb does not mean *to create*, but *to shape, to form;* and consequently we have no assertion, here or elsewhere in the Scriptures, of the absolute creation of the world out of nothing, by an act of divine power. The reasons for this opinion are: 1. That the etymological ground-meaning of the verb, as shown by that form of it which usually exhibits the primary sense, is *to cut, to hew, to shape* by hewing. 2. That it is sometimes used, in the Scriptures, where it can not be intended to express a creation out of nothing.

But, on the contrary, it should be observed: 1. That all verbs have, for their etymological ground-meaning, a physical act perceptible to the senses, from which proceed their secondary, which are the most usual, significations. 2. That this verb, out of the form which expresses the primary physical meaning, has always God for its subject, and is used only when something *new, not before existing*, is produced, brought into existence, by the power of God. See, for example, Ex. 34 : 10, properly, " Such as have not been created" (brought into existence) " in all the earth;" Num. 16 : 30, properly, "if Jehovah create a new thing;" Jer. 31 : 22; Isaiah 4: 5; 41: 20, " the Holy One of Israel has created it" (brought it into existence); 45 : 8; 48 : 7; 57: 19; 65: 17, 18. 3. That in this account of the creation, it is accurately distinguished from the Hebrew verb meaning *to make* either from nothing or from already existing material, and from the verb meaning *to form* out of such material, and hence is never accompanied by a word denoting the material of which a thing is made. 4. That in ch. 2 : 3 it is expressly said, " which God created in making it,"—that is, made by creation.

V. 2. The form of the earth, and its internal structure, show that it was originally in the state here described. How long it continued in that state is not indicated.

It was *waste and empty;* namely, without order or productiveness, a barren waste, empty of

over the face of the abyss; and the Spirit of God was brooding over the face of the waters.

3 And God said: Let there be light; and there was light. 4 And God saw the light, that it was good. And God divided 5 between the light and the darkness. And God called the light Day; and the darkness he called Night. And there was evening, and there was morning, one day.

6 And God said: Let there be an expanse in the midst of 7 the waters; and let it divide waters from waters. And God

---

all the beautiful varieties of organized life with which it was afterward filled. Compare the opposite description, in Psalm 104: 24, "The earth is full of thy riches."

Over the dark abyss the *Spirit of God was brooding*; imparting to lifeless matter powers which give it an active agency in working out the divine purposes. The Hebrew word *brooding* is highly significant; being used of fowls, *brooding* over their eggs and imparting the vivifying warmth. So the divine power is represented as acting upon the mass of inert matter, imparting the properties necessary to its proper organization, so as to fit it for sustaining vegetable life, and to be the abode of animated and intelligent beings.

V. 3. One of the most essential agencies of nature is *light*. Hence the production of it at this stage of creation, as being necessary for those processes of development which must precede the formation of vegetables and animals.

The nature of light, and its physical cause, are still among the unsettled problems of natural philosophy, and no satisfactory solution of them can be given. Hence, objections to the sacred narrative, founded on any of the theories of light and its production, are without just ground.

V. 5. *And there was evening;* namely, the close of a period of light by the coming on of darkness; *and there was morning*, the close of a period of darkness by the return of light; the two periods making a day.

This is the true idea of evening and morning. By *evening* is meant, in Hebrew as well as in English, the coming on of darkness after a period of light; in other words, the close of day by the coming on of night. There could be no evening, without a previous period of light.

Day began, therefore, with light and not with darkness; and one day continued, till the returning light marked the commencement of another.

The later custom of the Hebrews (Lev. 23: 32), of reckoning the day from evening to evening, was made necessary by the use of the lunar calendar, in the observance of their feasts and other commemorative seasons, which depended on the return of the new moon. Where the natural day is meant, as in Lev. 7: 15, it closes with the morning of the following day.

VV. 6, 7. These verses describe the effect of the formation of the earth's atmosphere, under the divine agency and direction, from its elements in the yet unorganized earth. The result was, as described in v. 7, the separation of the dense sea of vapors above, from the waste of waters below, by the intervening expanse.

The *expanse* (properly, what is *outspread*) is so called from its apparent limit in the blue vault above, where the heavenly bodies appear, and along which the fowls fly (v. 20). This is not inconsistent with the explanation here given of the separation of the waters. The sacred writer describes this process, as he does others, in terms suggested by the senses, as being most readily understood.

Observe that the sacred writer says, *God made the expanse*,—not, necessarily, created it; the atmosphere being composed of elements already existing. Compare No. 3, in the third paragraph on v. 1.

But what wisdom and power were necessary, to combine those elements in exact proportions fitted for the support of vegetable and animal life, and with a density suited to the transmission of light to the organ of vision; and so to adjust the elements of earth and air to each other, that, through thousands of ages, these delicate proportions should never be essentially disturbed!

And it was so; that is, it became fixed and established, just as God willed and ordered it.

made the expanse ; and he divided the waters which are under the expanse from the waters which are above the expanse ; and it was so. And God called the expanse Heavens. And there was evening, and there was morning, a second day.

9 , And God said : Let the waters under the heavens gather themselves to one place, and let the dry land appear ; and 10 it was so. And God called the dry land Earth, and the gathering together of the waters he called Seas ; and God saw that it was good.

11 And God said : Let the earth put forth shoots, herb setting seed, fruit-tree bearing fruit after its kind, in which is 12 its seed, above the earth ; and it was so. And the earth brought forth shoots, herb setting seed after its kind, and tree producing fruit, in which is its seed, after its kind ; and 13 God saw that it was good. And there was evening, and there was morning, a third day.

14 And God said : Let there be lights in the expanse of the heavens, for dividing between the day and the night ; and

---

V. 14. Lights: *or*, luminaries

VV. 9, 10. These verses describe the effects of the upheaving from the abyss of the portions of the earth which had now become solidified. These, as is proved by their structure, and by the substances composing them, had been formed under the waters ; and they were now, by the action of internal forces, raised above the surface. This was effected by the will of that almighty Power, who controls the agencies of nature, and is himself their efficient cause. As these solid portions are forced upward, the waters subside and " the dry land appears."

To *one place* means, apart, by themselves. That more than one receptacle is meant, is evident from the plural *seas*, in v. 10. By " the gathering together of the waters," is meant every such gathering.

VV. 11-13. The earth is now in a proper condition for producing and sustaining vegetable life. A suitable soil is formed, by the processes which have been going on among the primary elements of the earth, and by the exposure of its surface, now left dry, to the action of air, light, and warmth. But it could only be by a divine power that these elements originally produced the delicate and complicated organism of plants, with the wonderful endowment of vegetable life. For the vegetable life is not, any more than the animal life, the effect merely of a certain mechanical structure, with a certain combination of material elements. Both are divinely imparted principles, differing in their nature, but both communicating to inert matter peculiar powers of activity, growth, and strength.

And God said : Let the earth put forth shoots. From the earth sprang up, by the agency of divine power, these organized forms, endowed with vegetable life. The language expresses, in words, the will of the Creator, as declared by the exertion of his own power.

In which (fruit) *is its* (the tree's) *seed ;* that is, fruit-tree whose seed is in its fruit. *Above the earth ;* rising high above it, in distinction from the *herb*, just spoken of.

The different classes of vegetation here follow the order in which they are proved by science to have succeeded each other.

VV. 14-19. Institution of the two great lights, and their offices. These are : 1. To *divide*

let them be for signs and for seasons, and for days and years; and let them be for lights in the expanse of the heavens, for giving light on the earth; and it was so.

16 And God made the two great lights; the greater light for dominion over the day, and the lesser light for dominion over the night; and the stars. And God set them in the expanse of the heavens, to give light on the earth; and to rule over the day and over the night, and to divide between the light and the darkness; and God saw that it was good.

19 And there was evening, and there was morning, a fourth day.

20 And God said: Let the waters swarm with swarms of living beings; and let fowl fly above the earth, along the expanse of the heavens. And God created the great sea-monsters, and every living being that moves, with which the waters swarm, after their kind, and every winged fowl after its kind; and God saw that it was good. And God

---

V. 16. *Or*, great luminaries   *Ib. Or*, the greater luminary—the lesser luminary

between the day and the night, regulating the alternation of light and darkness. 2. To *be for signs*, and, as such, *for seasons*, by marking their return and duration, and *for days and years*. The last two are specially named, and in conjunction, as being the units of measure chiefly employed in the reckoning of time; while months, indicated by the phases of the moon, and the divisions of the year caused by the sun's progress between the equinoctial and solstitial points, are comprehended under the word *seasons*. 3. To give light on the earth.

Thus these heavenly bodies are the great regulators of life, on whose influences all its interests are made to depend, and whose motions chronicle the ages as they pass. Hence the dominion ascribed to them in Job 30 : 33,
    Knowest thou the ordinances of the heavens,
    or dost thou establish their dominion over earth?

It is said in v. 16: "God made" (not *created*; see No. 3, in the third paragraph on v. 1) "the two great lights." These bodies became lights to the earth, at the time when they were made its luminaries, or sources of light; and they were then "set" (v. 17) as lights for the earth, "in the expanse of the heavens."

The sun of our system is not a body of simple and uniform substance; nor is it known what changes were required in its physical constitution, after the creation of its substance, in order to make it the great luminary of our world. Hence the charge sometimes made against the sacred narrative, that it conflicts with the known truths of astronomy in regard to the structure of our planetary system, is shown by the teachings of that science to be without just ground.

Moreover, a certain condition of the earth's atmosphere was required. It was already fitted for the support of vegetable life, and for such transmission of the sun's influences as was necessary to that end. But the heavenly bodies could not be made luminaries of the earth, without a transparent medium, through which their light could be conveyed to it.

VV. 20-23. The sun has now become the great source of light and warmth to the earth, and the time has arrived for a higher stage of organic life, that of the animal creation. It begins with the lowest in the scale, the inhabitants of the waters; then follow the occupants of the air.

The account here given (vv. 20-23) indicates the ascending scale, from the lowest forms of animal life up to the highest, which science has traced in its vestiges in the earth itself.

V. 22. *Blessed them.* The blessing bestowed was the power of reproduction and of indefinite

blessed them, saying: Be fruitful, and multiply, and fill the
23 waters in the seas; and let fowl multiply on the earth. And there was evening, and there was morning, a fifth day.
24 And God said: Let the earth bring forth the living being after its kind, cattle, and reptile, and beast of the earth,
25 after its kind; and it was so. And God made the beast of the earth after its kind, and cattle after their kind, and every reptile of the ground after its kind; and God saw that it was good.
26 And God said: We will make man, in our image, after

multiplication, as expressed in the words which follow and define the meaning, namely, "Be fruitful, and multiply." It was expressed, of course not in words, but in the nature with which God endowed his creatures, and in the power of reproduction which he bestowed.

That the gift of conscious life, and the power of indefinite propagation of it, was truly a blessing, and was worthy of the divine Giver, will not be questioned by one who finds pleasure in witnessing its innocent enjoyments; nor will he doubt, that such provision for happiness, on a scale of inconceivable extent, is a worthy expression of the divine goodness.*

VV. 24–25. Another stage in the production of organic life, the creation of land animals.

The land is now, as well as the water and air, fitted to be the abode of animal life. Its surface is clothed with vegetation, and the air has become purified, and thus adapted to the support of animal life in its higher and more perfect forms.

VV. 24, 25. First, the irrational animals are brought into existence; and this accords with what science shows to have been the order of creation.

Let the earth bring forth. The bodies of animals are of the earth, being composed of the same material elements. Divested of its figurative form (so well suited to the tone of conception and representation in this chapter) the language means: Let there be living beings, of the substance of the earth. The boldly figurative form of the expression will not mislead the attentive reader, since it is immediately added (v. 25), "And God made the beast of the earth."

Beast of the earth: wild animals that roam the earth without restraint, in distinction from *cattle*, the domestic animals whose home is with man.

VV. 26–28. Last and highest stage in the production of organic life, the creation of man.

The world in its physical structure, and the earth itself, both in its physical constitution and in the capacities of its living occupants, have been fitted to subserve some other purpose than thus far appear in their history.

If we look to the earth, vast treasures of mineral wealth have been accumulated within its bosom, which there is none to use; and in its soil lie hidden boundless powers of productiveness, which there is none to call forth.

If we look to the heavens, there is none to investigate the laws that regulate their "dominion over the earth" and profit by their teachings, or even to be conscious of their influence, beyond a passing sensation terminating in itself. To every creature of the earth, outside of its own momentary sensations, creation is a blank; and all this expenditure of wisdom and power is without intelligible aim or purpose.

Looking to the moral aspects of the case, we see that thus far all the arrangements have been physical in their nature, ministering only to physical wants, and to enjoyments into which no moral element enters. The divine Architect of all is unrecognized in the wonders he has wrought, and among the living conscious beings his own hands have made.

The final act, the creation of one bearing the image and likeness of his Maker, capable of comprehending his works in all their extent and making them serviceable to himself, and of recognizing God in all, is proof of an intelligent and consistent plan, tending to and terminating in this, its crowning work.

V. 26. *We will make;* the language of purpose and resolve. The plural form does not nec-

* A beautiful illustration of this thought may be found in Paley's *Natural Theology*, ch. xxvi., on the goodness of the Deity, in the paragraph beginning, "Nor is the design abortive."

our likeness; and they shall rule over the fish of the sea, and over the fowl of the heavens, and over the cattle, and over all the earth, and over every reptile that creeps on the 27 earth. And God created the man, in his image; in the image of God created he him; a male and a female created 28 he them. And God blessed them; and God said to them: Be fruitful, and multiply, and fill the earth, and subdue it;

V. 26. *Or,* as our likeness

essarily express anything more than the dignity and majesty of the speaker; being often appropriated, by way of distinction, to personages of exalted rank and power.*

It has been held by many, however, that there is here, as in "*our image, our likeness,*" an intimation of the mystery of the divine personality, to be afterward more clearly revealed.

Man. The Hebrew is *adam,* kindred with the word meaning *ground.* It is first used strictly as a proper name (Adam) in ch. 4 : 25. It is here used collectively, as *man* is in English.

Image, and *likeness,* two words of nearly the same import, are used to express the thought more fully and strongly than could be done by any single term. *As our likeness* (margin), is a very probable rendering of the Hebrew; meaning, in our image, to be our likeness.

It was the spiritual nature of man that was made in the image and after the likeness of God; for God is spirit (John 4 : 24), and in no other than a spiritual sense could man be said to bear his image. How this is to be understood, we learn from what the apostle says of the "new man," in Eph. 4 : 24, where there is evident allusion (as appears from the parallel passage in Col. 3 : 10) to what is said here.

The rational, moral, and spiritual nature of man are all included in "the image" and "the likeness" of God, and were all essential to that supremacy which was given him over the earth and its occupants. The "image of God" did not, as some have thought, consist in that supremacy; man being said to bear the image of God, as one representing his sovereignty on earth. On the contrary, the sovereignty conferred on man presupposed those spiritual endowments, and was justified only by his fitness, through them, to exercise it.

A male and a female created he them; that is, one of each sex; thus declaring the Creator's law for the marriage relation, namely, that a man shall have but one wife, and a woman but one husband.

The reader will not fail to mark the peculiar glow and animation which characterize the expression in these verses. They contain the germ of the distinctive form of Hebrew poetry.

V. 28. *Fill the earth, and subdue it.* This requirement, in accordance with the design and scope of the first and more general account of the creation, respects the whole race of man; passing over the special provision for the first human pair, which belongs to the more particular account of them in the next chapter.

It was the will of the Creator, that the race of man should "fill the earth" (should occupy it), "and subdue it" (bring it under his control).

If we look at the earth, as prepared for the occupancy of man, we find little that is made ready for his use, but boundless material which his own labor and skill can fit for it.

The spontaneous fruits of the earth furnish a scanty and precarious subsistence, even to a few; but with skillful labor, it is made to yield an abundant supply for the "wants of every living thing."

On its surface, many natural obstacles are to be overcome. Forests must be leveled, rivers bridged over, roads and canals constructed, mountains graded or tunneled, and seas and oceans navigated.

Its treasures of mineral wealth lie hidden beneath its surface; and when discovered and brought to light, they are valueless to man, till his own labor subdues and fits them for his

---

* The rendering of the common English version, "Let us make," is not the meaning of the Hebrew. The questions, therefore, whether there was a consultation, and with whom it was held, and whether any other than the Divine Being (angels, as some have thought) took part in the work, are not raised by the language of the sacred writer.

and rule over the fish of the sea, and over the fowl of the heavens, and over every living thing that moves on the earth.

29 And God said: Behold, I have given to you every herb scattering seed, which is on the face of all the earth, and every tree, in which is the fruit of a tree, scattering seed, 30 to you shall it be for food; and to every beast of the earth, and to every fowl of the heavens, and to every thing that creeps on the earth, wherein is a spirit of life, all green herbage for food; and it was so.

31 And God saw all that he had made, and behold, it was very good. And there was evening, and there was morning, the sixth day.

1 And so were finished the heavens and the earth, and all 2 their host. And on the seventh day, God ended his work

service. The various useful metals lie in the crude ore, and must be passed through difficult and laborious processes before they can be applied to any valuable purpose. Iron, for example, the most necessary of all, how many protracted and delicate processes are required to separate it from impurities in the ore, to refine its texture, and to convert it into steel, before it can be wrought into the useful ax or knife, with the well tempered edge!

What an education for the race has been this labor of subduing the earth! How it has developed reflection, stimulated invention, and quickened the powers of combination, which would otherwise have lain dormant!

Nor are the collateral and remote less important than the direct and immediate results. He who takes a piece of timber from the common forest, and forms it into a useful implement, thereby makes it his own, and it can not rightfully be taken from him; since no one can justly appropriate to himself the product of another's skill and labor. So he who originally takes possession of an unappropriated field, and by his labor prepares it for use, thereby makes it his own, and it can not rightfully be taken from him. Hence arises the right of property, the origin and bond of civil society; and thus all the blessings of society, and of civiliz tion and government, are due to the divinely implanted impulse, "fill the earth, *and subdue it.*"

VV. 29, 30. Provision for the sustenance of man (v. 29), and of other animals (v. 30).

To man is assigned *every herb scattering seed* (propagated by seed) leaving him his choice among them of such as are suited to his nature and wants, as the different kinds of grain, pulse, etc.; and every fruit-tree in like manner, to choose among them what is suited to his taste, and adapted for his nourishment. To other animals is assigned *all green herbage*, without distinction.

V. 31. *God saw all that he had made, and behold, it was very good.* Nothing but what was good, *for its object*, could proceed from the allwise Creator. When men complain of imperfection in his works, it is because they propose other ends than those which he has in view.

The sixth day, being the last of the six days of creation, is for that reason distinguished by the definite article, as the completion of the series.

Ch. 2:1. There should be no division here, the first three verses belonging to the account given in the first chapter. The division should be made at the fourth verse, where another account begins.

VV. 1–3. *Institution of the Sabbath.*

Their host. This expression is often used of the heavenly bodies (as in Isaiah 45:12), moving like marshaled armies through the skies, and here includes by a familiar figure (*zeugma*) all the objects on the earth's surface.

V. 2. *Ended;* not *had ended*, which the form of the Hebrew verb here used never means.

which he made; and he rested on the seventh day from all ³ his work which he made. And God blessed the seventh day, and hallowed it; because on it he rested from all his work, which God created in making it.

⁴ THESE are the generations of the heavens and the earth,

The Creator did not cease from his work until the seventh day; and on that day, therefore, it came to an end. "He rested (ceased from the work of creation) on the seventh day," as is said in the following verse.

V. 3. *Blessed the seventh day*, distinguished it, above other days, by his special regard; *and hallowed it*, set it apart from common and worldly uses, and consecrated it as a season of sacred rest. His consecration of the day makes it sacred for all time; and his blessing has made it rich in temporal as well as spiritual benefits to the race of man.

The consecration of the seventh day (that is, of every seventh day, a seventh portion of time), was made from the beginning, for a reason of universal application, and therefore for all mankind. So long as men, in obedience to the divine requirement, labored six successive days and rested on the seventh, they were continually reminded of God, their creator and sovereign, whom they thus imitated and obeyed. The necessity of this to the maintenance of the knowledge of God among men is manifest; and its many other advantages render it one of the most important and salutary institutions of divine wisdom and goodness.

But it is held by many, that the Sabbath was not instituted at this time; principally on the ground, that in Ex. 16 : 5, and 22–30, it seems to be spoken of as a new institution, then for the first time established.

If so, it was done in a very incidental way, and not with the formalities which might be expected in such a case. In vv. 4 and 5, God announces his purpose to rain bread from heaven; and requires the people to gather it daily, and on the sixth day twice as much as on other days. In v. 23, Moses gives the explanation of this, namely, "To-morrow is the rest of the holy Sabbath unto Jehovah." It is said, moreover, in v. 29, "Jehovah has given you the Sabbath;" but of the gift of it there is no intimation in this connection.

This has not the appearance of a new institution, but rather of an ancient one which had fallen into disuse, as must have been the case with the Hebrews during their long bondage in Egypt; for they certainly would not be allowed to claim exemption, one day in seven, from the toil imposed by their task-masters. A fit opportunity was chosen for reviving its observance, namely, one which would signalize its weekly return, by withholding on that day the usual supply of bread.

Ch. 2 : 4—3 : 24. Second part of the first division: *Continued account of the creation, with special reference to the first human pair; their temptation and fall.*

The account of the creation is here resumed, but with special reference to man, and in order to prepare the way for the account of his temptation and fall, and of its consequences to the whole creation. Hence he is the leading subject of this section, and all other things are viewed in their relations to him, as the head and representative of all.

Jehovah God is the name by which the Divine Being is designated in this section. The Hebrew word rendered God (*Elohim*), being the intensive plural of the word meaning *worshiped*, denotes the supreme object of worship. To this is sometimes prefixed, as in this section, the special name Jehovah (the *Eternal*) by which the true God revealed himself, in distinction from the false gods worshiped among men. As a proper name, it should be retained, and not translated.

V. 4. This verse has by some been regarded as the conclusion of the preceding narrative. In their view, the writer means: "These (referring to what precedes) are the generations of the heavens and the earth." But to this there are decisive objections in the customary usage of the Hebrew; and the verse is now generally understood to be an introduction to what follows.

Generations. The import of this word here must be learned from its use in other passages. It properly means *bir'hs*, and by metonymy, *a record of births*. As such a record often contained incidents of family history (as in ch. 5, and especially in vv. 24, 29) the word came to be sometimes used of these alone. Thus in ch. 6, the ninth and following verses, under the heading

when they were created, in the day that Jehovah God made earth and heavens.

5 Now there was yet no plant of the field in the earth, and no herb of the field had yet sprung up; for Jehovah God had not yet caused it to rain on the earth, and there was no 6 man to till the ground. And there went up mist from the earth; and it watered all the face of the ground.

7 And Jehovah God formed the man of dust of the ground; and he breathed into his nostrils the breath of life, and the man became a living soul.

"generations of Noah," instead of a record of births, we find only the leading incidents of his own life and times.

So here, under the heading "generations of the heavens and the earth," we have a record of the continuation and further development of their own history, in events connected with them as parts of the same great plan.

VV. 5, 6. As man is the special subject of this section, what relates immediately to him is briefly stated again, and in the order which its relation to him naturally suggests. See remarks on v. 9 and v. 19. What is said here, and in vv. 8, 9, coincides in time with the account of the third day, in the first chapter.

V. 6. This language not inaptly describes the usual process of the formation of clouds, by vapors rising from the earth, and their descent in the form of rain. But the language may refer, as some suppose, to a time when mists enveloped the earth, and thus supplied the land with moisture.

V. 7. *Formed the man of dust of the ground.* See the remarks on ch. 1 : 27, the fifth paragraph. A comparison of the two passages shows that man has a higher spiritual nature, made in the likeness of God, as well as a material animal nature, kindred with that of the brutes.

Here it is said, that God *formed* the man (see No. 3 in the third paragraph on ch. 1 : 1), and it is added, "of dust of the ground;" while in ch. 1 : 27, God is said to have "*created* the man." But the difference is only apparent, and is occasioned by the difference in the writer's object in the two passages. In ch. 1 : 27 the statement is general, without any specification of man's relation to the material world. But here we are taught, that man's body is composed of the same substances as the ground from which it draws its sustenance, from which its waste is continually supplied, and to which its elements ultimately return. Chemistry detects in the animal frame the same elements as enter into the composition of the earth; and this fact is figuratively expressed in the statement, "formed the man of dust of the ground."

Breathed into his nostrils the breath of life; that is, animated him with a principle of life. The thought is most naturally expressed under this physical form, since the life of the body is dependent on the breath.

It is proper to add, that very able interpreters, whose opinions are entitled to respect (Delitzsch, Lange, Murphy, and others), suppose these words to express the imparting from God of that spiritual element, in which man's likeness to him consists. Hence they find here a recognition of the doctrine of the threefold nature of man, *body, soul,* and *spirit* (1 Thess. 5 : 23). But admitting the truth of the doctrine, it may still be questioned, whether they do not interpret into the passage more than is fairly interpreted out of it. They admit, moreover, that the Scriptures sometimes speak of man's nature as twofold (*body* and *soul*), including soul and spirit under one term. Here there seems to be no more implied than is recognized in Isaiah 2 : 22, where it is said, with probable reference to this passage: "Cease ye from man, in whose nostrils is breath;"* only breath, so frail a principle of life, and so easily extinguished! Hence it is added: "For wherein is he to be accounted of?" Of what account, as a refuge, is he!

A living soul. The Hebrew word (*nephesh*) here rendered *soul*, includes all beings that have

---

* Not, as in the common English version, "whose breath is in his nostrils;" for where else should it be? The objection is not to its place in the body, which is the proper one for it, but to its frail and perishable nature.

⁸ And Jehovah God planted a garden in Eden, on the ⁹ east; and there he put the man whom he formed. And Jehovah God caused to spring up out of the ground every tree that is pleasant to the sight, and good for food, and the tree of life in the midst of the garden, and the tree of knowledge of good and evil.

¹⁰ And a stream went forth from Eden, to water the garden; and from thence it parted itself, and became four ¹¹ heads. The name of the first is Pishon. This is that which

animal life; and hence it is applied to animals of the sea and land, in ch. 1 : 20, 21, 24, 30. The English word *soul* (like the German *Seele*), originally had this extent of meaning, as in vv. 20 and 30, in the margin of the common English version. But, as the word is now used, it would misrepresent the meaning in those passages.

What man was, the statement in ch. 1 : 27 leaves no room to doubt; for he was created "in the image and likeness of God." The Hebrew expresses by the same word, *nephesh*, not only the animal life, common to men and beasts, but also the higher nature of man, the rational soul, by which he is distinguished from brute beasts. The former is sometimes its exclusive sense; but it may also include the latter, where, as in this passage, it is equally pertinent. The term *soul* is, therefore, its proper English equivalent here.

V. 8. *Eden;* that is, delight, pleasure; as the plural is used in Psalm 36 : 8, "the river of thy pleasures." *On the east;* eastward, in reference to the position of the writer, and those immediately addressed by him. On the site of Eden, see the remarks on vv. 10–14.

V. 9. *Caused to spring up.* This fact is not here stated in its place in the actual order of events, which is already given in the first chapter. Man being the special subject of this section, his formation is stated first; and then follows the account of the provision already made for his subsistence. Compare the remarks on v. 19. If the sacred writer's object is thus kept in view, the perfect agreement of the two accounts, in the sequence of events, will be apparent.

Tree of life—tree of knowledge; see remarks on v. 17, and at the close of the third chapter.

VV. 10–14. Two of the rivers here mentioned, the Tigris and the Euphrates, are identified by their names; and it is useless to look for the site of Eden beyond the region of country to which they belong. An inspection of a correct map shows the accuracy of the description here given. All the principal rivers of this region have their origin within a short distance of each other, around a central body of water, and run thence in different directions, that is, are divided or parted thence, as the sacred writer expresses it. Of course, his object is not a minute topographical description, but a general and impressive conception, as a whole.

From thence it parted itself; namely, from Eden, its source; or from the garden, as it is not unreasonable to suppose that this embraced the region of Eden around the sources of these rivers. The idea of the sacred writer seems to be, that from Eden and the garden situated in it, as a centre, proceeded four principal streams, flowing thence in different directions. Of course he does not mean, that it *went forth* from Eden before it served to water the garden; for in that case, the garden would have been situated outside of Eden. Nor does he say, that a single stream or river, after passing through and watering the garden, then parted and became four; a gross conception of the writer's language, and one that does great injustice to his beautiful description.

The region of ancient Eden was, therefore, in the highlands of Armenia, around the sources of the Tigris and Euphrates. Its climate, as that of other parts of the earth, has undergone great change in the course of more than sixty centuries. Such a region, blessed with a genial climate, and clothed with perpetual verdure, was a fit abode for man, in his primæval innocence.

There is no necessity for assuming that the geographical features of this region have greatly changed; and though it is now difficult, through changes in the names of districts and rivers, to identify with certainty all that are mentioned here, yet, with a reasonable interpretation of the writer's language, enough remains to determine the site of ancient Eden, and to prove the accuracy the writer's description.

V. 11. *Pishon.* This river, it is said, " traverses the whole land of Havilah." By some it has

traverses the whole land of Havilah, where there is gold.
12 And the gold of that land is good. There is bdellium, and the onyx stone.
13 And the name of the second river is Gihon. This is that which traverses the whole land of Cush.
14 And the name of the third river is Tigris. This is that which goes on the east of Assyria. And the fourth river, that is Euphrates.
15 And Jehovah God took the man, and put him in the

been identified with the *Phasis* (flowing from the east into the Euxine Sea), and Havilah with the ancient Colchis, from the similarity in the consonant elements. By others the river is supposed to be the Araxes, called Phasis by an ancient writer. To both suppositions it is objected, that Havilah is elsewhere mentioned as a southern land. But the son of Joktan (ch. 10:29) from whom that region was named, is to be distinguished from the son of Cush (ch. 10:7) by whose descendants the more northern region was occupied; and the application of the word in this more ancient record need not be limited by a later usage.

V. 12. *Bdellium;* a substance well known in the time of Moses, for he refers to it in describing the appearance of manna, in Num. 11:7; but in the time of the oldest interpreters all certain knowledge of it was lost. Conjecture has suggested various precious stones, as the beryl, carbuncle, ruby, crystal, and also the pearl. It was probably a vegetable gum, much prized for burning as incense.

V. 13. The second river (*Gihon*) it is said, "traverses the whole land of Cush." A branch of the descendants of Cush (ch. 10:8-12) early took possession of the plains through which the Tigris and Euphrates flowed, built Babel by the latter and Nineveh near the headwaters of the former, and laid the foundations of the Babylonian and Assyrian empires. That they should have extended over this whole region, and that the name of Cush, the common ancestor, should have been given to a portion of it, though afterward restricted to a more southern region, is highly probable in itself.

It is not, therefore, an unreasonable admission, that the sacred writer was correct in speaking of Cush as the early name of a district in this region, and of a river flowing through it then called the Gihon; whether, with some, we suppose it to have been the ancient Cyrus (the Cur), or the Zabana, one of the largest confluents of the Tigris, rising near the sources of that river, and traversing one of the large districts just referred to, as occupied by the immediate descendants of Cush.

It is not to be expected, in such a case, that every point can be established by direct historical evidence. But it is clear, that the writer's representation is a possible one; and we are not forced to the conclusion, that it is an impossible combination of rivers and lands remote from one another, which could exist, therefore, only in the imagination, and could serve no purpose but to symbolize certain great truths of universal interest.

V. 14. *Tigris;* Hebrew, *Hiddekel*, the common name of the river Tigris, which, as well as that of the Euphrates in the next clause, was preserved through all ages; both rivers being too well known to lose their distinctive appellations, when once become familiar.

On the east of Assyria; either in its eastern part, or on the eastern side of it. The writer speaks of Assyria as it was in the earliest period of its history. The country began to be occupied by emigration from the west (ch. 10:11), and the progress eastward of the Tigris was of later date. The seat of government was originally west of the Tigris (as is shown by recent discoveries in the ruins of ancient cities of Mesopotamia), and continued to be so long after the time of Moses.

VV. 15-17. The account of man is here re-umed, and the terms are given on which he was to enjoy this state of felicity, provided by his Creator.

Took—and put, properly denotes transfer, from one place or condition to another. But under this form, the writer expresses nothing more than that special provision was made for man's necessities and enjoyment. It was not his natural and necessary condition, is the writer's mean-

¹⁶ garden of Eden, to till it, and to keep it. And Jehovah God commanded the man, saying: Of every tree of the ¹⁷ garden thou mayest freely eat. But of the tree of knowledge of good and evil, thou shalt not eat of it; for in the day that thou eatest thereof thou shalt surely die.

¹⁸ And Jehovah God said: It is not good that the man should be alone. I will make for him a helper, suited to him.

¹⁹ And Jehovah God formed out of the ground every beast of the field, and every fowl of the heavens. And he

---

ing, but one specially provided for him, and into which he *was brought*, so to speak, by the favor of his Creator.

To till it, and to keep it; that is, to cultivate the ground, and to guard its products from injury, the two principal occupations of the husbandman.

Occupation is essential to happiness; and not merely occupation of the mind, but of the body, such as will preserve it in a healthy condition, making it a fit abode and an efficient instrument of the soul that inhabits it. It was not till sin had changed man's relations to the Divine Being, that his relation to physical nature, and dependence on it, became a source of painful care and toil, of physical suffering, disease, and death.

V. 17. *Tree of knowledge of good and evil.* With this mode of designating the tree, compare the one in ch. 3:3, and the remarks at the end of that chapter.

What God, the gracious and all-wise Creator, wills and commands, that is his creature's good; what he forbids is his creature's evil.

Reversed (as in beings fallen away from God) the proposition stands: What the creature wills, that is his good; and what he wills not is his evil.

By disregarding the divine will, and deciding and acting on his own, man chose to know for himself what is good and what is evil. So the words of the Divine Being are to be understood, in ch. 3:22. (See the remarks on the passage.) The fact that consequences ensued, giving still further significance to the terms, does not conflict with the true interpretation of this language of the Creator.

Thou shalt not eat of it. The principle of conscious obedience to the divine will is the first step in moral progress, and the essential element of true happiness. Consequently, the conscious recognition of that will is the first condition of man's development as a moral being, and of his continued progress in holiness and happiness. Hence a test was required, to awaken that conscious recognition, and to give occasion for the exercise of his freedom of choice and action.

A test of obedience is, therefore, an expression of the truest love and care; and the more simple the test, the better it serves the purpose intended by the love that appoints it. Hence, numerous acts of obedience were not made the test. One act was forbidden; all else was allowed. Of the principle of obedience, no test could have been more simple and direct, or more easily apprehended; and hence it was a perfect test.

Thou shalt surely die. The nature and full extent of the threatened punishment, and how it would take effect, must be learned from the result, as stated in the next chapter.

VV. 18-24. The relation of the two sexes, and the nature of the marriage relation, are here shown by a more circumstantial account of their origin than is given in the first chapter. There man is represented more generally, in his relation to nature both animate and inanimate, as its constituted head and ruler. Here (second and third chapters) he is represented in his relation to history; and hence all the circumstances connected with the first great moral epoch in the history of the world are minutely detailed.

V. 19. *Jehovah God formed,* etc. Here, again, the sacred writer states the fact, without observing its chronological order. It was necessary to make the statement at this point in the narrative, in order to show that the creation of another being was required, as a suitable com-

brought them to the man, to see what he would call them; and whatever the man should call every living being, that should be its name.

20 And the man gave names to all cattle, and to the fowl of the heavens, and to every beast of the field; but for the man there was not found a helper, suited to him.

21 And Jehovah God caused a deep sleep to fall upon the man, and he slept; and he took one of his ribs, and closed
22 up the flesh in its place. And of the rib, which he took from the man, Jehovah God formed a woman, and brought
23 her to the man. And the man said: This now is bone of

* V. 20. O *, but for man, he found not

panion for man. The statement is not, therefore, in conflict with that given in the first chapter, but is inserted here where the connection requires it, though not in its chronological order.*
The object of the writer is still further apparent, from his mentioning only the occupants of earth and air, elements common to them and to man.
Out of the ground. Compare the remarks on ch. 1:24, and on ch. 2:7.
To see what he would call them; that is, how he would name them, from observing their structure, habits, etc. It would thus appear, whether he recognized, in the various beings brought before him, one suited to be his companion. But he could give no one a name that indicated any relation to man. It was not till the one formed expressly for him was brought, that he exclaimed, "This shall be called woman;" expressing, by that appellation, the relation to himself, which he recognized in the newly formed being.
That should be its name; indicating man's supremacy. By giving to each animal its name, according to its structure and capacities, he assigns to each its character and rank, and is thus the recognized lord of creation. Compare ch. 1:26, 28.
VV. 21-24. It is now made evident to man, that he is alone in the world of which he is the head. He is made ruler of a creation, full of inanimate and animate life, where he finds no companionship; abounding in the products of divine wisdom and goodness, in which none can intelligently participate with him. What is now to be done for him? To create another human being, wholly distinct in substance from himself, would introduce into the world a being independent of himself, antagonistic to him, and having no hold on his sympathies as a part of himself. As the creation of only one human pair is the point of unity for all the races of men,† so the mode of their creation is the point of unity for the two. They are one in nature, in substance, and in vitality; and in this relation of woman to man, as part of himself, is founded the moral relation of marriage, as an inseparable life-union.
V. 23. *This now,* etc.; the language of joyful surprise, on beholding the object of his long

* The rendering, "*had formed,*" assumed by some, is false translation, the Hebrew verbal form here used never having that sense. This rendering does, indeed, correctly represent the facts, but not the sacred writer's statement of them. It is interpretation, therefore, and not translation. The reader of the version is as competent to interpret the writer's language, as the translator is to do it for him; and it is his right to do it for himself.

† The proofs of this unity, existing in the organism of all these races, are well exhibited in the following compressed statement, by Prof. Delitzsch (Genesis, p. 200): "That the races of men are not species of one genus, but are varieties of one species, is proved by the agreement of the physiological and pathological phenomena in all men; the same anatomical structure, the same elementary powers and traits of mind, the same limits to the duration of life, liability to the same diseases, the same normal temperature of the body and the same mean frequency of the pulse, the same duration of pregnancy, the periodicity of the catamenia, the unrestricted fruitfulness of the cohabitation of all races with one another. Such sameness is nowhere found in the animal world, among the species of one genus."

my bones, and flesh of my flesh. This shall be called
24 Woman; because from man was she taken. Therefore shall a man leave his father and his mother, and shall cleave to his wife; and they shall be one flesh.
25 And they were both naked, the man and his wife, and were not ashamed.

1 Now the serpent was more crafty than any beast of the

and fruitless search. All other animals he had found associated in pairs, adapted in form and nature to each other. Now at length one is brought to him, suited to himself, "bone of his bone, and flesh of his flesh;" such as he himself, and of himself.

Man has now a fitting companion; formed by the divine Architect, after his own ideal of human beauty and loveliness; in person the counterpart of himself, but with softened and more graceful lines, and wanting his hardy strength, as one to be loved, cherished, and protected; his equal in range of thought, without his rugged vigor of intellectual strength; in all the traits, both of mind and person, fitted to soften, refine, and ennoble his nature.

V. 24. Whether we regard this as said by Adam, or as added by the sacred writer, it is a part of the divine ordinance of marriage. As such it is referred to by the Savior (Matt. 19:5), and by the apostle (Eph. 5:31); and it affirms, in words, the divine law of the marriage relation, already declared in the creation of one of each sex.

The language here is remarkable. It is the *man* who shall forsake all other relations, for this one. From the last clause of ch. 3:16 we may infer a change in woman's position, occasioned by the apostasy from God. In proportion as divine revelation has counteracted its evils, and brought man nearer to his original state, the position of woman in this relation has risen, and she has regained her rightful and salutary influence.

Shall be one flesh; an intimacy of union, a oneness, and a sameness, which can be expressed in no other terms.

The apostle (Eph. 5:28, 29) thus beautifully expands the thought: "So husbands ought to love their wives as their own bodies. He that loves his wife loves himself. For no one ever hated his own flesh, but nourishes and cherishes it."

V. 25. These words are intended to express perfect and childlike innocence. Shame is a species of self-reproach, and can not be felt by perfectly holy beings. The language here used is intelligible to all; and under every form of society, it would be understood to express absolute purity and innocence.

Ch. 3. *Account of the temptation and fall of man.*

In the moral condition and history of the race, there are fundamental problems, of which the Bible furnishes the only solution. One of these may be stated thus:

Man is conscious to himself, that whatever sinful acts he commits are his own acts; that they are the expression of his own free will, and that he himself, and no one else, is accountable for them.

At the same time, he perceives in himself an innate, natural tendency to evil, manifesting itself in the earliest developments of his moral consciousness, and of its own nature producing sinful acts.

He is conscious to himself that this innate tendency to evil does not justify or excuse his sinful acts, and that the tendency itself can not be justified or excused, any more than the acts to which it leads; and he holds himself blameworthy for the one as well as for the other.

These seeming discrepancies find their explanation in the facts here recorded. The individual man is not an isolated being, but stands in organic connection with a race estranged from God, and he shares the common guilt and common accountability. He can not disavow either, without disowning the moral instincts of his own nature.

The facts of human nature and human history require, therefore, for their explanation, such a transaction as is here recorded.*

---

* The writer here speaks only of the universal consciousness of depravity and guilt, irrespective of any *theory* of our connection with Adam's transgression and its consequences.

field which Jehovah God made. And he said to the woman: Is it even so, that God has said, Ye shall not eat of any tree of the garden?
2 And the woman said to the serpent: Of the fruit of the
3 trees of the garden we may eat. But of the fruit of the

V. 1. *Was more crafty,* etc. So the serpent has been represented in all ages. Compare Matt. 10: 16, "wise as serpents." The tempter having assumed the form of a serpent, the representation is consistently carried out; and hence the allusion here to its reputed craft.

That the serpent was merely the instrument of an evil spirit is apparent from the nature of the case, as well as from the testimony of the Scriptures.* It can not be supposed that the serpent could, of itself, devise and execute a plan for the deception and ruin of our first parents. The Savior says of the Evil One (John 8:44): "He was a murderer from the beginning. * * * When he speaks a lie, he speaks of his own; because he is a liar, and the father of it;" referring to the first act of deception on earth, of which he was the author. In 1 John 3:8, it is said: "The Devil sins from the beginning;" referring to this act. Compare Rev. 12:9 (and 20: 2): "The great dragon was cast down, the old serpent, called the Devil and Satan." In Rom. 16:20, the apostle says (with evident allusion to the curse pronounced on the serpent in v. 15 of this chapter): "The God of peace will shortly bruise Satan under your feet."

In order to understand how appropriate an instrument the serpent was for the tempter's purpose, we must divest ourselves of the common antipathy to it, and imagine how it appeared to the eye of Eve. Its motions are easy and graceful, and in beauty and brilliancy of coloring some species are unsurpassed by any other animal. Of course Eve could have no share in our prejudices against it.

The *speaking* of the serpent was the effect of supernatural influence. Before the habits of animals had, by long observation, come to be regarded as immutable laws of nature, a deviation from them could excite no such surprise as at present. See further remarks at the end of the chapter.

Is it even so; implying the unreasonableness of the prohibition.

Ye shall not eat of any tree of the garden, is an exaggeration of the divine prohibition, which well accords with the spirit and purpose of the tempter.

The tempter first aims to weaken the bond of childlike confidence and trust, which binds man to his Maker; infusing in its place a spirit of unbelief and distrust. The sure basis of simple trust in God, as the all-loving and the all-wise, once shaken, there is little left to be done.

VV. 2, 3. The woman corrects, in the second verse, the tempter's misstatement of the divine prohibition. But, in the third verse, she unnecessarily repeats the prohibition, and with an addition ("ye shall not touch it") which is noteworthy; indicating, perhaps, by this exaggeration of the command, that there was already awakened a feeling of impatience under the restraint imposed.

Observe that the tree, the fruit of which they were forbidden to eat, is here called "the tree

---

* That man must have been tempted into sin by an influence from without, not originating in himself, is very clearly and forcibly shown by Auberlen (*Göttliche Offenbarung,* p. 153):

"Though the sin of humanity rests on a free act of Adam, yet it can not have in this its ultimate ground. Everything that exists, and especially that which has personality, is attached by an intimate bond to its original. So must also the first human pair have been bound to God, by a native trait of the deepest piety. They had, as Melancthon, in his defense of the Augsburg Confession, so beautifully says, a pure, good, joyous heart toward God and all divine things; they lived in and from God, as the child lives in and from the mother. If now the thought of breaking loose from God, of spiritual parricide, had risen in *their* souls, then would they in their own inmost self have set themselves in opposition to God; evil would have been a thing not foreign to the nature of man, but man would have been the evil one himself,—he would have *satanized* himself. But then, too, it would be impossible to remove evil from the nature of man; humanity would no longer be capable of redemption. Inasmuch, therefore, as man is not a devil, it follows that there must be a devil. Evil in its human form, if it does not constitute the substance of the creaturely personality, and still leaves room for redemption, can be explained only through temptation."

tree which is in the midst of the garden, God has said: Ye shall not eat of it, and ye shall not touch it, lest ye die. **4** And the serpent said to the woman: Ye shall not surely **5** die. For God knows, that in the day ye eat thereof your eyes will be opened, and ye will be as God, knowing good and evil.

6 And the woman saw that the tree was good for food, and that it was a delight to the eyes, and that the tree was to be desired to make one wise; and she took of its fruit and ate, **7** and gave also to her husband with her, and he ate. And the eyes of both of them were opened, and they knew that

---

which is in the midst of the garden;" and this may have been the only mode of designating it before the fall.

In the language of the tempter (vv. 1 and 5), and of the woman in reply to him (v. 3), the name of the Divine Being is simply GOD. This is significant; the name used by the narrator himself, in this section, being invariably JEHOVAH GOD.

VV. 4, 5. Mark the confident tone of the tempter; an indication to us of what was passing in the mind of the woman, under his influence. For so the narrative is to be interpreted. Compare the different result in the case of the Savior (Matt. 5 : 3-10) when subjected to the like subtle influence.

The tempter here aims to infuse into the mind of the woman, first a doubt of the truth and certainty of the divine threatening ("ye shall not surely die"); and secondly a suspicion, that God was withholding from them a good, instead of guarding them against an evil ("God knows," etc.).

Your eyes will be opened, expresses the power of mentally apprehending things before unperceived and unknown; here, of course, both in an intellectual and moral sense.

Will be as God; in what respect, is stated in the following clause, "knowing good and evil;" knowing for yourselves, and able to choose between the evil and the good.

By these words, the tempter would awaken the feeling of self-exaltation, the longing for a higher development, in which they should attain to self-direction, and freedom of choice and action.

V. 6. In temptation, it is dangerous to deliberate. Half the tempter's work is done when he has gained a hearing. As she gazed on the tree, still unresolved, the forbidden object began to have charms never seen before.

The temptation is represented as addressing itself to the lower and sensual elements of man's nature ("the tree was good for food, and a delight to the eyes"), as well as to its higher aspirations ("was to be desired to make one wise"). And not without reason. For the result shows, that in the use and control of all his natural powers man became estranged from God (v. 22); that he was no longer in conscious and happy communion with him (vv. 7-10), as the source of his spiritual life and action, and his acknowledged and trusted sovereign.

To make one wise; in the sense insinuated by the tempter; for progress in real knowledge and wisdom was not interdicted by the divine prohibition.

The process of temptation was, therefore, a successful deception. Compare the apostle's statement of the case, 2 Cor. 11:3, "as the serpent beguiled Eve by his subtlety," and of the ordinary process of sin, Rom. 7:11, "deceived me." But the artifice was successful, only through the influence of unbelief and distrust of the divine word. Man disbelieved and distrusted God, and believed and trusted the deceiver, and was thus beguiled into sin. Faith in God would have been a sure defense against all the tempter's wiles.

V. 7. Effects of the transgression. Compare the apostle's brief and pointed summary (James 1:15): "Lust, having conceived, brings forth sin; and sin, when completed, brings forth death."

Their eyes were opened, means (as in v. 5), that they now perceived what they were not conscious of before.

They knew that they were naked. In place of conscious innocence and purity (ch. 2 : 25),

they were naked. And they sewed fig-leaves together, and made themselves aprons.

8 And they heard the voice of Jehovah God walking in the garden, at the breeze of the day. And the man and his wife hid themselves from the presence of Jehovah God, in the midst of the trees of the garden.

9 And Jehovah God called to the man, and said to him:
10 Where art thou? And he said: I heard thy voice in the garden, and was afraid, because I was naked, and hid myself.

11 And he said: Who has showed thee that thou art naked? Hast thou eaten of the tree, of which I commanded thee not to eat?

12 And the man said: The woman whom thou gavest to be with me, she gave me of the tree, and I ate.

V. 8. The voice; *or,* the sound

came the sense of guilt and shame. We are not to understand that there is allusion here to any physical effect of the eating of the forbidden fruit. So gross a conception is foreign to the spirit and purpose of the narrative. As the language in ch. 2 : 25 is an expression of purity and peace of mind, so the language used here is the expression of conscious guilt, of self-condemnation and shame. What is said in the remainder of the verse is a continuation of this figurative expression of the thought.

We are not to suppose, moreover, that the fruit itself had any effect. It was the transgression of the divine command that wrought the change. As obedience was the conscious recognition of the divine authority, and the condition of continued connection with the source of spiritual life and peace, so their disobedience was the conscious rejection of that authority, and forfeiture of spiritual life and enjoyment. Man's natural reason, with his appetites and passions, was now in the ascendant; no longer under the control and direction of that spiritual element of his nature, in which he bore the image of God, and lived in happy communion with him. Hence his dread of God, and conscious guilt and shame.

V. 8. All the circumstances of the narrative point to the intimate converse with the revealed Divinity, to which man in his primeval innocence was admitted. Nor should this seem strange to us. For what relation can be more intimate and endearing than that of the Creator to the being created by him? In what, beyond himself, could he take more delight, than in the being created by himself, and in his own image? What this intercourse had been, is represented under a form the most easily apprehended by us.

Voice, is probably the correct rendering here (compare, *thy voice*, in v. 10); though the marginal rendering *sound* (namely, of footsteps, etc.), would be admissible, as in 2 Samuel 5 : 24; 1 Kings 14 : 6; 2 Kings 6 : 32.

At the breeze of the day; toward evening, after the midday heat, when the cool breeze is accustomed to spring up.*

On vv. 8-10, compare the remarks on v. 7.

V. 11. *Who has showed thee that thou art naked?* How hast thou become conscious of this? Whence is this sense of guilt and shame? *Hast thou eaten,* etc. These questions recall the man from the consequences of his offense to the guilty act itself.

V. 12 is sometimes falsely interpreted, as an unworthy attempt of the man to cast the blame

---

* The same idea is expressed, in another form, in Cant. 2 : 17, and 4 : 6; properly, *till the day shall breeze.*

B

¹³ And Jehovah God said to the woman: What is this that thou hast done? And the woman said: The serpent beguiled me, and I ate.

¹⁴ And Jehovah God said to the serpent: Because thou hast done this, cursed art thou above all cattle, and above every beast of the field; on thy belly shalt thou go, and dust shalt ¹⁵ thou eat all the days of thy life. And I will put enmity between thee and the woman, and between thy seed and her seed; he shall bruise thee on the head, and thou shalt bruise him on the heel.

¹⁶ To the woman he said: I will greatly multiply the pains of thy pregnancy; in pain shalt thou bring forth children; and unto thy husband shall be thy desire, and he shall rule over thee.

V. 14. *Or, of all cattle, and of every beast*

---

of his offense on the woman. But the emphasis lies on the words, *whom thou gavest to be with me;* and he seeks to transfer the responsibility from himself to God, who gave him the companion by whose example he was betrayed into sin.

V. 13. *What is this that thou hast done?* The inquiry is an expression of surprise and displeasure, and of the fearful nature of the act and its consequences. It can not be denied, that her part in the transgression is regarded with special displeasure. Compare the severity of the punishment (v. 16), and the words of the apostle, in 1 Tim. 2:14.

V. 14. *Above all cattle*, etc., does not necessarily imply, as some have assumed, that other animals are accursed, though in a less degree. Even if this were true, the expression would be just, since the evil implied extends to all. Compare v. 17, and Rom. 8:20. *Of all cattle*, etc. (margin), refers to the instinctive dread and aversion with which all animals regard the serpent. *On thy belly shalt thou go.* We are not to infer from this that the serpent originally had a form different from its present one. The words, in their literal application to the serpent, imply that its natural structure and habits were made a perpetual memorial of the curse affixed to it. But in their real intent, they are a figurative expression of the humiliation of the tempter himself.*

V. 15. On the same principle, the subsequent relation between the evil spirit and man is aptly expressed by the enmity between the seed of the serpent and that of the woman, and by the nature of the injuries mutually inflicted. In this conflict, man is to have the ascendency. As this is true in the literal application of the words, so it is also in the higher one; for while the enemy of man shall inflict only partial injuries, he shall himself be finally subdued and crushed. Compare the apostle's evident allusion to this passage, in Rom. 16:20.

If we admit that in the transaction narrated in this chapter there is anything worthy of the divine and human parties to it, we must recognize here something more than the instinctive enmity between man and the serpent kind. It is evident that, along with this, there is still another and higher application of the words, which has gained for this verse the title of the *Protevangelium,* or the *First Gospel.*

It is certainly significant, that this is promised to the *seed of the woman.* She who had been foiled, in the first encounter with the wily enemy of the race, should triumph over and subdue him in her offspring. A gracious offset to the sentence of condemnation in the next verse!

V. 16. *Unto thy husband shall be thy desire;* an expression of subordination and dependence. *He shall rule over thee* expresses, not indeed what should be, but what would so generally be the

---

* This is true also of the expression, *dust shalt thou eat;* a reputed habit of the serpent, the ground of which is seen in Micah. 7:17, and which is here referred to as a part of its humiliation. A similar reference, with evident allusion to this passage, occurs in Isaiah 65:25.

¹⁷ And to the man he said: Because thou didst hearken to the voice of thy wife, and didst eat of the tree, of which I commanded thee, saying, Thou shalt not eat of it; cursed is the ground for thy sake. In sorrow shalt thou eat of it all ¹⁸ the days of thy life. And thorns and thistles shall it cause to spring up to thee; and thou shalt eat the herb of the ¹⁹ field. By the sweat of thy face shalt thou eat bread, till thou return to the ground; for out of it wast thou taken; for dust thou art, and unto dust shalt thou return.

²⁰ And the man called the name of his wife Eve; because she was the mother of all living.

²¹ And Jehovah God made for the man, and for his wife, garments of skin, and clothed them.

²² And Jehovah God said: Behold, the man has become as one of us, to know good and evil. And now, lest he stretch

---

effect of the apostasy on woman's relations in the married state. The stronger party in this relation, instead of being the natural guardian and protector of the weaker, would use his superior power to oppress and debase her. Such has always been the case, except so far as the influence of revelation has counteracted the evils of the fall.

VV. 17-19. There is a formal statement of the grounds of man's condemnation, for which there seems to have been no occasion in the case of the woman. In man's justification of himself (v. 12), it is implied that God was the occasion of the offense, in giving man for a companion one who had led him into sin. Observe the felicitous form of the refutation of this plea: In obeying the voice of the wife given thee, thou hast disobeyed the voice of God who gave her.

Cursed is the ground for thy sake; as a mark of the divine displeasure against sin. For the meaning of the expression, compare ch. 27:27, "as the smell of a field which Jehovah has blest;" on which his favor rests, making it fruitful, and fragrant with abundant increase. The curse consisted in rendering the ground unfruitful, or productive of useless and hurtful plants, adding to the labors of the husbandman. This blight of sin, on all the objects of nature, is referred to in Rom. 8:19-22.

Herb of the field; of the open field, wild and unsubdued, and requiring painful toil to fit it for use, and make it productive.

V. 19. Brief and impressive summary of human life! The literature of the world will be searched in vain for a parallel to this truthful and affecting statement.

By the sweat of thy face shalt thou eat bread, describes the condition of the race, and is true of all the race, as such. No man eats bread, but by the sweat of some man's face.

For out of it. This and the following clause may be taken together, as co-ordinate reasons for the statement, "till thou return to the ground;" or the second may be regarded as confirmative of the first, with the natural sequence, "and unto dust shalt thou return."

V. 20. *Eve;* that is, Life.

V. 21 expresses God's providential care for every human want. Sin has made the covering of the person necessary, and it is God's requirement. The first clothing of man is ascribed to him, on the principle, that what he requires and causes to be done, and gives the means and capacity to do, is his work.

V. 22. *As one of us, to know good and evil;* as one of us, in this respect, to know (for himself) good and evil, to decide for himself what is good and what is evil, without regard to the divine will. Thus his own will had become his supreme law, in place of the will of God; and thus he had become as God to himself.

Lest he . . . take also of the tree of life, and eat, and live forever. It is not meant, that by once partaking of this fruit, he would be forever secured against death. Nor is it implied

forth his hand, and take also of the tree of life, and eat, and
²³ live forever; therefore Jehovah God sent him forth from
the garden of Eden, to till the ground from whence he was
²⁴ taken. And he drove out the man; and he stationed on
the east of the garden of Eden the cherubim, and the flam-

that he had never yet partaken of it; for of this he might "freely eat" (ch. 2 : 16) so long as he continued obedient. But now, he is to be debarred from access to the tree of life; and thus the divine threatening, "in *the day* thou eatest thereof thou shalt surely die," was virtually fulfilled to the letter.

V. 23. The sentence commencing with the quoted words of the Divine Being, in the preceding verse, is left unfinished; the writer passing abruptly from the dramatic to the narrative form. Such transition is not necessarily a blemish in composition, but is often one of its highest excellences.

V. 24. *On the east of the garden;* indicating that the first direction of the race was eastward from Eden.

The cherubim and the flaming sword. The use of the definite *article*, in both cases, shows that these terms expressed well-known and familiar objects, or conceptions.

The *cherubim* were ideal forms, often occurring in the religious symbolism of the Hebrews. Here, in connection with the *flaming sword*, they represent the majesty and authority of Jehovah, in some visible manifestation, as in the terrors of the lightning-cloud. Compare the poetical description of Jehovah, appearing in his majesty and power, in Psalm 18 : 9-14, and 2 Samuel 22 : 11-15.

The conception of their form is not to be inferred from the description in Ezekiel, ch. 1 and ch. 10, which is peculiar to the visions of that prophet, as is also the description in ch. 41 : 18, 19. Compare the quite different conception of the form in Ex. 25 : 20, 37 : 9, and in 1 Kings 6 : 24.

To keep the way to the tree of life; denoting that there was no return to that state of immortality.

The penalty of the transgression (ch. 2 : 17) was, therefore, spiritual death (see the remarks on v. 7), and physical death as its immediate consequence; for "in the day" of his transgression, man was cut off from the source of life, and became a prey to death. Compare the use of the term *death* in such passages as Deut. 30 : 15, 19; Rom. 8 : 6; 7 : 9, 10, 13; Eph. 2 : 1, 5.

The profound truth of the representation in this chapter is admitted, even by those who do not accept the scriptural interpretation of it.

The Scriptures themselves are the only sure guide to the right interpretation. The passages bearing directly on this point, are the following: Eccl. 7 : 29, *God made man upright.* Rom. 5 : 12, *By one man sin entered into the world, and death by sin;* v. 14, *d ath reigned from Adam to Moses, even over those who sinned not after the likeness of Adam's transgression;* v. 15, *by the trespass of the one the many died;* v. 16, *the judgment came of one unto condemnation;* v. 17, *by the trespass of the one death reigned through the one;* v. 18, *through one trespass it came upon all men unto condemnation;* v. 19, *through the disobedience of the one man the many were constituted sinners.* 1 Cor. 15 : 22, *As in Adam all die.* 1 Tim. 2 : 14, *Adam was not deceived; but the woman, being deceived, has fallen into transgression.* 1 Tim. 2 : 13, *For Adam was first formed, then Eve.* 1 Cor. 11 : 8, *For the man is not of the woman, but the woman of the man.* Of the tempter it is said: 2 Cor. 11 : 3, *As the serpent beguiled Eve by his subtlety.* John 8 : 44, *He* (the Devil) *was a murderer from the beginning;* . . . *when he speaks a lie, he speaks of his own; for he is a liar, and the father of it.* Rev. 12 : 9 (and 20 : 2), *And the great dragon was cast down, the old serpent, called the Devil and Satan.*

It is evident from these statements (after making due allowance, in some instances, for a possible adoption of the mere imagery of the original passage), that there is recorded here a real transaction; that there was in reality an original state of innocence and happiness, free from the moral and physical evils that now afflict the race; that man, yielding to the suggestions of an evil spirit, apostatized from God, and forfeited the divine favor and his original state of innocence and happiness, and involved his whole posterity in guilt and ruin.

These are all the limitations, so far as I can recall them, which the Scriptures set to our inter-

ing sword, which turned every way, to keep the way to the tree of life.

pretation of the passage. Keeping to these plain scriptural views, and following their guidance, we may safely apply to it the common principles of interpretation.

The object of the preceding notes is simply to explain the sacred writer's language, following the form of conception in which he clothed his ideas. On some points, the following suggestions may aid the further reflections of the reader.

In regard to the tempter's mode of communicating with Eve, it matters not whether we suppose the serpent to have appeared visibly, and in actual bodily form, to the eye of Eve, addressing her in audible words, or that the communication was purely mental, the tempter appearing in this form to the mind of Eve.

Some have supposed that the *tree of knowledge of good and evil* was so called, because by eating of its fruit man came to know the difference between good and evil, that is, happiness and misery. To say nothing of the moral insignificance of the transaction, on such a supposition, it compels us to regard the words of the Divine Being, in v. 22, as "solemn irony," in allusion to the tempter's treacherous insinuation in v. 5. The imputation of such a sentiment to the Divine Being is too offensive and revolting to be entertained. The words are evidently a serious and earnest statement of a fact, the great fact in human history, on which the destiny of the race has turned; very far indeed from an ironical allusion to the base and treacherous artifice of the malignant deceiver.

Others suppose that the tree was so called, because by it man was to attain to the knowledge (or recognition) of moral good and moral evil. But how could the wise and gracious Creator have intended to interdict this knowledge to his intelligent and moral creature, made in his own image, and thereby frustrate his own purpose in creating him? To this they answer, that according to the divine will, man was to obtain this knowledge by obedience, namely, by *not* eating of the forbidden fruit; and that the statement in v. 22 means, that man has indeed attained to this knowledge (as was intended), but not in the *normal way*. If so, then the statement omits the essential point; and it must be admitted that the view seems rather to be interpreted into the passage, than out of it.

It is undoubtedly true, that man would have attained to the highest perfection of his nature by obeying the divine command; and that he could attain to it only by thus recognizing the divine will as his supreme law, and acting in conscious obedience to it. In this we see the gracious purpose of the Creator, in appointing the test. Compare the remarks on ch. 2:17.

The tree of life, if a literal tree is intended, was the visible medium through which a divine life-imparting power was communicated, and a token to man of his continued enjoyment of it, so long as he was obedient. Man, in his material nature, was of the earth, and tended back to earth; and the withholding of this divine influence was all that was necessary to enforce the divine decree, "unto dust shalt thou return."

But neither tree is spoken of elsewhere, as being literally a part of the reality in this transaction; and both may have been used as symbols of the great moral truths, that by disobedience man apostatized from God, and thereby forfeited the divine favor, and with it his spiritual life and his exemption from physical death.

The reality of the transaction, as viewed by our Lord and his apostles, is not affected by interpreting the whole passage as an embodiment of great moral truths in sensible imagery; in order to make them more readily intelligible to all degrees of intellectual culture, and to give them a stronger hold upon the mind. That this end is attained, every day's experience proves; for the child readily comprehends the lessons here taught, while they are more impressively conveyed, even to minds of the highest culture, than by any abstract form of conception and statement.

Are we to understand that the change in man's spiritual nature and relations was followed by a change in physical nature, and in the physical organization and habits of animals that prey on man and on one another?

Perhaps so. But not necessarily, unless we assume that the allwise God was taken by surprise; that He who sees the end from the beginning did not foresee the result of man's trial, and provide for it. The world which God prepared for man, and into which he was driven forth after his offense, was such as befits his state of alienation from God; such as God pronounced it to be, when he said, "Cursed is the ground for thy sake." Were it not for sin, it would do very well as it is.

¹ AND the man knew Eve his wife; and she conceived, and bore Cain; and she said: I have gotten a man, with Jehovah.

² And again she bore his brother, Abel. And Abel was a keeper of flocks; and Cain was a tiller of the ground.

³ And it came to pass, after a time, that Cain brought of
⁴ the fruit of the ground an offering to Jehovah. And Abel, he also brought of the firstlings of his flock, and of their fat.

⁵ And Jehovah regarded Abel and his offering; but Cain, and his offering, he did not regard. And Cain was angry exceedingly, and his countenance fell.

⁶ And Jehovah said to Cain: Why art thou angry? And
⁷ why is thy countenance fallen? Is there not, if thou doest well, a lifting up? And if thou doest not well, sin is crouching at the door; and toward thee is his desire; and do thou rule over him.

V. 7. *Or*, and thou shouldst rule

Ch. 4. First part of the second division: *Offspring of the first human pair; account of Cain and Abel, and of Cain's posterity.*
In this section, the name of the Divine Being is JEHOVAH.

V. 1. *I have gotten a man, with Jehovah;* her grateful acknowledgment of Jehovah's aid, in this her first experience of the special penalty of the transgression. *Cain;* that is, Gotten.

With Jehovah; either with his help, as the expression is now generally understood; or (as some suppose) conjoined with him, one associated with him, which is less probable.

V. 2. *Flocks;* embracing the smaller domestic animals, *sheep* and *goats*, in distinction from the larger classes, namely, oxen, horses, etc. The rendering of the common English version, *sheep*, is inaccurate.

V. 3. *After a time;* literally, *from* (that is, after) *the end of days*, which corresponds to our indefinite phrase, "after a time."

V. 4. *And of their fat;* to be burned on the altar, as afterward directed in Num. 18:17. The meaning is not, *of their fatlings*, as supposed by some. The fat of more than one is meant, as in Leviticus 9:19, and hence the use of the plural in the Hebrew.

But Cain, and his offering, he did not regard. The ground of the distinction seems to have been, that Abel's sacrifice recognized the principle of human guilt and its expiation (Heb. 9:22), which, in Cain's thank-offering, was overlooked and disregarded; and this is in harmony with his spirit and conduct, as shown in the remainder of the narrative.

V. 7. *A lifting up;* namely, of the countenance, the opposite of the expression, "his countenance fell," in v. 5.

Sin is crouching at the door. Sin (the evil disposition which beset him, and to which he was yielding) is personified as a lurking beast of prey, ready to spring upon its victim in an unguarded moment. Against this insidious enemy Cain is warned, and commanded to "rule over it."*

---

* It is beautifully said by Herder, *Spirit of Hebrew Poetry*, eighth dialogue: "God talks with him as with a sullen child; unriddles to him what slumbers in his heart, and like a beast of prey is lurking at the door. The near approach of sin could not be more truly or more fearfully pictured. And what God did with Cain, that he does with every one, if he will but give heed to his own heart, and to the voice of God."

8 And Cain told it to Abel his brother. And it came to pass, when they were in the field, that Cain rose up against Abel his brother, and slew him.
9 And Jehovah said to Cain: Where is thy brother? And he said: I know not. Am I my brother's keeper?
10 And he said: What hast thou done? The voice of thy
11 brother's blood cries to me from the ground. And now, cursed art thou from the ground, which opened her mouth
12 to receive thy brother's blood from thy hand. When thou tillest the ground, it shall no more yield to thee its strength. A fugitive and a wanderer shalt thou be in the earth.
13 And Cain said to Jehovah: My iniquity is greater than
14 can be borne. Behold, thou hast driven me out this day from the face of the ground, and from thy face must I hide myself; and I shall be a fugitive and a wanderer in the earth; and it will come to pass, that every one who finds me will slay me.
15 And Jehovah said to him: Therefore, whoever slays Cain,

V. 11. *Or*, of the ground   V. 13. *Or*, can be forgiven

V. 8. *Told it;* in what spirit, may be inferred from what follows.
V. 11. *From the ground;* in the sense that he has no longer a resting-place upon it, being henceforth "a fugitive and a wanderer;" or, that the curse proceeds *from* the ground (see margin), which "shall no more yield to him its strength."
V. 12. *Shall no more yield to thee its strength.* Such was the region to which the first homicide was driven forth, a fugitive from the abodes of men, and finding nowhere a resting-place.
V. 13. *My iniquity.* The Hebrew word occurs two hundred and twenty-nine times, and in the common version is correctly translated *iniquity*, in all except thirteen passages. In five it is translated *punishment*; in four, *punishment of iniquity*; twice it is translated *fault*, once *sin*, and once *mischief*. But there is no ground for these variations from the ordinary and proper rendering.
My iniquity is greater than can be borne. "To bear iniquity" means, to suffer its penalty; as in Lev. 19:8; 20:19. Cain's language is the utterance of conscious guilt and fear; of an overwhelming sense of the magnitude of his crime, and of the punishment it deserved and would surely meet. It is not the language of penitence, but of harrowing remorse and dread of future evil. This is clear from what follows. The words, "Every one who finds me will slay me," indicate his own sense of the desert of his crime against God and man.
The Hebrew may also be rendered, as in the margin, *can be forgiven;* expressing the same despairing sense of guilt and its inevitable punishment, the latter being the predominant thought, as the following words show.
V. 15. *Shall be avenged.* So the Hebrew verb must be rendered in v. 24, where there is direct reference to the statement made here.
Sevenfold. Jehovah himself was dealing with Cain for his crime; and it was necessary, by the threat of severe punishment, to check the spirit of private retaliation.
Set a sign for Cain; not, "set a mark upon Cain," as in the common English version. The sign, whatever it may have been, was such as to assure Cain of his safety, and to warn others against doing him harm.

CHAP. IV.   GENESIS.

it shall be avenged sevenfold. And Jehovah set a sign for Cain, that no one finding him should smite him.

16 And Cain went out from the presence of Jehovah, and dwelt in the land of Nod, on the east of Eden.

17 And Cain knew his wife; and she conceived and bore Enoch. And he was building a city; and he called the city after the name of his son, Enoch.

18 And to Enoch was born Irad. And Irad begot Mehujael; and Mehujael begot Methusael, and Methusael begot Lamech.

19 And Lamech took to himself two wives. The name of the one was Adah; and the name of the second was Zillah.
20 And Adah bore Jabal. He was father of those
21 who dwell in tents and with cattle. And his brother's name was Jubal. He was father of all who handle the
22 harp and the flute. And Zillah, she also bore Tubal-Cain, a maker of every cutting instrument of brass and iron. And the sister of Tubal-Cain was Naamah.

23 And Lamech said to his wives:

Adah and Zillah, hear my voice;
Wives of Lamech, give ear to my word.
For I have slain a man for my wound,
And a young man for my hurt.
24 For sevenfold should Cain be avenged;
And Lamech seventy and seven.

V. 16. *Nod;* meaning, Flight. *On the east of Eden,* indicates the continued direction of population toward the interior of Asia.

VV. 17-24. *Posterity of Cain.*

V. 17. *A city.* In its primary use the word meant, as here, the entrenched encampment of a migratory family or tribe, for temporary security of themselves and their flocks against wild beasts and robbers. So it is used in Num. 13 : 19, where we should translate: "and what are the cities they dwell in, whether in camps, or in strongholds." The statement here is not inconsistent, therefore, with the one made in v. 12.

V. 19. The first recorded instance of that violation of the marriage institution, which has been so desolating in its effects on society throughout the eastern world. Some have said that it is here mentioned without censure; but the mere mention of it, in connection with the institution of marriage in the second chapter, is condemnatory.

V. 20. Jabal is mentioned as father of the nomadic tribes of Asia; that is, as the one who first followed their mode of life.

V. 21. *The harp,* the generic name of stringed instruments, as the *flute* is of wind instruments.

V. 22. *Cutting instruments of brass and iron;* including weapons of war, with the invention of which the incident that follows is connected.

Naamah (*pleasing, lovely,* an appropriate female name) is here mentioned as having some important connection with the history, and very probably with the deed commemorated in the two following verses.

VV. 23, 24, are the oldest specimen of the poetical form of composition. It consists here of

25 And Adam knew his wife again. And she bore a son, and called his name Seth; For God has appointed me another seed in place of Abel. For Cain slew him. And to Seth, to him also was born a son; and he called his name Enos. Then began men to call on the name of Jehovah.

1 This is the book of generations of Adam. In the day that God created man, in the likeness of God made he him; 2 a male and a female created he them; and he blessed them, and called their name man, in the day when they were created. 3 And Adam lived a hundred and thirty years, and begot a son in his likeness, after his image, and called his name Seth. 4 And the days of Adam, after he begot Seth, were eight 5 hundred years; and he begot sons and daughters. And all

---

V. 25. *Or, because Cain slew him*

the parallelism of the lines in form and sense, the assonance and final rhyme, and the use of poetical words and forms.

These lines are preserved here as an illustration of the spirit of that period of violence and blood, which culminated in the state of society described in ch. 6:5, and 11-13, when " the earth was filled with violence." They celebrate the prowess of an ancient hero, who boasts that he had signally avenged his wrong upon his adversary, and that the vengeance promised to Cain was light, compared with what he had inflicted.

VV. 25, 26. *Another line of descent from Adam, worshipers of the true God.*
With the account of Lamech and his family, being the seventh generation from Adam through Cain, the character of that race is sufficiently shown; and the narrative now turns to another line of descent from Adam, the pious posterity of Seth.

V. 25. *Seth;* meaning, Appointed; namely, in place of him who was taken away.
For Cain slew him; the explanatory remark of the narrator. If these are the words of Eve, as many suppose, they should be translated as in the margin, " because Cain slew him; that is, *for the reason, that Cain slew him.* The former meaning seems to be the more appropriate one.

V. 26. *To call on the name of Jehovah,* means to utter his name, in prayer for divine aid, or, in a more general sense, in solemn acts of religious worship, as in ch. 12:8, 13:4, 21:33, 26:25; 1 Chron. 16:8; Psalms 79:6, 105:1, 116:17; Isaiah 12:4, 41:25, 64:7; Zeph. 3:9.
" To call on *the name* of Jehovah," is to recognize in him what the name expresses, the Eternal, the One Eternal God. The statement, that men now began to do this, shows that other and idolatrous worship was already practiced, and that the true God now began to be known and worshiped by this name.

There had now commenced that line of descent from Adam, in which God, in after-times, especially manifested himself by the covenant name Jehovah. Hence its use here by the narrator; while in the quoted language of Eve, in the preceding verse, the name of the Divine Being is God, and not Jehovah.

Ch. 5. Second part of the second division: *Genealogy from Adam, in the line of Seth, to Noah.*
In this section, the name of the Divine Being is God.

V. 1. *Book of generations;* see the note on ch. 2:4, second paragraph.
V. 3. *In his likeness, after his image;* in a spiritual and moral sense, as well as physically.
V. 5. The great age of man previous to the Flood, gradually diminishing for some generations after, till it reached its present usual limit, has been the subject of much discussion. Some have

the days that Adam lived were nine hundred and thirty years; and he died.

⁶ And Seth lived a hundred and five years, and begot Enos. ⁷ And Seth lived, after he begot Enos, eight hundred and seven ⁸ years, and begot sons and daughters. And all the days of Seth were nine hundred and twelve years; and he died.

⁹ And Enos lived ninety years, and begot Cainan. ¹⁰ And Enos lived, after he begot Cainan, eight hundred and ¹¹ fifteen years, and begot sons and daughters. And all the days of Enos were nine hundred and five years; and he died.

¹² And Cainan lived seventy years, and begot Mahalaleel. ¹³ And Cainan lived, after he begot Mahalaleel, eight hundred ¹⁴ and forty years, and begot sons and daughters. And all the days of Cainan were nine hundred and ten years; and he died.

¹⁵ And Mahalaleel lived sixty-five years, and begot Jared. ¹⁶ And Mahalaleel lived, after he begot Jared, eight hundred ¹⁷ and thirty years, and begot sons and daughters. And all the days of Mahalaleel were eight hundred and ninety-five years; and he died.

attempted to account for the change in the duration of human life by physical causes, namely, changes in the physical temperament of our world, in modes of living, etc. Others have maintained, that the age of man did not then greatly exceed that to which men are known to have attained in later times; some supposing that each name represents several generations; others, that the "year" was not a solar year as subsequently, but some equally defined period, as a lunar month, or a period of six months between the solstices or equinoxes, or a *season* of three months marked by the passage of the sun between the equinoctial and solstitial points, or (according to the ancient division of the year into spring, summer, and winter) a season of four months.

But this assumed meaning of the word *year*, making it a twelfth, or a half, or a third, or a fourth of the solar year, has no historical support; there being no evidence that such portions of time were ever made the unit of measure for long periods, such as the duration of human life, or were ever used for any other purpose than as fractions of the solar year.

It fails, moreover, in its application. For though it might explain the cases occurring in this chapter, it fails when applied to ch. 11, tenth and following verses, where some are mentioned as having sons at the age of thirty, and as living to the age of four or five hundred years.

The term of life, in man as in all other animals, is God's ordinance. The progress of a human being from infancy, through childhood, youth, and manhood, to old age, is a law of his constitution ordained by his Maker; and the length of time assigned for each, together with the secondary causes on which it depends, is also his appointment. Our belief that it was ever otherwise than at present, depends on our confidence in the record which asserts it. It is not an unphilosophical supposition, that man was originally so constituted, that his term of life should go on diminishing till it reached its minimum, and there remain stationary.

V. 6. The one mentioned in these genealogies is not always the first-born son. It is the one through whom the particular line traced in the genealogy was continued, and the others are passed over. Compare the third verse.

18 And Jared lived a hundred and sixty-two years, and be-
19 got Enoch. And Jared lived, after he begot Enoch, eight
20 hundred years, and begot sons and daughters. And all the
days of Jared were nine hundred and sixty-two years; and
he died.
21 And Enoch lived sixty-five years, and begot Methuselah.
22 And Enoch walked with God, after he begot Methuselah,
23 three hundred years, and begot sons and daughters. And
all the days of Enoch were three hundred and sixty-five
24 years. And Enoch walked with God; and he was not, for
God took him.
25 And Methuselah lived a hundred and eighty-seven years,
26 and begot Lamech. And Methuselah lived, after he begot
Lamech, seven hundred and eighty-two years, and begot
27 sons and daughters. And all the days of Methuselah were
nine hundred and sixty-nine years; and he died.
28 And Lamech lived a hundred and eighty-two years, and
29 begot a son. And he called his name Noah, saying:
This one will comfort us,
From our labor,
And from the toil of our hands,
From the ground,
Which Jehovah cursed.

V. 22. *Walked with God.* This expresses the most intimate converse, founded on a unity of spirit and purpose. (Compare Amos 3 : 3.) It is said of no other except Noah (ch. 6 : 9). It is not implied that no others of the race were devout men; but that Enoch was pre-eminently so, and as such was distinguished by the manner of his removal from earth (v. 24).

V. 24. *And he was not,* naturally expresses sudden and mysterious removal, or disappearance. Compare Isaiah 17 : 14; Job 27 : 19; Psalm 103 : 16. The phraseology and connection show that a removal from earth is meant; or as the apostle expresses it (Heb. 11 : 5), he "was translated, that he should not see death."

Was not, for God took him. Many have maintained that the Hebrew Scriptures contain no intimation of a future life, beyond the grave. But the thoughtful, reflecting Hebrew could not read this passage, without seeing in it decisive evidence of a state of happiness for the righteous after death. Length of life (so he would necessarily reason) is the promised reward of piety. Yet this man, specially distinguished as one who "walked with God," was taken away in the midst of his days, when he had barely attained to half the then usual age of man. And it is said, moreover, that "God took him;" that is, took him to himself, for such is the proper meaning of the word. He walked with God, and God took him to himself! What can this mean, but that He, with whom he held intimate converse on earth, took him to a still nearer and happier intercourse with himself, in a higher and purer state of being? On this view alone could the thoughtful Hebrew reader reconcile this statement with what he was elsewhere taught.

V. 29. *Noah;* meaning, Rest.

In the following words (which have the form of poetry in the Hebrew) there appears to be no reference to Noah's subsequent history, as given us in the sacred records. They seem rather

³⁰ And Lamech lived, after he begot Noah, five hundred and ³¹ ninety-five years, and begot sons and daughters. And all the days of Lamech were seven hundred and seventy-seven years; and he died.
³² And Noah was five hundred years old. And Noah begot Shem, Ham, and Japheth.

¹ AND it came to pass, that men began to be numerous on the face of the ground, and daughters were born to them. ² And the sons of God saw the daughters of men, that they were fair; and they took for themselves wives of all whom they chose.
³ And Jehovah said: My Spirit shall not forever strive with man, in their erring. He is flesh; and his days shall be a hundred and twenty years.

V. 3. *Or*, judge man

to express the pious and grateful feelings of poor, toil-worn parents on the birth of a son, from whom they hoped for aid and relief in the labors to which sin had subjected man.

From the ground. This may be taken, either with the first line, in the same relation to it as the second; or with the third line, in the sense of proceeding from the ground, as the source or occasion of painful toil.

The use of the word JEHOVAH by the pious Lamech, in a section where the narrator uses the word GOD, is explained by what has been said on the last clause of ch. 4 : 26.

V. 32. This statement is made in a general manner, without intending to be definite. Noah was of this age (is the meaning) at the birth of the first-born of the three sons here mentioned. For Shem is said (11 : 10) to have been a hundred years old, two years after the Flood. Hence Japheth, his elder brother (10 : 21), may have been born at the age of Noah here mentioned. Ham was the youngest of the three, as is stated in ch. 9 : 24.

Chs. 6–9. Third part of the second division : *Account of the Flood, and subsequent history of Noah.*

In this section, the name of the Divine Being is GOD; occasionally JEHOVAH, as in 6 : 3, 5, 6, 7, 8; 7 : 1, 5, 16; 8 : 20, 21; 9 : 26.

VV. 1–12. Intermarriages between the two races descended from Adam, and consequent general corruption.

V. 2. *Sons of God.* The worshipers of Jehovah are so designated in Deut. 14 : 1, Psalm 73 : 15, Prov. 14 : 26. It is a natural and appropriate designation, recognizing in them a divinely imparted principle, and the divine relation founded on it.

The descendants of Seth are meant, among whom, as a race, the worship of the true God was maintained; though, in process of time, it became with many a mere outward form, as their choice of wedded companions shows.

After such a use of the phrase *sons of God*, the word *men* takes a peculiar and special meaning, designating those in whom this divinely imparted principle is wanting,—men, and nothing more. By *daughters of men* are meant, therefore, not merely women, females of the human family, but those of a race estranged from the knowledge and worship of the true God.

Of all whom they chose; of all, without distinction, not regarding the race to which they belonged. Thus the bounds which separated the two races were broken over; and this resulted in universal irreligion and lawlessness.

V. 3. *Strive with man;* that is, admonish and reprove him. Margin, *judge man*, to the same effect; acting as judge, and condemning his sinful conduct to his own consciousness.

GENESIS.   CHAP. VI.

4   The men of violence were in the earth in those days. And also after the sons of God came in unto the daughters of men, they bore children to them. These were the mighty men, who of old were the men of renown.
5   And Jehovah saw that the evil of man was great in the earth; and every device of the thoughts of his heart was
6   only evil, all the day. And Jehovah repented that he made man on the earth, and he was grieved at his heart.
7   And Jehovah said: I will wipe off man, whom I created,

In their erring. The verb means, *to go astray* (as it is well rendered in Psalm 119:67), *to err* (from the right way), either consciously, or through inattention or ignorance. In Lev. 5:18, it is correctly rendered in the common English version, "wherein he erred;" as is also the corresponding noun, in Eccl. 5:6, "it was an error," and 10:5, "an error which proceedeth from the ruler."

Shall not forever strive with man. This course of probationary and punitive discipline shall not go on without end, but shall give place to the final act of retributive justice. For the sentiment, compare 1 Peter 3:19, 20.

He is flesh; frail, both physically and morally; depraved, as well as mortal, and as such shall be treated. But time shall be allowed him (the whole race of man) for repentance and reformation; and his days (the continuance of the race upon earth) shall be prolonged to a hundred and twenty years. The sacred writer here records the divine purpose—what God purposed in himself—not what he communicated of his designs. The exact number of years was determined by the event, and there is no reason to suppose that it was communicated beforehand.

Some take this for the limit of human life, from that time onward. But there is no indication that it was ever fixed at this number of years; and that it was not now thus limited, is shown in ch. 11:11-26.

It has also been taken for the interval of time "while the ark was preparing" (1 Pet. 3:20). But this is impossible. From the birth of Japheth (ch. 5:32) to the Flood (ch. 7:11) was a hundred years. When the direction for building the ark was given to Noah (vv. 13 and following) his sons were already grown to manhood (v. 18); and it could not, therefore, have been a hundred and twenty years before the Flood.

V. 4. *The men of violence;* with the definite article, as being the well-known and dreaded class of men, descendants of Cain, who were distinguished for deeds of violence, and (as may be inferred from this) for extraordinary stature and physical strength. (Compare Num. 13:32, 33). Hence "*The* men of violence;" that is, renowned as such.

The meaning of the passage may be stated thus: The descendants of Cain were an irreligions race, and some were distinguished for personal prowess and the oppressive use of it. Descendants of Seth intermarried with women of this race; and from this union sprang men distinguished for like character and conduct. Thus the whole race of man became corrupt.

V. 5. *Every device of the thoughts of his heart;* that is, all that the thoughts of his heart devise. *All the day;* the whole day, all the time, without intermission. Language could not describe more strongly the entire corruption of the race.

V. 6. We can not presume to fathom the depth of meaning in such language, when spoken of the infinite and all-perfect God. How the divine nature is affected by the guilt and folly of sin is unknown to us; but this language is designed to bring it as near to our conception as is possible for our finite and imperfect nature.

In 1 Sam. 15:29, it is said of God, "He is not a man that he should repent;" that is, as man repents. The unchanging God can not repent in such a sense as does changeful man, whose purpose of to-day may give place to another of to-morrow.

He was grieved at his heart, expresses the depth of sorrow, and the tender pity, with which divine love regards the base ingratitude of sin.

V. 7. *Will wipe off.* The verb is used in its primary literal meaning in Prov. 30:20, "she eats, and wipes her mouth;" Isaiah 25:8, "will wipe away tears;" 2 Kings 21:13, properly, "as one wipes the dish; he wipes, and turns it on its face." It is proper that the distinction

from the face of the ground; from man to cattle, to reptile, and to the fowls of heaven; for I repent that I made them. 8 But Noah found favor in the eyes of Jehovah.

9 These are the generations of Noah. Noah was a just man; perfect was he in his generations; Noah walked with 10 God. And Noah begot three sons, Shem, Ham, and Ja- 11 pheth. And the earth was corrupt before God; and the 12 earth was filled with violence. And God saw the earth, and behold, it was corrupted; for all flesh had corrupted its way upon the earth.

13 And God said to Noah: The end of all flesh is come before me; for the earth is filled with violence through them; and behold, I will destroy them with the earth.

14 Make thee an ark of cypress wood. With cells shalt thou make the ark, and shalt pitch it within and without with 15 pitch. And this is what thou shalt make it; three hundred cubits shall be the length of the ark, fifty cubits its breadth, 16 and thirty cubits its height. Light shalt thou make for the ark; and to a cubit shalt thou finish it above; and the

---

V. 14. *Or*, of resinous wood
·V. 16. *Or*, Lights shalt thou make   *Or*, them   *Or*, from above (*or*, upward)

should be made, here and in 7:4, 23, between this verb and the verb "destroy" in vv. 13, 17, and that the figurative form of the original should be preserved.

V. 9. *Generations.* See the remark on ch. 2:4, second paragraph. *In his generations;* through which his life extended.

V. 13. *Is come before me;* is present to my view; no longer a remote and distant thing, but near at hand, and about to take place. *With the earth;* which would be utterly laid waste, and in that sense destroyed.

V. 14. *An ark.* The word is used only here, and in Ex. 2:3, 5, of the ark of rushes, in which the infant Moses was exposed.

It properly means a box, or chest, and in shape was an oblong square. The ark was intended merely for floating on the water, and not for sailing. Vessels have been built in modern times, with the same construction and proportions, and have been found to carry a third more freight than ships of equal dimensions.

Cypress wood; used anciently in ship-building, for which it was well adapted by its lightness and durability. The same is true of the more comprehensive designation, *resinous wood* (margin), embracing the pine, fir, cypress, cedar, etc. But the more probable rendering is given in the text.

With cells; stalls for the various animals to be provided for.

V. 15. *Cubit;* the length of the fore-arm from the elbow to the end of the middle finger; variously estimated at from eighteen to twenty-one inches.

V. 16. *Light* (or, as in the margin, *lights*). The word used here is not the one rendered "window" in ch. 8:6.

To a cubit shall thou finish it above. The meaning of this expression is very obscure, from its extreme brevity, and from the uncertain reference of the pronoun (whether to "light," or to "the ark"), as well as the different uses of the word rendered *above*, and in the margin, *from above*, or *upward*. The pronoun *it* (or *them*) is usually referred to *light*, or collectively *lights*

GENESIS. CHAP. VII.

door of the ark shalt thou set in the side thereof; with lower, second, and third stories shalt thou make it.
17 And I, behold I bring the flood of waters upon the earth, to destroy all flesh, wherein is the breath of life, from under the heavens. All that is in the earth shall expire.
18 And I establish my covenant with thee; and thou shalt come into the ark, thou, and thy sons, and thy wife and the
19 wives of thy sons, with thee. And of all the living of all flesh, two of all shalt thou bring into the ark, to keep alive
20 with thee; a male and a female shall they be. Of the fowl after its kind, and of cattle after their kind, and of every reptile of the ground after its kind, two of all shall come to
21 thee, to keep them alive. And do thou take to thee of all food that may be eaten, and thou shalt gather it to thee; and it shall be to thee and to them for food.
22 And Noah did it. According to all that God commanded him, so did he.

1 And Jehovah said to Noah: Come thou, and all thy

V. 18. *Or*, And I will maintain my covenant

(margin); supposed by some to have been placed in the roof (*above*), and finished "to a cubit" in size. The other rendering, *to a cubit from above*, means, as some suppose, to a cubit's length, measuring from the top downward, that is, a cubit in height; or, as others think, to a cubit's distance from the top of the ark or its projecting roof, leaving the space of a cubit between it and the edge of the roof; or, according to others, "to a cubit" in width, extending "from above" downward through all the three tiers in the ark, giving light to each. The rendering, *to a cubit shalt thou finish it* (or *them*) *upward*, is supposed to mean, that it should be finished (terminated) at the height of a cubit, that is, should be made a cubit in height; the only supposition (with the similar one, the second given above) on which the word "finish" seems applicable, with this reference of the pronoun.

But on neither of these suppositions does the word "finish," bring to completion, seem very applicable, with this reference. The word more naturally refers to the finishing of the whole structure, by completing the inclosure above. *To a cubit* (in height) *shall thou finish it above* (or, *upward*) would then indicate the pitch of the roof or deck. That it would be nearly flat is no objection, that being the case also with the deck of a ship, and no other shape being equally safe.

The description is of course very general, as must be the case in describing such a structure in half a dozen lines; and much remains untold, in regard to light, ventilation, and other necessary arrangements.

From ch. 8 : 13 it has been inferred that light was not admitted at the *sides* of the ark; as, if it had been, Noah could have seen the state of the earth, without "removing the covering of the ark." But this is a misinterpretation of that passage. It is evident from ch. 8 : 5, that objects could be seen from the ark before the covering was removed; and this must have been made possible by the necessary provisions for ventilation and cleanliness.

Ch. 7 : 1-3. The forbearance of God, during the interval in which "the ark was preparing" (1 Peter 3 : 20), and the solemn admonitions enforced by such signal evidence of God's purpose of speedy retribution, seem to have failed to reclaim any from their evil course; and, as is usual

Chap. VII.   GENESIS.

house, into the ark; for thee have I seen righteous before
2 me in this generation. Of all clean cattle thou shalt take to
thee seven of each, a male and his mate; and of cattle
3 that are not clean two, a male and his mate; also of the
fowls of heaven seven of each, male and female; to keep
4 seed alive on the face of all the earth. For yet seven
days, and I will cause it to rain upon the earth forty days
and forty nights; and every being that I made will I wipe
off from the face of the ground.
5 And Noah did according to all that Jehovah commanded
him.
6 And Noah was six hundred years old, when the flood of
7 waters was upon the earth. And Noah went in, and his
sons, and his wife and the wives of his sons, with him, into
8 the ark, because of the waters of the flood. Of the clean
cattle, and of cattle that are not clean, and of the fowl, and
9 all that moves upon the ground, there went in two of each
to Noah into the ark, a male and a female, as God commanded Noah.

---

when such admonitions fail of the intended effect, had doubtless hardened them in impiety. Their history is written in the brief and impressive words of the Savior (Matt. 24:38): "They were eating and drinking, marrying and giving in marriage, . . . and knew not until the Flood came, and took all away." The formal reiteration of the testimony to Noah's piety in the midst of such a people, is well suited to the solemnity of the occasion; and the deep religious tone of the whole narrative exhibits a striking contrast to the frivolous traditionary accounts of this great catastrophe, found among almost all pagan nations.

The ark being now completed, after an interval of time of unknown length (see the note on ch. 6:3, last paragraph), Noah receives a more specific direction in regard to the number of *clean cattle* to be admitted into the ark. This does not conflict with the statement in ch. 6:19, 20, but is added as a further and special direction respecting this class of animals.

V. 2. *Clean;* such animals as "divide the hoof and chew the cud" (Lev. 11:2–8).

Seven of each. Either seven individuals of each class of animals, which is the most natural meaning of the expression; or seven pairs of each, which accords best with the following words, *a male and his mate.*

Observe that only clean *cattle* (domestic animals; see the note on ch. 1:24, 25, third paragraph) are thus distinguished. The number, therefore, would not be great.

The necessity for the speedy propagation of this class of animals, and the intended use of the male in sacrifice (ch. 8:20; compare Lev. 1:2, 3), appear to be the grounds of the distinction.

V. 4. The septimal division of time, observable in this narrative (compare ch. 8:10, 12), is a strong corroborative testimony to the primitive institution of the Sabbath. It is not probable that the division was suggested by successive changes of the moon, and was dependent on them; for these are not sufficiently definite and observable for such a purpose.

Forty days, etc. This may be here the exact number of days and nights during which the rain continued. But the number *forty* seems to be sometimes used, and may be here, for a long indefinite number. Compare, for example, Ex. 24:18; Num. 13:25; Deut. 9:9, 18, 25; 1 Kings 19:8; Judges 3:11, 5:31, 8:28, 13:1; 2 Sam. 15:7; Ezek. 29:11, 13.

V. 9. *Two of each,* is not at variance with the first direction given in the second verse. This

¹⁰ And it came to pass, after the seven days, that the waters
¹¹ of the flood were upon the earth. In the six hundredth year of Noah's life, in the second month, on the seventeenth day of the month, on that day were all the fountains of the great abyss broken up, and the windows of the heavens
¹² were opened. And the heavy rain was upon the earth forty
¹³ days and forty nights. On the selfsame day entered Noah, and Shem, and Ham, and Japheth, sons of Noah, and the wife of Noah, and the three wives of his sons with them,
¹⁴ into the ark; they, and every living thing after its kind, and all the cattle after their kind, and every reptile that creeps on the earth after its kind, and every fowl after its
¹⁵ kind, every bird of every sort. And they went in to Noah into the ark, two of each, of all flesh wherein is the breath
¹⁶ of life. And they that went in, went in a male and a female of all flesh, as God commanded him. And Jehovah closed up after him.
¹⁷ And the flood was forty days upon the earth; and the waters increased, and bore up the ark, and it rose up from
¹⁸ the earth. And the waters prevailed, and increased mightily

is the general direction for both clean and unclean, and does not exclude an additional and special one for the former.

V. 10. *After the seven days;* the seven days mentioned in the fourth verse. Hence the use of the definite article.

V. 11. *The second month.* The year commenced at the time of the autumnal equinox; and the seventeenth day of the second month fell in the first quarter of November, when the rainy season had begun.

The remainder of the verse expresses, in strong figurative language, the rush of waters to the earth's surface, from above and below, as though windows were opened in the heavens, and the fountains of the great abyss were broken up.

V. 13. *On the selfsame day* (namely, the seventeenth), the necessary arrangements were completed by the entrance of Noah and his family into the ark. What is stated in the next three verses had already taken place.

The words, *wife of Noah,* and *the three wives of his sons,* show that in Noah's family the original institution of marriage was preserved.

V. 16. *Closed up after him;* an expression of God's providential care, that watched over and preserved the ark through the storms and floods that followed.

VV. 17-20. The charm of the preceding narrative is the simple earnestness with which all the particulars are minutely detailed, and are fondly dwelt upon and reiterated. In the following verses the narrative proceeds with increasing animation, sketching rapidly and vividly the several stages of the great catastrophe. The following points in its progress are distinctly marked in the narration:

(V. 17.) The flood has now been a long time on the earth. The waters still increase, and rising higher and higher at length reach the ark, and lift it from its resting-place, and it is raised from the earth.

(V. 18.) The waters still prevail, and increase mightily upon the earth; and the ark now floats freely on the surface of the waters.

upon the earth; and the ark went upon the face of the waters. ¹⁹ And the waters prevailed mightily, mightily, upon the earth; and all the high mountains, that are under the whole heavens, were covered. ²⁰ Fifteen cubits upward did the waters prevail; 'and the mountains were covered. ²¹ And all flesh expired that moved upon the earth, of fowl, and of cattle, and of beast, and of every creeping thing that creeps upon the earth, and every man. ²² All in whose nostrils was the breath of a spirit of life, of all that was on the dry land, died. ²³ And every being was wiped off, which was upon the face of the ground, from man to cattle, to reptile, and to the fowl of the heavens; and they were wiped off from the earth, and there remained only Noah, and they that were with him in the ark. ²⁴ And the waters prevailed upon the earth a hundred and fifty days.

¹ AND God remembered Noah, and every living thing, and all the cattle that were with him in the ark; and God caused a wind to pass over the earth, and the waters subsided. ² And the fountains of the abyss and the windows of heaven were closed, and the heavy rain from heaven was restrained. ³ And the waters returned from off the earth continually; and the waters abated from the end of a hundred and fifty days. ⁴ And the ark rested in the seventh

(V. 19.) The flood still increases, and the waters prevail mightily, mightily, upon the earth, and cover all its mountains.

(V. 20.) The waters yet increase, the mighty masses still swelling upward, and rising fifteen cubits after the mountains were covered.

The whole description is marked by the glow and animation of an eye-witness of the scene.

V. 20. *And the mountains were covered;* that is, *were* (already) *covered,* equivalent to *when the mountains were covered.* Or this may be an emphatic repetition of the statement,—as much as to say, and the very mountains were covered.

V. 22. *A spirit of life.* The word rendered *spirit* is literally *breath* (like our word *spirit*), and with or without the word *life* (ch. 6 : 17) means *breath of life,* the vital breath, on which life is made dependent. Hence it comes to mean, as here, the principle of life, the vital spirit, whether in man or other animals. Compare Eccl. 3 : 19, 21.

V. 24. *Prevailed . . . a hundred and fifty days;* dating perhaps (as the word *prevailed* seems to indicate) from the stage of the flood described in v. 19, and terminating with that described in ch. 8 : 3, when the waters were abating. But see the remarks on ch. 8 : 4.

Ch. 8 : 4. *In the seventh month, on the seventeenth day of the month;* being five months, or a hundred and fifty days, from the entrance into the ark (ch. 7 : 11-13); which may have been the period intended in ch. 7 : 24.

Ararat was the name of a region of country in Armenia. Compare 2 Kings 19 : 37, and Isaiah

month, on the seventeenth day of the month, on the mount-
5 ains of Ararat. And the waters were abating continually until the tenth month. In the tenth, on the first of the month, were the tops of the mountains seen.

6 And it came to pass at the end of forty days, that Noah
7 opened the window of the ark which he made. And he sent forth the raven; and he went forth, going forth and returning, until the drying up of the waters from off the earth.

8 And he sent forth the dove from him, to see if the waters
9 were lightened from off the face of the ground. And the dove found not a resting-place for the sole of her foot, and she returned to him into the ark; for the waters were on the face of all the earth. And he put forth his hand, and took her, and brought her in to him into the ark.

10 And he waited yet another seven days; and again he sent
11 forth the dove from the ark. And the dove came in to him at evening; and lo, in her mouth an olive-leaf plucked off! And Noah knew that the waters were lightened from off the earth.

12 And he waited yet another seven days, and sent forth the dove; and she returned to him no more.

13 And it came to pass in the six hundred and first year, in the first month, on the first of the month, that the waters were dried up from off the earth. And Noah removed the

---

37 : 38 (in both properly *land of Ararat*), and Jer. 51 : 27, where it is mentioned in connection with *Minni*, another region of Armenia.

VV. 7-9. *He went forth, going forth and returning, until the drying up of the waters;* that is, he continued to go forth from the ark, and to return to it, till the waters were dried up. The raven, accustomed to feed on carrion, was daily tempted forth, to prey on the floating carcasses, returning to the ark for rest. But the dove (v. 9), finding neither resting-place nor her accustomed food, returned to the ark and remained there.

V. 10. *Another seven days,* shows that he had before waited seven days, when he first sent forth the dove (v. 8); and the same interval occurs a third time in v. 12, indicating an established septimal division of time.

V. 11. *Plucked off.* The freshness of the fracture showed that the leaf was plucked from the tree, and not picked up from the surface of the water.

By sending forth the dove, he might hope to obtain some indication of the state of the earth at a distance, beyond the sphere of vision from the ark. *Came in to him at evening,* implies that she had been long on the wing.

VV. 13, 14. *In the six hundred and first year,* of Noah's life; compare ch. 7 : 11.

The waters were now "dried up from off the earth;" and Noah removed the covering of the ark, and from its top, the highest point of view he could reach, saw no water on the face of the ground.

covering of the ark, and saw, and behold the face of the
14 ground was dry. And in the second month, on the seven
and twentieth day of the month, was the earth dried.

V. 14. The flood commenced (ch. 7 : 11) on the seventeenth day of the second month ; on the first day of the following year (ch. 8 : 13), after ten and a half months or about three hundred and eight days, the waters of the flood had disappeared from the surface of the ground; and after a month and twenty-seven days more (v. 14) " the earth was dried," and in a state to be trodden again by the foot of man and beast.
According to the statement in ch. 7 : 24, and 8 : 3, the flood was at least a hundred and fifty, or possibly (see the note on ch. 7 : 24) a hundred and ninety days in attaining its greatest height. The subsiding of the waters occupied about a hundred and sixty, or at the least, a hundred and twenty days. So gradual was the rise of the waters and their fall.
We can not fail to be impressed with the sobriety of the narrative, and with the truthful minuteness and consistency of all its details.

Traditions of the Flood are found among almost all known nations; an evidence, in itself, that they had their origin in an actual historical event; for the same tradition could not have sprung up casually, at so many and widely distant points.
But the Biblical narrative alone fulfills the required conditions, in the historical definiteness and consistency of its details, and in the deep religious and moral grounds which it furnishes for such an extraordinary interposition of divine justice.
It must be admitted that there are very great difficulties, not in the narrative, which is everywhere clear and consistent with itself, but in the nature of the case; and this might well be expected. It is just and reasonable, that Christian scholars should seek to disarm the objections of unbelievers, by so interpreting the narrative as to avoid these difficulties.
It is claimed that the narrative does not necessarily suppose a strictly universal flood, that is, a flood universal to all the divisions of the earth. The horizon of the writer, it is suggested, is to him the natural boundary of "the whole heavens" of which he speaks. This undoubtedly is the manner of the Holy Scriptures; and there is no valid objection to such an interpretation. Nor was it necessary, for the accomplishment of the divine purpose, that the flood should extend beyond the region occupied by living animals, or perhaps beyond the region occupied by man.
It is supposed, therefore, that the flood covered only such a portion of the earth, not large in extent, as was already inhabited by man, and consequently reached only such of the brute creation, and those mostly domestic animals, as were in his immediate neighborhood; the words " all flesh," " all in whose nostrils was the breath of life," referring to those within the writer's sphere of view. On these suppositions (and they can not be proved to be absolutely inconsistent with the narrative) the difficulties inherent in the nature of the case are greatly lessened, and perhaps wholly removed.
But it is not easy to reconcile them with the narrative. Nor do we rightly estimate the difficulties in the case, unless we bear in mind that the course of nature was then, in many respects, different from what we now observe. It is sufficient to refer to the age of man. The laws which have governed the multiplication of animals, in species and varieties, are not yet fully determined; nor can it be said, with any certainty, how many existed in the time of the Flood. The water on the earth's surface, as is well known, would, if evenly distributed over it at a uniform depth, more than cover its highest elevations. In the geological history of the earth, its continents, with their loftiest mountains, have been more than once submerged beneath the waters of the ocean; and though, in the process of cooling through many ages, the crust of the earth had acquired greater stability before it became the abode of man, yet since then great changes of level in the continents and in the bed of the ocean are known to have taken place, and such changes are even now going on, though at a very gradual rate. When we consider how very slight is the elevation of mountain ranges compared with the entire mass of the earth (not more than would be represented by the thickness of pasteboard on an artificial globe) it is evident that a comparatively slight elevation of the ocean bed, and corresponding depression of the dry land, would suffice to flood the whole earth.
It can not be doubted, of course, that the Almighty, who created all things, and has all the powers of nature under his control, was able to accomplish what is here narrated; and that

GENESIS.   CHAP. VIII.

¹⁵ ¹⁶ And God spoke to Noah, saying : Go forth from the ark, thou, and thy wife, and thy sons, and the wives of thy sons, ¹⁷ with thee. Every living thing that is with thee, of all flesh, of fowl, and of cattle, and of every reptile that creeps upon the earth, bring forth with thee, that they may breed abundantly in the earth, and be fruitful, and multiply on the earth.
¹⁸ And Noah went forth, and his sons, and his wife, and the ¹⁹ wives of his sons, with him. Every living thing, every reptile, every fowl, all that moves upon the earth, after their families, went forth from the ark.
²⁰ And Noah built an altar to Jehovah. And he took of all clean cattle, and of every clean fowl, and offered burnt-offer- ²¹ ings on the altar. And Jehovah smelled the sweet odor. And Jehovah said in his heart : I will not again curse the ground on account of man, for the device of the heart of man is evil from his youth ; and I will not again smite ²² every living thing, as I have done. During all the days of the earth, sowing and reaping, and cold and heat, and summer and winter, and day and night, shall not cease.

he could carry into effect any plan he devised for continuing the race of man and all other animals. In what manner it was done, is a fair question of interpretation.
Of the moral significance of this event, in the world's history, there can be no question ; nor is it possible to estimate the influence of such a fact, handed down through the nations by tradition and revelation. It has everywhere testified to the truth, " There is a God that judges in the earth ;" and the record of it can not be effaced from the world's literature, or from the minds of men.
VV. 20-22. The new era of the race commences more auspiciously than the first, with acts of piety and devotion, and with the solemn recognition of man's guilt, and of the atoning sacrifice. On this is founded the gracious purpose toward the new race, expressed in vv. 21, 22.
V. 20. The *altar*, and *burnt-offerings*, are here mentioned for the first time. For the latter, compare Lev. ch. 1.
V. 21. *Smelled the sweet odor*. The thought is expressed under a physical image. It was, of course, the spiritual significance of the offering that made it acceptable in the sight of God.
Said in his heart; purposed within himself. It is significant that this purpose, regarding the future of the race, is expressed in connection with Noah's act of faith, and with his accepted offering.
For the device, etc., has been thought to be the reason for the promised forbearance ; which appears, however, to be inconsistent with itself, and with what is said in ch. 6 : 5-7. The words seem rather intended to show, that this lenity is undeserved forbearance toward man. The connection of thought is : " I will not again curse the ground on account of man,"—for that only does he deserve,—" for the device of the heart of man is evil from his youth."
V. 22. *Sowing and reaping,* etc. By these are not meant divisions of the year, as some have regarded them. The principal occupations on which men depend for subsistence, and the alternations of temperature and of the seasons, with which these are necessarily connected, and of day and night, are specified, in order to show that the course of nature should ever after be regular and unbroken.

¹ AND God blessed Noah and his sons; and he said to ² them: Be fruitful, and multiply, and fill the earth. And the fear of you, and the dread of you, shall be upon every beast of the earth, and upon every fowl of the heavens, upon all with which the ground teems, and upon all the fishes of ³ the sea; into your hand are they given. Every moving thing that lives, to you shall it be for food; as the green ⁴ herb have I given you all. But flesh with its life, its blood, ye shall not eat.

⁵ But also your blood of your lives will I require; at the hand of every beast will I require it, and at the hand of man; at the hand of each one's brother will I require the ⁶ life of man. He that sheds the blood of man, by man shall his blood be shed; for in the image of God made he man.

Ch. 9 : 3. Here is the first express permission of the use of animal food. That it was already allowed can not be inferred from the dominion given to man over the lower animals, nor from the keeping of flocks (as in the case of Abel, ch. 4 : 2), which furnished milk and material for clothing, and were offered in sacrifice (ch. 4 : 4). If animal food was used, as is not improbable, it was done without divine permission.

V. 4. In regard to the *blood*, there are two restrictions. In this verse, the eating of blood is prohibited; "flesh with its life, its blood, ye shall not eat." For the ground of the prohibition see Lev. 17 : 11; the principle of life being contained in the blood, it was to be offered on the altar, "to make atonement for the soul," and was sacred to this use.

V. 5. *But also;* a further restriction, in regard to the blood of man. The blood of beasts may be shed, in sacrifices, and for the use of their flesh as food. But your blood shall not be shed, by man or beast, on penalty of death.

Your blood of your lives; that is, in which your life resides, or with which it is connected.

At the hand of every beast will I require it. Compare Exod. 21 : 28. Such is the sacredness of human life in the eye of God. It is not meant that the beast is morally guilty, or capable of being so; but the sanctity of human life must be vindicated by the death of its destroyer.

At the hand of each one's brother will I require the life of man. The obvious sense of the words is: For the life of every man I will hold his brother man accountable. Here is an accountability beyond the person of the manslayer. What that accountability is, is expressed in the following verse.

V. 6. *He that sheds the blood of man, by man shall his blood be shed.* Such is the accountability to which God holds man for the blood of his fellow-man; as he has said in the preceding verse, "at the hand of each one's brother will I require the life of man." The reason for this requirement is added: *For in the image of God made he man.* He that violates the sacredness of that image in his fellow-man, shall forfeit it in himself.

Unquestionably, God here requires that the murderer shall be punished with death, and holds men guilty who disregard the requirement. If he intended by these words (as they are sometimes evasively interpreted) merely to predict that men would, unauthorized and criminally, put the murderer to death, then they are out of place in the connection with his own requirement in the preceding verse, and he follows them here with a reason for the act ("for in the image of God made he man") that has no force or pertinence.

This was not a requirement of the Jewish law, to be abolished with it. It was made binding on all the races of men, descendants of Noah, and has never been revoked.

7 And you, be ye fruitful, and multiply; and bring forth abundantly in the earth, and multiply therein.

8 And God spoke to Noah, and to his sons with him, say-
9 ing: And I, behold, I establish my covenant with you, and
10 with your seed after you; and with every living being that is with you, of the fowl, of the cattle, and of every beast of the earth with you; of all that go forth from the ark of
11 every beast of the earth. And I establish my covenant with you; and all flesh shall not again be cut off by the waters of a flood, and there shall not again be a flood to destroy the earth.

12 And God said: This is a sign of the covenant which I make between me and you, and every living being that is
13 with you, for perpetual generations. My bow I set in the cloud, and it shall be for a covenant-sign between me and
14 the earth. And it shall come to pass, when I bring a cloud over the earth, that the bow shall be seen in the cloud.
15 And I will remember my covenant, which is between me and you, and every living being of all flesh; and the waters
16 shall no more become a flood to destroy all flesh. And the bow shall be in the cloud; and I will see it, to remember the perpetual covenant between God and every living being
17 of all flesh that is upon the earth. And God said to Noah: This is a sign of the covenant which I establish between me and all flesh that is upon the earth.

18 And the sons of Noah, who went forth from the ark, were Shem, and Ham, and Japheth. And Ham was the father of
19 Canaan. These were the three sons of Noah; and from these was the whole earth overspread.
20 And Noah, the husbandman, began and planted a vine-

V. 11. *Or*, I will maintain my covenant

V. 13. *My bow I set in the cloud.* Its previous occurrence was no reason why God should not make it a sign of his covenant; and these words do not imply that it had never been seen before. He *sets his bow in the cloud*, whenever it is seen there. It is not permanent and abiding, but occasional; and whenever it is seen in the cloud, he *sets it* there, as a covenant-sign; and the words, "My bow I set in the cloud," belong to every such appearance.

VV. 20–23. The impartiality and truthfulness of the narrative are shown by the freedom with which it exposes the faults of the most distinguished and highly commended of the personages whose lives it records. If there were extenuating circumstances in this case of Noah, as there probably were, they are unknown to us, and it is useless to conjecture them. It is better (as

CHAP. IX. GENESIS.

21 yard. And he drank of the wine, and was drunken; and he
22 uncovered himself within his tent. And Ham, the father of Canaan, saw the nakedness of his father; and he told it to
23 his two brothers without. And Shem and Japheth took the mantle, and laid it on the shoulders of them both, and went backward, and covered the nakedness of their father; and their faces were backward, and the nakedness of their father they did not see.
24 And Noah awoke from his wine; and he knew what his
25 younger son did to him. And he said:

> Cursed be Canaan;
> A servant of servants shall he be to his brethren.

26 And he said:

> Blessed be Jehovah, God of Shem;
> And let Canaan be servant to him.

27 God give enlargement to Japheth,
> And he will dwell in the tents of Shem;
> And let Canaan be servant to him.

---

remarked by Calvin) to leave them out of the question, and to learn rather, from this sad record, how vile and detestable a thing is drunkenness.

V. 20. *Began and planted a vineyard;* either made this his first occupation as a husbandman, or was the first who practiced this mode of husbandry.

V. 23. *The mantle;* the large square garment, worn over the shoulders and covering the whole body. It was also used at night, as a covering in sleep. See Ex. 22 : 26, 27, and Deut. 24 : 12, 13, where it should be rendered *mantle*, and not *raiment*. The definite article (*the mantle*) designates a garment of a particular kind.

VV. 25-27. In these predictions (having the form of poetry in the Hebrew) there are two divisions; the first containing the curse upon Canaan, the second the blessings on his two brothers; the former, for greater emphasis, being repeated after each of the two latter.

V. 25. *Cursed be Canaan.* The language is prophetic; anticipating, by a divinely given foresight, the future character and destiny of this line of Ham's posterity. These did not follow as consequences of the curse here pronounced, but were prophetically anticipated by it.

Canaan alone, not all the posterity of Ham, is the subject of it. See the list of his descendants in ch. 10 : 15-19. It was among them that the worst forms of idolatry prevailed, with all its nameless abominations and horrible atrocities, calling down the judgment of heaven here predicted.

V. 26. A beautiful turn is given to the blessing on Shem; namely, *Blessed be Jehovah, God of Shem!* This special relation to the Divine Being, with all its inestimable privileges, is thus indirectly and beautifully summed up, in a burst of grateful praise.

V. 27. *Japheth* means *spreading abroad, enlargement.*

He will dwell. It is a question whether Japheth is meant here; or whether *he*, the subject of this clause, refers to *God*, the subject of the preceding one.

This statement of the question shows, that one reference is grammatically as probable as the other. But the fact that Japheth is the object of blessing here, and the repetition of the words, "let Canaan be servant to him," seem to favor the former reference.

On the other hand, it is not unnatural that the patriarch, in blessing Japheth with unbounded enlargement, should revert to the favored lot of Shem in his narrower bounds, and should therefore say: *God give enlargement to Japheth; and he will dwell in the tents of Shem,*—his abiding

²⁸ And Noah lived, after the flood, three hundred and fifty ²⁹ years. And all the days of Noah were nine hundred and fifty years; and he died.

¹ AND these are the generations of the sons of Noah; Shem, Ham, and Japheth; and to them were born sons after the flood.
² The sons of Japheth; Gomer, and Magog, and Madai,
³ and Javan, and Tubal, and Meshech, and Tiras. And the

place, where he manifests his presence, will be there. The repetition, "let Canaan be servant to him," is not strange, since this belongs essentially to the blessing pronounced on Shem.

To this use of the words, *He will dwell*, it is objected, that the name Jehovah is the one under which God holds this relation to his people. But not exclusively; and his relation to them is quite as often spoken of under the more general name. It is further objected, that God is said to dwell in his tabernacle, on his holy hill, on Zion among the children of Israel, but never in the tents of Israel. This is good special pleading, but no argument. The idea to be expressed is, that God will dwell with his chosen people; and for this there is no more suitable expression than the one here used.

If Japheth is understood to be the subject of this clause, then the words, *dwell in the tents of Shem*, do not mean conquest and subjection of his territory, of which they are no suitable expression, but rather participation in the privileges and blessings of his lot, as of one admitted to his fireside. The same promise is expressed under another form, in ch. 12 : 3, and, more nearly under the form here used, in Isaiah 2 : 2, 3.

Chs. 10, 11. Third division: *Brief notices of the general history of man, from the Flood to the calling of Abraham.*

Ch. 10. Population of the earth by Noah's descendants.

This ancient ethnographic table is of great historical value, and has engaged the attention of many eminent scholars. Its statements are wonderfully comprehensive, and are found to be exact to the minutest details, so far as our knowledge from other sources enables us to verify them. By its aid we can trace satisfactorily the origin of many different nations, and their relation to each other.

The name of the founder of each race is usually given; but occasionally the gentilic name of the race itself (as *Jebusite*, etc., v. 16 and following), and with the Hebrew plural ending (*im*), designating the people, and sometimes also the country to which they gave the name, as *Kittim*, *Dodanim* in v. 4, *Mizraim* in v. 6, and *Philistim* in v. 14.

For the sake of uniformity in the table, the Hebrew plural ending (*im*) is retained throughout, though in some instances (*Philistim*, for example) the English plural ending is elsewhere used, as in ch. 21 : 32.

In the division of the earth, according to the table, the descendants of Japheth occupied by far the largest portion, on the north and west; those of Shem the middle portion, being a comparatively small tract of western Asia; those of Ham the southern part, though they are found at some points of the tract occupied by Shem's descendants.

VV. 2-4. *Gomer;* ancestor of the *Cimmerian* (properly, *Kimmerian**) race, whose earliest known seat was around the lake Mæotis (Sea of Azof), whence they passed into western Asia, and middle and northwestern Europe. Traces of the name are seen in the ancient *Cimmerian* (Kimmerian) Bosphorus, etc., and in the modern Crimea. It is probably identical with *Gimiri* in cuneiform inscriptions of the age of Darius. The same name appears in the Welsh *Kymry* (*Cymry*) unaltered; and in *Cimbri*, and the *Cimbrian* Chersonese (Denmark) by the euphonic insertion of *b* between the liquids *m* and *r*, as in *Cambria* and *Cumber*-land. The Celtic races, which have overspread so large a part of Europe, are from this source.

His sons were *Ashkenaz*, not identified with certainty, originally in the neighborhood of

---

* The consonant elements, *g* (and *k*, both palatals), *m*, *r*, are the same in both words, and the *k* is represented by *c* (originally the same sound) in the other examples.

sons of Gomer; Ashkenaz, and Riphath, and Togarmah.
⁴ And the sons of Javan; Elisha, and Tarshish, Kittim, and
⁵ Dodanim. From these were overspread the coasts of the Gentiles, in their lands, each according to his tongue, according to their families, in their nations.
⁶ And the sons of Ham; Cush, and Mizraim, and Phut, and
⁷ Canaan. And the sons of Cush: Seba, and Havilah, and

Armenia (Jer. 51 : 27); *Riphath*, probably inhabiting the Rhipæan (Carpathian) mountains; *Togarmah*, inhabitants of Armenia.

Magog, inhabitants of the Caucasus and neighboring regions, the western Scythians; mentioned in Ezek. 38 : 2, as the people (or country) of Gog, "the prince of Rosh,* Meshech, and Tubal."

Madai, the Medes. Modern scientific research has shown that this ancient and powerful people belonged, both in physical type and language, to the races with which they are here classed.

Javan; ancestor of the *Ionians* (older form, *Iaon*), to the Orientals the best known representatives of the Greek race, or Hellenic family. Branches:

Elisha, a name that probably appears in Æolis, a maritime district of Asia Minor (compare Ezek. 27 : 7, properly "coasts of Elisha"); *Tarshish*, who gave the name to the earliest settlements on the Mediterranean coast of Spain; *Kittim* (Chittim), a people of Cyprus, of which it became the name, and in a wider sense extended to the islands and coasts of the northern part of the Mediterranean Sea, including those of Greece and Italy; *Dodanim*,† supposed to be identical with the *Dardani* (a not unusual softening of the liquid *r* to a vowel), inhabiting Illyricum and Troas.

Tubal, the *Tiberini*, in Pontus.

Meshech, the *Moschi*, on the borders of Colchis and Armenia, a powerful ancient tribe.

Tiras; supposed ancestor of the *Thracians*.

V. 5. *In their lands;* the lands of which the Gentiles (pagan nations) severally took possession. *According to his tongue,* etc.; that is, in different nations, according to their different languages and origin.

VV. 6, 7. *Cush.* See the remarks on ch. 2 : 13. His descendants occupied the vast tract extending from Assyria through eastern Arabia into Africa. In Babylonia and adjacent regions the name is preserved in *Cuthah, Chuzistan, Cossæi,* etc. As a country, it sometimes denotes eastern Arabia, and more commonly Ethiopia. Branches:

Nimrod, first king of Babylonia and Assyria; *Seba,* supposed to have been the original name of *Meroe,* seat of an ancient Ethiopian kingdom in Africa; *Havilah* (see the remarks on ch. 2 : 11 and on v. 29, below); *Sabtah,* probably *Sabota* (*Sabbatha*), in southern Arabia; *Raamah* (properly Raghma), founder of *Rhegma,* a sea-port town on the Arabian coast of the Persian Gulf, whose sons, *Sheba*‡ and *Dedan,* founded trading colonies in that quarter (compare, *e. g.,* Ezek. 27 : 20, 22); *Sabtecha,* not identified.

The other sons of Ham were *Mizraim,* Egypt; *Phut,* not identified;§ and Canaan, whose bounds are given in v. 19.

---

* As properly translated. *Rosh* (according to the best authorities) is identical with *Rus* and *Russian,* and is the earliest trace of that powerful people. "The obliteration of it, by the authorized version, is one of the many remarkable variations of our version from the meaning of the sacred text of the Old Testament."—*Rev. Arthur P. Stanley, in Smith's Bible Dictionary,* art. Rosh.

† Or, as in some ancient copies, *Rodanim,* the *Rhodians.*

‡ On the Island Aval, in the Persian Gulf near the coast of Arabia, are the ruins of an ancient city of this name.—*Smith's Bible Dictionary;* art. Sheba, II.

§ In Jer. 46 : 9, he is spoken of (English Bible, Libyans) in connection with Cush and Ludim (English Bible, Ethiopians and Lydians) as belonging to Pharaoh's army. It is inferred that his posterity settled in Africa, and probably on the south of Egypt.

Sabtah, and Raamah, and Sabtechah. And the sons of Raamah; Sheba, and Dedan. ⁸ And Cush begot Nimrod. He began to be a mighty one ⁹ in the earth. He was a mighty hunter before Jehovah. Wherefore it is said: As Nimrod, a mighty hunter before ¹⁰ Jehovah. And the beginning of his kingdom was Babel, and Erech, and Accad, and Calneh, in the land of Shinar. ¹¹ From that land he went forth to Assyria, and built Nineveh, ¹² and Rehoboth-Ir, and Calah, and Resen between Nineveh and Calah; that is the great city.

VV. 8–12. An important historical document. Nimrod was of the second generation from Ham, and he laid the foundations of the Babylonian and Assyrian empires. Here, then, on the plains watered by the Euphrates and the Tigris, was the commencement of empire in the new era of the race.

The material used in building has served to perpetuate the remains of the cities mentioned in these verses. The bricks, of which the enormous structures were built, softening and crumbling soonest at the top where they were most exposed, fell and accumulated around the bases and sides, till a shapeless heap was formed, covering and protecting the lower parts; and these have remained uninjured for ages, buried out of sight beneath what seemed to be shapeless hills of earth. Recent excavations have brought some of them to light; and numerous inscriptions and pictorial representations, already discovered, reveal much of the history of those distant ages.

V. 8. *Began to be*, that is, became; the expression denoting his progress in power.

V. 9. *A mighty hunter;* in distinction from the quiet and peaceful occupation of the herdsman (ch. 25 : 27). *Before Jehovah*; in his view and estimation, denoting the highest degree of any quality or attainment. He is identical with the *Orion* of Greek mythology, the mighty hunter (and also king) commemorated by the constellation of that name.

V. 10. *Beginning of his kingdom;* the region over which he first ruled. This consisted of the four cities here named, in the land of Shinar. Recent discoveries, in the buried remains of cities in this region, make it evident that the seat of empire was originally in these cities on the lower Euphrates, and that the more northern one, on the upper waters of the Tigris, was of much later date.

Babel; elsewhere rendered *Babylon*, the Greek form of the name, which represents the city in its subsequent enlargement and splendor, and by which it is known in history. The simple Hebrew form is properly retained here, on account of a possible connection with the tower of that name. See the note on ch. 11 : 9.

The ruins of ancient Babylon, as rebuilt by Nebuchadnezzar (Dan. 4 : 30), perhaps not exactly on its earliest site, are found near Hillah, a small town on the Euphrates, about fifty miles to the south of Bagdad.

Erech. It is believed that this was the ancient Orchoe, and that its site is indicated by the remarkable mounds of *Warka* (Irak, Irka), about eighty miles to the south of the site of ancient Babylon.

Accad; found in inscriptions dug from the buried ruins of these ancient cities, as the gentilic name of a large and powerful branch of the Hamites. See the note on ch. 11 : 28.

Calneh. Its site is indicated by the great mounds of *Niffer*, on the Euphrates, about sixty miles further south than the site of ancient Babylon.

Shinar; the whole of the alluvial region through which the lower waters of the Euphrates and Tigris flow to the sea, subsequently known as Chaldæa, or Babylonia.

VV. 11, 12. *Nineveh;* the capital of the great Assyrian empire, so often mentioned in the later biblical history of the Jews.

This vast city, sixty miles in circumference, was the capital of an empire, which for more than five centuries was the ruling power in western Asia. About the year 625 before Christ, it was captured by the Medes and Babylonians, and was plundered and burnt. Its destruction

CHAP. X. GENESIS.

¹³ And Mizraim begot the Ludim, and the Anamim, and the ¹⁴ Lehabim, and the Naphtuhim, and the Pathrusim, and the Casluhim (whence came forth the Philistim) and the Caphtorim.
¹⁵ ¹⁶ And Canaan begot Zidon his first-born, and Heth, and the Jebusite, and the Amorite, and the Girgashite,

was so complete that it was never reoccupied, and in time all traces of its former magnificence disappeared, and even its site was unknown. Nothing was left to mark the place of the proud city but immense shapeless mounds of earth, burying beneath them the relics of its former grandeur, while their surface was occupied by scattered huts, or grazing flocks, or scanty harvests of grain. So wonderfully was fulfilled the prophecy of Nahum (ch. 3 : 11), "Thou shalt be hidden!"

These ruins are found on the east side of the Tigris, opposite Mosul, about two hundred and seventy miles further north than the site of ancient Babylon, occupying an area sixty miles in circumference. Excavations have disclosed the lower portions of magnificent palaces, adorned with sculptures, the alabaster walls and flooring covered with pictured representations, or written records, of the domestic annals and military conquests of the empire. Among these are numerous verifications of Jewish history, as recorded in the Bible.

The sites of the other four cities are supposed to be indicated by the principal ruins of ancient Nineveh, which mark its circuit in its widest extension. *Calah* is identified with the great mound of Nimroud, about twenty miles south of Mosul.

That is the great city; referring to Nineveh.

VV. 13, 14. On the *form* of these names, see the introductory note to this chapter, second paragraph.

Ludim, the Lydians of Africa. Compare the remark on vv. 6, 7, third paragraph, foot-note (§).
Anamim; not identified. *Lehabim;* the original orthography of *Lubim,* the Lybians (as the name should be written), a people of Africa, and probably on the south of Egypt. Compare Nahum 3 : 9, and the foot-note (§) just referred to. *Naphtuhim,* not satisfactorily identified. *Pathrusim,* inhabitants of Pathros in Egypt (Jer. 44 : 1, 15). It was probably upper Egypt, the mother country of Egypt proper. Compare Ezek. 29 : 14 (properly, *the land of their nativity,* origin). *Casluhim,* a people of Egypt, as inferred from the connection; supposed by some to have been the same as the Colchians, who are said by ancient writers to have been a colony from Egypt.

Philistim. The name means *emigrants;* and their migration is spoken of here, and in Deut. 2 : 23 (under the name Caphtorim), Jer. 47 : 4, and Am. 9 : 7. The importance of this event may be inferred from the passage last quoted, where it is compared with the deliverance of Israel from Egyptian bondage. This migration must have been very early, as they held their possessions in Palestine in the time of Abraham (Gen. 21 : 32, 34).

Elsewhere, as in Amos 9 : 7, and Jer. 47 : 4 (compare Deut. 2 : 23), they are said to have come from Caphtor. Hence there is some probability in the suggestion, that this parenthetic clause may have been accidentally transposed, and that it properly belongs after Caphtorim. But as there is no evidence of such a transposition, it is reasonable to suppose that more than one migration took place, either from different original points, or in passing over different countries. Of this there is another indication in the different names by which different divisions of them are designated, as Cherethites in Zeph. 2 : 5, and 1 Sam. 30 : 14, compared with v. 16.

Caphtorim; supposed by some to have been inhabitants of Crete, in favor of which is the designation of the Philistines, or a part of them, by *Cherethim,* Cretans. See the preceding paragraph. But later investigations seem to establish the fact, that Caphtor (allied to the ancient Egyptian name of *Coptos*) was in upper Egypt; and that the Cherethim were a neighboring and kindred people, who formed settlements on the island of Crete, and probably also on the coast of Palestine.*

VV. 15-20. *Canaan.* The country to which he gave the name was the tract lying between

---

* A full discussion of this interesting topic, for which there is not space here, may be found in the *Encyclopædia Britannica,* 8th ed., art. Ægypt, vol. viii., p. 419, and (by the same writer) in *Smith's Bible Dictionary,* art. Caphtor.

¹⁷ and the Hivite, and the Arkite, and the Sinite,
¹⁸ and the Arvadite, and the Zemarite, and the Hamathite;
and afterward were the families of the Canaanites spread
¹⁹ abroad. And the border of the Canaanites was from Zidon,
as thou goest to Gerar, unto Gaza; as thou goest to Sodom
²⁰ and Gomorrah and Admah and Zeboim, unto Lasha. These
are the sons of Ham, according to their families, according
to their tongues, in their lands, in their nations.
²¹ And to Shem, father of all the sons of Eber, eldest brother

the Mediterranean Sea on the west, and the river Jordan and Dead Sea on the east, extending from Zidon on the north as far as the southern extremity of the Dead Sea. Branches:
Zidon (as it should be written, as in ch. 49:13, Josh. 11:8, 19:28; Judges 1:31, etc.) name of the celebrated city of Phœnicia, now Saida, on the northern boundary of this tract.
Heth, ancestor of the Hittites, who occupied the country around Hebron, to the south of Jerusalem, and among whom Abraham dwelt for a time (ch. 23:4, 19). They were therefore of the race of Ham, and not of the "country" or "kindred" of Abraham and Isaac, as intimated in ch. 24:3, 4, and 28:1, 2.
Jebusites, in and around Jerusalem; *Amorites*, on the east and west coasts of the Dead Sea, and east side of the Jordan; *Girgasites*, westward from the Jordan (Josh. 24:11), but their position is not further determined; *Hivites*, chiefly at the base of Mount Hermon and in the valleys of Lebanon, found, at one period, at Shechem, ch. 34:2, compare also Josh. 9:7, 17, and 11:19; *Arkites*, at the base of Mount Lebanon; *Sinites*, in the northern part of the district of Mount Lebanon; *Arvadites*, on the Phœnician island Aradus (now *Ruad*), compare Ezek. 27:8, 11; *Zemarites*, traced in the local name Zemaraim, Josh. 18:22, and 2 Chron. 13:4; *Hamathites*, inhabitants of Hamath, chief city of upper Syria, on the Orontes.

V. 18. *Spread abroad;* over the territory of which the bounds are given in the following verse. Or the meaning may be, that *afterward* they spread abroad beyond their original bounds (given in the next verse), not only in Palestine, but in remote regions, settled by Phœnician colonists.

V. 19. *As thou goest to Gerar;* that is, on the way to, or in the direction of Gerar, which was the most southern city of Palestine, and near the Mediterranean Sea. The meaning is, that the territory extended, on the western side, from Zidon southward to Gaza. In a similar manner the boundary on the eastern side is then given, namely, as thou goest to Sodom, Gomorrah, Admah, and Zeboim (that is, by the route of those cities), as far as to Lasha,* at the head waters of the Jordan.
This description comes to us, as is shown by its terms, from a time anterior to the catastrophe in which the cities of the plain perished. (Ch. 19:24, 25; Deut. 29:23.)

V. 20. Compare the remark on v. 5.
V. 21. *Father of all the sons of Eber;* namely, in both branches of his descendants.
In the family of Eber occurred the division of the land by his descendants (v. 25); one branch remaining in the northern section, and the other occupying the southern. The latter are enumerated in this table, vv. 26-30; the former in the table given in the next chapter, vv. 18-26, continuing the line of descent in that branch to Abraham.
In these words, therefore, attention is directed to the fact, that these widely separated branches have a common ancestor in Shem; that he is father *of all* the sons of Eber, and not of those only who bear his name, in the line of Abraham and his descendants.
Eldest brother of Japheth; that is, the elder of his two brothers.
This agrees with the three other statements in regard to the relative ages of these sons of Noah. It appears from ch. 5:32, that the oldest was born when Noah was five hundred years old. Two years after this Shem was born; for he was a hundred years old two years after the

---

* Probably (as suggested by Dean Stanley, *Sinai and Palestine*, p. 288) the same as Laish, called also Leshem in Josh. 19:47, to which the name Dan was given after its capture by the Danites, as there related.

GENESIS.

²² of Japheth, to him also were children born. The sons of Shem; Elam and Asshur, and Arphaxad, and Lud, and ²³ Aram. And the sons of Aram; Uz, and Hul, and Gether, ²⁴ and Mash. And Arphaxad begot Shalah; and Shalah be- ²⁵ got Eber. And to Eber were born two sons. The name of one was Peleg, for in his days the land was divided; and ²⁶ the name of his brother was Joktan. And Joktan begot

V. 25. *Or, the earth was divided*

Flood (ch. 11 : 10), consequently in the six hundred and third year of Noah (ch. 7 : 11, and 8 : 13). As Ham is called "his younger son" (ch. 9 : 24), he must have been the youngest of the three.

In the table Ham is placed before Shem, apparently on account of the historical precedence of his immediate posterity, the earliest kingdoms having been founded by them (vv. 6–12). There is a reason, therefore, for stating here their actual relation in point of age.

VV. 22-24. *Elam* gave name to a tract extending northward from the Persian Gulf on the east of the Tigris, called by the ancient Greek geographers Susiana. The name is preserved in Elymais. *Asshur* gave name to Assyria. *Arphaxad*, supposed to be traced in the ancient name Arrapachitis, a province of Assyria; *Lud*, ancestor of the Asiatic Lydians, on the western coast of Asia Minor. *Aram* gave name to the tract on the northeast of Palestine, comprehending ancient Syria and Mesopotamia.

VV. 23, 24. *Uz* gave name to a tract of country (*land of Uz*) in northern Arabia, bordering on Babylonia on the east, and Idumæa and Palestine on the west; *Hul* is recognized, most probably, in the district (*Huleh*) round the bases of Lebanon, north of lake Merom; *Gether*, not identified; *Mash*, recognized in Mount Masius, part of the mountainous ridge which separated Armenia from Mesopotamia, between the Tigris and Euphrates; *Shalah*, not identified.

V. 25. *Eber;* ancestor of the Hebrews,* whose dwelling was beyond (on the east side of) the river Euphrates. See the note on ch. 14 : 13. With his two sons originated the great division of the line of Shem into the Abrahamic and Arabic races. This being the most important occurrence in the history of Shem's posterity, it is for that reason specially commemorated.

Peleg means *division:* a name given him, because in his time occurred the division of the tract occupied by Shem's descendants, between his branch of the family and that of his brother Joktan, who migrated into the neighboring region of Arabia.

Some translate as in the margin, *the earth was divided*,† and suppose that the dispersion spoken of in ch. 11 : 8, 9, is meant. But the other view is the more probable one.

VV. 26-29. The descendants of Joktan peopled southern Arabia, *Arabia Felix*, the rich province of Yemen, in its ancient extent. Their colonization of this tract is clearly established by the various traces they have left of their occupation of it, though some of the names here mentioned are not found among Arabic names in this region, and others are not yet fully identified.

Almodad is not yet traced in the name of any place or people; *Sheleph* is recognized in the name of the district Sulaf (Selfia, or Selef), and in that of the tribe Shelif (or Shulaf); *Hazarmaveth* is preserved almost letter for letter in the Arabic orthography of the name Hadramawt, as commonly written in English; *Jerah*, and *Hadoram*, not identified; *Uzal* is found in Awzal (the Hebrew and Arabic names being the same), the ancient name of the capital of Yemen; *Diklah*, not certainly identified; perhaps found in Dakala‡ (Hebrew Diklah); *Obal* is not identified, nor is *Abimael* satisfactorily determined; *Sheba* is recognized in the celebrated kingdom

---

* This word would regularly be written *Ebrew*, according to the analogy of other proper names in the English Bible, having the same initial letter in the original Hebrew.

† In Hebrew, as in other languages, the word meaning *earth* is often applied to some particular division of its surface, a country; as in v. 11 of this chapter, "out of that land," and in vv. 5, 20, 31, "in their lands," and ch. 12 : 1, "go from thy land, . . . to the land which I will show thee."

‡ The reader should observe that in all these ancient names *vowels* are of no account; serving only to facilitate the utterance of the consonants, which are the body and substance of the word, and varying greatly with accidental influences.

²⁷ Almodad, and Sheleph, and Hazarmaveth, and Jerah, and ²⁸ Hadoram, and Uzal, and Diklah, and Obal, and Abimael, ²⁹ and Sheba, and Ophir, and Havilah, and Jobab. All these ³⁰ were sons of Joktan. And their dwelling was from Mesha, ³¹ as thou goest to Sephar, a mountain of the East. These are the sons of Shem, according to their families, according to their tongues, in their lands, according to their nations.
³² These are the families of the sons of Noah, according to their generations, in their nations. And from these were the nations spread abroad in the earth, after the flood.

¹ AND the whole earth was of one speech and of one language.
² And it came to pass, as they journeyed eastward, that they found a plain in the land of Shinar; and they dwelt ³ there. And they said one to another: Come, let us make

of that name often mentioned in the Bible (1 Kings 10 : 1; Ps. 72 : 10); *Ophir*, not otherwise identified;* *Havilah*, see the remarks on ch. 2 : 11 and 13. The Arabian Havilah is supposed to be recognized in Khawlan, a district in the northwestern part of Yemen; *Jobab*, not yet identified with any Arabic name in this region.
V. 30. *Mesha* is supposed to have been the western, and Sephar the eastern limit of their original settlements, as their occupation of the country is thought to have advanced from the west eastward. The former is not clearly ascertained. The latter is recognized in Zafar (written also Dafar), the ancient celebrated seaport of the Himyarite kingdom, lying at the base of a high mountain.†
Of the East; namely, of Arabia, as lying eastward from Palestine (ch. 25 : 6; Job 1 : 3).
V. 31. Compare the remark on v. 5.
V. 32. *According to their generations;* that is, according to their different lines of descent from one or the other of Noah's three sons, and their immediate offspring.
Ch. 11 : 1-11. The Dispersion.
V. 1. *Of one speech and of one language.* By *speech* is meant utterance, or manner of speaking, and by *language* the words uttered and their various forms. Compare the remark on v. 7.
V. 2. *As they journeyed eastward;* with reference to the general bearing of their course, if they followed, as they would be likely to do, the valley of the Euphrates or of the Tigris. Viewed from the writer's position on the west, from which they were receding, this direction of their course, taking them further to the east, would naturally be expressed by him as in the text.
Land of Shinar. See the remark on ch. 10 : 10.
V. 3. *Bitumen,* a mineral pitch, very abundant in these plains. It bubbles up from crevices in the earth, and collects in pools or pits on the surface. It is much used for building, for coating boats, etc.

* It can hardly be doubted that the original settlement was in this region. But it is still an open question whether the Ophir spoken of in other passages (1 Kings 9 : 28; 10; 11) is to be sought in Arabia, or whether it was situated, as maintained by eminent geographers, at the mouth of the Indus. A full summary of the discussions on this interesting question is accessible to the English reader, in *Smith's Bible Dictionary*, art. Ophir.
† As stated by Wellsted, *Travels in Arabia*, Book II., ch. 24; another point of identification with "Sephar, a mountain of the East."

bricks, and burn them thoroughly. And they had brick for stone, and bitumen had they for mortar.

4 And they said: Come, let us build us a city, and a tower, and let its top be in the heavens; and let us make us a name, lest we be scattered abroad on the face of the whole earth.

5 And Jehovah came down to see the city and the tower,
6 which the sons of men were building. And Jehovah said: Behold, there is one people, and they have all one speech; and this they begin to do. And now there will not be with-
7 held from them anything which they purpose to do. Come, let us go down, and there confound their speech, that they may not understand one another's speech.

8 And Jehovah scattered them abroad from thence on the face of all the earth. And they ceased to build the city.

V. 4. *A city and a tower;* that is, a city including within its area a tower, or citadel. This was to be of immense height, impressing the beholder by its magnificence, and also furnishing a final retreat from an invading force.

Name is used here as in 1 Kings 4 : 31 (Hebrew text, 5 : 11); properly, *his name was in all the nations around.* To "make one's self a name," is to get renown. Compare Isaiah 63 : 12, 14; Jer. 32 : 20.

Lest we be scattered abroad. The object was concentration and power. To this the renown of a great name would contribute; and that would be secured by building a vast and celebrated city, for their common residence.

It matters not whether these were the motives and objects of the whole body of those engaged in the work, or only of the leaders, who controlled and directed them. In either case, this undertaking, originating in the desire of worldly renown, and of concentrated power, was directly opposed to the divine will (ch. 9 : 1, 7), and was signally rebuked and frustrated.

V. 5. *Came down,* etc.; expressed after our mode of conception, as is often the case in speaking of the divine intervention in human affairs. The meaning is, that he manifested his presence, and his cognizance of their acts, by the expression of his displeasure which en-ued.

V. 6. *This they begin to do;* implying, that this is only the beginning, and that they will go on to what is still worse, as indicated in the following words.

V. 7. *Confound their speech.* By *speech* is here meant, oral expression of thought, the utterance of thought in spoken words. The Hebrew word, here as in v. 1, is *lip* ("let us confound their lip"), by metonymy for what the lip utters. This, while it naturally means simply "utterance, or manner of speaking," when (as in v. 1) it is expressly distinguished from "language," as naturally expresses what is uttered by the lips, when no such distinction is made.

The use of this word furnishes no ground for the theories, suggested by some writers, as to the manner in which the confusion of tongues was effected.*

V. 8. *Scattered them abroad;* thus frustrating the first organized resistance to his expressed will (ch. 9 : 1, 7), and making the renewal of it impossible.

They ceased to build the city; that is, for the time, and on the scale and for the purpose at first intended. The divine purpose was accomplished by the interruption of the work and the means through which it was effected, though the building of the city was afterward resumed (ch. 10 : 10).

---

* Namely, in the primary sounds, or vocal elements of speech, as supposed by some; or in the forms and grammatical structure of language, as with still less reason is assumed by others.

9 Therefore is its name called Babel; because there Jehovah confounded the speech of all the earth; and from thence did Jehovah scatter them abroad on the face of all the earth.

10 These are the generations of Shem. Shem was a hundred years old, and begot Arphaxad, two years after the

V. 9. *Babel;* that is, confusion. The simple Hebrew name is retained here (see the note on ch. 10 : 10, second paragraph) on account of its etymological import, and its historical connection with the tower of the same name.

In the neighborhood of the existing ruins of Babylon, and, as there is some reason to suppose, within the limits of its ancient walls in their widest extent, is the remarkable ruin of Nebuchadnezzar's temple; "a solitary pile, rising suddenly from the vast expanse of the desert," a hundred and fifty-three feet in height, and four hundred feet square at the base.* It is known among the native tribes as *Birs Nimrud* (Tower of Nimrod). An inscription, in the cuneiform character, shows that it was built by Nebuchadnezzar (about six hundred years before Christ), on the site, and on the "foundation platform," of a more ancient temple, "built by a former king," but left unfinished.

Dr. Oppert, one of the most distinguished among cuneiform scholars, thinks he finds proof, in his reading of the inscription,† that the site of this temple, and even its foundation, was the traditional one of the tower of the dispersion. The tradition can not be regarded as incredible in itself, when we consider how perfectly the bases of fabrics, composed of such materials, are concealed and protected for ages by the crumbling masses of the superstructure, from which they are now exhumed uninjured. But it is proper to add, that the reading of these inscriptions is still uncertain in many points; and that the statement on which Dr. Oppert rests his conclusion is differently read by other eminent scholars.

Confounded the speech of all the earth. The diversities in the languages of the earth present a problem, which philosophy has in vain labored to solve. Comparative philology has shown, however, that many different languages are grouped together by common affinities, as branches of the same family, all having the same original language for their common parent. Notwithstanding the great number and diversity of languages, they may all be traced to a very few original parent tongues. The difficulty lies in the essential and irreconcilable diversity between these several parent tongues, not the remotest affinities existing to indicate a common origin, or any historical relation; a problem for which speculative philosophy can find no solution.‡

VV. 10 and following. The narrative now takes up the line of Shem to Abraham.

It has been shown, in the history already given of man's repeated and general apostasy, that

---

* "The mound presents the appearance rather of a natural hill, crowned by a ruin, than that of a structure built entirely by the hand of man. Thirty-seven feet of solid brickwork, looking almost like a tower, stand exposed at the top; while below this, the original building is almost entirely concealed beneath the masses of rubbish which have crumbled down from the upper portion."—*Rawlinson's Herodotus,* vol. ii., App. iii., Essay iv., 13.

† Communicated by him to *Smith's Bible Dictionary* (appendix to art. "Tongues, confusion of"), and to the *Journal Asiatique,* 1857, ix., x.

‡ Schelling, in his Philosophy of Mythology, has well said: "Humanity can not have left that condition, in which there was no distinction of peoples, but only of races, without a spiritual crisis, which must have been of the deepest significance, must have taken place in the basis of the human consciousness itself. . . . . For we can not conceive of different peoples without different languages; and language is something spiritual. If difference of peoples is not something that was from the first, but is something that has arisen, then must this also hold true of the difference of languages. . . . . Here we fall in with the oldest account of the human race, the Mosaic writings; toward which so many are disinclined, only because they know not what to do with it, can neither understand nor use it. Genesis puts the rise of peoples in connection with the rise of different languages; but in such a way, that the confounding of language is the cause, the rise of peoples the effect."—*Einleitung in die Philosophie der Mythologie.*

¹¹ flood. And Shem lived, after he begot Arphaxad, five hundred years, and begot sons and daughters.

¹² And Arphaxad lived thirty-five years, and begot Shalah.

¹³ And Arphaxad lived, after he begot Shalah, four hundred and three years, and begot sons and daughters.

¹⁴ ¹⁵ And Shalah lived thirty years, and begot Eber. And Shalah lived, after he begot Eber, four hundred and three years, and begot sons and daughters.

¹⁶ ¹⁷ And Eber lived thirty-four years, and begot Peleg. And Eber lived, after he begot Peleg, four hundred and thirty years, and begot sons and daughters.

¹⁸ ¹⁹ And Peleg lived thirty years, and begot Reu. And Peleg lived, after he begot Reu, two hundred and nine years, and begot sons and daughters.

²⁰ ²¹ And Reu lived thirty-two years, and begot Serug. And Reu lived, after he begot Serug, two hundred and seven years, and begot sons and daughters.

²² ²³ And Serug lived thirty years, and begot Nahor. And Serug lived, after he begot Nahor, two hundred years, and begot sons and daughters.

---

without special interposition on the part of God none could enjoy, or would seek, his favor. This having been fully proved, the general history of the human race is pursued no further.*

The calling of Abraham (ch. 12), for which these verses prepare the way, commences the new era in the sacred history; and henceforth, the development of God's purpose of redemption, in connection with the history of Abraham's posterity, is the great theme of the Scriptures.

At the time of this call, the knowledge and worship of the true God seem to have become nearly extinct; see Josh. 24 : 2. The case of Melchisedek (ch. 14 : 18), shows that some remained faithful. There is no ground to suppose that Abraham himself was ever an idolater.†

* Auberlen, in his defense of the Scriptures as a divine revelation, has the following just thoughts on the historical value of these eleven chapters: "If we had not the first eleven chapters of Genesis, if we had, on the beginnings of the world and of humanity, only the myths of the heathen, or the speculations of philosophers, or the observations of naturalists, we should be in the profoundest darkness concerning the origin and nature of the world and of man. It is with these chapters on the one side, as with the prophecies of Scripture on the other. There we get the true light on the first, here on the last things; there on the foundation principles, here on the ultimate tendencies of history; there on the first cause, here on the object of the world; without which a universal history, or a philosophy of history, is impossible. But prophecy itself also has its roots in these chapters, on which all later revelation plants itself. Happily, these primeval records of our race, far more widely than we are aware, have penetrated our whole mode of thinking, and sway even those who believe they must reject the historical character of these accounts. These chapters maintain the consciousness, in humanity, of its own God-related nature, of its original nobility and its eternal destination."—*Auberlen, die göttliche Offenbarung*, p. 127.

† Compare the remarks on ch. 31 : 53, from which some infer that the God of Nahor and of Terah was not the same as the God of Abraham.

24 And Nahor lived twenty-nine years, and begot Terah.
25 And Nahor lived, after he begot Terah, a hundred and nineteen years, and begot sons and daughters.
26 And Terah lived seventy years, and begot Abram, Nahor, and Haran.
27 And these are the generations of Terah. Terah begot
28 Abram, Nahor, and Haran; and Haran begot Lot. And Haran died before Terah his father, in the land of his birth,
29 in Ur of the Chaldæans. And Abram and Nahor took to themselves wives. The name of the wife of Abram was Sarai; and the name of the wife of Nahor was Milcah,

---

V. 26. *Abram.* See the reason for the change of this name to *Abraham*, in ch. 17 : 5.

VV. 27-30. This brief account of Abraham's family connections is necessary, in order that the allusions to them, in the succeeding history, may be understood.

V. 28. *Ur*, the ancient capital of Chaldæa, on the site now marked by the great mound of Mugheir, and seat of the most celebrated temple of the *Moon-God*, as shown by numerous inscriptions dug out of the ruins.* These are about six miles west of the present channel of the Euphrates, near its junction with the Shat-el-Hie, and about a hundred and twenty-five miles from its mouth.

Chaldæans, an ancient people, of Cushite origin, occupying the lower part of the alluvial tract watered by the Euphrates. Their history has heretofore been involved in great obscurity; but much light has been thrown on it by the discovery of ancient inscriptions relating to them.†

V. 29. *Sarai.* For the change of this name to *Sarah*, see the remark on ch. 17 : 15.

---

* An account of it, with a drawing of the ruins of the temple, is given in *Smith's Bible Dictionary*, art. Ur.

† The chief points are contained in the following compressed statement: "The Chaldæans appear to have been a branch of the great Hamite race of *Akkad*, which inhabited Babylonia from the earliest times. With this race originated the art of writing, the building of cities, the institution of a religious system, and the cultivation of all science, and of astronomy in particular. The language of these *Akkad* presents affinities with the African dialects on the one side, and with the Turanian, or those of High Asia, on the other. It stands somewhat in the same relation as the Egyptian to the Semitic languages, belonging as it would seem to the great parent stock from which the trunk-stream of the Semitic tongues also sprung, before there was a ramification of Semitic dialects, and before Semitism even had become subject to its peculiar organization and developments. In this primitive Akkadian tongue, which I have been accustomed generally to denominate Scythic, from its near connection with the Scythic dialect of Persia, were preserved all the scientific treatises known to the Babylonians, long after the Semitic element had become predominant in the land—it was in fact the language of science in the East, as the Latin was in Europe during the Middle Ages. When Semitic tribes established an empire in Assyria in the thirteenth century B. C. they adopted the alphabet of the *Akkad*, and with certain modifications applied it to their own language; but during the seven centuries which followed of Semitic dominion at Nineveh and Babylon, this Assyrian language was merely used for historical records and official documents. The mythological, astronomical, and other scientific tablets found at Nineveh are exclusively in the Akkadian language, and are thus shown to belong to a priest-class, exactly answering to the Chaldæans of profane history and of the Book of Daniel. We thus see how it is that the Chaldæans (taken generally for the *Akkad*) are spoken of in the prophetical books of Scripture as composing the armies of the Semitic kings of Babylon and as the general inhabitants of the country, while in other authorities they are distinguished as philosophers, astronomers, and magicians, as, in fact, the special depositaries of science."—*Rawlinson's Herodotus*, Book I., ch. 181, foot-note.

daughter of Haran, the father of Milcah, and the father of ³⁰ Iscah. And Sarai was barren; she had no child.
³¹ And Terah took Abram his son, and Lot, son of Haran, his son's son, and Sarai his daughter-in-law, wife of Abram his son; and they went forth with them from Ur of the Chaldæans, to go to the land of Canaan. And they came ³² to Haran, and dwelt there. And the days of Terah were two hundred and five years. And Terah died in Haran.

¹ AND Jehovah said to Abram: Go from thy land, and

V. 1. *Or, from thy land, and from thy birthplace*

V. 31. *Terah took Abram his son*, etc. It seems, from the form of expression, that Terah took the lead in this movement; but we are not told by what motive he was induced to do it. On reaching Haran, he seems, for some cause, to have abandoned the design of proceeding further. Abraham received direction (ch. 12 : 1) to leave his kindred and his father's house, probably because they could not be prevailed on to accompany him.

Nahor either preceded or followed them as far as Haran, and remained there. This is evident from ch. 24 : 10, 29, and 27 : 43; a comparison of the last two passages showing that "the city of Nahor," mentioned in the first, was Haran.

They went forth with them. The form of the expression, in the Hebrew as well as in English, leaves it uncertain who are meant by "they," and who are meant by "them." Probably by "them" are meant Terah and Abram, the two who are most prominently before the mind, and "they" is an indefinite expression for all who accompanied them.

Haran, a city in the northwestern part of Mesopotamia.* It is not on the direct route from the supposed site of Ur (see the note on v. 28) to the land of Canaan. But the necessities of pasturage for their flocks and herds required a deviation from the shortest and most direct route. The ancient caravan route took this direction for a similar reason, as does the modern one by the neighboring city of Edessa.

And dwelt there. This shows that they made it their abode for some length of time, and not a mere resting-place in their journey onward.

V. 32. It is said in Acts 7 : 4, that Abraham went from Haran "after his father was dead." But if Terah was seventy years old (v. 26) at the birth of Abraham, his age when Abraham left Haran (at the age of seventy-five, ch. 12 : 4) would have been a hundred and forty-five years; and hence, according to the statement made in this verse, he would have lived sixty years after Abraham went from Haran.

It is not uncommon, however, to mention sons, not in the order of birth, but of precedence in history, as in the case of Noah's sons. See the remarks on ch. 10 : 21, the third and fourth paragraphs.

Abraham may, therefore, have been a younger son of Terah, but named first in the genealogy on account of his important relation to Hebrew history.

Chs. 12—50. Fourth division : *History of the Patriarchs.*

Chs. 12 : 1—25 : 10. First part of the fourth division: *Calling of Abraham* (12 : 1-3), *and his subsequent history.*

See the note on ch. 11 : vv. 11 and following, the third paragraph.

VV. 1-3. *Said to Abram*,† etc. This took place in Haran; as is evident from v. 4, where it is said that Abram "went forth from Haran" in obedience to this command.

---

* See Dr. Hackett's addition to the art. Haran, *Smith's Bible Dictionary*, American edition.
† The rendering, "had said" (common English version) is false translation, the Hebrew form never having that sense. It is a mere makeshift, to avoid an imaginary discrepancy with the statement in Acts 7 : 2, 3. See the remarks in the text (second paragraph), and Dr. Hackett's *Commentary on Acts*, 7 : 3, 4.

from thy kindred, and from thy father's house, to the land
2 that I will show thee. And I will make thee a great nation; and I will bless thee, and will make thy name great,
3 and thou shalt be a blessing. And I will bless them that bless thee, and him that curses thee will I curse. And in thee shall all the families of the earth be blest.
4 And Abram went, as Jehovah said to him; and Lot went with him. And Abram was seventy-five years old, when he went forth from Haran.
5 And Abram took Sarai his wife, and Lot his brother's son, and all their substance that they had gathered, and the persons that they had gotten in Haran, and they went

---

It is stated in Acts 7 : 3, that this was said to Abram "before he dwelt in Haran." So it was, without doubt; and it was the cause of his leaving "Ur of the Chaldæans to go to the land of Canaan," as related in ch. 11 : 31. In rehearsing the command, given on both occasions, Stephen uses the well-known form in which it was recorded here.
From thy land and from thy kindred. He was still in his own land (compare ch. 24 : 4, 10, where Haran is meant, as has been shown in the note on ch. 11 : 31, second paragraph) and among his kindred. These he must forsake, and with them his "father's house," to go to a strange land, of which he has no other intimation than the words, "which I will show thee." So true is it, that "he went forth" (as said by the apostle, Heb. 11 : 8) "not knowing whither he went."
V. 3. *Families.* By *family* is meant here, and often elsewhere, a people, or nation, regarded as one great family descended from a common parent. So the Jewish people, as the family of Abraham, is called in Micah 2 : 3, *against this family do I devise an evil,* and in Jer. 8 : 3, *the residue of them that remain of this evil family.*
In thee; or, as expressed in chs. 22 : 18, 26 : 4, *in thy seed.* In no sense can it be pretended that the nations of the earth have been blest in Abraham and his seed, except as the depositaries and guardians of that divine knowledge which through them has become the heritage of the nations, and as the chosen race of whom came the Messiah, the Redeemer of mankind. In this sense the promise, wonderful in the circumstances under which it was made, has been still more wonderfully fulfilled.*
V. 5. *Persons;* as the Hebrew word is properly rendered in the common English version, in ch. 14 : 21, *give me the persons, and the substance take to thyself,* and ch. 36 : 6, *all the persons of his house, and his cattle,* and in many other passages.
Persons that they had gotten; namely, the servants they had acquired, by birth or otherwise, during their residence in Haran.
That Abraham was the recognized head of a numerous body of retainers, holding various relations to him, is evident from ch. 14 : 13-16; where it is seen that he could bring into the field a body of servants trained to the use of arms, and with them was able to intercept and overcome the four victorious kings. The relation was one of mutual dependence; service, on the one side, being rewarded by protection and provision and the equal administration of justice on the other. For Abraham was a "prince" (ch. 23 : 6), a man of princely rank and authority, as well as a master; and in no other relation could his dependents obtain the like protection, as well as equal and exact justice in their dealings with one another. In the then existing state of society and government, the weak had no security but in the protection of a prosperous and powerful leader.

---

* "In the concluding words of the promise is expressed the utmost limit of all history; for beyond the blessing of all nations there can be nothing more."—*Baumgarten, Theolog. Commentar Zum Pentateuch,* I., 170.

forth to go to the land of Canaan; and they came into the land of Canaan.

6 And Abram passed through the land to the place of Shechem, to the oak of Moreh. And the Canaanite was 7 then in the land. And Jehovah appeared to Abram, and said: To thy seed will I give this land. And he built there an altar to Jehovah who appeared to him.

8 And he moved onward from thence to the mountain on the east of Bethel, and stretched his tent, with Bethel on the west and Ha-ai on the east. And he built there an altar to Jehovah, and called on the name of Jehovah.

9 And Abram continued removing toward the south country.

V. 6. *Or*, to the station of Shechem

VV. 6, 7. *Passed through the land*. From Haran he would enter Palestine on the north; and he would therefore *pass through the land* to Shechem, nearly in the geographical centre of the country. It lies in a quiet sheltered valley, between mount Gerizim on the south and mount Ebal on the north, opening westward on a distant view of the sea. In this "paradise of the Holy Land" was his first halting-place. Here, in the seclusion and repose of this lovely valley, Jehovah appears to him; and in the words, "to thy seed will I give this land," he is assured that this is the goal of his journeyings. Compare ch. 37 : 12, foot-note.

Oak of Moreh; probably its traditional name, from an earlier occupant of the ground. It is alluded to again in Deut. 11 : 30 (*oaks of Moreh*), and probably in Gen. 35 : 4, and Josh. 24 : 26; perhaps also in Judges 9 : 6 (*oak of the pillar*), compare Josh. 24 : 26, 27.*

The Canaanite was then in the land. The possession of the land was, therefore, prospective and not immediate. It was "by faith he sojourned in the land of promise, as a foreign land" (Heb. 11 : 9).

To thy seed will I give this land. He does not say "to thee;" for "he gave him no inheritance in it, not even a foot-breadth" (Acts 7 : 5).

He built there an altar to Jehovah. On the spot where Jehovah appeared to him, he commemorates the event by erecting an altar for his worship. The memory of this great event was perpetuated; and the place seems to have been regarded as a sanctuary for many generations. See the references in the second paragraph of the remarks on these verses, and especially Josh. 24 : 26.

The attentive reader of Abraham's history will note the interesting fact, that wherever he fixed his abode he *built an altar to Jehovah.* (See v. 8, and 13 : 4, 18.) Every place where he dwelt became a temple of the Eternal God. Thus his whole life was a witness to that faith in the One God, which is the groundwork of the civilization of our age, and is diffusing its blessings around the world.

V. 8. *Ha-ai*, as the name should be written. It signifies *the ruins*, and was doubtless given to the place after its destruction by Joshua, who "burnt it, and made it a heap forever" (Josh. 8 : 28). It was most natural to speak of a place by the name under which it was known in the writer's time, though it may have borne a different one at the date of the transaction narrated.

Called on the name of Jehovah. See the remarks on ch. 4 : 26.

V. 9. *Continued removing;* as the necessities of pasturage required. His flocks and herds

---

* Some think it is also mentioned in Judges 9 : 37, under the name *Oak of the magicians* (or, *Oak of enchantments*), in allusion to the ear-rings, supposed to be *amulets*, buried by Jacob "under the oak which is by Shechem" (Gen. 35 : 4).

10 And there was a famine in the land. And Abram went down to Egypt to sojourn there; for the famine was griev- 11 ous in the land. And it came to pass, as he drew near to enter into Egypt, that he said to Sarai his wife: Behold now, I know that thou art a woman of fair countenance. 12 And it will come to pass, that the Egyptians will see thee, and will say: This is his wife. And they will slay me, 13 and will let thee live. Say, I pray thee, thou art my

having consumed the sustenance in the vicinity of his encampment, he removed to another unoccupied region, and there remained till that in like manner was exhausted, and then moved onward again.
The south country; the southern border of Canaan.* Compare ch. 13 : 1, where it said that "Abraham went up from Egypt to the south country."
VV. 10-20. Abraham's sojourn in Egypt.
V. 10. *There was a famine in the land;* a not unfrequent occurrence, in a country depending for its fertility on the local rains. Egypt, on the contrary, was the granary of the ancient world; its fertility depending on the annual overflow of the Nile, fed by the periodical rains at its sources in the highlands.
V. 11. *Of fair countenance.* Sarah was now about sixty-five years old (compare ch. 17 : 17, with 12 : 4), an age at which some women, in modern times, have been in the maturity of their personal charms. What is said of her here is not at all strange, considering the age to which she lived (a hundred and twenty-seven years, ch. 23 : 1), and the highly favorable circumstances of her life, passed in the open country, and in rural occupations and enjoyments.
V. 13. *Thou art my sister.* We learn from ch. 20 : 12 that this was true; probably in the same sense that Lot, Abraham's nephew, is called his brother (14 : 14), being his brother's son; for that she was not the daughter of Terah, Abraham's father, is evident from ch. 11 : 31, where she is called his daughter-in-law. It has been generally supposed, and with great probability, that Sarai was the same as Iscah (11 : 29), and was therefore the half niece of Abraham.†
We also learn from ch. 20 : 13, that from the beginning of their wanderings it was understood between Abraham and Sarah (compare v. 5 of that chapter) that she should pass for his sister. This precaution was innocent and harmless in itself; and Calvin's censure is too severe when he says (on ch. 20 : 12) that this dissembling, by revealing only part of the truth, was a falsehood in fact, though not in words. The censure would be just, if the object had been to deceive others to their injury. But the object was personal safety; and the injury to others arose from their own violation of the duties of hospitality and the rights of strangers. Persons traveling, or sojourning, where the full knowledge of their relations exposes them to danger, are not bound to disclose all that concerns themselves, and in no way concerns others. This principle is often acted on, and without any violation of moral duty; but whether wisely and prudently, the circumstances of the case must decide.
Abraham consulted her honor, no less than his own safety, in adopting this expedient. For if she had been deprived of him, her only protector, her fate would have been worse than his. But while he passed for her brother, none but honorable proposals would be made to her as his sister; and these could be evaded, or postponed, till they should remove to a place of safety. That she should be taken without consent, by royal authority, was a contingency not likely to be foreseen.

---
* So the common English version properly renders the word in chs. 20 : 1 and 24 : 62; and should have rendered it so in ch. 13 : 1, where it represents Abraham as going up from Egypt "into the south."
† Terah had two wives (compare the statement in ch. 20 : 12, "she is the daughter of my father, but not the daughter of my mother"), and "it may be that by one of them he had Haran, and by the other Nahor and Abram; and that Nahor and Abram married the daughters of their older half-brother Haran, Nahor the elder and Abram the younger niece."—*Delitzsch, Comm. über die Genesis,* 3te Ausg., p. 327.

sister, that it may be well with me for thy sake; and my soul shall live because of thee.

14 And it came to pass, when Abram was come into Egypt, that the Egyptians saw the woman that she was very fair. 15 And the princes of Pharaoh saw her, and they commended her to Pharaoh; and the woman was taken to the house 16 of Pharaoh. And he showed kindness to Abram for her sake; and he had flocks and herds, and he-asses, and men-servants and maid-servants, and she-asses, and camels. 17 And Jehovah smote Pharaoh and his house with great 18 plagues, on account of Sarai, Abram's wife. And Pharaoh called Abram, and said: What is this that thou hast done to me? Why didst thou not tell me that she is 19 thy wife? Why saidst thou, She is my sister, so that I should take her to me for a wife? Now, therefore, behold thy wife; take her and go.

20 And Pharaoh commanded men concerning him; and they brought him on his way, him and his wife, and all that he had.

1 And Abram went up from Egypt, he, and his wife, and all that he had, and Lot with him, to the south country.

V. 13. *Or*, may be well with me through thy means

V. 15. *Pharaoh*, the royal title of the ancient Egyptian kings, meaning *the Sun*, as the earthly representative of the god of that name. In the Bible, it commonly stands for the king of Egypt; sometimes followed by the proper name of the individual who bore the title (as Pharaoh Necho, 2 Kings 23 : 29, Pharaoh Hophra, Jer. 44 : 30), and sometimes with the addition *king of Egypt*, as in 1 Kings 3 : 1.

There is reason to believe that the Pharaoh of this passage was not a native prince, but was one of the Shepherd kings (Hyksos), who ruled over lower Egypt, bordering on Canaan, from about 2080 years before Christ, when the country was overrun by the incursion of an Arabian race, known in history as the Shepherds. The territory was nearly contiguous, therefore, to the "south country" (v. 9), and the language of the dominant races was the same in both. On the eastern frontier, toward Canaan, was a royal residence for a portion of the year, the Zoan mentioned in Num. 13 : 22, and referred to in Psalm 78 : 12, 43, as the scene of the plagues in Egypt.

VV. 17-19. That this divine interposition was timely and effectual, for the protection of Sarah, is evident from all the circumstances narrated. The dread it inspired was also effectual for Abraham's safety; and he was dismissed, with reproaches indeed, but also with an honorable safe-conduct.

V. 20. *Brought him on his way;* that is, accompanied him, as an honorable escort and safe-guard. The same Hebrew word is used in ch. 18 : 16, where it is said, that Abraham "went with them, to bring them on their way."

Ch. 13 : 1-13. Return of Abraham and Lot from Egypt. Division of the land between them.

2 And Abram was very rich in cattle, in silver, and in gold.
3 And he went on in his journeyings from the south country, and unto Bethel, unto the place where his tent was at the
4 beginning, between Bethel and Ha-ai, to the place of the altar which he made there at the first. And there Abram called on the name of Jehovah.
5 And Lot also, who went with Abram, had flocks, and
6 herds, and tents. And the land could not bear them, that they might dwell together; for their substance was great, and they could not dwell together.
7 And there was strife between the herdsmen of Abram's cattle, and the herdsmen of Lot's cattle. And the Canaan-
8 ite and the Perizzite were then dwelling in the land. And Abram said to Lot: Let there be no strife, I pray thee, between me and thee, and between my herdsmen and thy
9 herdsmen; for we are brethren. Is not the whole land before thee? Separate thyself, I pray thee, from me; if to the left-hand, then I will go to the right; and if to the right-hand, then I will go to the left.
10 And Lot lifted up his eyes, and saw all the plain of the

V. 3. *Went on in his journeyings.* See the remark on ch. 12 : 9.

VV. 6, 7. *The land could not bear them, that they might dwell together.* It did not furnish pasturage sufficient for their numerous flocks and herds. Hence the strife between their herdsmen for the occupation of the pasture-grounds; a strife that was rendered perilous to their common safety by the presence of the Canaanite and the Perizzite in the land. Or this allusion may be made to them, to show that the resources of the land were yet further restricted by their prior occupancy of it.

The *Perizzites* are not included in the table in ch. 10, and hence we have no light on their origin, and their relation to other occupants of Canaan.

V. 9. As the proposal for a separation came from Abraham, it was proper, as well as disinterested, that he should give his younger and less prosperous kinsman his choice in the proposed division of the country. It was equally proper that Lot should accept the generous offer of his more favored kinsman.

V. 10 describes the appearance of the valley-plain of the Jordan, as it was before the great catastrophe in which the five cities perished (ch. 19 : 24–29). From the lofty highlands on the west,* more than three thousand feet above the plain of the valley, the eye could trace the stream of the Jordan, winding its way through meadow-lands, and groves, and cultivated fields, and losing itself in a beautiful lake bordered by rich plains, that furnished subsistence to the thronged cities that dotted their surface. The great depression of the valley-plain, more than thirteen hundred feet below the level of the Mediterranean Sea, gave to this tract a tropical climate; and being all "a well-watered region," the more intense the heat the more active and vigorous was every form of vegetation. To the eye that beheld this scene, stretching far to the north and south, it seemed "like the garden of Jehovah, like the land of Egypt."

---

* The "mountain on the east of Bethel" (compare v. 3 with ch. 12 : 8) commands such a view. See *Stanley's Sinai and Palestine,* p. 217.

Jordan, that it was all a well-watered region (before Jehovah destroyed Sodom and Gomorrah) like the garden of Jehovah, like the land of Egypt, as thou goest to Zoar. ¹¹ And Lot chose for himself all the plain of the Jordan. And Lot removed eastward, and they separated themselves, ¹² each from his brother. Abram dwelt in the land of Canaan, and Lot dwelt in the cities of the plain, and pitched his tent as far as Sodom. ¹³ And the men of Sodom were wicked, and sinners against Jehovah exceedingly. ¹⁴ And Jehovah said to Abram, after Lot separated himself from him: Lift up now thine eyes and look, from the place where thou art, northward, and southward, and eastward, ¹⁵ and westward. For the whole land which thou seest, to ¹⁶ thee will I give it, and to thy seed forever. And I will make thy seed as the dust of the earth; so that if a man can number the dust of the earth, thy seed also shall be ¹⁷ numbered. Arise, walk through the land, in its length and in its breadth; for to thee will I give it. ¹⁸ And Abram removed his tent, and came and dwelt by the oaks of Mamre, which are in Hebron. And he built there an altar to Jehovah.

¹ And it came to pass, in the days of Amraphel king of

As thou goest to Zoar; namely, in that direction, and by the way of the river valley, leading to that city. Zoar was in the vicinity of Sodom (ch. 19 : 20, 22).

V. 12. *Canaan.* See the note on ch. 10 : 15-20.

Lot dwelt in the cities of the plain; namely, in one or another as he removed from place to place for convenience of pasturage; *and pitched his tent* (as he changed from time to time his place of encampment) as far to the south as Sodom. For the position of Sodom and the neighboring cities, see the remarks on ch. 19.

VV. 14-18. Renewal of the promise to Abraham.

Abraham is now separated from all earthly relations. He stands by himself, the representative of his race in the land destined for them. No obstacle now remains to the full recognition of him, on behalf of his seed, as its sole proprietor. In terms of singular beauty and expressiveness, he is told to view the land in all its extent, to move at will through its length and breadth, for to him and his seed it is given forever. He had already been promised that he should become a great nation; but now, his seed shall be as the dust of the earth, without number!

V. 18. *Oaks of Mamre.* We learn from ch. 14 : 13, that *Mamre* was an Amorite, who, with his brothers Eshcol and Aner (mentioned again in v. 24) was "in covenant with Abram." The word occurs in chs. 23 : 17, 19; 25 : 9; 35 : 27; 49 : 30; 50 : 13; but only as the name of the place, which it received from him as its earlier occupant.

Ch. 14. Invasion and plunder of the cities of the plain; rescue of the captives and their property by Abraham.

Shinar, Arioch king of Ellasar, Chedorlaomer king of Elam, 2 and Tidal king of nations, that they made war with Bera king of Sodom, and with Birsha king of Gomorrah, Shinab king of Admah, and Shemeber king of Zeboïm, and the 3 king of Bela (that is Zoar). All these joined together in the vale of Siddim (that is the salt sea).

The cities of the plain, after twelve years of subjection, as tributaries, to the king of Elam (ch. 10 : 22), threw off the yoke in the thirteenth year. †

In the following year, Chedorlaomer, king of Elam, and three neighboring confederate kings in the valley of the Euphrates, joined their forces in a military expedition against the countries westward, on the Mediterranean slope.

They entered this border land on the north, and subdued successively Dashan, Ammon, Moab, Edom, Amalek, the Amorites in their chief city, and the cities of the plain. On their homeward march, they were intercepted by Abraham near the ancient city of Dan (v. 14), and the captives and plunder they had taken were recovered.

VV. 1-3 contain a brief statement of the parties to the conflict described in vv. 8-10 ; and this statement is followed in vv. 4-16 by a full account of the cause of the invasion, and of its progress and result.

V. 1. *Shinar.* See the note on ch. 10 : 10.

Ellasar; identical with *Larsa* (the Greek *Larissa*), an ancient city of Lower Babylonia or Chaldæa, nearly midway between Ur (ch. 11 : 28) and Erech (ch. 10 : 10). It was one of the primitive capitals, as proved by the inscriptions, and probably older than Babylon.* Compare the remark on ch. 10 : 10, the first and fourth paragraphs.

Elam. See the note on ch. 10 : 22.

Chedorlaomer. A very high authority, on such subjects,† regards it as most probable, that Chedor aomer was identical with a leader of Chaldæan Elamites, who took possession of Babylonia (perhaps after the date of the transactions here narrated) and founded the second Hamite or Chaldæan dynasty, early in the twentieth century before Christ. His title is understood to mean, *Ravager of the West.*

King of nations. The word *nations* naturally suggests mixed races, united under one chief; but nothing is historically known of them.‡

V. 2. *Bela (that is Zoar).* Bela was the ancient, and Zoar the more modern name. Compare ch. 19 : 20, 22. The word *Bela* means *a swallowing up;* and according to a Jewish tradition, the place was so called from its having been often destroyed by earthquakes. The tradition is of little account, though the fact in itself is not improbable. But *Bela* occurs several times as the name of a person ;§ and it is quite as probable that the city was so called from i s founder and king, and that for this reason he is not mentioned by name.∥

The narrative of the transactions commemorated in this chapter is admitted by all scholars to be of very great antiquity, containing several names of places that had passed out of use and remembrance in later times; and hence the addition (here, and in vv. 3, 7, 17) of the more modern names, and the explanation (in vv. 6, 15) of localities that had become obscure, or could be made clearer by reference to one that had become more distinguished and was better known.

V. 3. *All these* (the five kings mentioned in the second verse) *joined together,* for defense against the common enemy.

In the vale of Siddim; where the battle was fought, as stated in v. 8. For the position of "the vale of Siddim," see the remarks on ch. 19.

---

* *Rawlinson, in Smith's Bible Dictionary,* art. Ellasar.

† Sir Henry Rawlinson, App. to Herodotus, Book I., Essay VI., 5, and 19, 20.

‡ Sir Henry Rawlinson suggests "*Median Scyths,* belonging to the old population" of the country (as above, § 20).

§ For example, of a king of Edom, ch. 36 : 32. See also ch. 46 : 21 (common English version *Belah,* properly *Bela*) and 1 Chron. 5 : 8.

∥ It should not be overlooked, that the city itself was a very inconsiderable one (ch. 19 : 20), and for that reason the name of its king may have been omitted in the ancient record of this transaction.

⁴ Twelve years they served Chedorlaomer; and in the ⁵ thirteenth year they rebelled. And in the fourteenth year came Chedorlaomer, and the kings that were with him, and smote the Rephaïtes in Ashteroth-Karnaim, and the Zuzim

---

V. 4 states the cause of the war referred to in the preceding verses, which lead to the disastrous battle in the vale of Siddim. It was the result of this battle that connected Abraham's history with these events; and hence it is the special object of the narrator, as appears from the first three verses.

VV. 5-12. The narrator (in vv. 5-7) sketches briefly and rapidly the progress of the invasion, till he comes to his special object, the battle in the vale of Siddim and its results. These he describes more in detail, in vv. 8-12.

It will be observed, that this invasion swept the whole of the extensive region, so important both in a commercial and military view, from the sea of Tiberias to the Arabian gulf, and subjected it to the then dominant power in western Asia. Thus early began that struggle for the mastery of this country, which in after-times so often made it the theatre of war between the Babylonian or Assyrian power on the east, and the Egyptian on the south.

Rephaïtes (as the name should be written). These were a gigantic race on the east of the Jordan, dwelling in Bashan and northern Gilead, "called land of giants" (*Rephaites*) Deut. 3 : 13, who were driven out by Moses, and of whom Og, king of Bashan, "who reigned in Ashtaroth and Edrei," his chief cities, was the last (Deut. 3 : 10, 11; Josh. 13 : 12). Other giant races of Canaanites are also included under this term; hence the name, "valley of Rephaïtes," 2 Sam. 5 : 18.

Ashteroth-Karnaim. The word *Ashteroth* is the Hebrew plural of *Ashtereth* (the Greek *Astarte*), name of a female divinity widely worshiped among the ancient inhabitants of Canaan; for example, by the Zidonians (1 Kings 11 : 33; 2 Kings 23 : 13), by the Philistines (1 Sam. 31 : 10,) and also on the east side of the Jordan, as is seen in this passage. The Israelites were often seduced into this debasing worship; see Judges 2 : 13, 10 : 6; 1 Sam. 7 : 3, 4; 12 : 10; 1 Kings 11 : 5, 33; 2 Kings 23 : 13.

This form of idolatry originated in the worship of the heavenly bodies ("the host of heaven," Deut. 4 : 19) regarded as presiding over the seasons, regulating their return, and dispensing their blessings.³ As Baal was the Sun-god, representing the sun's dominion over earth (and also the planet *Jupiter*, "the star of Jove, the guardian and giver of good fortune"), so Ashtereth represented the moon, and also the planet *Venus* "the goddess of love and fortune." Under the former character, the image of the idol bore on the head the figure of a crescent moon; and hence the name *Ashtereth-Karnaim* (literally, *Ashtereth of two horns*), the crescented, or moon-ed, Ashteroth. Here it has the plural form, Ashteroth; either from the number of images erected as objects of worship, or indicating different modifications of the same divinity.

The city was called *Ashteroth-Karnaim* from the worship of the goddess (or goddesses) of that name that prevailed there.† The name does not occur again in the Hebrew Scriptures; but *Karnaim* reappears, as a city of Gilead, in later Jewish history; see 1 Macc. 5 : 26, 43, 44; 2 Macc. 12 : 21, 26; Josephus, Ant. 12, 8, 4.‡

---

* Compare Job 31 : 26, 27, and the writer's note on the passage (*Book of Job, explanatory notes)*: The adoration of the heavenly bodies was the first departure from the worship of the Eternal God, their Creator; Idols, afterward worshiped, being only representatives of the sun, moon, and stars or planets. Compare Deut. 4 : 19, 2 Kings 23 : 5, Ezek. 8 : 16.

† The following statement is a sufficient refutation of the Jewish tradition, that the place was so called from "'its situation between two high-peaked hills:'" "Mr. Porter is very confident that 'Karnaim' refers to the figure of Ashteroth. At *Kunawât* (Kenath, Num. 32 : 42) in *Lejah*, the ancient Argob, he found 'a colossal head of Ashteroth, sadly broken, in front of a little temple, of which probably it was once the chief idol. The crescent moon which gave the goddess the name Carnaim (two-horned) is on her brow.' Elsewhere also among the massive ruins of the deserted cities there he saw 'sculptured images of Astarte, with the crescent moon,' showing how prevalent was this form of worship, and what was its characteristic symbol."— Dr. *Hackett*, in *Smith's Bible Dictionary*, vol. I., p. 176, 2d col.

‡ *Grove* (*in Smith's Bible Dictionary*, art. Ashteroth-Karnaim) who, with much probability,

GENESIS. CHAP. XIV.

⁶ in Ham, and the Emim in Shaveh-Kiriathaim, and the Horites in their mount Seir, unto El-paran (which is by ⁷ the wilderness). And they returned, and came to Enmishpat (that is Kadesh), and smote all the country of the

Emim; the ancient and probably original occupants of a region east of the Dead sea. Their territory was afterward held by the Moabites, who gave them this name (signifying *objects of dread, dreaded ones*) on account of their formidable stature and strength (Deut. 2 : 10, 11).
Shaveh-Kiriathaim means *plain of two cities* (or, *of the double city*), and was so called, apparently, from two contiguous cities on the same plain. The route taken by the invading force, and the order of their conquests, show that it was within the territory of the Moabites, before the northern half of it was wrested from them by Sihon king of the Amorites (Num. 21 : 26). *Kiriathaim* occurs in subsequent history as the name of a city in the territory assigned to the tribe of Reuben (Num. 32 : 37; Josh. 13 : 19); but it is not certain that it was the place spoken of here.
V. 6. *The Horites* (meaning *dwellers in holes* or *caves*) were the aboriginal inhabitants of the mountainous region called *Seir* (*rugged*), extending from the Dead sea to the Arabian gulf. Their ancestor was *Seir*, an appellation coincident with that of his home, whose descendants are given in ch. 36 : 20–30. They were dispossessed of their mountainous home by the posterity of Esau (Deut. 2 : 12, 22), and ceased to exist as an independent people.*
El-paran (oaks of Paran): *by the wilderness,* namely, the desert region between mount Sinai, Palestine, and Idumæa. Its position is not satisfactorily determined.†
V. 7. From El-paran, the southern limit of their conquests, they returned northward, and came to *En-mishpat* (fountain of judgment), so called from some unrecorded transaction which took place near it.‡
Kadesh, according to Dr. Robinson,§ is " in the western part of the 'Arabah south of the Dead sea, perhaps not far from the fountain 'Ain el-Weibeh, the most frequented watering-place in all that region."
Country of the Amalekites. By these are meant here an ancient pastoral people, dwelling between Egypt, Philistia, Edom, and the wilderness of mount Sinai.‖
Hazazon-amar (pruning, or felling, of the palm); called afterward En-gedi (2 Chron. 20 : 2), celebrated in ancient writers for its groves of palm-trees;¶ hence its ancient name.
Having thus completed a rapid sketch of the ravages of the invading army, the narrative now returns to its special object, namely, the occurrences which connected them with Abraham's history.

identifies it with *es-Sanamein,* " on the Haj route, about twenty-five miles south of Damascus, and to the northwest of the *Lejah.*"
* In Job 30 : 3–8 is a melancholy picture of the outcast remnant of such a race, drawn very probably from the case here referred to. See the writer's remarks on the passage (*Book of Job, second part, explanatory notes*).
† "Without doubt the later Elath (Deut. 2 : 8, or Eloth, 1 Kings 9 : 26) the important seaport town *Aila* on the northern extremity of the so-called Ælanitic gulf."—*Keil Bib. Commentar, Genesis,* p. 149. So Winer, Knobel, and Delitzsch. But see *Smith's Bible Dictionary,* art. Paran.
‡ Some explain it by reference to Num. 20 : 12, 13, and suppose that the name is used here by anticipation. But of this there is no probability.
§ *Hebrew Lexicon of Gesenius;* compare *Researches in Palestine,* vol. II., pp. 582 and 610.
‖ "A very ancient people (hence called 'first of the nations,' Num. 24 : 20), who in the time of the patriarchs (Gen. 14 : 7) already occupied the region southwest of Palestine, between the Edomites and the borders of Egypt. This is evident from Gen. 14 : 7, Ex. 17 : 8–16, Num. 13 : 29, 1 Sam. 15 : 7, compare Josephus, Ant. vi., 7, 3. They may also have had settlements among their kindred Canaanites in Palestine; hence a mountain in the tribe of Ephraim was called mount of the Amalekites (Judges 12 : 15), and hence also ch. 5 : 14 is to be explained."—*Gesenius, Ersch und Gruber's Encyclop.,* art. Amalek. Compare *Smith's Bible Dictionary,* art. Amalekites.
¶ *Josephus, Antiq.,* ix. 1, 2; *Pliny, Nat Hist.,* v. 17.

Amalekites, and also the Amorites that dwelt at Hazazon-tamar.

8 And there went out the king of Sodom, and the king of Gomorrah, and the king of Admah, and the king of Zeboïm, and the king of Bela (that is Zoar), and joined bat-
9 tle with them in the vale of Siddim; with Chedorlaomer king of Elam, and Tidal king of nations, and Amraphel king of Shinar, and Arioch king of Ellasar; four kings with the five.

10 And the vale of Siddim was full of bitumen-pits; and the kings of Sodom and Gomorrah fled, and fell there; and they that were left fled to the mountain.

11 And they took all the substance of Sodom and Gomor-
12 rah, and all their food, and went their way. And they took Lot the son of Abram's brother, and his substance, and went their way; and he was dwelling in Sodom.

13 And there came one that escaped, and told Abram the Hebrew. And he was dwelling by the oaks of Mamre the Amorite, brother of Eshcol, and brother of Aner; and these were in covenant with Abram.

14 And Abram heard that his brother was taken captive; and he drew out his trained men, born in his house, three

---

V. 9. The expression (in the last clause) is peculiar, as the proper grammatical arrangement would be, *five kings with four*. But there is a *material*, though not a *formal*, propriety in the writer's expression; making the *nearer* the leading subject, and the more remote the subordinate one. This requires the definite article (*with the five*) as in the Hebrew.

V. 10. *Bitumen-pits;* where this mineral pitch boiled up, or was dug out from the earth. This substance still abounds in that region, and is often thrown up from the bed of the Dead sea.

V. 13. *The Hebrew;* meaning *one from beyond*, namely, from beyond the river Euphrates, where the descendants of Eber (ch. 10 : 25) in one line of his posterity (ch. 11 : 16-26) dwelt before the migration of a part of them to Canaan. This appellation would naturally be given them by those among whom they came as immigrants from beyond the river.

The name Hebrew might be formed, as a patronymic, from the name Eber; but there is no evidence that this was the case.*

V. 14. *Unto Dan.* The noted city of this name, known as the northern landmark of Palestine, was originally called *Laish*, and did not receive the name *Dan* till long after the date of this record of these transactions. See Judges 18 : 7, 14, 27, 29, and also Josh. 19 : 47 (where the name is written *Leshem*). It is very improbable, therefore, that this city was the one which is here called Dan.

It is a further objection, that this city does not lie on either of the routes (one below the sea of Tiberias, the other below lake Merom) which lead from the valley of the Jordan by Damascus and Palmyra to Thapsacus on the Euphrates, and which the retiring forces would have taken

---

* See a full discussion of the subject in *Smith's Bible Dictionary*, art. Hebrew.

¹⁵ hundred and eighteen, and pursued after unto Dan. And he divided himself against them by night, he and his servants, and smote them, and pursued them unto Hobah (which is on the left of Damascus).
¹⁶ And he brought back all the substance. And also Lot his brother; and his substance, he brought back ; and also the women, and the people.
¹⁷ And the king of Sodom went out to meet him, after he returned from smiting Chedorlaomer and the kings that were with him, to the valley of Shaveh (that is the King's Dale).
¹⁸ And Melchizedek king of Salem brought forth bread and

on their homeward march; and further, that if they had proceeded as far north as the sources of the Jordan in the valley of Beth-rehob, they would then have taken the direct course through this valley by Hamath, instead of fleeing in the direction of Damascus.*

For these reasons, it is supposed that another place is meant here, namely, *Dan-jaan* in Gilead, mentioned in Deut. 34 : 1, and 2 Sam. 24 : 6.†

V. 15. The unexpected assault by night, and at three different points, accounts for the success of the attack against a much larger force. For this mode of attack, compare 1 Sam. 11 : 11; Job 1 : 17.

Hobah. A village, two miles north of Damascus, still bears this name.

On the left. In the Hebrew expression of the cardinal points, the person is supposed to face the east, when the north is on the left and the south on the right, the east before and the west behind.

V. 17. *The king of Sodom.* It is not improbable that by "kings of Sodom and Gomorrah," in v. 10, are meant the forces represented by them (brought by them into the field), and that the king of Sodom may have been among the survivors; otherwise, his successor is meant here.

The king's dale is mentioned again in 2 Sam. 18 : 18, as the place where Absalom "reared for himself a pillar," which, according to Josephus (Ant. VII., 10, 3), was two stadia (a quarter of a mile) from Jerusalem.

VV. 18-20. *Melchiz-dek* (king of righteousness), and *king of Salem* (king of peace), are highly significant, in view of the use made of this narrative in the seventh chapter of the epistle to the Hebrews.

It appears, from this record, that this exalted personage united in himself the offices of king and priest of the most high God. The latter relation Abraham recognized by giving him a tenth of the spoils.

Of the race to which he belonged, his parentage, his birth and death, nothing is known. Hence the statement in Heb. 7 : 3.

As far as the record goes, all is historical and certain, and free from mystery. All beyond this is groundless and worthless conjecture.‡

Here, then, is a Royal Priesthood, anterior to and independent of the Levitical order of priests, and recognized by Abraham himself, the ancestral head of that order. In no way could the subordinate and temporary relation of the Levitical priesthood to the primary and eternal priesthood of the Messiah be so clearly shown, as by the use made of this historical incident in the epistle to the Hebrews.

* *Keil, Biblische Commentar, Genesis,* 2te Aufl., p. 150.

† "The Dan of this passage, according to Deut. 34 : 1, belonged to Gilead, and is without doubt the same as the *Dan-jaan* mentioned in connection with Gilead in 2 Sam. 24 : 6, and is to be sought in the northern part of Peræa, southwest of Damascus."—*Keil* (as above).

‡ See a brief summary of worse than idle conjectures in *Smith's Bible Dictionary,* art. Melchizedek.

¹⁹ wine. And he was priest of the most high God. And he blessed him, and said: Blessed be Abram of the most high ²⁰ God, possessor of heaven and earth. And blessed be the most high God, who delivered thine enemies into thy hand. And he gave him a tenth of all.

²¹ And the king of Sodom said to Abram: 'Give me the ²² persons, and the substance take to thyself. And Abram said to the king of Sodom: I have lifted my hand to Jeho- ²³ vah, the most high God, possessor of heaven and earth, that not from a thread to a shoe-latchet will I take of all that is thine. And thou shalt not say: It is I that made Abram ²⁴ rich. Nothing for me, save what the young men have eaten, and the portion of the men who went with me, Aner, Eshcol, and Mamre; they shall take their portion.

¹ AFTER these things, the word of Jehovah came to Abram, in vision, saying: Fear not, Abram. I am a shield to thee; thy reward is exceeding great.

² And Abram said: Lord Jehovah, what wilt thou give me? For I go childless; and the heir of my house, he is

V. 19. *Or,* founder of heaven and earth.   V. 22. *Or,* founder of heaven and earth

By *Salem* is meant Jerusalem; and this ancient name occurs, as a poetic archaism, in Psalm 76 : 2, and is retained in the compound name Jerusalem.
The "bread and wine" seem intended for refreshment. A sacramental use, which some have imagined to be intended, has no warrant in the connection.
V. 20. *Gave him a tenth of all;* as he had a right to do, this being less than his proper share of the rescued spoils.
VV. 21-24. Abraham declines, and with very marked emphasis, the proffered reward for his disinterested service. For the grounds of this, there is no occasion to look beyond his own generous spirit, and his resolution to be under no obligation to the king, even in appearance. But he is just as well as generous; and claims for his partners their share of the recovered spoils (v. 24).
V. 22. *Have lifted my hand to Jehovah;* in token of recognition of him, as witness to the oath.
Ch. 15. Confirmation of the covenant with Abraham.
V. 1. *After these things.* The preceding chapter gives a vivid picture of the perils and uncertainties, to human view, of Abraham's occupancy of the land of promise. Jehovah now appears, and reassures him with the words: "Fear not, I am a shield to thee;" and adds, in view of his steadfast faith and unwavering trust, "thy reward is exceeding great."
In vision; that is, in the mental perception, whether in dream or trance (Job 4 : 13; Acts 22 : 17, 18). Compare below, vv. 12 and 17.
Thy reward. Compare the statement of the case in Rom. 4 : 3-5. It was on the ground of his faith alone, and as a gift of grace, that he was promised this great reward.
V. 2. *I go* (that is, go on, continue) *childless.* Or, as others understand the expression, *I go* (that is, go away, pass away) *childless;* shall die childless. But the former is more probably the meaning.

GENESIS. CHAP. XV.

3 Eliezer of Damascus. And Abram said: Behold, to me thou hast not given seed; and behold, one of my household will be my heir.
4 And behold, the word of Jehovah came to him, saying: This shall not be thy heir; but one that shall come forth from thine own bowels, he shall be thy heir.
5 And he brought him forth abroad, and said: Look now toward heaven, and number the stars, if thou shalt be able to number them. And he said: So shall be thy seed.
6 And he believed in Jehovah; and he reckoned it to him for righteousness.
7 And he said to him: I am Jehovah, who brought thee out from Ur of the Chaldæans, to give thee this land to
8 possess it. And he said: Lord Jehovah, whereby shall I know that I shall possess it?
9 And he said to him: Take for me a heifer three years old, and a she-goat three years old, and a ram three years

---

Eliezer. Probably the head steward and confidential servant of Abraham, "that ruled over all that he had" (ch. 24 : 2).
Of Damascus. This city was on one of the principal routes between Mesopotamia and Palestine. There are intimations in ancient writings of Abraham's temporary residence in its vicinity.
V. 5. *If thou shalt be able;* if, upon making the trial, thou shalt prove able to do it.
It is now well known, that the number of stars that can be counted with the naked eye, though seemingly innumerable, is really very small; and Abraham's posterity, unless it far exceeded that number, would have been quite inconsiderable. This shows, along with many similar cases, that the Scriptures speak of such subjects according to the common apprehension of them; and this we ought to expect in a divine book, intended for the instruction of all, and not of the favored few.
V. 6. Compare Rom., ch. 4.
V. 7. A night had intervened; and on the following day (compare v. 5 with v. 12) Jehovah reminds Abraham, that it was he who brought him from Ur of the Chaldæans; and that his purpose in this was to give him the land to possess it. In regard to this further promise, namely, that his posterity shall rightfully possess the land, Abraham desires some outward token that shall assure him of the divine purpose. This is granted him.
VV. 9–17. We have here one of the most impressive ceremonies known to ancient times. The party, or parties, to a covenant (here there was but one,* as intimated in Gal. 3 : 20) passed between the severed bodies of slain beasts, symbolizing what was due to a violation of the compact.† Jehovah, in like manner, condescends to confirm his covenant, by causing a symbol of his presence to pass between the divided victims (v. 17).
V. 9. *Three years old;* that is, of full age, when it is a perfect animal. The animals here mentioned were accounted clean, for sacred uses, and hence were selected for this religious rite.

* Those who represent this as a covenant to which two were parties, God being one and Abraham the other, misconceive the whole transaction. It was God's covenant with Abraham, and not Abraham's covenant with God.
† Compare the impressive reference to this ancient rite in Jer. 34 : 18-20.

¹⁰ old, and a turtle-dove, and a young pigeon. And he took to him all these; and he divided them in the midst, and laid each one's part over against its fellow; but the birds he did not divide.

¹¹ And birds of prey came down upon the carcasses; and Abram drove them away.

¹² And the sun was about going down, and a deep sleep fell upon Abram; and behold, a horror of great darkness ¹³ falling upon him. And he said to Abram: Know surely, that thy seed shall be a sojourner in a land that is not theirs, and will serve them; and they will afflict them four ¹⁴ hundred years. And the nation which they will serve I judge; and afterward they shall come out with great sub-¹⁵ stance. And as for thee, thou shalt go to thy fathers in ¹⁶ peace; thou shalt be buried in a good old age. And in the fourth generation they shall return hither. For the iniquity of the Amorites is not yet full.

V. 10. *Laid each one's part over against its fellow;* that is, he laid one half of each animal over against its other half. *The birds he did not divide;* did not "divide them asunder," as directed in Lev. 1 : 17.

V. 11. *Birds of prey came down*, etc. This would naturally follow the exposure of dead bodies in the open field, and would therefore, together with the act of guarding them, be an essential feature in a complete picture of the scene. Perhaps this is all that is intended. But by some it is regarded as an omen of hostile attempts on the part of heathen adversaries, which should be successfully repelled.*

V. 12. As the sun is going down, a deep sleep falls upon Abraham; and in it, a shuddering sense of great darkness, settling down upon him. In this state of insensibility to outward objects, his inward sense is conscious of the divine presence, and receives the prophetic revelation.

Deep sleep. The same Hebrew word is used to express the supernatural sleep that fell upon Adam (ch. 2 : 21).

V. 13. *Four hundred years;* the prophetic round number, for the more exact historical period of four hundred and thirty years, in Ex. 12 : 40.

V. 16. *Generation* is here equivalent to a hundred years or more (v. 13), in accordance with the term of human life at that time.

Is not yet full. Their course of evil is not yet fully run, and the divine purposes are not fully accomplished by them in their chosen career of guilt. This is the key to many of the dark ways of Providence, as regards individuals as well as nations; and all human history is the illustration of this divine forbearance and delayed but sure justice.

---

* "This is no unmeaning trait, but has a significance bearing on the future founding of the theocracy. Birds of prey were regarded by the Hebrews and others as impure (Lev. 11 : 13; Plutarch, Romulus, ix.), and are therefore symbols of impure heathen; here of the Egyptians, who would not let Israel go, and accordingly would have hindered the consummation of the covenant at Sinai, but were foiled by the zeal of Israel's leaders. To them the hawk was especially sacred; and under the image of the hawk, symbol of the sun, they represented the deity, and especially their supreme god, the Sun-god Osiris."—*Knobel, die Genesis erklärt,* 2te Aufl., p. 153.

17 And the sun was gone down, and darkness came on. And behold, a furnace of smoke and fiery flame, that passed between those pieces.
18 On that day did Jehovah make a covenant with Abram, saying: To thy seed I give this land, from the river of Egypt unto the great river, the river Euphrates;
19 the Kenites, and the Kenizzites, and the Kadmonites,
20 and the Hittites, and the Perizzites, and the Rephaïtes,
21 and the Amorites, and the Canaanites, and the Girgashites, and the Jebusites.

1 AND Sarai, the wife of Abram, bore him no child. And she had an Egyptian maid-servant, and her name was

---

The delayed occupancy of Palestine by the Israelites for the reason here assigned, their oppression in the land of Egypt and deliverance from it by divine power, are among the most important events of history, in the extent of their influence on human welfare.

V. 17. A glowing furnace, enveloped in smoke and outbursting flame, symbolized the divine presence. The consuming fire, breaking through the enveloping smoke, is an apt emblem of the divine power, veiling itself and only partially revealed.

It is uncertain whether this scene passed before Abraham's mental vision, during the supernatural sleep that fell upon him (v. 12), or whether he awoke and beheld it with the bodily eye. The former view seems to be the more probable one; as the covenant confirmed by this rite, and expressed in the following verses, was then communicated, and doubtless in the same manner as the prophetic revelation in vv. 13-16.

The covenant being the free grant of Jehovah (compare ch. 6 : 18), he alone executes the rite in confirmation of it.

V. 18. *From the river of Egypt*, etc. The kingdom of Israel, in its most prosperous period, had this extent of territory. See 1 Kings 8 : 65. *River of Egypt;* here the Pelusiac or most eastern branch of the Nile.

These are the terms of this divine deed of gift. The subsequent history of the Israelites, in connection with it, is an instructive commentary on the relation of human action to the declared purpose of God.

VV. 19-21. These verses seem not to have been a part of the divine communication to Abraham, but to have been added by the sacred writer, specifying the principal nations by whom this territory was occupied.

Kenites; in the region south of Palestine and bordering on Egypt (1 Sam. 15 : 6, 7).

Kenizzites (in the common English version written also *Kenezites*, in Num. 32 : 12, Josh. 14 : 6, 14, where the Hebrew is the same as here), a people of Edom, descendants of Kenaz (ch. 36 : 11).

Kadmonites (not elsewhere mentioned), meaning *eastern*, and supposed to have occupied the part of this territory toward its eastern limit.

Hittites; see the remarks on ch. 10 : 15, 16, third paragraph.

Perizzites; see ch. 13 : 7, 34 : 30; Josh. 17 : 15; Judges 1 : 4, 5.

Rephaites; see the remarks on ch. 14 : 5-12, third paragraph.

Canaanites; see ch. 10 : 19. *Amorites, Girgashites, Jebusites;* see the remarks on ch. 10 : 15-20, fourth paragraph.

Ch. 16. Hagar, Sarah's maid-servant, given by her mistress to Abraham for a wife. Birth of Ishmael.

The transaction here recorded is not defensible on any grounds of Christian morality. But it is to be observed, in the first place, that neither of the parties to the marriage relation was wronged by it, since it was proposed and urged by the wife, and for her own gratification

² Hagar. And Sarai said to Abram : Behold now, Jehovah has withheld me from bearing. Go in, I pray thee, unto my maid-servant. It may be, that I shall be built up from her. And Abram hearkened to the voice of Sarai.
³ And Sarai, the wife of Abram, took Hagar the Egyptian, her maid-servant, after Abram had dwelt ten years in the land of Canaan, and gave her to Abram her husband, to
⁴ be his wife. And he went in unto Hagar, and she conceived. And she saw that she had conceived ; and her mistress was despised in her eyes.
⁵ And Sarai said to Abram : My wrong be upon thee. I myself gave my maid-servant into thy bosom ; and she saw that she had conceived, and I was despised in her eyes. Jehovah judge between me and thee.
⁶ And Abram said to Sarai : Behold, thy maid-servant is

---

and benefit ; and secondly, that it was in accordance with the custom of the age, and at a time when such an expedient, for the benefit of the interested party in the marriage relation, was condemned by no precept of the divine law then promulgated.

Sarah voluntarily yielded her rights as a wife, a relation which seemed to her to have failed of its object, in order that she might obtain children whom she could call her own, and in whom her name and memory would be perpetuated. It seems that Abraham did not seek it, and only yielded to the importunities of his wife. We have no reason, from the whole narrative, to think that these importunities fell short of what is recorded in a similar case (ch. 30 : 1), "Give me children, or else I die." The result showed that compliance, in such a case, is not the easiest or safest policy.*

Calvin and others think it an extenuating circumstance, that the object was good, namely, to make sure of the child of promise before it should be too late. It is not clear how this would help the case, even if the supposition were true ; and of this there is no indication in the language of the narrative.

V. 1. *An Egyptian maid-servant.* She probably became a member of the household during Abraham's temporary abode in Egypt. See the statement in ch. 12 : 16.

V. 2. *I shall be built up from her;* namely, in a family of children proceeding from her, and borne by her as mine. See ch. 30 : 3.†

V. 3. *To be his wife.* She took the place and relation of a wife, which Sarah voluntarily relinquished for her own advantage. See the introductory remarks on this chapter.

VV. 5, 6. *My wrong be upon thee ;* namely, in case I am not redressed by the punishment of the offender.

I myself gave, etc. She pleads, as the reason why she should be redressed, that to her own self-denying act Abraham owed the prospect of an heir, and Hagar the ground of her insolent and ungrateful triumph.

Thy maid-servant is in thy hand. Abraham concedes to Sarah the right, which truly belonged to her, to deal with her own maid-servant as she deemed just and proper. Hagar, by her

---

* In beautiful contrast is the relation between Elkanah and Hannah (*nomen carissimum*), as indicated in his language, "Am not I better to thee than ten sons ?" (1 Sam. 1 : 8.)

† There is the same allusion in the Hebrew word for *son*, and its feminine form for *daughter*, from a verb meaning *to build.* So also the word for *house* (properly *building*, from the same verb) often stands for a numerous progeny, or race. See, for example, Ruth 4 : 11, "like Rachel and like Leah, which two built the house of Israel ;" and compare the numerous expressions like " house of Jacob" (Psalm 114 : 1), " house of Judah" (2 Sam. 2 : 4).

in thy hand. Do to her that which is good in thine eyes. And Sarai dealt harshly with her, and she fled from her face.

7 And the angel of Jehovah found her by the fountain of water in the wilderness, by the fountain in the way to
8 Shur. And he said: Hagar, Sarai's maid-servant, whence camest thou, and whither art thou going? And she said: I am fleeing from the face of Sarai, my mistress.
9 And the angel of Jehovah said to her: Return to thy mistress, and submit thyself under her hands.
10 And the angel of Jehovah said to her: I will greatly multiply thy seed, and it shall not be numbered for multitude.
11 And the angel of Jehovah said to her: Behold, thou art with child, and shalt bear a son, and shalt call his name Ishmael; because Jehovah hearkened to thy affliction.
12 And he will be a wild man, his hand against every man, and every man's hand against him. And before the face of all his brethren will he dwell.
13 And she called the name of Jehovah, who spoke to her, Thou God of vision. For she said: Do I even see, here after the vision?
14 Therefore the well was called Beer-lehai-roi. Behold, it is between Kadesh and Bered.

---

unjustifiable demeanor toward her mistress, had forfeited any claim she might otherwise have had on his protection.

V. 7. *Angel of Jehovah;* one of the divine messengers so often mentioned in the Old Testament; for example, Judges 6 : 11, 21; 13 : 3, 16, 20; 2 Sam. 24 : 16. Compare, in the New Testament, Matt. 1 : 19; Luke 1 : 11; Acts 5 : 19.

In the way to Shur. Shur was near the eastern boundary of Egypt; compare ch. 25 : 18, "Shur, that is before Egypt, as thou goest toward Assyria." She was returning, therefore, to her native country.

V. 11. *Ishmael;* meaning, God hears.

V. 12. *Before the face of all his brethren will he dwell* (make his abode). This is by some understood to mean, in their vicinity and neighborhood, and that he should not be reckoned an outcast because he was born of a bondwoman. But the meaning is rather, he will dwell at large, in sight of all his kindred, maintaining his separate and independent nationalities, apart from and in the sight of all; a characteristic trait of the wandering Ishmaelite tribes of Arabia.

VV. 13, 14. *God of vision;* who permits himself to be seen, to be an object of vision, and whom one may see and live.

In the following clause, *do I see* (behold the light) is the same as, do I live; and the words, *here after the vision* mean, here where I beheld this sight, the holy place where God appeared through his angel.

Beer-lehai-roi means, well of living vision; where one lived after the vision (the beholding)

¹⁵ And Hagar bore a son to Abram. And Abram called
¹⁶ the name of his son, whom Hagar bore, Ishmael. And Abram was eighty and six years old, when Hagar bore Ishmael to Abram.

¹ AND Abram was ninety and nine years old. And Jehovah appeared to Abram, and said to him: I am God,
² Almighty; walk before me, and be perfect. And I will set my covenant between me and thee, and will multiply thee exceedingly.
³ And Abram fell on his face; and God talked with him,
⁴ saying: As for me, behold my covenant is with thee, and
⁵ thou shalt become a father of a multitude of nations. And thy name shall no more be called Abram, but thy name shall be Abraham; for a father of a multitude of nations
⁶ have I made thee. And I will make thee fruitful exceedingly, and I will make nations of thee, and kings shall
⁷ come forth from thee. And I will establish my covenant between me and thee, and thy seed after thee in their generations, for an everlasting covenant, to be a God to
⁸ thee and to thy seed after thee. And I will give to thee, and to thy seed after thee, the land of thy sojournings, the whole land of Canaan, for an everlasting possession; and I will be their God.
⁹ And God said to Abraham: And as for thee, my cov-

of a divine messenger. It was supposed that a mortal could not look on such a being and live. Compare Judges 6 : 22, 23, 13 : 22.

Kadesh; see the remarks on ch. 14 : 7, second paragraph. *Bered* is not mentioned elsewhere, and nothing is known of its position.

Ch. 17. The covenant of circumcision with Abraham and his posterity.

The stipulations of this covenant are the following: On the part of Jehovah (vv. 4-8), the grant to Abraham of a numerous and powerful progeny (vv. 4-6), the establishment of his covenant with him and his posterity to be their God (v. 7), and the gift of the land of Canaan as their inheritance (v. 8); on the part of Abraham and his posterity (vv. 9-14), the circumcision of every male throughout all generations.

The obvious design of this covenant was to set apart a people for a special purpose (see remarks on ch. 11 : vv. 10 and following), and to keep them distinct from others by a peculiar national sign, till that purpose should be accomplished.

V. 1. *Walk before me;* as in my presence and sight, and by implication, in accordance with my will and requirements. *Be perfect;* omitting nothing of all that is required.

V. 5. *Abraham;* meaning, father of a multitude.

V. 8. *Of thy sojournings,* from place to place, as a stranger without a fixed abode. The plural is significant of his frequent change of abode.

enant shalt thou keep, thou, and thy seed after thee in
10 their generations. This is my covenant, which ye shall
keep, between me and you and thy seed after thee: Every
11 male of you shall be circumcised. And ye shall circumcise the flesh of your foreskin; and it shall be a cov-
12 enant-sign between me and you. And at the age of eight
days every male of you shall be circumcised, in your generations, he that is born in the house, and bought with
13 money of any stranger, who is not of thy seed. He that
is born in thy house, and he that is bought with thy
money, shall surely be circumcised; and my covenant shall
14 be in your flesh for an everlasting covenant. And the
uncircumcised male, the flesh of whose foreskin is not circumcised, that soul shall be cut off from his people; he
has broken my covenant.
15 And God said to Abraham: As for Sarai thy wife, thou
shalt not call her name Sarai, for Sarah shall be her name.
16 And I will bless her, yea and will give thee a son from
her; and I will bless her, and she shall become nations;
kings of peoples shall be from her.
17 And Abraham fell on his face, and laughed; and he said
in his heart: Shall a child be born to him that is a hundred years old? And Sarah, shall she that is ninety years
old bear?
18 And Abraham said to God: Would that Ishmael might
live before thee!
19 And God said: Nay, Sarah thy wife shall bear thee a
son, and thou shalt call his name Isaac. And I will estab-

VV. 12, 13. The requirement in v. 10, of the circumcision of every male, extends to him "that is born in the house, and bought with money of any stranger, who is not of thy seed." Being a national sign, it is required of all who are admitted within the pale of the nation.

V. 14. *Shall be cut off from his people;* shall not be reckoned as one of them.

V. 15. *Sarah;* meaning, princess; so called as the mother of future nations and their kings.

V. 17. *Laughed;* not at the apparent improbability of what is promised, expressing doubt and unbelief, but at its strangeness,'an expression both of surprise and joy.

V. 18. *Before thee;* namely, in thy sight, and by implication, with thin approval and by thy favor. Abraham, with a natural affection for the child already born to him, desires that he may be the promised heir. This is evident from the form of the reply in the first clause of the following verse, showing that God had something better than this in reserve for him.

V. 19. The name *Isaac* (kindred with the word meaning *to laugh*) is a gentle reminder of the effect produced on Abraham by the promise in vv. 15, 16. See the remark on v. 17. The name

lish my covenant with him for an everlasting covenant, for his seed after him.
20 And as for Ishmael, I have heard thee. Behold, I have blessed him, and made him fruitful, and multiplied him exceedingly. Twelve princes shall he beget, and I will
21 make him a great nation. But my covenant I will establish with Isaac, whom Sarah shall bear to thee at this set time, in the following year.
22 And he finished talking with him; and God went up from Abraham.
23 And Abraham took Ishmael his son, and all that were born in his house, and all that were bought with his money, every male among the men of Abraham's house, and he circumcised the flesh of their foreskin in that very
24 day, as God had spoken with him. And Abraham was ninety and nine years old, when he was circumcised in the
25 flesh of his foreskin. And Ishmael his son was thirteen years old, when he was circumcised in the flesh of his
26 foreskin. In that very day was Abraham circumcised, and
27 Ishmael his son. And all the men of his house, born in the house, and bought with money of the stranger, were circumcised with him.

1 AND Jehovah appeared to him by the oaks of Mamre; and he was sitting at the door of the tent in the heat of
2 the day. And he lifted up his eyes and saw, and behold, three men standing over against him. And he saw, and ran to meet them from the door of the tent, and bowed

---

is significant also of another occurrence, related in ch. 18 : 12, and allusion is made to it again in ch. 21 : 6.

V. 20. *And made him fruitful*, etc.; in God's purpose, is meant. What he has determined is spoken of as in effect already done.

Ch. 18. Jehovah appears to Abraham. Renewed promise of a son. Destruction of Sodom foretold.

V. 2. *Three men.* Three personages in human form. Such was their appearance, and as such they were received and hospitably entertained by Abraham. Their true character becomes apparent to the reader in the progress of the narrative. That Jehovah thus manifested himself, in intercourse with the patriarchs, is not more strange than that "the Word became flesh and dwelt among us."

Standing over against him. It is the manner of eastern travelers, when soliciting hospitality, to remain standing at a respectful distance till invited to approach.

3 himself toward the earth. And he said: My Lord, if now I have found favor in thy sight, pass not on, I pray thee, 4 from thy servant. Let a little water, I pray thee, be fetched, and wash your feet, and recline under the tree. 5 And let me fetch a morsel of bread, and strengthen ye your heart; after that ye shall pass on; for therefore do ye pass by your servant. And they said: So do, as thou hast spoken.
6 And Abraham hastened into the tent to Sarah, and said: Make ready quickly three seahs of fine flour, knead 7 it, and make hearth-cakes. And Abraham ran to the herd, and took a calf tender and good, and gave it to the 8 servant; and he made haste to dress it. And he took curd and milk, and the calf which he had dressed, and set it before them; and he stood by them under the tree, and they ate.
9 And they said to him: Where is Sarah thy wife? And 10 he said: Behold, in the tent. And he said: I will surely

V. 3. *My Lord.* He recognizes the chief personage, on whom the other two are attendants, and salutes him with the title commonly used in addressing a person of distinction.

V. 4. As only sandals were worn on the feet, it was an essential part of eastern hospitality to provide water for washing the feet of the guest. Compare ch. 19 : 2, 43 : 24; Judges 19 : 21.

V. 5. *For therefore do ye pass by your servant;* that is, turn aside to his home on your way. It was accounted an honor and a privilege to entertain a stranger, and was accepted as a favor conferred by him. Hence Abraham's words, "for therefore do ye pass by your servant," are a courteous acknowledgment of the honor intended him.

V. 6. *Seah,* a dry measure, supposed to be one-third of the ephah (Ruth 2 : 17, 18), or about one peck and a half.

Hearth-cakes; cakes baked on the hearth (not in an oven), either under hot embers, or on heated stones.*

V. 8. *Curd.* In ancient times, the people of the east used milk in its natural state, curdled milk (curd), and the same with the whey pressed out (cheese, Prov. 30 : 33, properly, *the pressing of milk brings forth cheese*), and cream (Psalm 55 : 21, in the common English version, *butter*). At the present day, they separate the fatty particles of the milk from the whey and the caseine, by agitation in a common water-skin, which is partly filled with milk and suspended from a frame, and is then regularly moved to and fro with a jerk, till the separation is effected.† But of such a practice in ancient times there is no sure indication.

V. 9. *They said;* a common and very natural indefiniteness of expression in familiar and unstudied narrative. The question proceeded from the party of guests; but which of them was the speaker is not indicated. That it was the chief personage may be inferred from v. 1).

V. 10. *And he said;* namely, he who appeared to him (v. 1) in the person of his principal guest. Compare v. 13.

* As is still practiced in the east. "The women in some of the tents were kneading bread, and baking it in thin cakes in the embers or on iron plates over the fire."—*Robinson, Biblical Researches,* vol. ii., p. 180.

† *Robinson's Biblical Researches,* vol. ii., p. 180. See also the American edition of *Smith's Bible Dictionary,* addition to the article Butter.

return to thee at the reviving season; and behold, Sarah thy wife shall have a son. And Sarah was listening at the door of the tent; and that was behind him.

11 And Abraham and Sarah were old, far gone in years. It had ceased to be with Sarah after the manner of women.
12 And Sarah laughed within herself, saying: After I am decayed, shall I have pleasure, my lord being old also?
13 And Jehovah said to Abraham: Wherefore is this, that Sarah laughed, saying: Is it even so, that I shall indeed
14 bear, when I am old? Is anything too hard for Jehovah? At the set time I will return to thee, at the reviving season, and Sarah shall have a son.
15 And Sarah denied, saying: I did not laugh. For she was afraid. And he said: Nay, but thou didst laugh.
16 And the men rose up from thence, and looked toward Sodom. And Abraham went with them, to bring them on the way.
17 And Jehovah said: Shall I conceal from Abraham what
18 I am about to do; seeing that Abraham shall surely become a great and mighty nation, and all the nations of the
19 earth shall be blessed in him? For I have known him, in

At the reviving season; when this season revives, returns again, after passing away with the departing year. By a beautiful and natural figure, the seasons of the year are conceived as dying out and passing away with it, and as reviving again with the succeeding one.

The expression corresponds to the one used in ch. 17 : 21, "at this set time in the following year;" namely, when this set time, or season, returns.

V. 12. *Laughed within herself;* a secret feeling of the incongruity of the promise with the actual circumstances of the case. Compare the remarks on ch. 17 : 17. There may have been here more of doubt and distrust, as seems to be intimated by the grave but mild rebuke that follows.

V. 13. *Jehovah said.* The reader is now apprised that it is Jehovah who is speaking. This was clearly understood by Abraham, though we are not told in what manner it was made known. He interprets her thought in language that expresses its full import.

V. 15. The statement, *I did not laugh*, was true in the sense intended, namely, that there was no outward expression of laughter. The reply, "Nay, but thou didst laugh," showed her that one was dealing with her who knew her inmost thoughts.

V. 16. *Looked toward Sodom;* took the way leading to that city.—*To bring them on the way* (see the remark on ch. 12 : 20). He accompanied them as an expression of respect and courtesy, and perhaps to act as their guide.

VV. 17-22. On the way, the chief personage, in whom Jehovah manifested himself, resolves to impart to Abraham his purpose respecting Sodom; and the reasons for this special mark of confidence are assigned in vv. 18, 19.

V. 19. *I have known him.* Here, and often elsewhere,* *to know* has the special meaning, to regard, to make an object of attention and care; by implication, to make choice of for one's

* Compare Amos 3 : 2, "*you only have I known, of all the families of the earth.*"

order that he may command his children and his house after him, and they may keep the way of Jehovah, to do righteousness and justice; that Jehovah may bring upon Abraham that which he has spoken of him.

20 And Jehovah said: Because the cry of Sodom and Go-
21 morrah is great, and because their sin is very grievous, I will go down now, and will see whether they have done altogether according to the cry of it that is come to me; and if not, I will know.

22 And the men turned from thence, and went toward Sodom; and Abraham stood yet before Jehovah.

23 And Abraham drew near, and said: Wilt thou even take
24 away the righteous with the wicked? Perhaps there are fifty righteous in the midst of the city. Wilt thou even take away and not spare the place, for the sake of the
25 fifty righteous within it? Far be it from thee to do after this manner, to slay the righteous with the wicked, that

---

V. 20. *Or*, the cry against

self and admit to near and intimate relationship. Compare James 2:3, "and he was called, Friend of God." The purpose of this choice is stated in the following words.

V. 20. *Jehovah said.* He now declares, in the hearing of Abraham, the purpose of his coming.

The cry of Sodom; namely, of the abominations committed there; the name of the place put for what belongs to it and especially characterizes it.

This is commonly understood as meaning, the cry concerning Sodom (as in the margin, *the cry against Sodom*). But the more natural construction and meaning is, that their own acts cry to heaven against them. Compare Isaiah 59:12, "our sins testify against us," and Jer. 14:7, "our iniquities testify against us."

V. 22. The two subordinate personages depart, and proceed on their way to Sodom (ch. 19:1), and Abraham remains standing before Jehovah.

From the place where they now stood (ch. 19:27, 28) Abraham beheld, on the following morning, the smoke that rose from the doomed cities. An eminence, distant about an hour and a half eastward from Hebron where Abraham dwelt (compare v. 1 of this chapter with ch. 13:18), commands a remote view of the region of the Dead Sea.*

VV. 23-32. Abraham's intercession on behalf of the righteous in Sodom.

Abraham infers what may be the fate of the city, from what he knows of the character of its people.

There is no parallel, even in sacred history, to the scene which follows. With earnestness, but with unaffected humility, devout courtesy, and a reverent freedom, the patriarch presses his suit on behalf of the few righteous men in Sodom. On the other hand, Jehovah receives the intercession of his servant graciously, and admits the reasonableness of his plea by granting all that he desires.

Abraham begins with the very moderate supposition, that there may be fifty righteous in the city. There is a beautiful aptness in the turn given to the first plea for a slight abatement of this number: "Wilt thou for five destroy the whole city?" The whole passage is singularly felicitous and beautiful, in conception and expression.

---

* Robinson, *Biblical Researches*, vol. ii., pp. 188, 189, and p. 449, note.

the righteous should be as the wicked; far be it from thee. Shall not the Judge of all the earth do right?

26 And Jehovah said: If I shall find in Sodom fifty righteous in the midst of the city, then I will spare all the place on their account.

27 And Abraham answered and said: Behold now, I have taken upon me to speak to my Lord, and I am dust and ashes. 28 Perhaps the fifty righteous will lack five. Wilt thou for five destroy the whole city? And he said: I will not destroy it, if I shall find there forty and five.

29 And yet again he spoke to him, and said: Perhaps there will forty be found there. And he said: I will not do it for the sake of the forty.

30 And he said: Let not my Lord be angry, I pray, and I will speak. Perhaps there will thirty be found there. And he said: I will not do it, if I shall find thirty there.

31 And he said: Behold now, I have taken upon me to speak to my Lord. Perhaps there will be twenty found there. And he said: I will not destroy it for the sake of the twenty.

32 And he said: Let not my Lord be angry, I pray, and I will speak but this once. Perhaps there will ten be found there. And he said: I will not destroy it for the sake of the ten.

33 And Jehovah went away, when he had finished talking to Abraham; and Abraham returned to his place.

1 AND the two angels came to Sodom at evening; and Lot was sitting in the gate of Sodom. And Lot saw, and rose up to meet them; and he bowed with his face toward the earth. 2 And he said: Behold now, my Lords, turn aside, I pray, into the house of your servant, and pass the

---

V. 33. *Jehovah went away.* See ch. 19 : 24.
Ch. 19. Sodom destroyed. Deliverance of Lot and his family. Origin of Moab and Ammon.
V. 1. *And the two angels came to Sodom.* The definite article (*the two angels*) shows that these are the two personages already spoken of in ch. 18 : 22, as being then on their way to Sodom. They still appear, however, as men (vv. 10, 12), and as such are received and entertained by Lot.
V. 2. *Wash your feet.* Compare the remark on ch. 18 : 4.

night, and wash your feet; and ye shall rise up early, and go on your way. And they said: Nay, for we will pass
3 the night in the street. And he pressed them very earnestly; and they turned aside to him, and entered into his house; and he made them a feast, and baked unleavened cakes, and they ate.
4 Before they lay down, men of the city, men of Sodom, surrounded the house, both young and old, all the people
5 from the farthest limit. And they called to Lot, and said to him: Where are the men who came in to thee this night? Bring them out to us, that we may know them.
6 And Lot went out to them, to the doorway, and shut
7 the door behind him. And he said: Do not, I pray, my
8 brethren, do wickedly. Behold now, I have two daughters, who have not known a man; let me, I pray, bring them out to you, and do to them as is good in your eyes. Only to these men do nothing; for therefore came they under the shadow of my roof.
9 And they said: Stand back. And they said: This one came in to sojourn, and he will needs be judge. Now will we deal worse with thee than with them. And they pressed hard upon the man, upon Lot, and came near to
10 break the door. And the men put forth their hand, and drew Lot into the house to them; and they shut the door.
11 And the men that were at the door-way of the house they smote with blindness, both small and great; and they wearied themselves to find the door-way.
12 And the men said to Lot: Whom else hast thou here? Son-in-law, and thy sons, and thy daughters, and all that
13 thou hast in the city, bring out from this place. For we are about to destroy this place, because their cry is great

---

V. 4. What follows shows the justice of the impending catastrophe, that so suddenly and utterly consumed the city and its guilty inhabitants. The men who surrounded Lot's house were not gathered from some single infected district of the city, but "all the people from the farthest limit" were represented there. The ten righteous men, whose presence would have saved the city, were not found.
V. 12. *Son-in-law;* in case thou hast any, is implied in the form of expression. On the contrary, he says, "thy sons and thy daughters," as Lot was known to have them.
V. 13. *Their cry.* See the remark on ch. 18 : 20.

in the presence of Jehovah; and Jehovah has sent us to destroy it.

14 And Lot went out, and spoke to his sons-in-law, who married his daughters, and said: Arise, go forth from this place; for Jehovah is about to destroy the city. And he was as one that jested in the eyes of his sons-in-law.

15 And when dawn arose, the angels hastened Lot, saying: Arise, take thy wife, and thy two daughters who are at hand, lest thou be consumed in the iniquity of the city.

16 And he lingered; and the men laid hold on his hand, and on the hand of his wife, and on the hand of his two daughters, through Jehovah's compassion for him, and they brought him forth and set him without the city.

17 And it came to pass, when they had brought them forth abroad, that he said: Escape for thy life; look not behind thee, and stay not in all the plain; escape to the mountain, lest thou be consumed.

18 And Lot said to them: Not so, I pray, my Lord.
19 Behold now, thy servant found favor in thy sight, and thou hast magnified thy kindness, which thou didst show me, in saving my life; and as for me, I can not escape to
20 the mountain, lest the evil overtake me, and I die. Behold now, this city is near to flee thither, and it is a little one. Let me, I pray, escape thither, (is it not a little one?) and my soul shall live.

21 And he said to him: Behold, I have accepted thee in this thing also, that I will not overthrow the city of which
22 thou hast spoken. Haste, escape thither; for I can do

V. 15. *Who are at hand;* in distinction from his married daughters, who were residing with their husbands, and chose to remain with them.

V. 16. *He lingered;* unwilling to leave so many whom he loved, and who could not be persuaded to go.

V. 17. *To the mountain;* in the mountain range of Moab. See the remark on v. 30.

V. 19. The relations of time are accurately distinguished in this verse, and should not be overlooked by the reader. *Thy servant found favor* (namely, at the first, in being selected as an object of the divine compassion) *and thou hast magnified thy kindness* (in this present wonderful deliverance), *which thou didst show* (at the first, in purposing to save me). *In saving my life* is connected in sense with *hast magnified thy kindness.*

The evil; the threatened evil, which was about to fall upon the city. Since it would extend over "all the plain" (as intimated in v. 17) Lot feared it might overtake him before he could reach the mountain. He therefore pleads for a nearer refuge.

GENESIS. CHAP. XIX.

nothing until thou come thither. Therefore the name of the city was called Zoar. ²³ The sun came forth upon the earth as Lot entered into ²⁴ Zoar. And Jehovah rained upon Sodom and upon Gomor- ²⁵ rah brimstone and fire from Jehovah out of heaven. And he overthrew those cities, and all the plain, and all the inhabitants of the cities, and that which grew from the ground.

²⁶ And his wife looked back from after him, and she became a pillar of salt.

²⁷ And Abraham got up early in the morning to the place ²⁸ where he stood before Jehovah. And he looked out toward Sodom and Gomorrah, and toward all the land of the plain, and saw, and behold, the smoke of the land went up as the smoke of a furnace.

V. 22. *Zoar;* meaning little.
VV. 23–25. The sacred writer records in these few lines, with characteristic brevity, a catastrophe that has made its mark indelibly on the face of the earth and on human history.
The record has a fearful significance; showing with what ease He who controls the elements "turned to ashes the cities of Sodom and Gomorrah," and "made them an example of those who should afterward live ungodly." If we had always access, as we have here, to his secret counsels, we should read in all such occurrences a like purpose and a similar lesson.

V. 26. *Looked back.* This is evidently a mild form of expression, implying more than is directly said.* Instead of following close upon her husband's steps, she turned her face toward the home she unwillingly left, and while he barely escaped the storm, she was overtaken by it and perished.
Became a pillar of salt. It is not said that she was changed into that substance; but, incrusted with it, she became "a pillar of salt." See the remarks below.

VV. 27, 28. *To the place where he stood;* a distance of about an hour and a half from his abode in Hebron. See the remark on ch. 18 : 22. From this eminence the modern traveler has a distant view of the region of the Dead Sea; and Abraham, standing there, could distinctly see the smoke of the land, as it went up.

The valley of the Jordan and Dead Sea is a deep chasm, or fissure, in the rocky crust of the earth,† extending in length more than a hundred and fifty miles, from the slopes of Mount Hermon to the plain south of the Dead Sea, with a breadth of from five to twelve miles. The depth of this wonderful chasm has been ascertained, within a few years, by scientific measurement. At the surface of the Sea of Galilee it is found to be six hundred and fifty-three feet below the level of the Mediterranean Sea; and at the surface of the Dead Sea it is thirteen hundred and sixteen feet below that level. The greatest depth of the Dead Sea is thirteen hundred and eight feet. At its lowest point, therefore, this chasm is more than twenty-six hundred feet below the ocean level.‡ It is the most remarkable of the natural features of Palestine; and scientific

---

* As is implied also in the Savior's use of her example (Luke 17 : 32), as a warning not to "turn back."
† It is a part of the deep and broad fissure by which Syria is cleft from north to south, extending from Antioch to the eastern branch of the Red Sea.
‡ "The traveler who stands on the shore of the Dead Sea has reached a point nearly as far below the surface of the ocean as the miners in the lowest levels of the deepest mines of Cornwall."—*Smith's Bible Dictionary,* art. Palestine (36).

CHAP. XIX.   GENESIS.

29 And it came to pass, when God destroyed the cities of the plain, that God remembered Abraham, and he sent

observers describe it as the most extraordinary depression known to exist on the surface of the earth.

This chasm extends onward, though not at the same depth, to the northeastern fork of the Red Sea, the Gulf of Akaba. It is crossed a few miles south of the Dead Sea by a line of cliffs, composed of chalky earth, varying in height from fifty to a hundred and fifty feet. Through this barrier breaks the great water-course, in which the waters of this chasm flow northward to the Dead Sea from a line about sixty miles to the south of it. Beyond that the water flows southward to the Red Sea. The elevation at this point has not been ascertained, but it must be considerably above the lowest level of the Jordan; and as the Red Sea has nearly the same level as the Mediterranean, the Jordan could never have flowed onward into the former, with the present configuration of the country.

This vast chasm, moreover, is evidently of the same age to which the present general configuration of the earth's surface belongs. This clearly appears in the condition of the strata upheaved and broken by the forces that produced the chasm,* and in all the geological features of the country. It is the unanimous conclusion of the most eminent naturalists, that within the whole historic period of the earth, since its occupation by man, the Jordan has flowed into what is now the Dead Sea, at nearly its present level, though probably with more limited extent of surface.†

But at the period to which this chapter refers, the sea, and the face of the country in its vicinity, were greatly changed by some convulsion of nature.‡ There are evidences of volcanic action; and among them, besides small fragments of sulphur, nitre, and pumice-stone, occasionally found, are immense quantities of fossil salt, either in large masses at single localities,§ or spread over the surface of the plains.

The Dead Sea is forty-six miles in length, and is of very uniform width, its greatest breadth being a little more than ten miles. At about one-fourth of the distance from its southern extremity, it is nearly crossed by a low peninsula from the eastern side, dividing the northern from the southern portion; and while the former is more than thirteen hundred feet deep, at its greatest depression, the latter has a depth of only about thirteen feet of water. The northern portion is in the form of a deep basin, descending rapidly on all sides to a great depth, while the southern portion is an extensive flat covered with shallow water. This flat plain continues onward from the southern margin of the sea, with a gradual and very slight change of elevation; so slight that when the sea is swollen a few feet by the winter rains, the water overflows it to a distance of two or three miles.‖ It is probable that the sea once occupied only the basin which forms its northern part, and that its waters have by some cause been made to overflow the low plain at its southern extremity.

There is evidence of the existence of bitumen beneath this southern portion of the sea. When its bed is violently disturbed and broken up, as by the earthquake in 1834, and by another in 1837, considerable quantities of bitumen are brought to the surface, and even in large masses,

---

* "Caused by the forcible rending and falling in of the aqueous strata, resulting from the eruption and elevation of the basalt which bases it almost from its commencement to the Dead Sea."—*Newbold, Journal of the Royal Asiatic Society*, vol. xvi., art. ii., p. 23.

† "The changes which occurred when the limestone strata of Syria were split by that vast fissure which forms the Jordan Valley and the basin of the Salt Lake, must not only have taken place at a time long anterior to the period of Abraham, but must have been of such a nature and on such a scale as to destroy all animal life far and near."—*Smith's Bible Dictionary*, art. Sodom, vol. iii., p. 1341.

‡ There need be no apprehension that the reality of the miracle, in the destruction of these cities, will be affected by ascribing it to the agency of the elements of nature, which are all under the control and at the bidding of their Maker. The miracle consists, not in the material agency employed, but in the evidence of a divine power present and directing it; and this evidence is furnished in the whole account of this transaction, in chs. 18, 19.

§ Near the southern extremity of the sea is a huge pile, from a hundred to a hundred and fifty feet high, and five geographical miles in length, the whole body of which is "a solid mass of rock-salt."—*Robinson's Biblical Researches*, vol. ii., p. 482.

‖ *Robinson's Biblical Researches*, vol. ii., p. 672.

Lot out of the midst of the overthrow, when he overthrew the cities in which Lot dwelt.

30 And Lot went up out of Zoar, and dwelt in the mountain, and his two daughters with him; for he feared to dwell in Zoar. And he dwelt in a cave, he and his two daughters.

---

but always in this southern portion of the sea.* This accords with the statement in ch. 14 : 3, that the "vale of Siddim" (said in v. 10 to be "full of bitumen-pits") is the "Salt Sea;" the sea, in its present extent, covering what was once the vale of Siddim.†

From the earliest times to which the tradition can be traced, when the localities of this region were better known than at present, and names and places now obliterated by time were familiar, the region south of the Dead Sea has been spoken of as the site of the doomed cities. With this agree the names of places that can still be traced,‡ and the present features of the country, combining natural sources of fertility§ (compare ch. 13 : 10) with a desolation, such as the sacred writers describe in speaking of the site of those cities (Deut. 29 : 23; Zeph. 2 : 9).

Vestiges of these cities are spoken of, as then existing, by writers who lived near the commencement of the Christian era. A recent traveler (De Saulcy) thinks he has discovered traces of them. But his views have not been confirmed by the observations of others.

V. 30. *Zoar* was on the border of Moab (as attested by Jerome), on the east side of the Dead Sea, at the base of the mountains near its southern extremity.∥

Feared to dwell in Zoar; lest a fate similar to that of Sodom might overtake it, which he may have had reason to apprehend from the similar character of its inhabitants.

Dwelt in a cave; in the limestone formation of which the mountains of Moab near the Dead Sea chiefly consist.

---

* "After the earthquake of 1834, a considerable quantity was found floating in small pieces, which were driven ashore and gathered. After the great earthquake of January 1, 1837, in which Safed was destroyed, a large mass of asphaltum was found floating in the water,—one said like a house, another like an island,—to which the Arabs swam off, and cut it up with axes, and gathered enough to sell for two or three thousand Spanish dollars. In both cases, the asphaltum was found in the southern part of the sea."—*Robinson's Biblical Researches,* vol. ii., p. 672.

† The author of the article "Siddim," in *Smith's Bible Dictionary,* can escape this conclusion only by assuming the statement in ch. 14 : 3, "that is the Salt Sea," to be a misapprehension. But setting aside the inspiration of the writer, and regarding him only as a human witness to an event so near his own age, we can hardly question that he was better informed on this point than we are, who at such a distance of time can only infer an opinion from data in many respects imperfect.

Dean Stanley suggests (*Sinai and Palestine,* p. 289, foot-note) that "this phrase may merely mean, that the region in question bore both names;" and he compares "En-Mishpat which is Kadesh," etc. But the cases are quite different. There is here a change of character as well as name; what was a *vale* became a *sea*. With regard to what he there justly remarks on the meaning of *emek* (translated *vale*) it is to be observed, that the term is properly applied to this region, as terminating the "long and broad valley" of the (modern) 'Arabah, this part of it bearing the specific name *Emek Siddim*.

‡ "The cities which were destroyed must have been situated on the south of the lake as it then existed; for Lot fled to Zoar which was near to Sodom; and Zoar, as we have seen, lay almost at the southern end of the present sea."—*Robinson's Biblical Researches,* vol. ii., p. 602.

§ "Even to the present day, more living streams flow into the ghor (valley) at the south end of the sea, from wadys [ravines] of the eastern mountains, than are to be found so near together in all Palestine; and the tract, although now mostly desert, is still better watered, through these streams and by the many fountains, than any other district throughout the whole country." —*Robinson* (as above).

∥ *Robinson's Biblical Researches,* vol. ii., p. 649, last paragraph.

³¹ And the firstborn said to the younger: Our father is old, and there is no man in the earth to come in to us ³² after the manner of all the earth. Come, let us make our father drink wine, and we will lie with him, that we may preserve a seed from our father. ³³ And they made their father drink wine that night. And the firstborn went in, and lay with her father; and he knew not when she lay down, and when she arose. ³⁴ And it came to pass on the morrow, that the firstborn said to the younger: Behold, I lay yesternight with my father. Let us make him drink wine this night also; and do thou go in and lie with him, that we may preserve a seed from our father. ³⁵ And they made their father drink wine that night also. And the younger arose, and lay with him; and he knew ³⁶ not when she lay down, and when she arose. And both the daughters of Lot were with child by their father. ³⁷ And the firstborn bore a son, and she called his name ³⁸ Moab. He is the father of Moab to this day. And the younger, she also bore a son, and she called his name Ben-ammi. He is the father of the children of Ammon to this day.

¹ AND Abraham removed from thence toward the south country, and dwelt between Kadesh and Shur, and he

---

VV. 31–36. The conduct of the two daughters shows the fearful influence of familiarity with vice. They had grown familiar with it in its vilest forms, till they were capable of the most revolting crime themselves.

VV. 31, 32. *Is old;* and (as is implied) will not marry again, to continue the race.

To preserve a seed from our father; so that the family may not become extinct.

VV. 37, 38. *Father of Moab to this day.* The idea is, that he is represented to this day in the Moabites, of whom he was the father.

Ben-ammi; meaning, son of my people, an indication of her solicitude for the preservation of the race.

Thus originated the Moabites and Ammonites, among whom prevailed the most horrible and revolting abominations of heathenism. The record was preserved here, apparently, for two important ends: first, to show the fearful dangers from the social influences to which Lot exposed his family by dwelling in Sodom; and secondly, to deepen and perpetuate, in the minds of God's people, their horror of the abominations practiced among these heathen nations, by associating their origin with this unnatural crime.

Ch. 20. Abraham's sojourn in the land of the Philistines.

V. 1. *The south country.* See the note on ch. 12:9, second paragraph.

Dwelt, etc. The meaning is, he dwelt in the tract of country lying between Kadesh and Shur

GENESIS. CHAP. XX.

² sojourned in Gerar. And Abraham said of Sarah his wife: She is my sister. And Abimelech, king of Gerar, sent and took Sarah.

³ And God came to Abimelech in a dream by night, and said to him: Behold, thou diest, on account of the woman whom thou hast taken; for she is married to a husband. ⁴ And Abimelech had not come near her. And he said: ⁵ Lord, wilt thou slay even a righteous nation? Did not he himself say to me: She is my sister? And she, she herself also said: He is my brother. In the integrity of my heart, and in the innocency of my hands have I done this.

⁶ And God said to him in a dream: I myself also knew that

(occupied it for pasture-grounds), and sojourned (abode for a time, as a passing stranger) in the city of Gerar.

Kadesh; see the remark on ch. 14 : 7, second paragraph. *Shur;* see the remark on ch. 16 : 7, second paragraph.

Gerar (ch. 1) : 19), an ancient city of the Philistines (see ch. 21 : 34; 26 : 1), lying to the south of Gaza, near the Mediterranean Sea.

V. 2. *She is my sister.* See the remarks on ch. 12 : 13.

Sent and took Sarah. Sarah had not borne children, and all the circumstances of her life had been favorable to the preservation of a matronly comeliness to an advanced age.* There is nothing, therefore, incredible in the narrative. Nor is it necessary to assume, with a very able biblical interpreter,† that Abimelech was not induced by her personal appearance to add her to his household, but by the desire to form an alliance by marriage with Abraham; a supposition for which the narrative furnishes no ground.

VV. 3-7. The case stands thus. Abimelech had, without knowing the extent of the injury he was doing, taken to himself the wife of another man. A great wrong was done; but, as to the full extent of it, unintentionally and in ignorance.‡ The evil is arrested by divine interposition; and he is apprised both of the extent of the wrong, and of its fatal consequences to himself if persisted in. At the same time the assurance is given him of safety, on his making restitution, and at the intercession of the injured party; thus recognizing, at once, the law of redress and of forgiveness. He must seek and obtain the forgiveness and intercession of the injured party, before he could receive forgiveness from God.

Abimelech pleads that he was innocent; namely, of the more grievous wrong actually though unintentionally done. His plea, thus far, is admitted; and he is made to suffer no more than is necessary to arrest the injury, unless he should knowingly persist in it.

It is clear, that in all this he was both justly and tenderly dealt with. For though guiltless in intention of the greater crime, yet he had wrongfully taken that which was not his own, without the owner's consent. It was one of the arbitrary acts of unrestricted power, so common where the sovereign's will is the only law, appropriating whatever is fancied, without so much as saying, "by your leave."§

God interposes effectually on behalf of his injured servant, and shows the peril of inflicting harm on his chosen ones. On this and similar cases (ch. 12 : 14-20), compare Psalm 105 : 14, 15.

V. 6. *Withheld thee;* by the illness which already threatened his life (v. 3), and is spoken of in v. 17.

---

* She was now eighty-nine years of age. Compare ch. 17 : 17, 21, with ch. 21 : 2.

† *Delitzsch, Commentar über die Genesis,* 3te Ausg., p. 403.

‡ Compare the similar case of the apostle Paul (1 Tim. 1 : 13); who was forgiven a still greater offense, and for a like reason.

§ Abimelech's self-justification only shows that he was ignorant of the relation of the injured parties, and not that he acted with the approval and consent of either.

in the integrity of thy heart thou didst this; and I withheld thee, even I myself, from sinning against me. Therefore I did not permit thee to touch her. Now therefore return the man's wife; for he is a prophet, and he will pray for thee, and thou shalt live. And if thou dost not return her, know that thou shalt surely die, thou and all that are thine.

8 And Abimelech rose early in the morning, and called all his servants, and spoke all these words in their ears; and the men feared exceedingly.

9 And Abimelech called Abraham, and said to him: What hast thou done to us? And in what have I sinned against thee, that thou bringest on me and on my kingdom a great sin? Deeds that should not be done hast thou done with me.

10 And Abimelech said to Abraham: What sawest thou, that thou didst this thing?

11 And Abraham said: Because I thought, surely there is no fear of God in this place, and they will slay me on account of my wife. And also in truth she is my sister, the daughter of my father, but not the daughter of my mother; and she became my wife. And it came to pass, when God caused me to wander from my father's house,

---

V. 7. *And all that are thine.* Such is the course of Providence, as daily observed; and such it must be from the nature of the social laws that bind households and communities in one. In these relations men often suffer for wrongs done by others; but none ever suffer to the extent of their own deserts.

V. 8. *Feared;* already alarmed by the sickness that had invaded the household of the king (v. 17), and now still more by its declared origin in the displeasure of a Deity able to inflict such a penalty.

VV. 9-11. Abimelech appears to great advantage in all this transaction, with the single exception of his arbitrarily taking possession of the person of Sarah; and even this, in those eastern despotisms, is only an assertion of the royal prerogative. How much of the magnanimity he here displays is due to the severe lesson he had received, is uncertain; but it is evident, from the whole account of him in this chapter, that he was no common personage.

What sawest thou, that thou didst this thing? The meaning is not, as some suppose, what hadst thou in view (what was thy intention) in doing this; but rather, what didst thou see, in the character of the people, in the customs of the country, that led thee to take this course? To this Abraham's words in the following verse are a direct answer.

I thought, etc. There is no ground for supposing that in this he was mistaken, and that there was not sufficient occasion for the apprehension he felt. The consideration with which he was afterward treated by Abimelech was very probably due to the divine interposition on his behalf. Compare ch. 21 : 22.

V. 12. *Daughter of my father.* See the note on ch. 12 : 13. The word *daughter*, like the word *son*, is often used with this latitude of meaning.

that I said to her: This is thy kindness which thou shalt show me; at every place whither we shall come, say of me, he is my brother.

14 And Abimelech took sheep, and oxen, and men-servants, and maid-servants, and gave them to Abraham, and 15 returned to him Sarah his wife. And Abimelech said: Behold, my land is before thee; dwell where it is good in thine eyes.

16 And to Sarah he said: Behold, I have given a thousand pieces of silver to thy brother. Behold, that is to thee a covering of the eyes for all that has happened with thee and with all. And she was redressed.

17 And Abraham prayed to God; and God healed Abimelech, and his wife, and his handmaids, and they bore chil-
18 dren. For Jehovah had fast closed up every womb of the house of Abimelech, because of Sarah, Abraham's wife.

1 AND Jehovah visited Sarah as he had said; and Jehovah
2 did to Sarah as he had spoken. And Sarah conceived, and

V. 16. *Or*, he is to thee   *Ib. Or*, for all that are with thee   *Ib. Or*, was reproved

V. 16. *A covering of the eyes.* By this is meant a peace-offering, as an expiation or atonement for an offense; namely, a gift or present to hide a fault from the view of the offended party. So Jacob says (ch. 32 : 20): "I will cover his face with the present;" that is, will hide my fault from his view,—in other words, will appease him.
To thy brother, he says, delicately concealing his knowledge of their true relation.
And with all; because all in her household shared in the dishonor of their mistress.
According to the marginal reading, the meaning is: "He (Abraham, thy husband) is to thee a covering of the eyes for all that are with thee," to protect thee from the unlawful gaze of others. *And she was reproved;* namely, for not availing herself of that protection.
This conception of the passage, though expressive of far less delicacy on the part of Abimelech, is in itself both striking and just. But there seems to be one decisive objection to it; namely, that in this view, the words with which Abimelech commences this remark to Sarah ("Behold, I have given a thousand pieces of silver to thy brother") have no significance as addressed to her.*

V. 17. *His wife.* In countries where a plurality of wives is allowed, one is often designated as *the wife,* in distinction from the others, who are also wives, but in a subordinate relation.

Ch. 21. Birth of Isaac. Hagar and Ishmael sent away. Covenant between Abraham and Abimelech.

V. 1. *Visited Sarah.* God is said *to visit* one, when he specially manifests his presence, either in kindness or severity. For instances of the former, see ch. 50 : 24, Ruth 1 : 6, 1 Sam. 2 : 21, Jer. 29 : 10, Zeph. 2 : 7; of the latter, Job 35 : 15, Psalm 59 : 5, Isaiah 26 : 14, Jer. 9 : 9, 49 : 8, Amos 3 : 14.
As he had said. See chs. 17 : 21; 18 : 10, 14.

* In the article, "Covering of the Eyes" (*Smith's Bible Dictionary*, American edition) I have given a summary of the various interpretations of the difficult phraseology in this passage.

bore to Abraham a son in his old age, at the set time of which God had spoken with him.

3 And Abraham called the name of his son that was born
4 to him, whom Sarah bore to him, Isaac. And Abraham circumcised Isaac his son, when eight days old, as God
5 commanded him. And Abraham was a hundred years old, when Isaac his son was born to him.
6 And Sarah said:
>God has prepared for me laughter;
>Every one that hears will laugh with me.

7 · And she said:
>Who tells to Abraham,
>Sarah nurses children?
>For I have borne a son to his old age.

8 And the child grew, and was weaned. And Abraham made a great feast on the day that Isaac was weaned.
9 And Sarah saw the son of Hagar the Egyptian, whom
10 she bore to Abraham, making sport. And she said to Abraham: Drive out this handmaid and her son; for the son of this handmaid shall not be heir with my son, with Isaac.
11 And the thing was very grievous in the eyes of Abraham, on account of his son.
12 And God said to Abraham: Let it not be grievous in thine eyes, on account of the lad, and on account of thy

---

V. 7. *Or*, a son of his old age.

V. 3. *Isaac.* See the remark on ch. 17 : 19.
V. 4. *As God commanded him;* in ch. 17 : 12.
V. 6. *Has prepared for me laughter.* For the allusion (to the name *Isaac*) see the note on ch. 17 : 19. *Will laugh with me;* an expression of joyful surprise and wonder, at the incredible and yet actual event.
V. 7. *Who tells to Abraham.* In the excess of her joyful triumph, she imagines that it will be a coveted honor to be the bearer of the happy message.*
In the Oriental mind, whenever feeling rises above its ordinary tone it expresses itself, as here, in the poetic form.
V. 9. *Making sport;* of the new household wonder, as is evident from the indignation it excited.
V. 12. *Hearken to her voice;* as the instrument in God's providence of accomplishing his own purpose, expressed in ch. 16 : 12.

* "Who would have said" (common English version) is not authorized by the Hebrew form of the verb, and the sentiment is tame and flat compared with the true sense.

handmaid. In all that Sarah says to thee, hearken to her
13 voice; for in Isaac shall thy seed be called. And also the
son of the handmaid, I will make him a nation; for he is
thy seed.
14 And Abraham rose early in the morning, and took
bread, and a water-skin, and gave it to Hagar, putting it
on her shoulder, and the child, and sent her away. And
she went, and wandered in the wilderness of Beer-sheba.
15 And the water was spent from the skin; and she laid
16 the child down under one of the bushes. And she went
and sat down over against him a good way off, as it were
a bowshot. For she said: Let me not see the death of
the child. And she sat over against him, and lifted up
her voice and wept.
17 And God heard the voice of the lad. And an angel of
God called to Hagar out of heaven, and said to her:
What ails thee, Hagar? Fear not; for God has heard the
18 voice of the lad, where he is. Arise, lift up the lad, and
hold him fast in thy hand; for I will make him a great
nation.
19 And God opened her eyes, and she saw a well of water.
And she went, and filled the skin with water, and gave
the lad to drink.

V. 14. Harsh as this treatment of Hagar appears, Abraham's conduct is not to be blamed. Sarah's demand was "very grievous in his sight" (v. 11); but he was divinely instructed to comply with it (v. 12).

A water-skin. In the East, water and other liquids are carried, on a journey, in the skins of animals.* The skin is stripped whole from the body of the animal (a sheep, goat, or kid), after cutting off the head and feet; so that when distended with any liquid it has the form of the animal from which it is taken.

Beer-sheba. For the origin of the name see v. 31. Abraham was now residing here, on the border of the wilderness in which she wandered; compare vv. 22 and 31.

By *wilderness* is meant a region better fitted for pasturage than for tillage, and for that reason suffered to remain in its natural wild state. Hence the English name; the Hebrew name meaning, a place to which cattle are driven for pasturage.

V. 17. *Where he is;* where he now lies, helpless and perishing.

V. 18. *Hold him fast in thy hand;* as one whose duty it is to support and encourage him, with hopeful confidence, instead of yielding to despair and leaving him to perish.

V. 19. *Opened her eyes;* caused her to perceive what she was not before aware of, namely, a fountain in the neighborhood which had been concealed from her view.

* "It was not a 'bottle,' in our sense of the word, but a *water-skin*, according to the Hebrew, which Abraham took and placed on the shoulder of Hagar, when he sent her forth into the desert."—*Dr. Hackett's Illustrations of Scripture*, 8th ed., p. 45.

²⁰ And God was with the lad; and he grew, and dwelt in ²¹ the wilderness, and became as he grew up an archer. And he dwelt in the wilderness of Paran. And his mother took for him a wife out of the land of Egypt.
²² And it came to pass at that time, that Abimelech, and Phichol the captain of his host, spoke to Abraham, saying: ²³ God is with thee in all that thou doest. Now, therefore, swear to me here by God, that thou wilt not deal falsely with me, nor with my son nor with my son's son. According to the kindness that I have done to thee shalt thou do to me, and to the land wherein thou hast sojourn- ²⁴ ed. And Abraham said: I will swear.
²⁵ And Abraham reproved Abimelech on account of the well of water, which Abimelech's servants violently took ²⁶ away. And Abimelech said: I know not who did this thing. And thou also hast not told me; and I also have not heard it, except this day.
²⁷ And Abraham took sheep and oxen, and gave them to Abimelech; and they two made a covenant.
²⁸ And Abraham set seven ewe lambs of the flock by ²⁹ themselves. And Abimelech said to Abraham: What are they, these seven ewe lambs which thou hast set by them- ³⁰ selves? And he said: The seven ewe lambs thou shalt take from my hand, that they may be for me a witness that I dug this well.
³¹ Therefore he called that place Beer-sheba; because there they both swore.

V. 21. *Wilderness of Paran;* see the remark on ch. 14 : 6, second paragraph.

VV. 22–32. Covenant between Abimelech and Abraham.

Abimelech proposes a covenant of peace and amity, to which Abraham assents. But before it is consummated, Abraham proposes as a preliminary step (vv. 25, 26, and 28–30) to settle an existing dispute, lest it should be a future source of discord. What is said in vv. 23, 24, 27, 31, 32, relates to the covenant proposed by Abimelech; vv. 25, 26, and 28–30 have reference to the preliminary step required by Abraham.

V. 27. Abraham shows his readiness to enter into this league of amity, by making the customary present from the party immediately benefited by it (compare 1 Kings 15 : 19); the unmolested use of Abimelech's territory (ch. 20 : 15) being an immediate benefit to Abraham, while the advantages to Abimelech were prospective and remote.

VV. 28–30. In making this present, Abraham sets apart a portion of it, the acceptance of which would be an acknowledgment, and a perpetual witness, of his right to the well in dispute.

V. 31. *Beer-sheba;* well of the oath, or (as it might also mean) well of seven, with reference to what is stated in vv. 28–30.

GENESIS. CHAP. XXII.

32 And they made a covenant at Beer-sheba. And Abimelech rose up, and Phichol the captain of his host, and they returned to the land of the Philistines.
33 And he planted a grove in Beer-sheba; and he called there on the name of Jehovah, the eternal God.
34 And Abraham sojourned in the land of the Philistines many days.

1 AND it came to pass after these things, that God tried Abraham. And he said to him: Abraham! And he said: 2 Here I am. And he said: Take now thy son, thine only one, whom thou lovest, Isaac, and go to the land of Moriah; and offer him there for a burnt-offering upon one of the mountains of which I will tell thee.

About twenty-five miles south of Hebron, near the southern border of Palestine, modern travelers find two very deep wells, about two hundred yards apart.* They mark the site of the ancient town of Beer-sheba, and the place so often the temporary abode of the ancient patriarchs.†

Ch. 22. Abraham is commanded to offer up Isaac. Family of Nahor.

As a trial of Abraham's faith in God, and of his obedience to the will of God, he is required to offer up his son for a burnt-offering.

It was no part of the divine purpose, as is evident from the sequel, that this bloody sacrifice should be accomplished. The requirement was made as a test of Abraham's faith and obedience; and it was made for his sake, that he might more fully know himself, and in what relation he stood to the Divine Being. On the moral purpose and uses of such a test, see the remarks on ch. 2 : 17, fifth and sixth paragraphs.

V. 1. *Tried.* So the Hebrew word is properly expressed in 2 Chron. 32 : 31, "God left him, to try him."

V. 2. *Land of Moriah;* the region or district of Moriah. According to 2 Chron. 3 : 1, the eminence on which Solomon's temple was built was called mount Moriah. The name does not occur elsewhere in the Old Testament; but it seems to have been the ancient name by which the region was known to Abraham.‡ The objections urged by some recent biblical critics§ are not decisive against the earlier view.

* "The larger one is twelve and a half feet in diameter, and forty-four and a half feet deep to the surface of the water; sixteen feet of which at the bottom is excavated in the solid rock. The other well lies fifty-five rods west-southwest, and is five feet in diameter and forty-two feet deep. The water in both is pure and sweet, and in great abundance; the finest indeed we had found since leaving Sinai. Both wells are surrounded with drinking-troughs of stone for camels and flocks; such as were doubtless used of old for the flocks which then fed on the adjacent hills. The curb-stones are deeply worn by the friction of the ropes in drawing up water by hand."—*Robinson's Biblical Researches*, vol. i., p. 300.

† "Here then is the place where the patriarchs Abraham, Isaac, and Jacob often dwelt, and here Abraham dug perhaps this very well. . . . Over these swelling hills the flocks of the patriarchs once roved by thousands, where now we found only a few camels, asses, and goats." —*Robinson*, as above, p. 302.

‡ "The name is very ancient, and the chroniclist has revived it, as he has much else belonging to the ancient treasures of the language."—*Delitzsch, Commentar über die Genesis*, 3te Ausg., p. 415.

§ *Smith's Bible Dictionary*, art. Moriah; *Stanley's Sinai and Palestine*, 2d ed., p. 251. The grounds in favor of the earlier view are very satisfactorily stated by *Knobel* (*die Genesis erklärt*, 2te Aufl., p. 191).

³ And Abraham rose early in the morning, and saddled his ass, and took his two servants with him, and Isaac his son; and he cleaved the wood for a burnt-offering; and he rose up, and went to the place of which God told him. ⁴ On the third day Abraham lifted up his eyes, and saw ⁵ the place afar off. And Abraham said to his servants: Do ye remain here with the ass; and I and the lad will go yonder, and worship, and return to you. ⁶ And Abraham took the wood for the burnt-offering, and laid it upon Isaac his son; and he took in his hand the fire and the knife; and they went both of them together. ⁷ And Isaac spoke to Abraham his father, and said: My father! And he said: Here am I, my son. And he said: Behold the fire, and the wood; but where is the lamb for ⁸ a burnt-offering? And Abraham said: God will provide himself the lamb for a burnt-offering, my son. And they went both of them together. ⁹ And they came to the place of which God told him. And Abraham built there the altar, and laid the wood in order, and bound Isaac his son, and laid him on the altar upon the wood. ¹⁰ And Abraham stretched forth his hand, and took the ¹¹ knife to slay his son. And an angel of Jehovah called to

---

V. 4. *On the third day.* The distance from Beer-sheba where Abraham dwelt (v. 19), to Jerusalem is a little over forty miles.

Saw the place afar off. To the view stated above, that mount Moriah was the place of the offering, it is objected that this eminence is not visible at a distance.* But the locality with which it is connected is distinctly visible from a high ridge on the traveled route, at a distance of about three miles.†

There seems to be no good ground, therefore, for setting aside the view of the older interpreters, that this extraordinary transaction prefigured a far more important event, which took place on the same spot. In this view it has a significance which explains and justifies it.‡

* *Stanley, Sinai and Palestine* (as above): "There is no elevation, nothing corresponding to the 'place afar off,' to which Abraham '*lifted up* his eyes.'" The words, "lifted up," should not have been italicised, as though they implied a looking upward to an elevated object. Persons are said to lift up their eyes to see objects on a level with them, as in ch. 24: 63, 64; and Lot lifted up his eyes to see, from the heights east of Bethel, the plain of the Jordan far below him· (ch. 13: 1.).

† "Here" [on the ridge of Mar Elyas] " we got our first view of the Holy City,—the mosque and other high buildings standing on mount Zion without the walls."—*Robinson's Biblical Researches*, vol. i., p. 323.

‡ The parallel is traced by Melito, one of the earliest Christian writers belonging to the second century, in an interesting fragment preserved to us from his writings in the *catena in Genesin*. —*Routh, Reliquiæ Sacræ*, I., 116, and *Migne, Patrologiæ Cursus*, V., 1215.

him out of heaven, and said: Abraham! Abraham! And
12 he said: Here am I. And he said: Stretch not forth thy
hand against the lad, nor do anything to him. For now
I know that thou fearest God, and hast not withheld thy
son, thine only one, from me.
13 And Abraham lifted up his eyes, and saw, and behold a
ram behind him, caught in the thicket by his horns. And
Abraham went and took the ram, and offered him up for
a burnt-offering, in place of his son.
14 And Abraham called the name of that place Jehovah-
jireh. As it is said at this day: In the mount of Jehovah
it will be provided.
15 And the angel of Jehovah called to Abraham a second
16 time out of heaven, and said: By myself have I sworn,
says Jehovah, that because thou hast done this thing, and
17 didst not withhold thy son, thine only one, I will greatly
bless thee, and will greatly multiply thy seed as the stars
of heaven, and as the sand which is upon the sea shore;
18 and thy seed shall possess the gate of his enemies. And
in thy seed shall all the nations of the earth be blessed;
because thou hast hearkened to my voice.
19 And Abraham returned to his servants; and they rose
up and went together to Beer-sheba; and Abraham dwelt
at Beer-sheba.
20 And it came to pass after these things, that it was told
to Abraham, saying: Behold, Milcah, she has borne chil-
21 dren to Nahor thy brother; Uz his firstborn, and Buz his
22 brother, and Kemuel the father of Aram, and Chesed, and

V. 14. *Jehovah-jireh;* meaning, Jehovah will provide (compare v. 8).
From this divine interposition, and the commemoration of it in this memorial name, arose the proverbial saying, "In the mount of Jehovah" (where he records his name, Ex. 20 : 24) "it will be provided." He will not be called upon in vain.

VV. 15-18. Abraham was sustained in this severe trial by a sublime faith in the rectitude and wisdom of Him who required the sacrifice. The test has shown him to be a true representative of that faith to all who should come after him; and this is here recognized and commemorated in the solemn repetition of the promises already made.

VV. 20-24. A brief record is here made of the family of Nahor, as being necessary to the understanding of the subsequent history. Compare ch. 11 : 29.

It was told to Abraham. On this knowledge he acted in selecting a wife for Isaac, as related in ch. 24.

She also has borne children; alluding to the birth of a son to Sarah, her sister or sister-in-law.

²³ Hazo, and Pildash, and Jidlaph, and Bethuel. And Bethuel begot Rebekah.

These eight did Milcah bear to Nahor, Abraham's broth-
²⁴ er. And his concubine, whose name was Reumah, she also bore Tebah, and Gaham, and Thahash, and Maachah.

¹ AND the life of Sarah was a hundred and twenty-seven
² years, the years of the life of Sarah. And Sarah died in Kirjath-arba; that is Hebron in the land of Canaan. And Abraham came to mourn for Sarah, and to weep for her.
³ And Abraham stood up from before his dead, and spoke
⁴ to the sons of Heth, saying: I am a stranger and a sojourner with you. Give me a possession of a burying-place with you, that I may bury my dead out of my sight.
⁵ And the sons of Heth answered Abraham, saying to

The two names *Uz* (not *Huz*, as in the common English version), and *Aram*, occur in the enumeration of Shem's immediate descendants, in ch. 10 : 22, 23. The former is the name of a son of Aram and grandson of Shem (ch. 10 : 23), and of a son of Nahor (in this passage), and of a son of Dishan and grandson of Seir (ch. 36 : 28), and of the country of Job (Job 1 : 1). It is not improbable, therefore, that this coincidence of names indicates a "fusion of various branches of the Semitic race in a certain locality."*

Buz was ancestor of the tribe to which Elihu the *Buzite* belonged (Job 32 : 2).

V. 24. *His concubine.* A concubine was a wife, though of a rank inferior to the one who properly bore the name, and was usually of servile condition. The relation was inconsistent with the original institution of marriage, and with the true and proper relation of the sexes. But as an existing civil institution, it was regulated by the Mosaic law in the interest and for the protection of the weaker party,† till a more advanced civilization under the increasing influence of divine truth should abolish it.‡

Ch. 23. Death of Sarah. Purchase of the field and cave of Machpelah for a burying-place.

V. 2. *Kirjath-arba* § (City of Arba §) was the original Canaanitish name of the place afterward called Hebron; compare Joshua 14 : 15, Judges 1 : 10. In its vicinity were the oaks of Mamre (ch. 13 : 18) where Abraham often dwelt, and where he was now dwelling, having left Beer-sheba.

Came to mourn for Sarah; namely, to the place appointed for the public ceremonial.

VV. 3, 4. *Sons of Heth.* See the note on ch. 10 : 15-20, third paragraph.

I am a stranger and a sojourner with you, explains the necessity of his present appeal to them. As a stranger, and not a citizen, he has no landed possession which he can call his own and permanently occupy. As a sojourner, and not a visitor or passing traveler, he needs a place of burial for his dead. *A possession,* etc.; a property in land, for a burying-place.

* *Smith's Bible Dictionary,* art. Uz, where further evidences of this are given. "There was an old Semitic and a younger Nahorite Aram; there was an old Aramæan and a younger Nahorite Uz. Nahorites, migrating beyond the Euphrates, blended with older primitively related races, and the younger mixed races shared the name of the older."—*Delitzsch, Commentar über die Genesis,* 3te Ausg., p. 422.

† See *Smith's Bible Dictionary,* art. Concubine, and Marriage, I., third paragraph.

‡ Compare what the Savior says, on an analogous case, in Matt. 19 : 8.

§ Not so called from the individual of that name mentioned in Joshua 14 : 15. The name of the place was of earlier origin; that of the person referred to was either derived from it, or was a mere coincidence.

6 him: Hear us, my lord. Thou art a prince of God among us. In the choice of our sepulchres bury thy dead. None of us will withhold from thee his sepulchre, that thou mayest not bury thy dead.
7 And Abraham stood up, and bowed himself to the peo-
8 ple of the land, to the sons of Heth. And he talked with them, saying: If it be your mind to bury my dead out of my sight, hear me, and intercede for me with Ephron son
9 of Zohar, that he may give me the cave of Machpelah, which is his, which is at the end of his field. For the full price shall he give it me in the midst of you, for a possession of a burying-place.
10 And Ephron was sitting in the midst of the sons of Heth. And Ephron the Hittite answered Abraham in the hearing of the sons of Heth, of all that enter in at the gate
11 of his city, saying: Nay, my lord, hear me. The field I give thee, and the cave that is therein, to thee I give it; in the sight of the sons of my people I give it thee; bury thy dead.
12 And Abraham bowed himself before the people of the
13 land. And he spoke to Ephron in the hearing of the people of the land, saying: But if thou wilt, pray hear me. I give the price of the field; take it of me, and I will bury my dead there.
14 And Ephron answered Abraham, saying to him: My

VV. 5, 6. The sons of Heth address him as a "prince of God;" one to whom God has given a princely rank and authority, by the wealth bestowed on him and the number of his servants and dependents. Compare the remarks on ch. 12 : 5, third paragraph.

VV. 7-9. Abraham courteously declines the proffered use of another's sepulchre for the burial of his dead.

If it be your mind to bury my dead; to furnish a place of burial, in order that it may be done, is the meaning.

Cave of Machpelah. The field and the cave were before Mamre (v. 17), and therefore contiguous to Abraham's place of abode. The hills of Palestine, being a limestone formation, abound in caves; and these were often used as places of burial.

V. 10. *Hitti'e;* the gentilic name of one who belonged to the tribe of Heth. *Of all that enter in at the gate of his city;* that is, of all the inhabitants of the town. It is called *his city* because it was his residence; not, as some suppose, because he was its chief or magistrate.

V. 13. *But if thou wilt;* meaning, either, wilt part with the field, or, as is more probable, wilt listen to my request.

VV. 14, 15. With admirable delicacy, Ephron evades and at the same time complies with Abraham's desire, that he would name the purchase-money. Instead of saying, the land is worth so much (as in the common Eng'ish version, where the delicate turn of the expression is lost), he alludes to its value as a thing too inconsiderable to be taken into account.

¹⁵ lord, hear me. Land worth four hundred shekels of silver, what is that between me and thee? So bury thy dead.
¹⁶ And Abraham hearkened to Ephron. And Abraham weighed to Ephron the silver, which he had spoken of in the hearing of the sons of Heth, four hundred shekels of silver, current with the merchant.
¹⁷ And the field of Ephron, that is in Machpelah, which is before Mamre, the field, and the cave that is therein, and all the trees that are in the field, that are in all its borders
¹⁸ around, were made sure to Abraham for a possession, in the sight of the sons of Heth, among all that enter in at the gate of his city.
¹⁹ And after this, Abraham buried Sarah his wife in the field of Machpelah before Mamre. That is Hebron, in the
²⁰ land of Canaan. And the field, and the cave that is therein, were made sure to Abraham for a possession of a burying-place, from the sons of Heth.

¹ AND Abraham was old, far gone in years. And Jehovah blessed Abraham in all things.
² And Abraham said to his servant, the elder of his house, who ruled over all that he had: Put, I pray thee,
³ thy hand under my thigh; and I will make thee swear by Jehovah, the God of heaven and the God of earth, that thou wilt not take a wife for my son of the daughters of

---

VV. 16-20. *Hearkened;* acceded to his proposal, implied in his words. The whole process of the sale is minutely stated, to show that all formalities were duly observed for securing the rightful ownership and the peaceful occupation of the place.

V. 20. *From the sons of Heth.* It was owned among them, by a member of their tribe; and it passed from their possession into that of Abraham.

Ch. 24. Marriage of Isaac.

VV. 2, 3. *The elder of his house;* that is, his chief servant, the head of his household, who had the direction of all his affairs, as stated in the following clause, "who ruled over all that he had." Compare, in ch. 50 : 7, "the servants of Pharaoh, the elders of his house;" that is, the high officers of his household, who were at the head of its several departments. Men of mature age and experience were required in these offices, and hence they are called *elders;* and this became a title of official rank and dignity.

It is commonly supposed, though without any special ground for the opinion, that this confidential servant was the Eliezer spoken of in ch. 15 : 2.

Put thy hand under my thigh; as a pledge of fidelity to the required promise. Compare ch. 47 : 29, 30. Among many ancient nations a peculiar sacredness was attached to this act, and to a promise confirmed by it. To this formal pledge was sometimes added an oath, as in this case (v. 3) and in the one recorded in ch. 47 : 29-31.

⁴ the Canaanites, in the midst of whom I dwell. But thou shalt go to my land, and to my kindred, and take a wife for my son, for Isaac.

⁵ And the servant said to him: Perhaps the woman will not be willing to follow me to this land. Must I needs bring thy son again to the land from whence thou camest?

⁶ And Abraham said to him: Beware that thou bring not ⁷ my son thither again. Jehovah, the God of heaven, who took me from my father's house, and from the land of my kindred, and who spoke to me, and who swore to me, saying: To thy seed will I give this land; he will send his angel before thee, and thou shalt take a wife for my ⁸ son from thence. And if the woman shall not be willing to follow thee, then thou shalt be clear from this my oath; only, thou shalt not bring my son thither again.

⁹ And the servant put his hand under the thigh of Abraham his master, and swore to him concerning this matter.

¹⁰ And the servant took ten camels of the camels of his master, and went; for all the goods of his master were in his hand; and he arose, and went to Mesopotamia, to the city of Nahor.

¹¹ And he made the camels kneel down outside of the city by the well of water, at the time of evening, the time ¹² when the women who draw water go forth. And he said: Jehovah, God of my master Abraham, I pray thee, prosper me this day, and show kindness to my master Abra-¹³ ham. Behold, I stand by the fountain of water; and the daughters of the men of the city come out to draw water.

¹⁴ And it shall be that the damsel to whom I shall say: In-

V. 4. *To my land and to my kindred.* See the note on ch. 12 : 1–3, third paragraph.
V. 10. *City of Nahor.* This was Haran, as appears from v. 29 compared with ch. 27 : 43. For *Haran*, see the note on ch. 11 : 31, fourth paragraph.
V. 11. *He made his camels kneel down;* to rest themselves, as they were to proceed no further.
When the women who draw water go forth. This service was always performed by women, as is still the case in the East. It was done at evening, after the heat of the day was past; and enough was drawn for use till the evening of the following day. The expression in v. 13, "the daughters of the men of the city come out to draw water," shows that they were not servants, or persons of inferior rank.
V. 14. *Incline thy pitcher—that I may drink.* He would not trouble her to let down the

cline thy pitcher, I pray, that I may drink; and she shall say: Drink, and I will give thy camels drink also; her thou hast appointed for thy servant, for Isaac; and by this I shall know that thou showest kindness to my master.

15 And it came to pass before he had done speaking, that, behold, Rebekah came out, who was born to Bethuel, son of Milcah, the wife of Nahor Abraham's brother, and her 16 pitcher was upon her shoulder. And the damsel was of very fair countenance, a virgin, and a man had not known her. And she went down to the fountain, and filled her pitcher, and came up.

17 And the servant ran to meet her, and said: Let me swallow, I pray, a little water from thy pitcher.

18 And she said: Drink, my lord. And she hasted and let down her pitcher upon her hand, and gave him drink. 19 And when she had done giving him drink, she said: I will draw for thy camels also, until they have done drink-20 ing. And she hasted, and emptied her pitcher into the watering-trough, and ran again to the well to draw; and she drew for all his camels.

21 And the man was attentively observing her, and holding his peace, to know whether Jehovah had prospered his way or not.

22 And it came to pass, when the camels had done drinking, that the man took a ring of gold, half a shekel was its

---

V. 21. *Or*, was wondering at her

vessel upon her hand, but would drink from it as she leaned it forward upon her shoulder. Compare the remark on v. 18.

V. 15. *Rebekah.* Compare ch. 22 : 23.

V. 16. *Went down to the fountain.* This is also called a *well*, in v. 11. The earth around a natural fountain was sometimes excavated to a considerable depth, and walled up, in order that a sufficient supply of water might be collected. When the well was not deep, steps were formed in the wall, leading down to the water.

V. 17. Mark the modesty of the request—just a swallow of water from her pitcher!

V. 18. Mark also the courteous compliance with his request. She does not, as he had modestly proposed to himself (v. 14), lean the vessel forward that he might drink from it on her shoulder. With the courtesy then thought to be due to a stranger, she let down the pitcher from her shoulder, and presented it to him on her hand.

Drink, my lord; a style of address suited to the character in which he appeared. The train of camels with which he traveled (v. 10), and of servants necessarily attending on them, indicated wealth and the distinction it confers.

V. 20. *Watering-trough.* See the remarks on ch. 21 : 31, second paragraph, foot-note (*).

weight, and two bracelets for her hands, ten shekels of
23 gold was their weight. And he said: Whose daughter art
thou? Tell me, I pray. Is there in thy father's house a
place for us to pass the night?
24 And she said to him: I am the daughter of Bethuel the
son of Milcah, whom she bore to Nahor.
25 And she said to him: We have both straw and provender abundant, and a place to pass the night.
26 And the man bowed his head, and worshiped Jehovah.
27 And he said: Blessed be Jehovah, God of my master
Abraham, who has not let his kindness and his truth
depart from my master. I was in the way; Jehovah led
me to the house of my master's brethren.
28 And the damsel ran, and told these things at the house
of her mother.
29 And Rebekah had a brother, and his name was Laban.
30 And Laban ran to the man without, to the fountain. And
it came to pass, when he saw the ring, and the bracelets
on his sister's hands, and when he heard the words of
Rebekah his sister, saying, thus did the man speak to me,
that he came to the man; and behold, he was standing by
31 the camels at the fountain. And he said: Come in, thou
blessed of Jehovah. Wherefore dost thou stand without?
For I have prepared the house, and a place for the camels.
32 And the man came into the house. And he ungirded
the camels, and gave straw and provender for the camels,
and water to wash his feet, and the feet of the men that
33 were with him. And food was set before him. But he
said: I will not eat, until I have told my message. And
he said: Speak.
34 35 And he said: I am Abraham's servant. And Jehovah

V. 28. *Or*, to her mother's household.

V. 27. *I was in the way*, a stranger and wayfarer, and Jehovah led me to the place I was seeking.
V. 29. *Ran to the man without.* This is said in anticipation of the statement in the next verse, where we learn the reason for his haste to welcome the stranger. Laban here shows himself true to his character, as more fully exhibited in chs. 29–31.
V. 32. *And he,* meaning Laban. *Water to wash his feet.* Compare the note on ch. 18 : 4.

has blessed my master exceedingly, and he is become great; and he has given him flocks and herds, and silver and gold, and men-servants and maid-servants, and camels,
36 and asses. And Sarah, my master's wife, bore a son to my master after she became old; and he has given him all that he has.
37 And my master made me swear, saying: Thou shalt not take a wife for my son of the daughters of the Canaanites,
38 in whose land I dwell. But thou shalt go to my father's house, and to my family, and take a wife for my son.
39 And I said to my master: Perhaps the woman will not
40 follow me. And he said to me: Jehovah, before whom I walk, will send his angel with thee, and will prosper thy way; and thou shalt take a wife for my son of my family,
41 and of my father's house. Then shalt thou be clear from my oath, when thou comest to my family; and if they will not give her to thee, thou shalt be clear from my oath.
42 And I came this day to the fountain; and I said: Jehovah, God of my master Abraham, if now thou wouldst
43 prosper my way, on which I go! Behold, I stand by the fountain of water; and it shall be, that the virgin who comes forth to draw water, and I say to her: Let me, I
44 pray, drink a little water from thy pitcher; and she shall say to me: Drink thou, and I will draw for thy camels also; she is the woman whom Jehovah has appointed for my master's son.
45 Before I had done speaking in my heart, behold, Rebekah came forth, and her pitcher was on her shoulder; and she went down to the fountain, and drew water. And
46 I said to her: Let me drink, I pray. And she hasted, and let down her pitcher from upon her, and said: Drink, and I will give thy camels drink also. And I drank, and she gave the camels drink also.
47 And I asked her, and said: Whose daughter art thou? And she said: The daughter of Bethuel, son of Nahor,

---

V. 42–48. A beautiful trait in this charming picture of Oriental life and manners is the variety of form and expression in relating the same occurrences; first as given by the narrator himself

whom Milcah bore to him. And I put the ring upon her face, and the bracelets upon her hands.

48 And I bowed my head, and worshiped Jehovah; and I blessed Jehovah, God of my master Abraham, who led me in the way of truth, to take the daughter of my master's brother for his son.

49 And now, if ye will deal kindly and truly with my master, tell me; and if not, tell me; that I may turn to the right hand, or to the left.

50 And Laban and Bethuel answered and said: The thing proceeds from Jehovah; we can not speak to thee evil or 51 good. Behold, Rebekah is before thee; take her, and go, and let her be the wife of thy master's son, as Jehovah has spoken.

52 And it came to pass, when Abraham's servant heard their words, that he bowed down to Jehovah, to the earth.

53 And the servant brought out vessels of silver, and vessels of gold, and garments, and gave them to Rebekah. And he gave precious things to her brother and to her mother.

54 And they ate and drank, he and the men that were with him, and passed the night. And they rose up in the morning, and he said: Send me away to my master.

55 And her brother and her mother said: Let the damsel abide with us some days, perhaps ten; after that she 56 shall go. And he said to them: Delay me not, since Jehovah has prospered my way. Send me away, that I may go to my master.

57 And they said: We will call the damsel, and let us

---

to the reader, and then as repeated by him in the mouth of the servant to his little company of interested listeners. The artless variations of the same story amuse and delight without wearying the reader.

V. 47. *I put the ring upon her face.* The Hebrew word translated *ring* meant both *ear-ring* and *nose-ring*. It has the former meaning in ch. 35 : 4, "and the rings which were in their ears." That the latter is meant here may be inferred from the expression, "upon her face." The use of such an ornament is a matter of taste, and seemed to them as suitable as the wearing of ear-rings does to us.

V. 50. *Evil or good;* that is, favorable to your object or unfavorable. In other words, we have nothing to say; it proceeds from Jehovah, and is not a matter for us to decide. He has already determined it.

V. 56. *Since Jehovah has prospered my way;* since all is accomplished for which I came.]

⁵⁸ inquire at her mouth. And they called Rebekah, and said to her: Wilt thou go with this man? And she said: I will go.

⁵⁹ And they sent away Rebekah their sister, and her nurse, ⁶⁰ and the servant of Abraham, and his men. And they blessed Rebekah, and said to her: Thou art our sister; do thou become thousands of ten thousands, and let thy seed possess the gate of those who hate thee.

⁶¹ And Rebekah arose, and her maidens, and they rode upon the camels, and followed the man. And the servant took Rebekah, and went.

⁶² And Isaac had come from a journey to Beer-lehai-roi; ⁶³ and he was dwelling in the south country. And Isaac went out to meditate in the field, at the coming on of evening. And he lifted up his eyes, and saw, and behold camels coming.

⁶⁴ And Rebekah lifted up her eyes, and saw Isaac; and ⁶⁵ she alighted from the camel. And she said to the servant: Who is this man, that is walking in the field to meet us? And the servant said: It is my master. And she took the vail and covered herself.

⁶⁶ And the servant related to Isaac all the things that he had done.

⁶⁷ And Isaac brought her into the tent of Sarah his mother.

V. 63. *Or, to mourn*

V. 60. *Thou art our sister;* and therefore shalt go with our prayers and blessings,—as expressed in the words that follow.

VV. 62-67. The meeting of Isaac with Rebekah, and their marriage.

V. 62. *Beer-lehai-roi;* see ch. 16: 14. He was dwelling in *the south country* (see the remarks on ch. 12: 9, second paragraph), and therefore not far from the well of that name.

V. 63. *To meditate in the field;* an indication of the contemplative character of his mind, averse to business affairs, and unskilled in the practical concerns of life.

In the margin the word is rendered, *to mourn*. The death of his mother, about three years before, was yet fresh in his remembrance, and a touching allusion is made to it again in the last clause of v. 67.

VV. 64, 65. Observing the approach of one whose appearance indicated wealth and rank, she alighted from the camel as an expression of respect.

On learning from the servant who it was, she took the vail* and covered herself. This was customary, and was the natural dictate of true delicacy. The first recognition of the bride he had never seen must not be before witnesses.

V. 67. She was conducted to the tent of Sarah, where she would be surrounded by the at-

---

* That part of the complete female dress is meant, and hence the use of the definite article; not, "a vail," as though it was no necessary part of the full female equipment.

And he took Rebekah, and she became his wife; and he loved her. And Isaac consoled himself after the death of his mother.

1 AND again Abraham took a wife, and her name was
2 Keturah. And she bore to him Zimran, and Jokshan, and
3 Medan, and Midian, and Ishbak, and Shuah. And Jokshan begot Sheba, and Dedan. And the sons of Dedan were
4 Asshurim, and Letushim, and Leummim. And the sons of Midian; Ephah, and Epher, and Hanoch, and Abidah, and Eldaah. All these were sons of Keturah.
5 6 And Abraham gave all that he had to Isaac. And to

tendants of the former mistress of the household, and by her own maidens (v. 61) who accompanied her from the paternal home.

The betrothal had taken place at her own father's house (vv. 50, 51).* The marriage consisted in the ceremony of her removal to the home of her husband, and his recognition of her as his wife and the mistress of his household.

Ch. 25 : 1-10. Marriage of Abraham with Keturah. His death and burial.

V. 1. *And again Abraham took a wife.* Abraham lived seventy-five years after the birth of Isaac, or about thirty-eight years after Sarah's decease.

From the order of the narrative we should naturally infer that the marriage with Keturah took place after the decease of Sarah. But in 1 Chron. 1 : 32 she is called "Abraham's concubine;"† and in the sixth verse of this chapter, "the concubines which Abraham had" are spoken of in the plural, as if he had more than one.‡ No more can fairly be inferred from this, however, than that Keturah, though a wife, was not by birth of the same rank and dignity as the wife by the first marriage.

VV. 2–4. The descendants of Keturah seem to have blended, to some extent, with those of Ishmael, and with them formed the roving tribes of Arabia and the adjacent territory.

Zimran; found, perhaps, in the Zamereni, in the interior of Arabia.

Sheba and Dedan; pastoral tribes on the borders of Idumea, perhaps connected with the commercial tribes of the same name, descendants of Raamah son, of Cush,§ on the Persian Gulf (ch. 10 : 7, note, second paragraph).

Asshurim, Letushim, and Leummim; names of Dedan's sons, with the Hebrew plural form (*im*) denoting tribes descended from them. Compare ch. 10, note, second paragraph.

Midian. The Midianites occupied the wilderness on the north of the peninsula of Arabia, and extended northward along the eastern border of Palestine, and to the south into the interior of the peninsula of Sinai, and along the eastern coast of the Elanitic Gulf.

VV. 5, 6. *Gave all that he had to Isaac;* in accordance with the divine purpose, as declared in chs. 15 : 4, 17 : 8, 21 : 12.

In compliance with this declared purpose, Abraham took the precaution, "while he yet lived," to send away his other sons, provided with the means of independent subsistence.

---

* Bethuel acts a subordinate part; for it lies in the nature of polygamy, that, in the divided interests of the father, a brother should take charge of the special rights of his sister by the same mother, and be her representative.—*Tuch, Kommentar über die Genesis,* p. 407.

† See the note on ch. 22 : 24.

‡ Hence some have inferred that this marriage took place during the lifetime of Sarah; but apparently on insufficient grounds. Keil, for example, in addition to the above circumstances, suggests that the youngest of Keturah's sons would otherwise have been too immature to be dismissed from the parental care and oversight, being only from twenty-five to thirty years of age.—*Biblischer Commentar über die Bücher Mose's,* 2te Aufl., p. 193.

§ *Smith's Bible Dictionary,* art. Sheba, II., and Dedan.

the sons of the concubines, which Abraham had, Abraham gave gifts, and sent them away from Isaac his son, while he yet lived, eastward, to the land of the East.

7 And these are the days of the years of Abraham's life 8 which he lived, a hundred and seventy-five years. And Abraham expired, and died in a good old age, old and 9 full. And he was gathered to his people. And Isaac and Ishmael, his sons, buried him in the cave of Machpelah, in the field of Ephron son of Zohar the Hittite, 10 which is before Mamre; the field which Abraham purchased from the sons of Heth. There was Abraham buried, and Sarah his wife.

11 And it came to pass after the death of Abraham, that God blessed Isaac his son. And Isaac dwelt by Beer-lehai-roi.

12 And these are the generations of Ishmael, son of Abraham whom Hagar the Egyptian, Sarah's maid-servant, bore 13 to Abraham. And these are the names of the sons of Ishmael, by their names, according to their generations: the

---

Concubines. See the remarks on v. 1. *Land of the East;* a comprehensive term for regions lying eastward from Palestine, including Mesopotamia and Babylonia, but denoting especially the district of Arabia and the wilderness on the north of it.

V. 8. *Full;* in the sense of sated, satisfied (as when one has had enough), as in Prov. 30 : 9, "Lest I be full, and deny thee." Compare the expression, "full of days," in ch. 35 : 29.

Was gathered to his people. He was not buried among them, nor in their vicinity, but in a foreign land and far remote from where their remains reposed. If he had been buried beside and among them, the phrase might be understood to mean merely, that his remains were deposited with theirs. But as the case stands, the phrase implies the belief, with which the Hebrew Scriptures are pervaded,* of the continued, separate existence of the soul, after the death of the body, in another state of being where all are gathered who have passed from this life. See an instructive example of this use of the phrase in ch. 49 : 33.

This conclusion can be evaded only by assuming that the phrase originated in the practice of burying the deceased of the same family or race in a common burying-place,† and by use became simply a technical expression for burial. But its use here in that sense, with the emphatic addition "to his people," is too glaringly incongruous to be admitted. Compare ch. 15 : 15, "thou shalt go to thy fathers in peace."

V. 11. *Beer-lehai-roi.* See the note on ch. 24 : 62, and the references there given.

VV. 12-18. A brief notice of the sons of Ishmael, and of his death.

---

* Compare the note on ch. 5 : 24; and see, in the writer's remarks on Job 26 : 5 (Part First, philological notes, and Part Second, explanatory notes) the evidence of this belief impressed on the language itself in the term used for the disembodied spirit, that part of man which survives death. This evidence is unhappily effaced from the scriptures of the Old Testament in the common English version, where this term is improperly rendered *dead*, and is thus confounded with another Hebrew word which is properly so rendered. See also the article DEAD, added to the American edition of *Smith's Bible Dictionary.*

† See the writer's remarks on Job (Part Second, explanatory notes), ch. 27 : 19.

firstborn of Ishmael, Nebaioth; and Kedar, and Abdeel,
14 15 and Mibsam, and Mishma, and Dumah, and Massa, Hadad
16 and Temah, Jetur, Naphish, and Kedemah. These are the sons of Ishmael, and these are their names, by their villages, and by their encampments; twelve princes according to their peoples.
17 And these are the years of the life of Ishmael, a hundred and thirty-seven years. And he expired, and died,
18 and was gathered to his people. And they dwelt from Havilah unto Shur, that is before Egypt, as thou goest to Assyria. Before the face of all his brethren he abode.
19 And these are the generations of Isaac, son of Abraham.
20 Abraham begot Isaac. And Isaac was forty years old when he took Rebekah, daughter of Bethuel the Aramite of Padan-aram, sister of Laban the Aramite, for his wife.
21 And Isaac entreated Jehovah on account of his wife, for

Nebaioth; ancestor of the Nabathæans, a very ancient and powerful people, inhabiting Arabia Petræa.
Kedar; one of the most enterprising and renowned of the Ishmaelite races, on the northwestern part of the peninsula of Arabia and near the borders of Palestine. See allusions to "the glory of Kedar," "archers, the mighty men of the sons of Kedar" (Isaiah 21 : 16, 17), to "the princes of Kedar" (Ezek. 27 : 21), to "the tents of Kedar" (Cant. 1 : 5).
Dumah (Isaiah 21 : 11), ancestor of an Ishmaelite tribe whose habitation and name are identified in the town called *Dooma-el-Jendel*, in the northwestern part of the peninsula of Arabia.
Hadad (not *Hadar*, as in the common English version), as in 1 Chron. 1 : 30.
Tema (Job 6 : 19, Isaiah 21 : 14, Jer. 25 : 23), founder of a tribe called after him, whose name is recognized in *Teyma*, a town near the borders of Syria and on the pilgrim-caravan route to Damascus. Hadad and Tema are connected here, probably as dwelling together and apart from the other tribes.
Jetur gave name to the district called (in its Greek form) *Iturœa*, in northern Palestine. *Jetur* and *Naphish** are mentioned among the Hagarites (1 Chron. 5 : 19) who were subdued by the sons of Reuben, Gad, and Manasseh (vv. 18-22).
Kedemah; compare the *Kadmonites* (differing only in the gentilic termination) in ch. 15 : 19.
V. 16. *Their villages,* their permanent settlements; *their encampments,* their temporary and movable abodes as they migrated from place to place.
Twelve princes according to their peoples; each people having its own prince, as an independent nationality by itself.
V. 18. *From Havilah* (ch. 10 : 29) *to Shur* on the eastern border of Egypt. *As thou goest to Assyria;* on the way to that land.
Before the face of all his brethren. Compare the remark on ch. 16 : 12.
Ch. 25 : 19-27 : 46. Second part of the fourth division. *Family history of Isaac.*
After the brief notice of Ishmael and his sons, in vv. 12-18, the general subject of this fourth division is resumed in the account of Isaac.
V. 20. *Padan-aram;* meaning, Plain of Aram, and including Mesopotamia and the wilderness west of the Euphrates, in distinction from the mountainous region parallel with the coast of the Mediterranean Sea.
V. 21. *Was barren.* She continued so about twenty years after her marriage; compare v. 20 with the last clause of v. 26.

* Inaccurately written *Nephish* in the common English version 1 Chron. 5 : 19.

she was barren. And Jehovah was moved by his entreaty, and Rebekah his wife conceived.

²² And the children struggled together within her. And she said: If so, wherefore am I thus? And she went to ²³ inquire of Jehovah. And Jehovah said to her: Two nations are in thy womb, and two peoples from thy bowels will be separated; and one people will be stronger than the other people; and the elder will serve the younger.

²⁴ And her days to be delivered were completed; and ²⁵ behold, there were twins in her womb. And the first came out red, all over like a hairy mantle; and they called ²⁶ his name Esau. And after that came out his brother, and his hand had hold of Esau's heel; and his name was called Jacob. And Isaac was sixty years old when they were born.

²⁷ And the lads grew up. And Esau became a man skilled in hunting, a man of the field; and Jacob was a plain ²⁸ man, dwelling in tents. And Isaac loved Esau, because he relished game; and Rebekah loved Jacob.

²⁹ And Jacob was seething pottage; and Esau came from ³⁰ the field, and he was faint. And Esau said to Jacob: Give me to eat, I pray thee, of the red, that red, for I am

---

V. 22. *Or,* If so, wherefore am I?

V. 22. *If so;* if such be the case. In this her first experience of this phenomenon of her condition, it seems to her an omen of evil.

Why am I thus? Meaning, either, thus affected, an expression of surprise and wonder; or, why am I in this condition, namely, why should I have desired it?

Wherefore am I (marginal rendering), that is, wherefore do I yet live, accords with her sanguine and impulsive temperament, as exhibited in ch. 27 : 46. But the rendering of the text is probably the true one.

V. 23. *Two peoples* (proceeding) *from thy bowels will be separated,* will be at variance with each other; or, as the words may mean, *will be separated* (at variance) from birth.

V. 25. *Esau;* meaning, hairy.

V. 26. *Jacob;* meaning, he takes by the heel,—a supp'anter. Compare Hosea 12 : 3.

V. 27. *Plain;* that is, quiet and orderly in his tastes, habits, and manner of life, in marked contrast with the wild and adventurous life of his brother.

VV. 29–34. We have here an incident of family history, illustrating the character of the two brothers, and exerting an important influence on their subsequent relations. As Esau once returned from a hunting excursion, faint with fatigue and hunger, he found Jacob preparing a rustic meal of boiled lentiles. Jacob tests his brother's estimate of the value of the birthright by demanding it in exchange for the food which Esau's hunger required; and Esau shows how little he prized it by yielding to the demand. The transaction is to be regarded as one of those providential occurrences by which the characters of men are brought to light.

V. 30. *Of the red, that red.* The expression is indicative of eagerness and haste. *Edom;* meaning, red.

31 faint. Therefore was his name called Edom. And Jacob
32 said: Sell me this day thy birthright. And Esau said: Behold, I am about to die; and what is that to me,
33 a birthright! And Jacob said: Swear to me this day. And he swore to him. And he sold his birthright to Jacob.
34 And Jacob gave Esau bread and pottage of lentiles. And he ate and drank, and rose up, and went his way. And Esau despised the birthright.

1 AND there was a famine in the land, besides the first famine that was in the days of Abraham. And Isaac went to Abimelech, king of the Philistines, to Gerar.
2 And Jehovah appeared to him, and said: Go not down
3 to Egypt; dwell in the land of which I tell thee. Sojourn in this land, and I will be with thee and will bless thee; for to thee, and to thy seed, I will give all these lands; and I will establish the oath which I swore to Abraham
4 thy father. And I will multiply thy seed as the stars of heaven, and will give to thy seed all these lands; and in thy seed shall all the nations of the earth be blessed.

V. 4. *Or,* shall . . . account themselves blessed

V. 32. *What is that to me, a birthright!* The form of expression is peculiarly contemptuous, indicating the worthlessness of this right in his estimation. Compare the sacred writer's comment in v. 34.

V. 34. *Despised the birthright;* not "his birthright" (as in the common English version), but the institution itself; including not only the temporal advantages of precedence in rank as head of the tribe and heir to the family estate, but also, in this case, the more important spiritual blessings of the covenant with the race of Abraham.*

Ch. 26. Isaac's sojourn in Gerar. Esau's marriage.

V. 1. *In the land;* namely, of Canaan, to which Isaac had returned from the "south country," where he had resided (ch. 24: 62). *A famine.* Compare the remark on ch. 12: 10.

Gerar. See the note on ch. 10: 19. This city was on the main route to Egypt, the granary of the old world (ch. 12, note on v. 10), from which supplies of food could easily be obtained. Here Isaac dwelt (v. 6), in accordance with the direction given in the two following verses.

Abimelech; the royal title borne by the kings of the land, and not the name of an individual monarch. Compare 1 Sam. 21: 11 with the superscription of Psalm 34. The same person who is mentioned by his proper name Achish in the former passage, in the latter is called Abimelech.

V. 4. *Shall all the nations of the earth be blessed.* The Hebrew verb may be translated as in the margin, "shall—account themselves blessed;" that is, shall by the same faith appropriate to themselves the blessings promised to Abraham and his seed.

---

* "With a selfish and profane spirit (Heb. 12: 16) he thought only of himself, not of his posterity, and preferred what was at hand, the present, to the invisible and future."—*Delitzsch, Commentar über die Genesis,* 3te Ausg., p. 445.

⁵ Because Abraham hearkened to my voice, and kept my charge, my commandments, my statutes, and my laws.
⁶ ⁷ And Isaac dwelt in Gerar. And the men of the place asked concerning his wife. And he said: She is my sister; for he feared to say, my wife, lest the men of the place kill me on account of Rebekah. For she was of fair countenance.

⁸ And it came to pass that he was there a long time. And Abimelech, king of the Philistines, looked out at the window, and saw, and behold Isaac was sporting with ⁹ Rebekah his wife. And Abimelech called Isaac, and said: Behold, she is surely thy wife; and how saidst thou, she is my sister? And Isaac said to him: Because I said, lest I die on account of her.

¹⁰ And Abimelech said: What is this that thou hast done to us? Well-nigh had one of the people lain with thy wife, and thou wouldst have brought a trespass upon ¹¹ us. And Abimelech charged all the people, saying: He that touches this man or his wife shall surely be put to death.

¹² And Isaac sowed in that land; and he received in that ¹³ year a hundred-fold; and Jehovah blessed him. And the man became great, and went on increasing until he be- ¹⁴ came very great. And he had possessions of flocks, and possessions of herds, and many servants. And the Philis- ¹⁵ tines were jealous of him. And all the wells which his

---

V. 4. *Or*, account themselves blessed

VV. 6-11. Compare the similar conduct of Abraham, chs. 12 : 11-13, and 20 : 2-13.
V. 7. *She is my sister;* that is, a near relative by blood, the terms brother and sister including relatives of any degree. Compare chs. 14 : 16; 29 : 12, 15.
V. 10. *Well-nigh*, etc. His meaning is, there was nothing to prevent it, and it was very likely to occur.
This passage in the life of the patriarch has been the occasion of much reproach on the part of the avowed enemies of revelation, and even some Christian writers (as in the similar case of Abraham) have condemned his conduct with unsparing severity. For a different view of the case, see the remarks made on ch. 12 : 13.*
VV. 14, 15. *Were jealous of him;* of his increasing wealth and power (compare v. 16). The Philistines of this region seem to have been a pastoral people, and the presence among them of

---

* When that note was penned, the writer was not aware that the propriety of the patriarch's conduct had been ably shown by Waterland (*Scripture Vindicated*, on Gen. xii. 13; Works, vol. iv., pp. 189-190), in a minute and careful analysis of the case.

father's servants dug in the days of Abraham his father, the Philistines stopped them, and filled them with earth. 16 And Abimelech said to Isaac: Go from us; for thou art 17. much stronger than we. And Isaac went from thence, and pitched his tent in the valley of Gerar, and dwelt there. 18 And Isaac dug again the wells of water which they dug in the days of Abraham his father; for the Philistines stopped them after the death of Abraham; and he called their names after the names by which his father called them. 19 And the servants of Isaac dug in the valley, and found 20 there a well of living water. And the herdsmen of Gerar strove with the herdsmen of Isaac, saying: The water is ours. And he called the name of the well Esek; because they disputed with him. 21 And they dug another well; and they strove for that also; and he called the name of it Sitnah. 22 And he moved onward from thence, and dug another well; and for that they did not strive. And he called the name of it Rehoboth, and said: For now Jehovah has made room for us, and we shall be fruitful in the land. 23 And he went up from thence to Beer-sheba. 24 And Jehovah appeared to him on that night, and said:

one so much more prosperous than themselves was a cause of jealousy and apprehension. Hence the stopping of the wells (v. 15) on which he depended for water, as the most effectual means of compelling him to remove.

V. 17. *In the valley of Gerar;* in the same valley in which the city of Gerar lay, but apparently farther up the country and nearer the head of the valley.

The Hebrew word here rendered *valley* means strictly the hollow which serves as the watercourse of a mountain stream, sometimes put for the stream itself; full in the rainy season, and during the melting of the winter snows, but often quite dry in summer, and in seasons of drought (compare 1 Kings 17 : 7).*

V. 19. *A well of living water.* In digging they struck a vein which supplied the well with fresh fountain water. This was greatly preferred to the cisterns (also called wells) which were so constructed, often in the solid rock, as to collect the rain and snow water, and preserve it cool through the dry season.

VV. 20-22. *The water is ours;* as being within the territory which they regarded as belonging to them. *Esek;* meaning, dispute. *Sitnah;* meaning, opposition. *Rehoboth;* meaning, room.

V. 23. He found it desirable, probably for convenience of pasturage, to remove to Beersheba. For the origin and meaning of the name, see the note on ch. 21 : 31, and compare the remarks below on v. 33.

* See the striking description of such a stream in Job 6 : 15-18.

I am the God of Abraham thy father. Fear not, for I am with thee; and I will bless thee, and will multiply thy seed, 25 for the sake of Abraham my servant. And he built there an altar, and called on the name of Jehovah. And he stretched his tent there; and there the servants of Isaac dug a well.

26 And Abimelech went to him from Gerar, and Ahuzzath 27 his friend, and Phichol chief captain of his host. And Isaac said to them: Wherefore do ye come to me, when ye hate me, and have sent me away from you?

28 And they said: We saw certainly that Jehovah was with thee; and we said, let there be now an oath between us, 29 between us and thee, and let us make a covenant with thee, that thou wilt do us no evil, as we have not touched thee, and as we have done thee only good, and have sent thee away in peace. Thou art now blessed of Jehovah.

30 And he made them a feast; and they ate and drank. 31 And they rose early in the morning, and they swore one to another. And Isaac sent them away, and they went from him in peace.

32 And it came to pass on that day, that the servants of Isaac came, and told him concerning the well which they had dug. And they said to him: We have found water. 33 And he called it Shebah. Therefore the name of the city is Beer-sheba to this day.

34 And Esau was forty years old; and he took for a wife

V. 26. *Phichol* (meaning, mouth of all; that is, one who speaks for all, the director and leader,) seems to have been the title of the military commander, and not the proper name of an individual. *His friend* (minister); 1 Kings 4 : 5; 1 Chron. 27 : 33, properly *the king's friend*.

VV. 32, 33. Here again it is mentioned, as in v. 25, that the servants of Isaac dug a well. As flocks and herds increased in number, a greater supply of water was required. In the immediate vicinity of this place, besides the two large wells mentioned in the second paragraph of the note on ch. 21 : 31, five smaller wells are still found, at a considerable distance from them, grouped together in the bed of the valley. The two former are on the northern bank and near the margin of the valley, and on the low hills a little further north are the ruins of a small town.

There is no ground, therefore, for supposing that there are two different accounts (here and in ch. 21 : 28–31) of the digging of the same well and of the origin of the name. The name originated in the transaction recorded in ch. 21; and it was historically connected with the occurrences related in both passages.

It will be observed that the name *Shebah* (meaning oath), given to the well here spoken of, differs from *sheba* in the name *Beer-sheba*. In Hebrew the forms differ still more, though both may have the same meaning. Compare the note on ch. 21 : 31, first paragraph.

GENESIS. CHAP. XXVII.

Judith the daughter of Beeri the Hittite, and Bashemath
35 the daughter of Elon the Hittite. And they were a bitterness of spirit to Isaac and to Rebekah.

1 AND it came to pass, when Isaac was old, that his eyes were dim, so that he could not see. And he called Esau his eldest son, and said to him: My son! And he said to
2 him: Here am I. And he said: Behold now, I am old; I
3 know not the day of my death. Now therefore take, I pray, thy weapons, thy quiver and thy bow, and go out
4 to the field, and hunt game for me. And make for me savory meats, such as I love, and bring them to me, that I may eat; in order that my soul may bless thee before I die.
5 And Rebekah was listening when Isaac spoke to Esau

VV. 34, 35. The *Hittites* (sons of Heth, ch. 10 : 15, note, third paragraph), occupying the region around Hebron where Abraham often dwelt, were Canaanites of the race of Ham, and Abraham would not allow a wife to be taken for Isaac from among them (ch. 24 : 3). It is another significant indication of the reckless character of Esau, that he not only took two wives, but chose them both from this irreligious race.

Ch. 27. Jacob obtains the paternal blessing.

It was the purpose of the aged and infirm patriarch to establish Esau in all the rights and prerogatives of the firstborn, by bestowing on him the paternal blessing, and so to perpetuate through him and his offspring the blessings of the promised seed. That this was contrary to the divine purpose is clearly indicated elsewhere (ch. 25 : 23), and was apparent in the development of the characters of the two brothers.

This chapter is a striking illustration of the truth, with which all human history is pervaded, that God works out his purposes by overruling men's weaknesses, and their wrong devices, for the accomplishment of his own just ends.[*]

VV. 1-4. *When Isaac was old.* He was at this time about a hundred and thirty-seven years of age.[†]

That my soul may bless thee. The arrangements for this solemn observance have been unjustly characterized as merely sensual. On the contrary, the patriarch would make the bestowment of the blessing a joyful as well as solemn occasion, a season of festivity, of devout thanksgiving for temporal and spiritual mercies.

VV. 5-10. Rebekah knew, from the divine communication made to her (ch. 25 : 23) that Isaac was about to bestow the paternal blessing in opposition to the divine will, as well as to her own maternal preference (ch. 25 : 28). To prevent this, she resorts to a stratagem, indefensible in every view, and the source of lifelong trouble and sorrow to herself and her favorite son.

[*] "God permitted Isaac to be deceived, to show that it was not by the will of man that Jacob, contrary to the order of nature, was raised to the rights and honors of the firstborn."— Calvin *in librum Geneseos*.

[†] As ascertained by the following comparison of dates, in which the due allowance for fractions of years would but slightly vary the result: Joseph was thirty-nine years old (ch. 41 : 46, and 45 : 6) when Jacob went down to Egypt at the age of one hundred and thirty years (ch. 47 : 9), and consequently was born when Jacob was ninety-one years old. As this occurred in the fourteenth year of Jacob's service with Laban (ch. 30 : 25, and 29 : 18, 21, 27), his flight took place in his seventy-seventh year, and consequently in the hundred and thirty-seventh year of Isaac's age (ch. 25 : 26).

his son. And Esau went to the field to hunt for game, to bring it.

6 And Rebekah spoke to Jacob her son, saying: Behold, I heard thy father speaking to Esau thy brother, saying: 7 Bring me game, and make for me savory meats, that I may eat; and I will bless thee before Jehovah, before my death.

8 Now therefore, my son, hearken to my voice, in regard 9 to what I command thee. Go now to the flock, and take for me from thence two good kids of the goats; and I will make them savory meats for thy father, such as he loves. 10 And thou shalt bring it to thy father, that he may eat; in order that he may bless thee before his death.

11 And Jacob said to Rebekah his mother: Behold, Esau my brother is a hairy man, and I am a smooth man. 12 Perhaps my father will feel of me, and I shall be in his eyes as a mocker; and I shall bring upon me a curse, and not a blessing.

13 And his mother said to him: Upon me be thy curse, my son; only hearken to my voice, and go take them for 14 me. And he went, and took them, and brought them to his mother. And his mother made savory meats, such as his father loved.

15 And Rebekah took the garments of Esau her eldest son, the precious ones, which were with her in the house, and 16 clothed Jacob her younger son. And the skins of the kids of the goats she put upon his hands, and upon the smooth 17 parts of his neck. And she gave the savory meats and the bread, which she prepared, into the hand of Jacob her son.

Was listening; an indication of her watchfulness over the interests of a darling son.

V. 12. *As a mocker;* as one who deals lightly with sacred things, making a mock of a serious and solemn observance.

VV. 13, 14. She takes upon herself the whole responsibility; and Jacob suffers his fears and scruples to be overruled by her maternal authority, siding as it does with the advancement of his own interests.

VV. 15–17. His best apparel is selected, as suited to the solemnity and the festive character of the occasion. Compare the remarks on vv. 1–4, second paragraph.

The skins of the kids of the goats. The Oriental camel-goat is meant, whose dark silky hair was used by the Romans as an artificial substitute for the human hair.*

* *Tuch, Kommentar über die Genesis,* p. 430.

GENESIS.   Chap. XXVII.

¹⁸ And he came to his father, and said: My father! And ¹⁹ he said: Here am I; who art thou, my son? And Jacob said to his father: I am Esau, thy first-born. I have done as thou didst say to me. Arise, I pray, sit and eat of my game, in order that thy soul may bless me.

²⁰ And Isaac said to his son: How is this, that thou hast found it so quickly, my son? And he said: Because Jehovah thy God prospered me.

²¹ And Isaac said to Jacob: Come near now, that I may feel of thee, my son, whether thou art my very son Esau ²² or not. And Jacob came near to Isaac his father; and he felt of him, and said: The voice is the voice of Jacob, but ²³ the hands are the hands of Esau. And he discerned him not, because his hands were as the hands of Esau his brother, hairy; and he blessed him.

²⁴ And he said: Art thou my very son Esau? And he ²⁵ said: I am. And he said: Bring it near to me, that I may eat of my son's game, in order that my soul may bless thee. And he brought it near to him, and he ate; and he brought him wine, and he drank.

²⁶ And Isaac his father said to him: Come near now, and ²⁷ kiss me, my son. And he came near, and kissed him. And he smelled the smell of his garments, and blessed him, and said:

See, the smell of my son is as the smell of a field,
Which Jehovah has blessed.

V. 20. *Jehovah thy God prospered me.* It is one of the most fearful perils of deviation from the right way, that no bound is set to it. The transgressor knows not whither it will lead him. Jacob begins with deception, follows it up with falsehood, and ends with profaning the sacred name of Jehovah, by attributing its success to his favor. Years of wandering from the beloved home, of toil and privation (ch. 31 : 40), and anxious fears (ch. 32 : 6-8), are the divine comment.

V. 23. *He blessed him;* greeted him with a blessing.* There is no reference here to the formal blessing recorded in vv. 27-29.

VV. 27-29. *The smell of his garments;* fragrant with the balmy air and the fresh odors of the open fields.†

Has blessed with his favor; made it productive, rich in abundant harvests, and perfumed with their fresh fragrance.

---

* As was usual at meeting and parting. See ch. 47 : 7, 10; 2 Kings 4 : 29, in the Hebrew, "if thou meet a man bless him not, and if a man bless thee answer him not." Compare the courteous and pious greeting of Boaz and his reapers, Ruth 2 : 4.

† Compare Cant. 4 : 11, "the smell of thy garments is as the smell of Lebanon."

28 And God give thee of the dew of heaven,
And of the fatness of the earth,
And abundance of corn and new wine.
29 Let peoples serve thee,
And nations bow down to thee.
Be lord of thy brethren,
And let thy mother's sons bow down to thee.
Cursed be every one that curses thee,
And blessed be every one that blesses thee.
30 And it came to pass, when Isaac made an end of blessing Jacob, and Jacob was but just gone out from the presence of Isaac his father, that Esau his brother came
31 from his hunting. And he also made savory meats, and brought them to his father. And he said to his father: Let my father arise, and eat of his son's game, in order that thy soul may bless me.
32 And Isaac his father said to him: Who art thou? And he said: I am thy son, thy first-born, Esau.
33 And Isaac trembled with exceedingly great trembling. And he said: Who then is he that hunted game, and brought it to me, and I ate of all before thou camest, and blessed him? Yea, blessed shall he be!
34 When Esau heard the words of his father, he cried with a great and exceedingly bitter cry. And he said to his father: Bless me, me also, my father.
35 And he said: Thy brother came with deceit, and took thy blessing.
36 And he said: Is not his name called Jacob? And he

New wine. By this is meant wine of the first year, the product of the season; and hence it is usually coupled as here with corn, or with corn and oil, as the yearly product of the land. It is obvious, therefore, that nothing further is to be inferred from the use of this particular term. Compare Hosea 4 : 11.

The words of the patriarch take the poetic form, as is customary with the Hebrews whenever feeling rises above its ordinary tone.

The blessing awards to its recipient whatever belonged of right to the first-born, and places him at the head of the chosen race.

VV. 32, 33. *Who art thou?* He does not say here (as in v. 18), Who art thou, my son? In his astonishment and alarm, he does not recognize his son, and demands who this intruder is.

Yea, blessed shall he be. He can not retract the blessing already pronounced. The Hebrew patriarch, in the character of priest and prophet, regarded himself as the instrument of the divine will, and what had passed his lips was beyond recall.

V. 36. *Jacob;* meaning *Supplanter* (compare ch. 25 : 26), one who takes another by the heel

has supplanted me these two times. He took my birthright; and, behold, now he has taken my blessing. And he said: Hast thou not reserved for me a blessing?

37 And Isaac answered and said to Esau: Behold, I have made him thy lord, and all his brethren have I given to him for servants, and with corn and new wine have I sustained him. And now what can I do for thee, my son?

38 And Esau said to his father: Hast thou but one blessing, my father? Bless me, me also, my father. And Esau lifted up his voice, and wept.

39 And Isaac his father answered and said to him:
Behold, from the fatness of the earth shall be thy dwelling,
And from the dew of heaven from above.

40 And by thy sword thou shalt live,
And thy brother shalt thou serve.

V. 39. *Or*, Behold, of the fatness of the earth shall be thy dwelling,
And of the dew of heaven from above.

---

to throw him down. To the Hebrew, Esau's words would read: "Is not his name called Supplanter? And he has supplanted me these two times."

V. 39. *From;* that is away from. His dwelling should be away from the fatness of the earth (its fruitful soil), and from the dew of heaven (its fertilizing influence). With this accord the descriptions of this region by ancient writers, and by modern travelers who have visited it. Compare Mal. 1:3.* Hence the patriarch adds, "by thy sword thou shalt live," as having no other means of subsistence.

The word might also be translated as in the margin, being the same word that is so translated twice ("of the dew"—"of the fatness") in v. 28. But the version in the text is doubtless the true one.†

V. 40. *By thy sword thou shalt live;* by war and plunder, as illustrated in his own history, and in that of his posterity.

And thy brother shalt thou serve; shalt be the inferior and subordinate power, unable to contend with him on equal terms. This is qualified in the following words, "as thou rovest at will, thou wilt break his yoke from off thy neck." Both statements are fully verified in the history and relations of the two races. The one became a great and prosperous kingdom; the

---

* Properly: *and made his mountains a waste, and his heritage desert tracts.* The connection shows that the prophet refers to the original distinction made between the two brothers in the allotment of their inheritance.

† A verbal correspondence with v. 28 was probably intended. But the connection of words is here quite different; and this, as well as the evident intention of the speaker, requires the other sense, which is equally common. As to the connection, the word *give* (in v. 28) is properly followed by the partitive sense ("give thee of the dew of heaven"), while it could not be said, "thy dwelling shall be of the dew of heaven," in any sense. As to the intention of the speaker, it seems clear that Isaac, after saying in v. 37, "And now what can I do for thee, my son?" would not have promised him the very same blessings of a fruitful soil and genial climate, which he had just allotted to Jacob; nor would he after this have added, "and by thy sword thou shalt live," as though he would have no other means of subsistence.

And it shall be, as thou rovest at will,
Thou wilt break his yoke from off thy neck.

41 And Esau purposed evil against Jacob, on account of the blessing with which his father blessed him. And Esau said in his heart: The days of mourning for my father are at hand, and I will slay Jacob my brother.

42 And the words of Esau her eldest son were told to Rebekah. And she sent and called Jacob her younger son, and said to him: Behold, Esau thy brother is about to 43 avenge himself on thee, by slaying thee. Now therefore, my son, hearken to my voice, and arise, flee to Laban my 44 brother, to Haran, and abide with him a few days, until 45 thy brother's fury turn away; until thy brother's anger turn away from thee, and he shall forget what thou hast done to him, and I will send and bring thee from thence. Why should I be deprived of you both together in one day?

46 And Rebekah said to Isaac: I am weary of my life because of the daughters of Heth. If Jacob takes a wife of the daughters of Heth, such as these of the daughters of the land, for what to me is life!

---

other never attained to permanent power and influence, and though many times mastered and temporarily subjected, restlessly asserted their independence.

As thou rovest at will, impatient of control, and defying all restraint. The words describe the wild and free habits of a race which can not be held in permanent subjection.

V. 41. *Purposed evil against Jacob;* watching his opportunity, when he might at length wreak his vengeance on him, without incurring his father's displeasure, as intimated in the following words.

V. 45. A fine touch of maternal feeling betrays itself in the words, *Why should I be deprived of you both;* of one by death, of the other by a crime worse than death.

V. 46. Compare the statement in ch. 26 : 35. Rebekah here shows her shrewdness and tact, in the means by which she obtained Isaac's assent, and his parting blessing.

The reader will not fail to note the artless truthfulness of this interesting and affecting narrative. The whole scene, as here depicted, is wonderfully true to nature, all the parties speaking and acting in harmony with their several characters.

Jacob seems to have yielded wholly to the guidance of his mother's stronger will (vv. 13, 14), but not without the calm and calculating forethought shown by him on other occasions, as in ch. 25 : 31–33, and ch. 30 : 31–43. Both acted on the false principle, that the end sanctifies the means; and both were signally rebuked (notes on vv. 5–10, and v. 20), though their conduct was divinely overruled for good; see introductory remarks, second paragraph.

Esau appears here as elsewhere, a strong, ardent nature, impetuous and violent in feeling as in action, as ready now to take the life of his offending brother, as he was to load him with caresses and kindness in after years, when the keen sense of wrong had passed away in the stirring excitements of a wild and roving life.

There is a mild, spiritual beauty in the whole of Isaac's character and career. In infancy,

¹ AND Isaac called Jacob and blessed him; and he commanded him, and said to him: Thou shalt not take a wife ² of the daughters of Canaan. Arise, go to Padan-aram, to the house of Bethuel thy mother's father, and take for thee a wife from thence, of the daughters of Laban thy ³ mother's brother. And God Almighty bless thee, and make thee fruitful, and multiply thee, that thou mayest ⁴ become an assemblage of peoples; and give to thee the blessing of Abraham, to thee and to thy seed with thee, that thou mayest possess the land of thy sojournings, which God gave to Abraham.

⁵ And Isaac sent away Jacob. And he went to Padan-aram, to Laban son of Bethuel the Aramite, brother of Rebekah the mother of Jacob and Esau.

⁶ And Esau saw that Isaac blessed Jacob, and sent him away to Padan-aram, to take for himself a wife from thence, when he blessed him, and commanded him, saying: Thou shalt not take a wife of the daughters of Canaan, ⁷ and Jacob hearkened to his father and to his mother, and

---

the pet of the household, in childhood taught the bitterest lesson of self renunciation and sacrifice, he grew up averse to action, patient of injuries, trustful, and forgiving. Of his contemplative character mention is made in ch. 24 : 63; and of the tender sorrow with which his mother's memory was cherished there is a beautiful record in v. 67. "Resist not evil, but overcome evil with good," was his life-principle, as exemplified in his intercourse with Abimelech and his herdsmen, in ch. 26 : 15-31. When invited to move further off, because he was the stronger party (v. 16), he patiently obeyed. When violently deprived of his rights in the wells he had caused to be dug, he moved further on and dug others (vv. 19-22). His fondness for Esau is an instance of the natural attraction of contrasts, often seen in life. His forgiveness of Jacob's deception, and recognition of a higher will than his, shows his readiness to accept the correction of his own misdirected zeal.

There was nothing in the circumstances of his life to require or develop those commanding traits which distinguished the person and mission of Abraham, and have made his name a household word. But his character shines with a mild and steady radiance, as the dutiful son, the affectionate and constant husband, the kind indulgent father, and the quiet peace-loving citizen.

Piety was the leading trait of his character; and it is specially recorded of him, as of Abraham, that where he paused for a temporary abode, in his migrations, he erected an altar to Jehovah. See ch. 26 : 25.

Chs. 28-50. Third part of the fourth division. *Family history of Jacob.*

Ch. 28. Jacob's journey to Padan-aram. Esau's marriage with a daughter of Ishmael. Jacob's night-vision, and his vow.

VV. 1-4. Isaac here follows the example of Abraham in ch. 24, and directs Jacob to seek a wife among his own kindred. He now bestows on him the blessing of Abraham, apparently convinced of his error in having intended the blessing of the first-born for Esau.

Padan-aram; see the note on ch. 25 : 20. *Of thy sojournings;* see the note on ch. 17 : 8. *Laban;* see ch. 24 : 29. *Bethuel;* see ch. 22 : 20-23.

⁸ went to Padan-aram. And Esau saw that the daughters ⁹ of Canaan were evil in the eyes of Isaac his father. And Esau went to Ishmael and took, in addition to his wives, Mahalath daughter of Ishmael Abraham's son, a sister of Nebaioth, to be his wife.

¹⁰ And Jacob went forth from Beer-sheba, and went toward ¹¹ Haran. And he lighted upon a certain place, and passed the night there, because the sun was setting. And he took one of the stones of the place and put it under his head; and he lay down in that place.

¹² And he dreamed; and behold a ladder set up on the earth, its top reaching to heaven; and behold angels of ¹³ God ascending and descending on it. And behold Jehovah standing above it; and he said: I am Jehovah, the God of Abraham thy father, and the God of Isaac. The land whereon thou liest, to thee will I give it, and to thy seed. ¹⁴ And thy seed shall be as the dust of the earth; and thou

---

V. 9. *Went to Ishmael;* that is, to his family, for Ishmael died some years before.* *Nebaioth;* see ch. 25 : 13.

V. 10. From Beer-sheba, in the southern limits of Palestine, he would proceed northward on his way to Haran in the northwestern part of Mesopotamia, passing by Bethel, the ancient Luz (v. 19). Beyond this, his route is not here traced.

He was compelled to leave his father's home stealthily (ch. 27 : 43, "flee to Laban my brother") through fear of Esau, and without the conveniences of traveling with which Abraham's servant made the journey (ch. 24 : 10). It is possible that a change in Isaac's worldly estate may have made this necessary.

V. 11. *A certain place.* By this is meant an open unoccupied space of ground, clear of all encumbrance, with nothing to prevent his occupation of it.†

The place (another rendering) means the well-known place, rendered memorable by the extraordinary occurrences connected with it, as related in this chapter. Compare the allusion made to them, long after this, in ch. 35 : 1–3.

He lighted upon it; by chance, as we are accustomed to say, his steps being directed to it without any human guidance.

V. 12. *And he dreamed*, etc. In this vision, a ladder is seen, connecting earth and heaven. Jehovah appears above it; and on it angels, his messengers, are passing from him to earth, and returning from earth to him.

The import of the vision seems very obvious. It is an instructive image of the real though unseen connection of the heavenly agencies with the affairs of earth. Its special design here is to give Jacob the assurance of an ever-active providential agency, though invisible to him, through which the promises that follow shall surely be accomplished. The record of it conveys the like assurance to all who have faith in an overruling Providence, and commit themselves to its care.

V. 14. *In thee—and in thy seed;* see the remarks on ch. 12 : 3.

---

* Ishmael was fourteen years older than Isaac (compare ch. 16 : 16 with ch. 21 : 5), and died at the age of a hundred and thirty-seven (ch. 25 : 17). As Isaac was of that age at this time (see the note on ch. 27 : 1–4), Ishmael must have died fourteen years before.

† So the word is used in Isaiah 28 : 8; properly, "there is no place," no empty and unoccupied space.

shalt spread abroad, to the west and to the east, and to the north and to the south; and in thee shall all the 15 families of the earth be blessed, and in thy seed. And behold I am with thee, and will keep thee in all the way that thou goest, and will bring thee back to this land; for I will not leave thee until I have done what I have spoken to thee.

16 And Jacob awoke from his sleep. And he said: Surely 17 Jehovah is in this place; and I knew it not. And he was afraid, and said: How dreadful is this place! This is no other than the house of God, and this is the gate of heaven.

18 And Jacob rose early in the morning, and took the stone that he put under his head, and set it for a pillar, 19 and poured oil on the top of it. And he called the name of that place Bethel. But Luz was the name of the city at the first.

20 And Jacob vowed a vow, saying: If God will be with me, and keep me in this way that I am going, and will 21 give me bread to eat, and raiment to put on, and I return in peace to my father's house, then shall Jehovah be my 22 God; and this stone, which I set for a pillar, shall be a house of God, and of all that thou givest me I will surely give the tenth to thee.

V. 16. *Jehovah is in this place;* manifests himself here also, though far from the abode of his chosen worshipers, where he is accustomed to reveal himself.

V. 17. *Was afraid* expresses the dread naturally inspired in sinful erring man by the conscious presence of the Divine. Compare Isaiah 6 : 5.

V. 18. In commemoration of the vision, and to mark the spot,* he erects on it a pillar, appropriately using the stone on which his head rested during the vision of the night.

Poured oil on the top of it, in token of the sacred purpose for which he set it up, and to which he consecrated it by this act. It was thus set apart to a holy use. Compare Ex. 30 : 26-30.

V. 19. *Bethel—Luz.* Compare ch. 35 : 6, 48 : 3; Josh. 16 : 2, 18 : 13; Judges 1 : 23. It is inferred from Josh. 16 : 2, that the place to which Jacob gave the name Bethel was not the exact site of the city, though the latter, from its proximity, was afterward called by that name.

The writer, in narrating things which occurred long before, might mention the place either by its later name which it bore in his own time, as in ch. 12 : 8, 13 : 3, or by its earlier name as in ch. 48 : 3.

V. 22. *Shall be a house of God;* compare ch. 35 : 1-7, already referred to. *Will give the tenth to thee;* a recognition and acknowledgment of him as giver of the whole.

---

* That it might be identified in future time. Compare the use afterward made of this place, ch. 35 : 1-7.

¹ AND Jacob lifted up his feet, and went to the land of ² the sons of the East. And he saw, and behold a well in the field; and behold there three droves of sheep lying by it, for out of that well they watered the droves; and the ³ stone on the mouth of the well was great. And thither were all the droves gathered; and they rolled the stone from the mouth of the well and watered the sheep, and put back the stone on the mouth of the well, in its place.
⁴ And Jacob said to them: My brethren, whence are ye? ⁵ And they said: We are from Haran. And he said to them: Do ye know Laban son of Nahor? And they said: ⁶ We know him. And he said to them: Is he well? And they said: He is well; and behold, Rachel his daughter is coming with the sheep.
⁷ And he said: Behold, it is yet high day; it is not time that the cattle should be gathered together. Water the ⁸ sheep, and go, feed them. And they said: We can not, until all the droves are gathered together, and they roll the stone from the mouth of the well, and we water the sheep.

V. 2. *Or*, and the stone, a great one, was on the mouth of the well

Ch. 29. Jacob continues his journey to Padan-aram. Meeting with Rachel at the well. Marriage with Leah and with Rachel.

V. 1. *Lifted up his feet and went;* a mode of expression by which the Hebrew indicates anything of formal and grave import, as in this case the undertaking of a long and difficult journey. Compare the similar purport of the phrase, "He opened his mouth and taught them," Matt. 5: 2. *Land of the sons of the East;* here referring specially to Mesopotamia, included in Padan-aram; see the note on ch. 25: 20. Compare ch. 25: 5, 6, note, third paragraph.

V. 2. *The stone on the mouth of the well* refers to the practice, still common in the East, of guarding the mouth of a well by covering it with a heavy stone, not easily removed.*
V. 3 describes what was customarily done, not what was done at this particular time.

VV. 6–8. *Is coming;* is on the way, this being the hour at which all who used the well were expected there with their flocks. It is not necessarily meant that she is near, or in sight; see the remark in the next paragraph.

Water the sheep, and go feed them; said, apparently, for the purpose of securing a meeting with his kinswoman in private.

We can not, etc.; it being the rule, that the stone should not be removed, till all who used the well were present with their flocks.

---

* "In approaching the ancient Sychar, I passed a well, the mouth of which was stopped with a stone so large that the united strength of two men would be required to move it."—*Dr. Hackett's Illustrations of Scripture*, 8th ed., p. 91.

⁹ And while he was yet speaking with them, Rachel came with her father's sheep; for she kept them.
¹⁰ And it came to pass, when Jacob saw Rachel the daughter of Laban his mother's brother, and the sheep of Laban his mother's brother, that Jacob came near and rolled the stone from the mouth of the well, and watered the flock of Laban his mother's brother.
¹¹ And Jacob kissed Rachel, and lifted up his voice and wept.
¹² And Jacob told Rachel that he was her father's brother, and that he was Rebekah's son. And she ran and told her father.
¹³ And it came to pass, when Laban heard the tidings of Jacob his sister's son, that he ran to meet him, and embraced him, and kissed him, and brought him to his house. And he related all these things to Laban.
¹⁴ And Laban said to him: Surely thou art my bone and my flesh. And he abode with him a month of days.
¹⁵ And Laban said to Jacob: Because thou art my brother, shouldst thou therefore serve me for nothing? Tell me, what shall be thy wages?
¹⁶ And Laban had two daughters. The name of the eldest was Leah, and the name of the younger was Rachel.
¹⁷ And Leah's eyes were weak; but Rachel was of beautiful form, and of beautiful countenance.
¹⁸ And Jacob loved Rachel; and he said: I will serve thee seven years for Rachel thy younger daughter.
¹⁹ And Laban said: It is better that I give her to thee, than that I should give her to another man. Abide with me.

V. 9. *While he was yet speaking.* The conversation, of which a part is given, was continued till Rachel came with her father's sheep.
For she kept them; as is still done by women in the East.*
V. 12. *Her father's brother;* meaning his near kinsman, the word being often used with this latitude of meaning.
V. 14. *A month of days;* that is, fully numbered; an entire month, with its full complement of days.
V. 17. *Leah's eyes were weak.* This is regarded by the Orientals as a great defect, bright and sparkling eyes being an essential element in feminine beauty.

* "Just beyond El-Arish, the last town in Egypt before entering Palestine, we saw, at a little distance from our path, a flock of sheep, so immensely large as to excite our wonder. . . . Three women were watching them."—*Dr. Hackett's Illustrations of Scripture*, 8th ed., p. 105.

²⁰ And Jacob served for Rachel seven years. And they were in his eyes as a few days, for the love he had for her.

²¹ And Jacob said to Laban: Give me my wife, for my days are completed, that I may go in to her.

²² And Laban gathered together all the men of the place,
²³ and made a feast. And it came to pass in the evening, that he took Leah his daughter, and brought her to him;
²⁴ and he went in to her. And Laban gave her Zilpah his maid-servant, as a maid-servant to Leah his daughter.

²⁵ And it came to pass, that in the morning, behold, it was Leah. And he said to Laban: What is this thou hast done to me? Was it not for Rachel that I served with thee? Wherefore then hast thou deceived me?

²⁶ And Laban said: It must not be so done in our place,
²⁷ to give the younger before the first-born. Complete this one's week; and we will give thee this one also, for the service which thou shalt serve with me yet seven other years.

²⁸ And Jacob did so, and completed her week; and he

VV. 21-23. The betrothal with Rachel had taken place seven years before (vv. 18, 19), and she was now to become his wife by the simple ceremony described in vv. 22, 23. No other was required; compare the note on ch. 24 : 67, second paragraph. In such a case, the deception here practiced was an easy matter.

It is plain that this was no marriage, and that it was not binding as such on Jacob by any principle of morals, or any law divine or human. Hence he could justly claim, as his lawful wife, her to whom he had been betrothed, and whose place in the bridal chamber had been fraudulently taken by another, without his knowledge.

The divine law of marriage required him to forsake all others, and cleave to her alone. That he acted otherwise is to be ascribed to the rude state of society, and to the requirements of the age and place (v. 26) in which he lived. The Bible records such things simply as historical facts, being responsible only for the truth of the record; and they are instructive as showing what human life and society have been under peculiar and ever-varying influences. Its own teachings can not be mistaken; and the civilization which has grown up under their guidance and influence attests their truth and efficacy.

VV. 25-27. Morning comes, and Jacob discovers that he, in his turn, is the victim of a cruel deception.* But remonstrances avail nothing; Laban pleading now, what he was careful not to disclose before, the custom of the place. Jacob is required to "complete this one's week," thus recognizing her before all as his wedded wife, and after that he can have his betrothed one, the wife of his choice, for another seven years' service.

This one's week; the week during which the usual marriage festival continued. See Judges 14 : 12, and Tobit 11 : 19. Laban stipulates that Jacob shall not withdraw himself from Leah during the continuance of this festival, and at the end of it Rachel shall be given him, and for her he shall serve another seven years.

* "Thus he who cheated Esau is cheated by Laban, and sin is punished by sin."—*Keil, Biblischer Kommentar,* 2te Aufl., p. 213.

GENESIS. Снар. XXX.

²⁹ gave him Rachel his daughter for his wife. And Laban gave to Rachel his daughter Bilhah his maid-servant to be ³⁰ her maid-servant. And he went in also to Rachel; and he loved Rachel more than Leah. And he served with him yet seven other years.

³¹ And Jehovah saw that Leah was hated, and he opened ³² her womb; and Rachel was barren. And Leah conceived, and bore a son, and she called his name Reuben. For she said: Jehovah has looked on my affliction; for now my husband will love me.

³³ And she conceived again, and bore a son. And she said: Jehovah has heard that I am hated, and he has given me this one also; and she called his name Simeon.

³⁴ And she conceived again, and bore a son; and she said: Now this time will my husband be joined to me, because I have borne him three sons. Therefore was his name called Levi.

³⁵ And she conceived again, and bore a son; and she said: Now will I praise Jehovah. Therefore she called his name Judah. And she ceased from bearing.

¹ AND Rachel saw that she bore no children to Jacob. And Rachel envied her sister; and she said to Jacob: Give me children, or else I die.

² And Jacob's anger was kindled against Rachel; and he

VV. 30, 31. *Went in also to Rachel.* See the remarks on vv. 21-23, third paragraph.

Leah was hated; was disliked and neglected, as was natural, she having been the means by which Jacob was defrauded. Yet he had taken her to be his wife for the sake of gaining another whom he preferred, and thus she in her turn was wronged; and his twofold wrong was visited on him, by making the hated one fruitful and the other barren.

V. 32. *Reuben* (See, a son!) is the triumphant appellation she gives to her first-born, when she finds that, not only a child, but a son is given her.

VV. 33-35. With a more subdued gratitude (for she had not won, as she hoped, her husband's regard) she calls her second son *Simeon* (a hearing) as a memorial that God has again heard her. *Levi* (a joining). *Judah;* meaning, praised (namely, praised be Jehovah).

Ch. 30. Birth of other children to Jacob. His new contract for service with Laban.

VV. 1-4. Rachel's longing for offspring is expressed with even childish simplicity and impatience. But the longing itself is nature's voice, implanted by God, and pleasing in his sight.*

To satisfy in some measure this longing, she resorts to an expedient common in that age and country. Compare the introductory remarks on the sixteenth chapter.

* "The chaste desire for offspring is the highest aim of a virtuous marriage."—*Delitzsch, über die Genesis,* p. 465.

121

said: Am I in place of God, who has withheld from thee the fruit of the womb?

3 And she said: Behold my handmaid Bilhah; go in to her, and she shall bear upon my knees, that I also may be built up from her.

4 And she gave him Bilhah her maid-servant for a wife; and Jacob went in to her.

5 6 And Bilhah conceived, and bore a son to Jacob. And Rachel said: God has judged me, and has also heard my voice and given me a son. Therefore she called his name Dan.

7 And Bilhah, Rachel's maid-servant, conceived again, and
8 bore a second son to Jacob. And Rachel said: With wrestlings of God have I wrestled with my sister; yea, I have prevailed. And she called his name Naphtali.

9 And Leah saw that she had ceased from bearing; and she took Zilpah her maid-servant and gave her to Jacob for a wife.

10 And Zilpah, Leah's maid-servant, bore a son to Jacob.
11 And Leah said: Good fortune! And she called his name Gad.

12 And Zilpah, Leah's maid-servant, bore a second son to

V. 3. *Upon my knees*, instead of the birth-stool then in use;* indicating by this that she claimed the offspring as her own. The common explanation, shall bear a child to be taken on my knees by me as its mother,† falls far short of the meaning of the phrase.

Be built up from her. See the remark on ch. 16 : 2.

V. 6. *Has judged me.* To judge one, in the scriptural use of the phrase, is to take cognizance of his case as a judge, to see that justice is done him and that he is protected in his rights. Rachel considered herself the rightful wife of Jacob, and as such entitled to the rights of maternity, with its privileges and honors, of which she had hitherto been deprived.

And has also heard my voice, etc.; an evidence that her cause was right and the judgment in her favor. *Dan;* meaning Judge (or, he judges).

V. 8. *Wrestlings of God;* either inspired by him, such as he alone has power to cause, or wrestlings with him, namely in prayer.‡

With my sister; as competitor with her for the divine favor. It was with God she wrestled in prayer (if we adopt the second explanation), but it was in competition with her sister and rival.

Naphtali; meaning, wrestled-for (won by wrestling).

V. 11. *Gad;* meaning, good fortune. The comment on the name, in ch. 49 : 19, is suggested by its resemblance to another word meaning *troop.*

---

* See Ex. 1 : 16. Its use is approved and adopted in some modern countries.

† Compare Job 3 : 12 (properly, "why were the knees ready for me") and the writer's remark on it, *Book of Job*, Part Second, explanatory notes.

‡ *Wrestlings of God*, namely, in which God acts as judge in determining the issue, as interpreted by some, is more remote from the simple and natural construction of the phrase.

GENESIS. CHAP. XXX.

¹³ Jacob. And Leah said: Happy am I! For the daughters will call me happy. And she called his name Asher.

¹⁴ And Reuben went in the days of wheat-harvest, and found mandrakes in the field, and brought them to Leah his mother. And Rachel said to Leah: Give me, I pray, ¹⁵ of thy son's mandrakes. And she said to her: Is it a small matter that thou hast taken my husband, and wouldst thou take my son's mandrakes also? And Rachel said: Therefore he shall lie with thee to-night for thy son's mandrakes.

¹⁶ And Jacob came from the field in the evening. And Leah went out to meet him, and said: Thou must come in to me; for surely I have hired thee with my son's mandrakes. And he lay with her that night.

¹⁷ And God hearkened to Leah; and she conceived and ¹⁸ bore a fifth son to Jacob. And Leah said: God has given my reward, because I gave my maid-servant to my husband. And she called his name Issachar.

¹⁹ And Leah conceived again, and bore a sixth son to ²⁰ Jacob. And Leah said: God has endowed me with a good dowry. Now will my husband dwell with me, because I have borne him six sons. And she called his name Zebulun.

²¹ And afterward she bore a daughter; and she called her name Dinah.

²² And God remembered Rachel; and God hearkened to

V. 13. *The daughters* (namely, of the race that shall spring from me) will call me happy, for such know how to prize the blessing. *Asher* (happy).

VV. 14–16. We have here another instructive incident of this unhappy connection, showing the jealousies and bickerings that necessarily grew out of it, and embittered the lives of all the parties to it.

Mandrakes (mentioned in the Scriptures only here and in Cant. 7:13) were supposed to promote fruitfulness, and hence were desired by Rachel, who had yet borne no children.

VV. 17–21. *God hearkened to Leah.* Every desired gift is from above, bestowed like the sunshine and rain (Matt. 5:45) without reference to desert. When the sacred writer says that "God hearkened to Leah" and bestowed the desired blessing, he teaches us to recognize this truth, leaving out of view the desert of the recipient as well as the nature and grounds of the desire.

She claims the merit of having yielded her place to her maid-servant for her husband's sake, and regards this gift as her reward. *Issachar;* meaning, reward (or, there is reward).

Zebulun; dwelling (with one), intimacy. *Dinah,* meaning vindication; a name afterward given her from the occurrences related in ch. 34.

VV. 22–24. *Hearkened to her.* See the note on vv. 17–21, first paragraph. *My reproach;* so

²³ her, and opened her womb. And she conceived, and bore a son; and she said: God has taken away my reproach. ²⁴ And she called his name Joseph, saying: Jehovah add to me another son!

²⁵ And it came to pass, when Rachel had borne Joseph, that Jacob said to Laban: Send me away, and let me go ²⁶ to my place and to my land. Give me my wives and my children, for whom I have served thee, and let me go; for thou thyself knowest my service with which I have served thee.

²⁷ And Laban said to him: If now I have found favor in thine eyes! I have divined that Jehovah blessed me on thy account. ²⁸ And he said: Name to me thy wages, and I will give it. ²⁹ And he said to him: Thou thyself knowest how I have ³⁰ served thee, and how thy cattle have been with me. For it was little which thou hadst before I came, and it increased to a multitude; and Jehovah has blessed thee at

---

barrenness was regarded, as being an adverse visitation of Providence, which denied a boon prized and sought by all. Compare Luke 1 : 25.

The gift of a first son she receives as an earnest of yet more, and calls his name *Joseph* (May He add!).

The reader will not look for a true religious sentiment, though there is much semblance of it, in such a rivalry as is here disclosed. Both parties to it were competitors for Jacob's good will; and both hoped for success, as the worldly often do in seeking their selfish ends, from the divine blessing on their own devices. God overrules all for ultimate good, and through such instruments as these works out his wise and beneficent ends; and herein are seen the wisdom and the mystery of his providence.

In this disclosure of the interior life of Jacob's household we have an instructive picture of the evils of polygamy, in its legitimate results as here described. The chaste relations of husband and wife, with their refining and ennobling influences, give place to a cold and selfish sensuality. The peace of the domestic fireside is destroyed by conflicting rival interests. The paternal home, the sanctuary where God intended that all divine influences should centre and harmonize, in the development and growth of the human spirit into the likeness of God, is made the scene of discord and strife. It is no wonder, that from such a nursery proceeded such characters as are some of those described in the subsequent family history of Jacob.

VV. 25-28. The fourteen years of service for Leah and Rachel being now ended, Jacob asks to be released, and to be allowed to depart in peace with his wives and children, having faithfully performed the required service.

If now, etc. The implied request is more forcibly urged than if expressed in words.

I have divined. To *divine* means to ascertain what is secret or obscure, or lies yet in the future, by omens, incantations, and the like. See ch. 44 : 5, 15. It also means (as it perhaps does here) to conjecture such things by one's own sagacity and observation. I perceive by omens, may be the meaning here.

VV. 29, 30. Jacob declines any stipulated wages, and claims instead a share in the annual increase of the flocks. After forcibly stating, in these verses, how greatly Laban's estate had

my footstep; and now, when shall I also do aught for my own house?

31 And he said: What shall I give thee? And Jacob said: Thou shalt not give me anything. If thou wilt do for me 32 this thing, I will again feed thy flock and keep it. I will pass through all thy flock to-day, removing from thence every one that is speckled and spotted, and every one that is brown among the sheep and spotted and speckled among 33 the goats. And such shall be my wages. And my righteousness shall answer for me in time to come, when it shall come before thee concerning my wages; every one that is not speckled and spotted among the goats and brown among the sheep, that is stolen with me.

34 And Laban said: Behold, let it be according to thy word.

35 And he removed on that day the he-goats that were striped and spotted, and all the she-goats that were speckled and spotted, every one in which there was any white,

---

increased under his care, while no provision had been made for his own family, he proposes terms more just to himself in the following verses.

At my footst p; as they followed my guidance, wherever I led them.

V. 32. In the East, white is the normal color of sheep, very few being black or brown, while that of the goat is dark or gray, seldom white or spotted with white. Hence Jac b's proposal, to take for his wages such of the annual increase as were not of the normal color, seemed to be a very moderate one, and was readily accepted by Laban.

Such (namely, the portion of the flock so marked in the future*) *shall be my wages;* for the year's service, is meant, as appears from the subsequent narrative in the thirty-seventh and following verses. It is plain that a division was made every year; and hence Laban's repeated change of the terms of the contract, complained of by Jacob in ch. 31 : 6, 7.

V. 33. The rectitude of my conduct shall answer for me (on my part); and if any other than are now designated shall be found in my flocks, let it be accounted stolen with me (that is, the same as stolen), and be restored to you as its rightful owner.

Or the meaning may be : My righteou-ness (the righteousness of my cause) shall answer for me; that is, I will trust to it for my reward. Any other than are now designated shall be accounted as stolen with me, and as belonging to you the rightful owner, the remainder being mine.

The latter accords with the peculiar style of Oriental bargaining, and is probably the true meaning.

When it shall come before thee concerning my wages; when the subject of my wages shall come before the · for adjustment, from year to year.

VV. 35, 36. *And he;* namely, Laban (acting in conjunction with Jacob, see v. 32), as is evident from the last clause of this verse and v. 36.

---

* Not the portion already so marked, and now to be removed from the flock. For, in the first place, Jacob received nothing from Laban (v. 31, "thou shalt not give me anything"); and secondly, the portion thus separated Laban "gave into the hand of his sons" (v. 35). Jacob's wages, moreover, were not to be paid in advance, but from the increase of the flock at the end of the season.

and all the brown among the sheep, and gave them into
⁸⁶ the hand of his sons. And he put three days' journey between himself and Jacob; and Jacob fed the flock of Laban that remained.

³⁷ And Jacob took rods of green poplar, and hazel, and plane-tree, and peeled white streaks in them, laying bare ³⁸ the white that was on the rods. And the rods which he peeled he placed in the troughs, the watering-troughs of water where the flocks came to drink, before the flocks. ³⁹ And they conceived when they came to drink. And the flocks conceived before the rods; and they brought forth striped, speckled, and spotted.

⁴⁰ And the lambs Jacob parted; and he set the face of the flock toward the striped and all the brown, in the flock of Laban. And he put his own droves by themselves, and put them not to the flock of Laban.

⁴¹ And it came to pass, whenever the flocks that were strong conceived, that Jacob laid the rods before the eyes of the flocks in the troughs, that they might conceive by ⁴² the rods. And when the flocks were feeble, he laid them not; and the feebler were Laban's, and the stronger Jacob's.

Gave them into the hand of his sons; that they might be kept separate from the rest, since those produced with such marks in future were to belong to Jacob. For the same reason (v. 36) "he put three days' journey between himself and Jacob."

VV. 37–40. In order to enlarge his own share of the annual increase, Jacob avails himself of a natural law of reproduction in animals, affecting the color of their offspring, which he had learned by observation, or from others. The uses he made of this knowledge for his own advantage are called by Dr. Chalmers (Scripture Readings, i., 60) "sneaking artifices." It may be so; but business men, in most callings, seem to think it fair and honorable to make use of their superior knowledge for their own benefit. There is, however, a wide range in the choice of means; and in the selection of these men betray their differences of character. But the circumstances of the case are also to be taken into account. In this case, Jacob was dealing with one whose selfishness knew no bounds, and scrupled at no artifice or trick (compare ch. 29 : 23), and who repeatedly changed the terms of this contract in order to gain something for himself; see ch. 31 : 7, 8. One can not read the statement in ch. 31 : 38–42, without feeling that there is much to excuse, if it does not justify, the use made by Jacob of his superior skill.

V. 40. The expression is very brief, and the sense somewhat obscure. The meaning seems to be, that Jacob parted the lambs, the abnormal in color from the rest, and set the face of the flock toward the former; the clause, "in the flock of Laban," being explanatory of "face of the flock," limiting it to the part that remained to Laban.

Put his own droves by themselves, etc. He drove his own cattle to pasture and to watering by themselves, apart from Laban's, that their increase might not be affected by the normal colors that prevailed in what fell to Laban's share.

VV. 41, 42. Another use of this same device. Jacob employed it only when the more vigorous

⁴³ And the man increased exceedingly; and he had numerous flocks, and maid-servants, and men-servants, and camels, and asses.

¹ AND he heard the words of Laban's sons, saying: Jacob has taken all that belonged to our father; and of that which belonged to our father has he made all this wealth. ² And Jacob saw the countenance of Laban, and behold, it was not toward him as formerly. ³ And Jehovah said to Jacob: Return to the land of thy fathers, and to thy kindred; and I will be with thee. ⁴ And Jacob sent and called Rachel and Leah to the field, ⁵ to his flock. And he said to them: I see your father's countenance, that it is not toward me as formerly. But ⁶ the God of my father has been with me. And ye yourselves know that with all my power I have served your ⁷ father. And your father has deceived me, and changed my wages ten times; but God suffered him not to do ⁸ me harm. If he said thus: The speckled shall be thy wages, then all the flock bore speckled. And if he said thus: The striped shall be thy wages, then all the flock ⁹ bore striped. And God took away the cattle of your father, and gave them to me. ¹⁰ And it came to pass at the time that the flock conceived,

---

of the flocks were brought to the watering place, omitting it when the feebler flocks came, and thus secured for himself the best part of the annual increase.

V. 43. *The man increased.* Jacob himself, in ch. 31 : 9, ascribes this to the special favor of God. See the remarks on ch. 31 : 10-13, the last paragraph.

Ch. 31. Jacob's flight from Padan-aram. Covenant between Jacob and Laban.

VV. 1-3. Jacob is now divinely directed (v. 3) to return to his home. It was evident, however, from what is stated in vv. 1, 2, that he would not be allowed to go in peace, with the wealth which he had acquired. He therefore proposes to depart secretly; and takes an opportunity (v. 10) when Laban and his servants were fully occupied, and probably would not be informed immediately of his movements.

I will be with thee. Jacob is thus assured of the divine presence and protection; but he does not, on that account, neglect the proper precautions for securing his own safety. He may have thought it well to act on the same principle, after the suggestion made to him in the dream (v. 10).

V. 4. The movement he was about to undertake required secrecy, and he therefore sends for them to the field, where he could consult with them in private, and mature his plans, without risk of disclosure.

VV. 7, 8. We have here a further development of Jacob's relations with Laban. It is evident that, in dealing with such a man, the odds were greatly against him.

VV. 10-13. The dream first related (in v. 10) seems to have occurred near the commence-

that I lifted up my eyes, and saw in a dream, and behold, the he-goats that leaped upon the flock were striped, speckled, and piebald.

¹¹ And an angel of God said to me in a dream: Jacob! ¹² And I said: Here am I. And he said: Lift up now thine eyes, and see all the he-goats that leap upon the flock, striped, speckled, and piebald; for I have seen all that ¹³ Laban does to thee. I am the God of Bethel, where thou didst anoint a pillar, where thou didst vow to me a vow. Now arise, go forth from the land, and return to the land of thy kindred.

¹⁴ And Rachel and Leah answered and said to him: Have ¹⁵ we yet any portion or inheritance in our father's house? Are we not regarded by him as aliens? For he has sold ¹⁶ us, and has also quite devoured our money. For all the wealth which God has taken from our father, that is ours and our children's. Now then, all that God has said to thee, do.

¹⁷ And Jacob rose up, and set his sons and his wives upon ¹⁸ the camels. And he brought away all his cattle, and all his goods which he had gathered, the cattle of his getting, which he had gathered in Padan-aram, to go to Isaac his father, to the land of Canaan.

---

ment, if not before, of his final and successful arrangement with Laban. It may have suggested his devices, or have been suggested by them; or the same train of waking thoughts may have suggested both.*

The second dream is of higher significance, and occurred near the close of his connection with Laban; see the last sentence of v. 13.

In relating this to his wives, to account to them for his successful competition with Laban he says nothing of the means by which he himself sought to insure it. The dream implies no judgment on these means; and only reminds him, that it was the divine favor that thwarted and punished the grasping and cruel avarice of Laban.†

V. 15. *Aliens;* as if not of his own family and kindred.

Has quite devoured our money; instead of bestowing on us any portion of what we brought him by our marriage.

V. 17. *The camels;* the definite article denoting that they are those already spoken of in ch. 30: 43.

* *Piebald;* sprinkled over with spots, differing from *speckled* (v. 33) in their size, the latter denoting smaller spots or specks, and from *spotted* (v. 33) in their number and distribution, the latter not necessarily implying more than one.

† Whatever judgment may be formed of Jacob's own conduct, the reader of the narrative will admit the justice of his complaint, when he says (in v. 42): "Thou wouldst now have sent me away empty."

19 And Laban had gone to shear his sheep; and Rachel
20 stole the teraphim that belonged to her father. And Jacob stole away unawares to Laban the Aramite, in that he told him not that he was about to flee.
21 And he fled, he and all that he had. And he rose up, and passed over the river; and he set his face toward mount Gilead.
22 And it was told Laban on the third day, that Jacob had
23 fled. And he took his brethren with him, and pursued after him seven days' journey; and he overtook him in mount Gilead.

V. 20. *Heb.*, stole the heart of Laban the Aramite

V. 19. Rachel, taking advantage of her father's temporary absence, stole the *teraphim* that belonged to him.

Teraphim were small images, kept as domestic idols or household gods. This was one of the practices of heathen superstition often met with in the Old Testament. Among the Hebrews, it was not so much a form of idolatry as a corrupting superstition engrafted on the true religion. Laban, in v. 30, calls these images his gods; and in ch. 35 : 4, "strange gods" are spoken of, in connection with another superstitious observance, as being in Jacob's family after his return to his home in Palestine. It is not necessary to suppose that they were strictly objects of worship. They were held in superstitious veneration as dispensers of good fortune, and as a protection against evil influences. They were also consulted as oracles; Zech. 10 : 2, properly, "the teraphim have spoken vanity."*

V. 20 (margin). *Stole the heart of Laban;* that is, put his sagacity and foresight at fault (heart in Hebrew denoting the understanding and reason), robbing him of it, so to speak, by his own superior craft.

The heart being, in the Hebrew conception, the seat of feeling as well as of understanding, this phrase may also have (as in 2 Sam. 15 : 6) the same sense as it has in English.†

V. 21. *The river.* So the Euphrates, from the importance of its geographical position and political relations, is often mentioned without further designation. See Ex. 23 : 31; Josh. 24 : 2, 3 (common English version "the flood," properly "the river"); 2 Sam. 10 : 16; 1 Kings 4 : 24; 1 Chron. 19 : 16; Ezra 4 : 10, 16, 8 : 36; Neh. 2 : 7, 9, 3 : 7; Isaiah 7 : 20.

Mount Gilead. Not any single eminence is here meant, but the mountain tract of that name. The route taken by Jacob on his return is clearly indicated.‡

V. 23. *His brethren;* the kindred of his own tribe. They were accompanied, doubtless, by their servants and dependents, and together were too numerous to be successfully resisted by Jacob. Compare v. 29.

* In the common English version they are called *teraphim* in Judges 17 : 5, 18 : 14, 17, 18, 20; Hosea 3 : 4; and improperly *images* (or *image*) in Gen. 31 : 19 (margin, *teraphim*) 34, 35 ; 1 Sam. 19 : 13, 16; 2 Kings 23 : 24; Ezek. 21 : 21 (margin, *teraphim*); and *idolatry* in 1 Sam. 15 : 23; and *idols* in Zech. 10 : 2 (margin, *teraphim*). As another object, quite different from this, is designated by the Hebrew word properly rendered *image*, the two should not be confounded by using the same English word for both.

† Lange, in his commentary, takes it in this sense here; understanding by *heart* an object of affection, and referring to what Laban says in vv. 26, 28. But though Laban might affect the sentimental, it is not so probable that the sacred writer, who is speaking here, would give him credit for it.

‡ "Jacob, having passed the Euphrates, . . . struck across the desert by the great fountain at Palmyra, then traversed the eastern part of the plain of Damascus, and the Plateau of Bashan, and entered Gilead from the northeast."—*Smith's Bible Dictionary,* art. Gilead.

24 And God came to Laban the Aramite in a dream by night, and said to him: Take heed to thyself, that thou speak not to Jacob either good or bad.
25 And Laban came up with Jacob. And Jacob pitched his tent in the mountain; and Laban with his brethren pitched in mount Gilead.
26 And Laban said to Jacob: What hast thou done, that thou didst steal away unawares to me, and bear off my
27 daughters, as captives of the sword? Wherefore didst thou flee away secretly, and steal away from me? And thou didst not tell me, that I might send thee away with
28 mirth and songs, with tabret and harp; and didst not suffer me to kiss my sons and my daughters. Now hast
29 thou done foolishly. It is in the power of my hand to do you harm. But the God of your father spoke to me yesternight, saying: Take heed to thyself, that thou speak not to Jacob either good or bad.
30 And now, if thou wouldst needs go, because thou greatly longedst for thy father's house, wherefore didst thou steal my gods?
31 And Jacob answered and said to Laban: Because I was afraid; for I said: Lest thou take thy daughters from me
32 by force. With whomsoever thou shalt find thy gods, let him not live. Before our brethren discern for thyself what

---

V. 24. *Either good or bad;* leaving him no discretion or choice in the matter, and forbidding him to interfere with Jacob in any way, for good or ill.

V. 25. *The mountain;* a particular eminence, rendered memorable by the transaction recorded in vv. 44–49; compare v. 54.

In mount Gilead; in the same mountain tract, and in the vicinity of the eminence on which Jacob had encamped.

V. 27. *Tabret and harp;* as in Job 21:12, the accompaniment of mirth and festivity.

V. 29. He uses the plural, *you, your,* connecting Jacob with his family, and particularly with his sons, to whom, as well as to Jacob, Isaac held the relation of father in the Hebrew use of the word.

V. 31. *I said: Lest thou take,* etc. It would be rhetorically more correct to say, *Lest he take.* But such graceful negligence of mere form is characteristic of the unstudied manner of the sacred writer.

V. 32. *Let him not live.* He knew not, as stated in the last clause of the verse, that Rachel was the guilty one. As head of all his household, and living under no civil government, he was the sole magistrate, and vested with full power to restrain or punish crime. The expression means no more than that he would screen the offender from no deserved punishment.

Before our brethren, namely, the friends of both parties; that should Laban find anything belonging to him it might be claimed and restored in their presence, and in failure of this Jacob's innocence be vindicated. Compare v. 37.

is with me, and take it to thee. For Jacob knew not that Rachel stole them.

33 And Laban went into Jacob's tent, and into Leah's tent, and into the tent of the two maid-servants, and found them not. And he went out of Leah's tent, and came into the tent of Rachel.

34 And Rachel took the teraphim and put them in the camel's saddle, and sat upon them. And Laban felt 35 through all the tent, and found them not. And she said to her father: Let it not displease my lord that I can not rise up before thee; for the custom of women is upon me. And he searched, and found not the teraphim.

36 And Jacob was angry, and chided Laban. And Jacob answered, and said to Laban: What is my trespass, what 37 is my sin, that thou dost hotly pursue after me? For thou hast felt through all my goods; what hast thou found of all thy household goods? Set it here before my brethren and thy brethren, and they shall judge between us both.

38 These twenty years have I been with thee; thy ewes and thy she-goats have not cast their young, and the rams 39 of thy flock I have not eaten. What was torn by beasts I brought not to thee; I myself bore the loss of it. Of my hand didst thou require it, what was stolen by day, 40 and what was stolen by night. Thus I was; by day heat

---

V. 34. A saddle, so constructed as to be easy and comfortable for women on a journey, would be a convenient seat for their use in the tent, while halting for the night or for a few days' repose. Such are now in use in Eastern countries.*

Felt through. The word is purposely chosen to express the minuteness of his search, groping with his hands where he could not see. One can not help a feeling of satisfaction, that his unmanly impertinence was thwarted.

V. 36. *Answered;* namely, to the charge of theft (in v. 30) and the attempt to prove it by search.

VV. 33 and following. Still more to expose the unreasonableness and injustice of Laban's conduct, in thus pursuing after him as a thief and a robber, Jacob recounts his own faithful labors and the hardships he endured in Laban's service, and the attempts to defraud him of his just reward.

V. 40. In Eastern climates, the intolerable heat by day is often followed by as excessive cold at night.†

---

* See the article *Furniture*, added by Dr. Hackett to the American edition of *Smith's Bible Dictionary.*

† " It happened to me frequently to need all the precaution I could adopt, in order to guard against the cold at night, even when the heat of the preceding day had been as great as could well be borne."—*Dr. Hackett, Illustrations of Scripture,* 8th ed., p. 136.

consumed me, and cold by night; and my sleep fled from my eyes.

⁴¹ Thus have I been twenty years in thy house. I served thee fourteen years for thy two daughters, and six years for thy flock; and thou hast changed my wages ten times.

⁴² Unless the God of my father, the God of Abraham, and the fear of Isaac, had been for me, surely thou wouldst now have sent me away empty. My affliction and the toil of my hands God has seen, and he rebuked it yesternight.

⁴³ And Laban answered, and said to Jacob: The daughters are my daughters, and the sons are my sons, and the flocks are my flocks, and all that thou seest, it is mine. And what can I do this day for my daughters, for these, or for their sons whom they have borne?

⁴⁴ Now therefore come, let us make a covenant, I and thou; and let it be for a witness between me and thee.

⁴⁵ And Jacob took a stone, and set it up for a pillar.

⁴⁶ And Jacob said to his brethren: Gather stones. And they took stones, and made a heap; and they ate there upon

⁴⁷ the heap. And Laban called it Jegar-sahadutha; and Jacob called it Galeed.

⁴⁸ And Laban said: This heap is a witness between me and thee this day. Therefore its name was called Galeed;

⁴⁹ and Mizpah, for he said: Jehovah watch between me and

⁵⁰ thee, when we shall be hidden one from the other. If thou shalt afflict my daughters, or if thou shalt take wives beside my daughters, no man is with us; see, God is witness between me and thee.

V. 42. *Fear*, by a common and natural metonymy, is put for the object feared; He whom Isaac feared, regarded with reverence and holy fear.

Had been for me; as the same Hebrew form and sentiment are expressed in Psalm 56:9, "God is for me."

V. 46. Eating together was a testimony of friendship, and a mutual pledge of it. The heap of stones, on which this was done, stood as a perpetual witness of the pledge.

V. 47. *Jegar-sahadutha*, in the Aramæan tongue, a sister dialect of the Hebrew spoken by Laban t' e Aramite, means *mound of testimony*. *Galeed* has the same meaning in Hebrew.

VV. 49, 50. *Mizpah* means a watching, or a place of watching, a watch-tower.

When we shall be hidden (by distance) *one from the other*, and neither will be able to watch the other. *No man is with us;* can then be present with us both, to act as witness for both.

What is related in this paragraph (vv. 48-50) may have taken place at a meeting of Jacob and Laban by themselves, apart from all others. There would then be a peculiar and solemn significance in the words, "No man is with us; see, God is witness between me and thee."

⁵¹ And Laban said to Jacob: Behold this heap, and behold ⁵² the pillar, which I have cast between me and thee. This heap be witness, and the pillar be witness, that neither will I pass over this heap to thee, nor wilt thou pass over ⁵³ this heap and this pillar to me, for harm. The God of Abraham and the God of Nahor shall judge between us; the God of their father. And Jacob swore by the fear of his father Isaac. ⁵⁴ And Jacob offered sacrifice on the mountain; and he called his brethren to eat bread. And they ate bread, and passed the night in the mountain. ⁵⁵ And Laban rose early in the morning, and kissed his sons and his daughters, and blessed them. And Laban went away, and returned to his place.

¹ And Jacob went on his way. And angels of God met ² him. And Jacob said, when he saw them: This is God's host. And he called the name of that place Mahanaim.

V. 53. *The G..d of their father.* The addition of this, after the verb, seems intended to intimate that by "the God of Abraham" and "the God of Nahor" is meant also "the God of their father," as being one and the same.* Influenced by filial feeling, Jacob swore "by the fear of his father Isaac" (*fear*, as in v. 42), meaning, by Him whom his father Isaac feared.

V. 55. Laban had given good cause for what is said of him in vv. 14, 15. But the most selfish natures have the instinct of natural affection, and are often deeply moved at a final parting with its objects.

Ch. 32. Jacob proceeds on his way; is met by angels. One in the form of man wrestles with him.

VV. 1, 2. *Went on his way;* southward, toward the river Jabbok (v. 22).

On his way, he receives an assurance that he is journeying under the divine protect'on. In what manner he was made aware of the presence of this celestial convoy is not stated. It may have been in a night vision, as in ch. 28 : 12 (for "met him" implies no more than that it occurred on the way), or in the manner related in 2 Kings 6 : 17.† In some way he received assurance once more of what was divinely promised him (ch. 31 : 3) "I will be with thee."

Mahanaim; meaning, two camps (or, two hosts), that of the angels encamping near him for his protection, and his own.

---

* If so, the true God continued to be acknowledged among the immediate ancestry of Abraham; and we are to understand Joshua 24 : 2, as meaning, that with this knowledge were connected idolatrous superstitions and practices, such as prevailed in Laban's family (v. 19, and note), and even in the family of Jacob, ch. 35 : 2, 4.

Some think that Laban, with his confused notions of God, here confounds the God of Abraham with the false gods worshiped by Nahor and their father; and that Jacob, to avoid sharing in this error, swears by the God of his own father Isaac. But this seems like refining, and not very happily, on the simple directness of the sacred writer's statement.

† "Jacob beheld them during his march (?), and therefore when he was awake; not inwardly, but externally to himself or above him, but whether with the bodily or the spiritual eye (compare 2 Kings 6 : 17) can not be determined."—*Keil, Commentar über die Genesis,* 2te Aufl., p. 225.

³ And Jacob sent messengers before him to Esau his ⁴ brother, to the land of Seir, the country of Edom. And he commanded them, saying: Thus shall ye say to my lord, to Esau, thy servant Jacob says thus: I have sojourn-
⁵ ed with Laban, and remained till now. And I have oxen and asses, flocks, and men-servants and maid-servants; and I have sent to tell my lord, that I may find favor in thy sight.
⁶ And the messengers returned to Jacob, saying: We came to thy brother, to Esau; and indeed he is coming to meet thee, and four hundred men with him.
⁷ And Jacob was greatly afraid, and he was distressed. And he divided the people that were with him, and the flocks, and the herds, and the camels, into two bands.
⁸ And he said: If Esau shall come to the one band, and smite it, then the other band that is left will escape.
⁹ And Jacob said: O God of my father Abraham, and God of my father Isaac, Jehovah, who said to me, Return to thy land and to thy kindred, and I will deal well with
¹⁰ thee. I am not worthy of the least of all the mercies, and of all the truth, which thou hast shown to thy servant; for with my staff I passed over this Jordan, and now I
¹¹ have become two bands. Deliver me, I pray, from the hand of my brother, from the hand of Esau; for I fear him, lest he shall come and smite me, the mother with the
¹² children. And thou thyself hast said, I will surely deal well with thee, and will make thy seed as the sand of the sea, which can not be numbered for multitude.

V. 3. *Seir.* See ch. 14 : 6, and note. *Edom* (ch. 25 : 30) was the later name of this region.*
V. 4. *I have sojourned with Laban,* a stranger in a foreign land, away from home and country, is his claim on a brother's sympathy and forgiveness.
V. 6. *Four hundred men with him.* Compare ch. 27 : 40, "By thy sword shalt thou live."
V. 10. *With my staff;* with nothing but my staff, that being all my wealth.
Over this Jordan; now not far distant, and reminding him of the different circumstances in which he crossed it then and now.
V. 11. *The mother with the children;* not sparing even the mother and her tender offspring. This addition defines his meaning in the preceding clause, and shows that his anxiety was chiefly for them.

---

* "The narrow mountainous tract (about a hundred miles long by twenty broad) extending along the eastern side of the Arabah, from the northern end of the gulf of Elath to near the southern end of the Dead Sea."—*Smith's Bible Dictionary,* art. Edom.

13 And he lodged there that night. And he took of that which had come into his hand a present for Esau his 14 brother; two hundred she-goats and twenty he-goats, two 15 hundred ewes and twenty rams, thirty milch camels and their colts, forty heifers and ten steers, twenty she-asses, 16 and ten young asses. And he gave them into the hand of his servants, each drove by itself. And he said to his servants: Pass over before me, and put a space between drove and drove. 17 And he commanded the foremost, saying: When Esau my brother shall meet thee, and ask thee, saying: Whose art thou, and whither art thou going, and whose are these 18 before thee? Then thou shalt say: Thy servant Jacob's; it is a present sent to my lord, to Esau; and behold, he also is behind us. 19 And he commanded the second, also the third, also all that followed the droves, saying: After this manner shall 20 ye speak to Esau, when ye find him. And say also: Behold, thy servant Jacob is behind us. For he said: I will appease him with the present that goes before me, and afterward I will see his face. Perhaps he will accept me.

V. 13. *Or, which came at his hand* V. 20. *Heb., I will cover his face with the present*

V. 13. *Into his hand;* into his possession. The Hebrew may also be translated (as in the margin) *at his hand;* namely, by his side, with him.
V. 15. *Young asses;* full grown, and fit for bearing burdens and for other labor, as in Isaiah 30 : 6 (English version correctly, "young asses"), and v. 24 (English version, "young asses," properly *that till the ground*), and for riding, as in Judges 10 : 4 (English version, "ass colts").
VV. 16-20. Here again Jacob shows his worldly wisdom. The disposition of this princely present in several droves, following one another at intervals (v. 16), was such as to repeat the favorable impression made by each, as they successively came before Esau accompanied with a conciliatory message. The announcement made with the first, and repeated with each succeeding one, "thy servant Jacob is behind us," would give time for reflection and kindly impressions, before their meeting.†
V. 20 (margin). *Will cover his face;* that is, will appease him. See the note on ch. 20 : 16, first paragraph.
V. 20. *Will accept me.* To accept one means to receive him graciously, and deal kindly with him; if as a suitor for some favor (ch. 19 : 21), it implies that his request is favorably heard and granted; if as an intercessor for others (Job 42 : 8, 9), that he is graciously heard on their behalf.

* Not *foals* (in this passage) as in the common English version, for then the number would be the same as that of the dams.
† The number of those who had charge of the present, and successively made their appearance with their several messages, was also an expression of consideration and respect for the personage to whom it was delivered.

21 And the present went over before him; and he himself lodged that night in the encampment.
22 And he rose up that night, and took his two wives, and his two maid-servants, and his eleven sons, and passed
23 over the ford of Jabbok. And he took them, and sent them over the brook, and sent over that which he had.
24 And Jacob was left alone. And a man wrestled with
25 him till the rising of the dawn. And he saw that he prevailed not against him; and he touched the hollow of his thigh, and the hollow of Jacob's thigh was out of joint as
26 he wrestled with him. And he said: Let me go, for the dawn is rising. And he said: I will not let thee go, ex-

---

V. 22. *That night;* the same that is mentioned in v. 13.
Passed over; in the person of his family is meant, for he himself remained behind in the place of the encampment (vv. 21, 24).*

VV. 24–32. The mysterious occurrence here related had a deep significance for Jacob's subsequent character and mission, as well as in its wider influence in the sphere of revelation. The errors and weaknesses in Jacob's spiritual character required to be corrected and strengthened; and the wisdom of God selected the means best adapted to his spiritual state.

Left alone, in the silence of the night, he is visited by a celestial being in human form (compare ch. 18), with whom he maintains a struggle till the dawn.

Three points are to be noted here: First, the celestial visitor presents himself to Jacob as an antagonist, but only to test him. Secondly, he does not prevail against him (v. 25 and note), and yet by a touch (or stroke) disables and renders him helpless. Thirdly, he declares Jacob to be the successful contestant, saying: "thou hast striven . . . and hast prevailed."

The divine lesson is, that Jacob in his own strength is helpless, and in his weakness is strong; that he prevails in that importunity of prayer, "I will not let thee go except thou bless me," which has become the watchword of the church in all ages.

Some would resolve this account into a merely figurative representation of the power of prayer, under the striking and familiar image of wrestling for a prize. To many minds this view may seem to be the most reasonable and instructive. But to the view itself there are the following objections: First, so purely spiritual a conception of the scene does not accord with the stage of spiritual development to which Jacob had attained, as is clear from his previous record. Secondly, it is not in harmony with God's method of dealing with men, at this early stage in the spiritual development of the race, as is shown in all the records of this book. Thirdly, it does not agree with the terms of the account, especially the evident allusion to a physical disability inflicted at this time (vv. 25, 31).

V. 24. *A man;* one in human form. Compare v. 30, and ch. 18 : 1, 2.

V. 25. *That he prevailed not against him;* that Jacob maintained the contest, and would not be overcome. It was a trial, not of physical force merely, but of moral purpose and persistency.

Hollow of his thigh; referring to the hip joint, the position of which is indicated by the external hollow of the thigh. The anatomical reference to the *socket* of the thigh, which receives the ball of the thigh-bone, may be intended as supposed by some, but is not so probable.

V. 26. *The dawn is rising;* announcing the return of day and of its appropriate duties.
It may be true also, that this mysterious being did not choose, on this occasion, to manifest himself otherwise than he had done in the solemn stillness and darkness of the night.

---

* "Jacob, as chief director of all, remained on the spot, in order to see that no one was left behind, and at last he was there alone."—*Knobel, die Genesis erklärt,* 2te Aufl., p. 258.

²⁷ cept thou bless me. And he said to him: What is thy ²⁸ name? And he said: Jacob. And he said: Thy name shall no more be called Jacob, but Israel; for thou hast ²⁹ striven with God, and with men, and hast prevailed. And Jacob asked and said: Tell, I pray, thy name. And he said: Wherefore is this, that thou askest for my name? And he blessed him there.

³⁰ And Jacob called the name of the place Peniel; for I have seen God face to face, and my soul was delivered. ³¹ And the sun rose upon him as he passed over Penuel. And he limped on his thigh. ³² Therefore the children of Israel do not eat of the sinew of the thigh, which is on the hollow of the thigh, unto this day; because he touched the hollow of Jacob's thigh, the sinew of the thigh.

¹ AND Jacob lifted up his eyes and saw, and behold, Esau was coming, and with him four hundred men. And he divided the children to Leah, and to Rachel, and to the ² two maid-servants. And he put the maid-servants and their children foremost, and Leah and her children after, ³ and Rachel and Joseph last. And he himself passed on before them; and he bowed himself to the earth seven times, until he came near to his brother.

V. 28. *Israel;* meaning, one who strives with God, and (by implication) has power with him.
And with men; that is, as he had already striven successfully with men.
V. 29. *Wherefore is this, that thou askest for my name?* The refusal, implied in the question thus emphatically expressed, accords with the mysterious reserve in which the character of this personage is vailed. Compare the note on v. 26, second paragraph.
VV. 30, 31. *Peniel;* meaning, face of God. *Penuel* (v. 31); another form of the word, with the same meaning.
My soul was delivered. See the remarks on ch. 16: 13, 14, third paragraph, and the references there given. On the contrary, compare the influence of a purer faith and more intimate walk with God, in the case of Abraham, ch. 19.
V. 32. *Do not eat of the sinew of the thigh.* No further notice of this observance occurs in the Old Testament. But in the Jewish traditions (compare Matt. 15: 2, Mark 7: 3), as collected in the *Talmud* written after the time of Christ, minute directions are given respecting it.
Ch. 33. Meeting of Jacob and Esau. Jacob comes into the land of Canaan. He purchases a piece of ground, and erects an altar to GOD THE GOD OF ISRAEL.
V. 1. *With him four hundred men.* See the reference in the note on ch. 32: 6.
Divided the children to Leah, etc.; to each her own, so disposing them that those dearest to him would be least exposed, and have opportunity to escape in case of danger.

CHAP. XXXIII.   GENESIS.

4 And Esau ran to meet him, and embraced him, and fell on his neck, and kissed him; and they wept.
5 And he lifted up his eyes, and saw the women and the children; and he said: Who are these to thee? And he said: The children whom God has graciously given thy servant.
6 And the maid-servants came near, they and their children, and they bowed themselves. And Leah also and her
7 children came near, and bowed themselves. And afterward Joseph and Rachel came near, and bowed themselves.
8 And he said: What meanest thou by all this drove that I met? And he said: To find favor in the sight of my
9 lord. And Esau said: I have abundance, my brother; keep what thou hast for thyself.
10 And Jacob said: Nay, I pray, if now I have found favor in thy sight, take my present from my hand; for therefore have I seen thy face, as if I saw the face of God,
11 and thou wast favorable to me. Take, I pray, my blessing that is brought to thee; because God has dealt graciously with me, and because I have all. And he pressed him and he took it.
12 And he said: Let us break up and go, and I will go before thee.

V. 4. All Jacob's precautions proved to be unnecessary, and only showed how timid a counselor is conscious ill desert.

Impulsive and generous in his nature, prompt to avenge and to forget an injury, Esau sees in him only the twin partner of his birth, the companion of his childhood's sports, the only and the long lost brother.

He was a model freebooter; and many such have given a startling brilliancy to the annals of that free-handed class of men, as free with what belongs to others as with their own. Natural affection, generous impulses, readiness to overlook injuries, scorn of revenge, have distinguished many who were the terror and scourge of their kind.

V. 5. *Who are these to thee?* That is, in what relation do they stand to thee?

VV. 8, 9. Jacob, by his mode of address ("my lord"), is careful not to remind Esau of the pre-eminence awarded to himself ("I have made him thy lord," ch. 27:37). On the contrary, Esau addresses him by the fraternal title, "my brother."

VV. 10, 11. Jacob pleads the favor already shown him by Esau, as the ground of a yet further favor, the acceptance of his expression of grateful joy.

To "behold the face of God" is to be received by him with favor (Job 33:26), as the "hiding of his face" is the withholding of his favor; Deut. 31:17; Job 13:24; Psalm 88:14.

My blessing; as being accompanied with fraternal greeting and well-wishes. Compare this use of the word in 1 Sam. 25:27, and 30:26 (properly, "Behold a blessing for you").

I have all; all things, namely of every kind, and nothing is wanting to me.

V. 12. *Let us break up;* in allusion to the breaking up of an encampment.

¹³ And he said to him: My lord knows that the children are tender, and the flocks and herds that give suck are with me; and if they drive them hard one day, all the ¹⁴ flock will die. Let my lord, I pray, pass on before his servant; and I will lead on in my slow way, at the pace of the cattle that are before me, and at the pace of the children, until I shall come to my lord, to Seir. ¹⁵ And Esau said: Let me now leave with thee some of the people who are about me. And he said: What need of this? Let me find favor in the sight of my lord. ¹⁶ ¹⁷ And Esau returned that day on his way to Seir. And Jacob removed to Succoth; and he built for himself a house, and for his cattle he made booths. Therefore the name of the place is called Succoth. ¹⁸ And Jacob came safe to the city of Shechem, which is in the land of Canaan, when he came from Padan-aram; ¹⁹ and he pitched his tent before the city. And he bought the part of the field where he stretched his tent, from the

---

V. 18. *Or,* came to Shalem, a city of Shechem

V. 13. Jacob courteously declines the proffered escort, knowing that he is safer without it. *The children;* compare the remark on v. 14. second paragraph.
The flocks and herds that give suck; such being kept in separate droves, for greater security and for special care.
V. 14. *In my slow way* is characteristic of the movement of herdsmen and their families, in distinction from the rapid unencumbered march of Esau and his men.
At the pace of the children. Jacob's own children rode on the camels (ch. 31 : 17); but there were others in the train belonging to his household servants and his numerous field-servants.
Until I shall come to my lord, to Seir. From this point, so far east of the Jordan, he would naturally proceed by the nearest route on the east side of the Dead Sea, if he intended to return to Beer-sheba, which he left twenty years before (ch. 23 : 10).
V. 17. *Removed;* compare the remark on ch. 12 : 9.
A house; more durable than the frail movable tent, and a better protection against storms and variations of heat and cold.
Booths, "of green boughs and branches interwoven, as a shelter from the sun." *Succoth;* meaning, booths.
The position of Succoth is not satisfactorily determined, and therefore the route by which Jacob came to Shechem (v. 18) is uncertain. There is no reason for supposing that he deceived his brother in regard to the route he intended to take. He remained at Succoth for a considerable time, as is evident from v. 17, and after an interval of unknown length (v. 1) resumed his course westward. In the mean time he may have changed his purpose, if he at first intended to pass east of the Dead Sea to southern Palestine.
V. 18 (margin). *To Shalem, a city of Shechem.* So the passage is understood by some, but on insufficient grounds.*
V. 19. *The part of the field* (that portion of the open field, outside of the inclosed city) on which he stretched his tent. Compare Josh. 24 : 32, and John 4 : 5.

---

* See the article *Shalem,* in *Smith's Bible Dictionary.*

hand of the sons of Hamor, father of Shechem, for a hun-
20 dred kesitas. And he erected there an altar, and called it
El-Elohe-Israel.

1   AND Dinah the daughter of Leah, whom she bore to
Jacob, went out to see the daughters of the land.
2   And Shechem, son of Hamor the Hivite, a prince of the
land, saw her; and he took her, and lay with her, and
3 humbled her. And his soul cleaved to Dinah the daughter
of Jacob, and he loved the damsel, and he spoke kindly to
4 the damsel. And Shechem spoke to Hamor his father,
saying : Take for me this damsel for a wife.
5   And Jacob heard that he had defiled Dinah his daughter.
And his sons were with his cattle in the field ; and Jacob
held his peace until their coming.
6   And Hamor, father of Shechem, went out to Jacob to
speak with him.
7   And the sons of Jacob came from the field, when they
heard it. And the men were grieved, and they were very
angry, because he committed folly in Israel in lying with

A *kesita* (pronounced *keseeta*) was a certain weight of gold or silver,* current as money in the patriarchal age. See Job 42 : 11. Its relative worth, in comparison with other representatives of value, is uncertain. The supposition, drawn from a comparison of this passage with ch. 23 : 16, that it was four times the value of the shekel, rests on very uncertain data.
V. 20. *El-Elohe-Israel;* meaning, God, the God of Israel.
Ch. 34. The wrong done to Dinah, Jacob's daughter, and the vengeance taken by her brothers.
V. 1. It is inferred, from a comparison of all the circumstances, that Dinah was at this time from thirteen to fifteen years of age.†
V. 2. *Humbled.* Doubtless, a constrained compliance is meant here, though it is not necessarily implied in the use of the word. Compare Deut. 21 : 14, 22 : 24, 29; Judges 19 : 24; 2 Sam. 13 : 12, English version, *forced* (as in vv. 14, 22), margin, *humbled;* Lam. 5 : 11, English version, *ravished.*
The Hivite ; see the remarks on ch. 10 : 15-20, fourth paragraph.
Prince ; the head, or chief, of a tribe (Num. 7 : 2) or family (Num. 3 : 24, English version, "chief"). See the note on v. 19.
V. 7. *Folly.* What is impious, immoral, contrary to the divine will and to the requirements of man's spiritual nature, the Bible calls *folly;* while piety, obedience to God's commands and to his will expressed in the laws of our nature, are accounted the true wisdom. The profound moral truth of this biblical conception should not be lost by substituting for it, as is sometimes done, the more general expression, *impiety, wickedness,* or *shame,* in which the specific and profoundly truthful thought of the sacred writer is left out of view. Compare Psalm 14 : 1 ; Job 1 : 22 ; Judges 20 : 6.

* Or, not improbably, a coin ; see *Smith's Bible Dictionary,* art. Money, 3, second paragraph.
† In Eastern countries, females are marriageable at twelve (and sometimes ten) years of age.

the daughter of Jacob; and such a thing should not be done.

8 And Hamor talked with them, saying: The soul of Shechem my son longs for your daughter. I pray you, 9 give her to him for a wife. And make marriages with us; give your daughters to us, and take our daughters for 10 you. And ye shall dwell with us, and the land shall be before you; dwell, and traffic therein, and get possessions therein.

11 And Shechem said to her father and to her brothers: Let me find favor in your eyes, and what ye shall say to 12 me I will give. Lay upon me ever so much purchase-money and gift, and I will give as ye shall say to me; and give me the damsel for a wife.

13 And the sons of Jacob answered Shechem and Hamor his father with deceit. And they spoke, because he defiled 14 Dinah their sister, and said to them: We can not do this thing, to give our sister to one that is uncircumcised; for 15 that is a reproach to us. Only on this condition will we consent to you; if ye will be as we are, that every male 16 of you be circumcised, then will we give our daughters to

---

V. 7. *Or*, is not done   V. 10. *Or*, dwell, and traverse it

Margin, *Is not done;* is altogether unknown in Israel.
V. 8. *Your daughter*, he says, addressing them all, though she held that particular relation to only one of them, and was otherwise related to the rest. She is designated (as remarked by *Knobel*) by her relation to her father, but with reference also to the others.
V. 10. *Shall be before you* (as in ch. 20 : 15, "my land is before thee, dwell where it is good in thine eyes"), to choose for yourselves where ye will dwell.
V. 12. The custom of the age required (as in the case of Jacob, ch. 29 : 18–20 and 27) that a price in money, or an equivalent in service, should be paid to the father in return for his daughter in marriage. See Ex. 22 : 17; 1 Sam. 18 : 25.*
And gift; for the bride herself.
V. 13. *Sons of Jacob.* Simeon and Levi, brothers of Dinah by the same mother, are specially meant.† Compare v. 25, and the remarks on ch. 24 : 67, second paragraph, foot-note.
V. 14. *A reproach to us;* such an act being a shame and a reproach, as violating the divine covenant, and the fundamental law of their own nationality (ch. 17 : 9-14).

* In Ex. 22 : 16, 17, the last clause of the former verse should be rendered, "he shall surely purchase her for his wife," and in the latter, "he shall weigh out silver according to the purchase-money of virgins." In 1 Sam. 18 : 25, "dowry" (in the English version) should be *purchase-money.* A different view is taken in *Smith's Bible Dictionary*, art. Marriage, III., but is not well sustained.

† The milder spirit of Reuben (ch. 37 : 21, 22) may account for his not being named in this connection.

you, and take your daughters for us, and will dwell with
¹⁷ you, and be one people. But if ye will not hearken to us, to be circumcised, then will we take our daughter, and go.
¹⁸ And their words were good in the sight of Hamor, and
¹⁹ in the sight of Shechem, Hamor's son. And the young man delayed not to do the thing, because he delighted in the daughter of Jacob. And he was honored above all his father's house.
²⁰ And Hamor, and Shechem his son, came to the gate of their city; and they spoke to the men of their city, saying:
²¹ These men are peaceable with us, and will dwell in the land, and traffic therein; and the land, behold, it is broad on both hands before them; let us take their daughters to
²² us for wives, and give our daughters to them. Only on this condition will the men consent to dwell with us, to be one people, that every male among us be circumcised, as
²³ they are circumcised. Their cattle, and their substance, and every beast of theirs, will they not be ours? Only let us consent to them, and they will dwell with us.
²⁴ And they hearkened to Hamor and to Shechem his son, all they that went out of the gate of his city; and they were circumcised, every male, all that went out of the gate of his city.

V. 19. *His father's house.* A *tribe* was divided into *families*, and each family into *households* (*fathers' houses*, or *ancestral houses*); see Ex. 6 : 14, 15. Over these households were *heads*, as they are termed in Ex. 6 : 14, or *chiefs* as termed in 1 Chron. 29 : 6, or *princes* as in 2 Chron. 5 : 2 (English version "chief," properly *princes*), compare v. 2 of this chapter.

Honored above all his father's house; accounting for the favorable reception of the proposal by his father, and by the people of the city.

V. 20. *Gate of their city;* referring to the broad open space at the city gate, alluded to in Job 29 : 7,

"When I went forth to the gate by the city,
And placed my seat by the broad way."

This was a place of public resort, where justice was administered, and other public business transacted. See the references in the writer's note on Job 5 : 4 (*Book of Job*, Part Second, explanatory notes).

Their city. See the remark on v. 24, second paragraph.

V. 21. *On both hands,* right and left;—there is room enough for them.

V. 24. *All they that went out of the gate of his city.* This, like the corresponding phrase, "all that enter in at the gate of his city," in ch. 23 : 10, means all the inhabitants of the town. But in both passages, the phrase is chosen with reference to the manner of consulting them, namely, as they passed out or in through the gate.

His city, as being his place of residence, and not because he was its magistrate or chief (ch. 23 : 10).

GENESIS. CHAP. XXXIV.

25 And it came to pass on the third day, when they were sore, that two of the sons of Jacob, Simeon and Levi, Dinah's brothers, took each one his sword, and came upon 26 the city boldly, and slew every male. And Hamor and Shechem his son they slew with the edge of the sword; and they took Dinah from the house of Shechem, and went forth.

27 The sons of Jacob came upon the slain, and plundered 28 the city, because they defiled their sister. They took their flocks, and their herds, and their asses, and that which 29 was in the city, and that which was in the field. And all their wealth, and all their little ones, and their wives, they took captive and plundered, and all that was in the house.

30 And Jacob said to Simeon and to Levi: Ye have troubled me, to make me a stench among the inhabitants of the land, among the Canaanites and among the Perizzites. And I am few in number, and they will collect together against me, and smite me; and I shall be destroyed, I and my house.

31 And they said: Should he deal with our sister as with a harlot?

V. 25. *On the third day;* the critical day, when the inflammation and fever were at their height.*
Simeon and Levi. Compare the comment on this bloody revenge, in ch. 49 : 5-7. Reuben, also a brother of Dinah by the same mother, seems to have taken no part in it. Compare the remark on v. 13, foot-note. Only the leaders, Simeon and Levi, are mentioned; but their armed followers of course are included.
Came upon the city boldly; having nothing to fear, in the disabled condition of its inhabitants.
V. 26. *Went forth;* satisfied with their revenge, and taking no part, apparently, in the subsequent plundering of the place.
V. 29. *In the house;* in distinction from " in the field," v. 28. They plundered every house.
V. 30. *Among the Canaanites and among the Perizzites.* Compare a similar allusion, in ch. 13 : 7, to the perils apprehended from these prior occupants of the country.
V. 31. The provocation, it must be conceded, was great, and such as has often been avenged with equal severity, in the world's history. To us, in our social relations, the reparation for the wrong proposed by Shechem seems the most honorable and desirable adjustment, and best for the injured parties. But it was not so regarded among people of the East; and passion ruled on both sides.

* "This operation, as is well known, is no light matter. If not performed skillfully and with care, the loss of blood and the inflammation may prove fatal. Grown persons, after submitting to it, must lie in bed and keep quiet for three days; and often the healing is not effected till after thirty-five or forty days."—*Delitzsch, Commentar über die Genesis,* 3te Ausg., p. 495.

¹ And God said to Jacob: Arise, go up to Beth-el, and dwell there. And make there an altar to God, who appeared to thee when thou wast fleeing from the face of Esau thy brother.

² And Jacob said to his household, and to all that were with him: Put away the strange gods that are among you,
³ and cleanse yourselves, and change your garments. And let us arise and go up to Beth-el; and I will make there an altar to God, who answered me in the day of my distress, and was with me in the way which I went.

⁴ And they gave to Jacob all the strange gods which were in their hand, and the rings which were in their ears; and Jacob hid them under the oak which is by Shechem.

⁵ And they removed; and the terror of God was upon the cities that were around them, and they did not pursue after the sons of Jacob.

⁶ And Jacob came to Luz which is in the land of Canaan (that is Beth-el), he and all the people that were with him.

Ch. 35. Jacob is directed to go to Beth-el, and dwell there. Death of Rachel, and of Isaac. This chapter records a new era of spiritual progress in the family of Jacob. Hitherto the divine favor has been shown in his worldly prosperity, accompanied with the promise of future blessings to the world through him and his race, and in the numerous and severe trials by which his character was tested, corrected, and strengthened, to prepare him for his mission.

He is now directed, in fulfillment of his vow (ch. 28 : 20-22), to build an altar to God in Beth-el and dwell there, making it "a house of God," as he had promised.* He therefore commands all who are in his household and service to put away their strange gods (Ex. 20 : 3), and after making the preparation of heart and life represented by outward cleansing and change of garments, to go with clean hearts and hands to the services of the sanctuary.

V. 2. *His household;* his own family, and household servants. *All that were with him;* those who had charge of his flocks and herds, and their families.

Strange gods. Rachel brought with her from Padan-aram the teraphim that belonged to her father (ch. 31 : 19, 34). Those in Jacob's service, who came with him from that country, might still retain the false views and practices which prevailed there, even among the descendants of Nahor. See the remarks on ch. 31 : 19, and v. 53, foot-note.

Cleanse yourselves, and change your garments; as a preparation for the sacred services. Compare Ex. 19 : 10, 20 : 4. It would be understood, of course, that to Him who "looks on the heart" (1 Sam. 16 : 7) the outward change is only an emblem of the change in the inward life.

V. 3. *Who answered me in the day of my distress;* thus binding me to the fulfillment of my vow (ch. 28 : 20-22).

V. 4. *Rings which were in their ears.* Such are meant as were worn, not for ornament, but as charms, or amulets, to guard against evil influences. Such superstitions, inconsistent as they are with the spirit of true piety, have often prevailed even among Christian people.

Under the oak. Compare the remarks on ch. 12 : 6, 7, second paragraph, foot-note.

V. 6. *That is Beth-el.* Compare the remarks on ch. 14 : 2, the second paragraph. The explan-

---

* As such it was long regarded, and resorted to. Compare Judges 20 : 18, 26, and 1 Sam. 10 : 3.

7 And he built there an altar; and he called the place El-beth-el, because there God appeared to him when he was fleeing from the face of his brother.

8 And Deborah, Rebekah's nurse, died; and she was buried below Beth-el under the oak, and the name of it was called Oak of Weeping.

9 And God appeared to Jacob again, when he came from
10 Padan-aram, and blessed him. And God said to him: Thy name is Jacob. Thy name shall no more be called Jacob, but Israel shall be thy name. And he called his name Israel.

11 And God said to him: I am God Almighty. Be fruitful and multiply; a nation, and an assemblage of nations, shall
12 be from thee, and kings shall come out of thy loins. And the land which I gave to Abraham and to Isaac, to thee will I give it, and to thy seed after thee will I give the land.

13 And God went up from him in the place where he spoke
14 with him. And Jacob set up a pillar in the place where

V. 8. *Or*, and he called the name of it

atory remark added here, "which is in the land of Canaan," and in v. 9, "when he came from Padan-aram," point to the same thing.

V. 7. *El-beth-el;* meaning, God of Beth-el, in allusion to God who appeared to him there (ch. 28 : 16-19).

V. 8. It is inferred, from what is here related, that Rebekah was no longer living, and that her aged nurse was now the care of the son, to whom she ministered in infancy and childhood.

Below B th-el; which was situated on a hill. *The oak;* with the definite article, as a well-known and familiar object.*

Oak of weeping; where they wept, at her burial. The name, and the occasion of it, are a beautiful tribute to the memory of an aged and faithful servant.

V. 8 (margin). *He called the name of it,* as the words may be rendered, expressing Jacob's grateful remembrance of her faithful service to his mother and to himself.

VV. 9-13. God appears to Jacob in Beth-el a second time, and repeats the promises before made to him.

Again, when he came from Padan-aram; as he had done before, when Jacob was on his way thither.

V. 10. *Israel shall be thy name.* These verses (9-12) may be regarded as a summary of the divine communications made to Jacob on his way back from Padan-aram, including the one recorded in ch. 32 : 29, or it may have been repeated on this occasion.

V. 13. *In the place.* He did not go away to some other place, as an earthly being would have done, but went up from the spot where he spoke with him.

VV. 14, 15. In commemoration of this event, Jacob again erects a pillar of stone, and offers

---

* "This is probably" (says *Dean Stanley, Sinai and Palestine,* p. 220) "the same oak as that referred to in 1 Sam. 10 : 3, though there translated 'plain,' and in 1 Kings 13 : 14." In the latter passage, the Hebrew word has the definite article, "under the oak."

he spoke with him, a pillar of stone; and he poured a
15 drink-offering thereon, and he poured oil thereon. And
Jacob called the name of the place, where God spoke with
him, Beth-el.
16 And they removed from Beth-el. And there was yet a
length of way to come to Ephrath, and Rachel was in
17 labor; and she had hard labor. And it came to pass,
when she was in hard labor, that the midwife said to her:
18 Fear not, for this also is a son for thee. And it came to
pass, as her soul was departing, (for she died,) that she
called his name Ben-oni. And his father called him Benjamin.
19 And Rachel died; and she was buried in the way to
20 Ephrath. That is Bethlehem. And Jacob set up a pillar
on her grave. That is the pillar of Rachel's grave to this day.
21 And Israel removed, and stretched his tent beyond Mig-
22 dal-eder. And it came to pass, when Israel was dwelling
in that land, that Reuben went and lay with Bilhah, his
father's concubine. And Jacob heard of it.
23 And the sons of Jacob were twelve. The sons of Leah;
Reuben, Jacob's first-born, and Simeon, and Levi, and

---

on it a drink-offering of wine, and consecrates it by an anointing with oil. Compare the note on ch. 28 : 18.

Called the name . . . *Beth-el;* not now for the first time, for the place already bore this name (v. 1, and ch. 28 : 19).

V. 16. *Removed,* for convenience of pasturage (ch. 12 : 9). A temporary change of abode, for such a purpose, is not inconsistent with the direction given in v. 1.

Ephrath; afterward called Bethlehem (v. 19). It means *fruitful,* corresponding to Bethlehem, which means *house of bread.*

V. 17. *This also is a son for thee.* She encourages her with the assurance that this also, as well as the first-born, is a son. The birth of a son was a blessing specially desired. Compare ch. 29 : 32 and note, and ch. 30 : 24.

V. 18. *Ben-oni;* meaning, son of my anguish. *Benjamin;* son of the right hand.

V. 20. *Rachel's grave.* Compare 1 Sam. 10 : 2.

V. 21. *Migdal-eder;* meaning, tower of the flock (Micah 4 : 8), a watchtower built for the use of herdsmen in watching and guarding their flocks. Compare 2 Chron. 26 : 10. The connection shows that it was not far from Bethlehem, but its position is not otherwise known. The expression in Micah 4 : 8, "O tower of the flock," is probably an allusion to this passage.

V. 22. Compare ch. 49 : 4.

VV. 23-26. Sons of Jacob. He is now approaching the paternal home. He went forth from it with only his staff (ch. 32 : 10), and now returns to it the father of twelve sons. As the object is to show how greatly he had been blessed in the exile from his home, the births of all are naturally included in one general statement (v. 26, last clause), without minute specification which the context readily supplies.

GENESIS.   CHAP. XXXVI.

²⁴ Judah, and Issachar, and Zebulun. The sons of Rachel; ²⁵ Joseph and Benjamin. And the sons of Bilhah, Rachel's ²⁶ maid-servant; Dan, and Naphtali. And the sons of Zilpah, Leah's maid-servant; Gad, and Asher. These are the sons of Jacob, that were born to him in Padan-aram.
²⁷ And Jacob came to Isaac his father, to Mamre, to Kirjath-arba, (that is Hebron,) where Abraham and Isaac sojourned.
²⁸ And the days of Isaac were a hundred and eighty years. ²⁹ And Isaac expired, and died, and was gathered to his people, old and full of days. And Esau and Jacob, his sons, buried him.

¹ AND these are the generations of Esau. He is Edom.
² Esau took his wives of the daughters of Canaan, Adah the daughter of Elon the Hittite, and Aholibamah the ³ daughter of Anah the daughter of Zibeon the Hivite, and

V. 27. *Mamre.* Compare ch. 13 : 18, and 23 : 19. *Kirjath-arba.* See ch. 23 : 2, and note. It is not meant that Jacob now saw his father for the first time after his return to Canaan; but that he now removed, with all his family, and his flocks and herds, and his whole retinue of herdsmen and other servants, to the vicinity of his father's abode.
V. 29. *Was gathered to his people.* See the remarks on ch. 25 : 8, second paragraph.
Full of days. Compare ch. 25 : 8, note, first paragraph.
The date of Isaac's death is here anticipated in the narrative, for he lived some years after Joseph was sold into Egypt (ch. 37).*
The sacred writer closes the account of Isaac and of Esau with this chapter and the following one, reserving the remainder of the book for the fortunes of Jacob and his family.
Ch. 36. Descendants of Esau.
Here is interposed a brief account of Esau's descendants, giving such information as is necessary for understanding subsequent allusions to them.
The chapter consists of seven divisions. First division, vv. 1—8. Origin of the Edomites.
V. 1. *Generations.* Compare the remarks on ch. 2 : 4, second paragraph. *Edom;* see the note on ch. 32 : 1–3, third paragraph.
VV. 2, 3. *Took his wives;* that is, took them with him when he departed to another land (v. 6). The sentence commencing here is continued on to the sixth verse, and this clause is resumed in the first clause of that verse.
Of the daughters of Canaan. Compare ch. 26 : 34, 27 : 46, 28 : 8. This refers only to the first two, from whom Bashemath is expressly distinguished as "Ishmael's daughter."
The superscription in the first verse, "These are the generations of Esau," indicates that this is an ancient record of the family of Esau. In the names of his wives, in these two verses, it varies from the account already given in chs. 26 : 34 and 28 : 9. It should be observed, however, that the accounts agree in the most important points; namely, first in the number of his wives, each making it three; secondly, in the fact that two of them were Canaanites, one of these being a Hittite; and thirdly, that the other was a daughter of Ishmael, and sister of Nebaioth.

* Compare the remarks on ch. 27 : 1–4, foot-note. It appears, from a comparison of the dates there given, that Joseph was twenty-nine years of age when Isaac died. As Joseph was sold into Egypt at the age of seventeen (ch. 37 : 2), Isaac must have lived twelve or thirteen years after that event.

147

⁴ Bashemath, Ishmael's daughter, sister of Nebaioth;—and Adah bore to Esau Eliphaz, and Bashemath bore Reuel, ⁵ and Aholibamah bore Jeush, and Jaalam, and Korah; these are the sons of Esau, that were born to him in the

As the three statements agree in these striking and essential points, there can be little doubt that the same persons are meant in all of them.* The mere difference of names would be of little account, since they were significant of personal qualities and traits of character, or of incidents in personal history, and hence not unfrequently changed as new circumstances occurred. The most remarkable of these changes, and apparently the most difficult one, is satisfactorily explained; as all might be, without doubt, if we had, as in this case, the historical links of connection which led to them, but which are naturally omitted in a document not intended for purposes of explanation and conciliation, and necessarily very brief.

It has been suggested, with great appearance of probability,† that the Ana mentioned in v. 2 is the one spoken of in v. 24 as the discoverer of "the warm springs in the wilderness;" and that from this circumstance he was afterward known by the name *Beeri*, meaning "a man of wells," a discoverer of them. In this genealogical record he would naturally be mentioned by his original name, while in the historical account (ch. 26 : 34) he would be more readily known by the one which superseded it. He might be a *Hittite*, as he is called in ch. 26 : 34, and yet be properly classed here (vv. 20, 24) with the *Horites* ; for the latter is not a gentilic name, but a designation derived from a certain mode of life.‡ Zibeon, his father, is here called a *Hivite*,§ whilst Beeri, in ch. 26 : 34, is called a *Hittite*; perhaps on the ground that the latter was a general designation of the inhabitants of Canaan, as in Joshua 1 : 4.∥

Aholibamah; meaning, tent of the height. She is called Judith in ch. 26 : 34, and this was doubtless her proper personal name. The name Aholibamah, as its meaning indicates, seems to have been given her from historical circumstances connected with her relation as wife of Esau,¶ and hence would naturally be used here, in a purely Edomitish document.

Daughter of Zibeon. The word "daughter" is here used in the wider sense which it often bears. She was the granddaughter of Zibeon, as is shown in vv. 24, 25. So the term *son* is sometimes applied to a grandson, or even a remoter lineal descendant.

The daughter of Elon, the second of Esau's wives, is called Bashemath (fragrant) in ch. 26 : 34, and Adah (ornament) in this passage. On the contrary, the third wife of Esau is called Mahalath (a stringed instrument of music, a lute) in ch. 28 : 9, and is here called Bashemath.** Of this change of names, and their still more remarkable interchange, the brief record has preserved no explanation.††

---

* The difference of names has been explained on the supposition that in the long interval of time, about forty years, the one first named in the previous account had died without issue, and that another wife by a subsequent marriage is mentioned here. The supposition is not improbable in itself, and may be the true explanation. It is idle to pretend that there is a discrepancy between these accounts, when they can be reconciled on suppositions that are perfectly reasonable, and could doubtless be proved to be true if we had the connecting links necessarily omitted in so brief a statement.

† *Hengstenberg, Beiträge zur Einleitung ins A. T.*, vol. iii., p. 273.

‡ "Each of the accounts gives us just the information we might expect [from it]. In the narrative, where the stress is laid on Esau's wife being of the race of Canaan, her father is called a Hittite; whilst in the genealogy, where the stress is on Esau's connection by marriage with the previous occupants of Mount Seir, he is most naturally and properly described under the more precise term Horite."—*Smith's Bible Dictionary*, art. Beeri.

§ It has been suggested that this may be an error of transcription; the difference between the Hebrew words for *Horite* and *Hivite* being only the difference between the letter ר and the letter ו, which are less distinguishable in manuscript than in their more exact printed forms.

∥ *Hengstenberg, Beiträge ins A. T.*, vol. iii., p. 275.

¶ Compare *Smith's Bible Dictionary*, art. Aholibamah.

** The Samaritan copy of the Hebrew text, and the Samaritan version of it, retain the name Mahalath. But in such a case, there is ground to suspect an attempt at conciliation, to avoid an obvious difficulty.

†† Compare *Smith's Bible Dictionary*, art. Bashemath.

⁶ land of Canaan;—and Esau took his wives, and his sons, and his daughters, and all the persons of his house, and his cattle, and all his beasts, and all his substance that he gathered in the land of Canaan, and went to a land away ⁷ from his brother Jacob. For their substance was great, so that they could not dwell together; and the land of their sojournings could not bear them on account of their cattle. ⁸ And Esau dwelt in mount Seir. Esau, he is Edom.
⁹ And these are the generations of Esau, father of Edom in mount Seir.
¹⁰ These are the names of Esau's sons; Eliphaz, son of Adah the wife of Esau, Reuel, son of Bashemath the wife of Esau.
¹¹ And the sons of Eliphaz were Teman, Omar, Zepho, and ¹² Gatam, and Kenaz. And Timna was concubine to Eliphaz, Esau's son; and she bore to Eliphaz Amalek. These were the sons of Adah, Esau's wife.
¹³ And these are the sons of Reuel; Nahath and Zerah, Shammah and Mizzah. These were the sons of Bashemath, Esau's wife.

VV. 6, 7. *And Esau took his wives.* The first clause in v. 2 is resumed here, and the sentence commenced there is completed in this verse.

Went to a land away from his brother Jacob. In dismissing Jacob with his final blessing, Isaac added the significant words (ch. 28 : 4), "that thou mayest possess the land . . . which God gave to Abraham." Esau was doubtless aware that he could not have his father's countenance in resisting the claim of Jacob and his posterity to the possession of the country. He therefore took all that he had, and retired to another land, "away from his brother Jacob."

This occurred during Jacob's absence in Padan-aram,* and was a precautionary measure which the prudence of Isaac would naturally suggest, and one which the interests of both parties required.

It will be observed, that no cause of separation is mentioned, except (as in the case of Abraham and Lot, ch. 13 : 6) that "the land could not bear them, on account of their cattle." The omission is perhaps explained by the fact alluded to in the remarks on vv. 2, 3, third paragraph. In such a record nothing more could be expected.

V. 8. *Mount Seir.* See the remarks on ch. 14 : 6, and on ch. 32 : 1-3, third paragraph, footnote.

Second division, vv. 9-14. The three chief branches of the Edomites.

V. 11. *Teman.* See the remarks on v. 42.

V. 12. *Timna,* the Horite (v. 22) is mentioned here as having borne *Amalek* to Eliphaz. A remnant of his race, dwelling in mount Seir, were exterminated in the time of Hezekiah (1 Chron. 4 : 41-43).

* Some suppose that it occurred after his return, and that this statement refers to Esau's final and permanent abandonment of the land of Canaan, and settlement in mount Seir. But the supposition is unnecessary, as shown by the remark in the text, and does not accord with the previous history. Compare, for example, ch. 32 : 3, and 33 : 16.

¹⁴ And these were the sons of Aholibamah, daughter of Anah the daughter of Zibeon, Esau's wife; and she bore to Esau Jeush, and Jaalam, and Korah.

¹⁵ These were princes of the sons of Esau; the sons of Eliphaz the first-born of Esau, prince Teman, prince Omar, ¹⁶ prince Zepho, prince Kenaz, prince Korah, prince Gatam, prince Amalek. These were the princes of Eliphaz, in the land of Edom. These were sons of Adah.

¹⁷ And these were sons of Reuel, Esau's son; prince Nahath, prince Zerah, prince Shammah, prince Mizzah. These were the princes of Reuel, in the land of Edom. These were sons of Bashemath, Esau's wife.

¹⁸ And these were sons of Aholibamah, Esau's wife; prince Jeush, prince Jaalam, prince Korah. These were the princes of Aholibamah, the daughter of Anah, Esau's wife.

¹⁹ These were the sons of Esau, and these were their princes. He is Edom.

²⁰ These are the sons of Seir the Horite, the inhabitants of the land; Lotan, and Shobal, and Zibeon, and Anah, ²¹ and Dishon, and Ezer, and Dishan. These were the princes of the Horites, the sons of Seir, in the land of Edom.

²² And the sons of Lotan were Hori and Hemam; and the sister of Lotan was Timna.

²³ And these are the sons of Shobal; Alvan and Manahath and Ebal, Shepho and Onam.

²⁴ And these are the sons of Zibeon; both Ajah and Anah. He was Anah who found the warm springs in the wilderness, as he fed the asses of Zibeon his father.

Third division, vv. 15-19. Princes descended from Esau.

V. 17. *These;* namely, these princes of Esau's line, continuing the enumeration commenced in v. 15, under the heading, "these were princes of the sons of Esau."

V. 18. *These;* as in v. 17.

Fourth division, vv. 20-28. Descendants of Seir, father of the original occupants of the country.

Seir's immediate descendants are given here, in this record of "the generations of Esau" (v. 1), on account of the intermarriage of some of them with Esau's descendants.

V. 20. *Seir the Horite.* See the remarks on ch. 14 : 6.

V. 22. *Timna.* She is mentioned, and her relation to Lotan, on account of her connection with Eliphaz, spoken of in v. 12.

V. 23. Of the sons of Shobal, the first three are grouped together, as are also the last two, for some reason which is not now apparent.

V. 24. *The warm springs.* These are frequent in that region, as attested by ancient writers

GENESIS.   CHAP. XXXVI.

²⁵ And these are the sons of Anah; Dishon, and Aholibamah the daughter of Anah.
²⁶ And these are the sons of Dishon; Hemdan, and Eshban, and Ithran, and Cheran.
²⁷ These are the sons of Ezer; Bilhan, and Zaavan, and Akan.
²⁸ These are the sons of Dishan; Uz, and Aran.
²⁹ These were princes of the Horites; prince Lotan, prince
³⁰ Shobal, prince Zibeon, prince Anah, prince Dishon, prince Ezer, prince Dishan. These were princes of the Horites, according to their princes, in the land of Seir.
³¹ And these are the kings that reigned in the land of Edom, before there reigned a king of the sons of Israel.
³² And there reigned in Edom Bela, son of Beor; and the name of his city was Dinhaba.
³³ And Bela died; and Jobab son of Zerah, of Bozrah reigned in his stead.
³⁴ And Jobab died; and Husham, of the land of the Temanites, reigned in his stead.
³⁵ And Husham died; and Hadad son of Bedad,. he who

and by modern travelers.* The value of their sanitary properties made the discovery an important one, and worthy to be thus commemorated.
V. 25. *These are the sons.* This is the standing formula in a table of genealogy, and it is therefore used here, though there is but one son to be mentioned.
Aholibamah; not the one mentioned in v. 2, who was daughter of Anah the son of Zibeon (v. 24).
V. 28. *Uz.* Compare the remarks on ch. 22 : 20-24, fourth paragraph.
Fifth division, vv. 29, 30. Princes of this race.
V. 30. *According to their princes;* that is, as their princes were severally named in their several tribes.
Sixth division, vv. 31-39. Kings of Edom.
V. 31. *Before there reigned a king of the sons of Israel.* This may have been added at a later period, as explanatory remarks occasionally were (ch. 14 : 2, note, second paragraph).
It is remarkable that none of these kings was a son or descendant of his predecessor. The government was, therefore, an elective monarchy, existing cotemporaneously with the narrower sway of the princes of tribes already spoken of, which it probably represented in one executive head.
V. 33. *Bozrah* was one of the chief cities of the Edomites.† See Isaiah 34 : 6, 63 : 1; Jer. 49 : 13, 22; Amos 1 : 12.
V. 34. *Land of the Temanites.* See the remark on v. 42.
V. 35. There is an allusion here to some battle, not elsewhere on record, in which the Edomites gained a victory over the Midianites, in the territory of Moab.

* Compare *Smith's Bible Dictionary*, art. Mules, and the art. Anah, in the American edition.
† "There is no reason to doubt that its modern representative is *el-Busaireh*, which was first visited by Burckhardt, and lies in the mountain district to the southeast of the Dead Sea, between Tufileh and Petra."—*Smith's Bible Dictionary*, art. Bozrah.

smote Midian in the country of Moab, reigned in his stead. And the name of his city was Avith.

³⁶ And Hadad died; and Samlah, of Masrekah, reigned in his stead.

³⁷ And Samlah died; and Saul, of Rehoboth by the River, reigned in his stead.

³⁸ And Saul died; and Baal-hanan, son of Achbor, reigned in his stead.

³⁹ And Baal-hanan, son of Achbor, died; and Hadar reigned in his stead. And the name of his city was Pau. And the name of his wife was Mehetabel, daughter of Matred, the daughter of Me-zahab.

⁴⁰ And these are names of princes of Esau, according to their families, according to their places, by their names; ⁴¹ prince Timnah, prince Alvah, prince Jetheth, prince ⁴² Aholibamah, prince Elah, prince Pinon, prince Kenaz, ⁴³ prince Teman, prince Mibzar, prince Magdiel, prince Iram. These were princes of Edom, according to their habitations in the land of their possession. He is Esau, father of the Edomites.

V. 37. *Rehoboth;* meaning, streets, and hence of frequent use in names of cities. By "the river" is meant the Euphrates (ch. 31 : 21, and note), where a name corresponding to Rehoboth is still found.*

Seventh division, vv. 40–43. Other princes of Esau's race.

These are mentioned here according to their *places* (v. 40), or *habitations* (v. 43), as well as their families and names. It is a list of princely residences; that is, of towns or cities occupied as such, and hence deserving to be commemorated. Only eleven are mentioned, though the Edomite tribes were at least thirteen in number (vv. 11–14), some having been apparently wandering tribes without a fixed abode.

It has been suggested,† that 1 Chron. 1 : 51 may perhaps furnish the explanation of this second list of princes (compare vv. 15–19) in Esau's line. The expression, "Hadad died also, and the princes of Edom were," etc., may intimate the extinction at his death of the regal dignity, and a return to the simple tribal relation, with its hereditary princedoms.

V. 42. *Kenaz.* Compare the note on ch. 15 : 19–21, third paragraph.

Teman; a celebrated district in the northeastern part of Idumæa, distinguished for its wise men (Jer. 49 : 7), and as the residence of Eliphaz, the most sagacious and profound of the speakers opposed to Job (Book of Job, chs. 2 : 11, 4 : 1, 15 : 1, 22 : 1). In Amos 1 : 12, it stands as the representative of Idumæa.

V. 43. *According to their habitations,* which bore the same names. They are mentioned by the names of the settlements founded by them, and named after them. Compare the first paragraph of the remarks under this seventh division.

---

* "It is not strange, where personal distinction paved the way to the throne," [compare the note on v. 31, second paragraph,] "that even a foreigner, Saul of Rehoboth by the River, attained to the regal dignity."—*Tuch, Kommentar über die Genesis.*

† *Bertheau, die Bücher der Chronik erklärt,* 1 Chron. 1 : 51; *Delitzsch, Commentar über die Genesis,* 3te Ausg., p. 511.

1 AND Jacob dwelt in the land of his father's sojournings, in the land of Canaan.
2 These are the generations of Jacob. Joseph, being seventeen years old, was tending the flock with his brothers, and he was a lad with the sons of Bilhah and with the sons of Zilpah his father's wives. And Joseph brought evil report concerning them to their father.
3 And Israel loved Joseph above all his sons, for a son of old age was he to him, and he made him a full length garment.
4 And his brothers saw that their father loved him above all his brothers; and they hated him, and could not speak to him peaceably.
5 And Joseph dreamed a dream, and he told it to his brothers; and they hated him yet the more.
6 And he said to them: Hear, I pray, this dream which
7 I dreamed. For, behold, we were binding sheaves in the midst of the field; and behold, my sheaf arose, yea and stood upright; and behold, your sheaves stood around, and bowed down to my sheaf.
8 And his brothers said to him: Shalt thou indeed reign over us? Or shalt thou indeed bear rule over us? And they hated him yet the more, for his dreams and for his words.

Ch. 37. Family history of Jacob resumed. Joseph sold into Egypt.
The family history of Jacob is here resumed, from ch. 35, after the brief notice of Esau's descendants in ch. 36.
V. 1. *Jacob dwelt* . . . *in the land of Canaan.* The reader's attention is recalled to this fact (compare ch. 35 : 27) as a proper introduction to the further account of Jacob and his family.
V. 2. *These are the generations.* Compare the remark on ch. 2 : 4, second paragraph.
He was a lad with the sons of Bilhah, etc. They had the oversight and direction of the flock, and of the field servants, and he was a lad (servant-boy) with them, for the lighter service of errands and the like. Compare vv. 13, 14.
V. 3. *A full length garment;* covering the whole person, the body of the garment extending to the feet, and the sleeves to the wrists. Such garments were worn only by persons exempted from manual labor, and were indicative of rank and wealth. The injudicious partiality of Jacob conferred this distinction on the favorite child of his old age. On the contrary, the ordinary dress, such as was worn by persons engaged in active employments, extended but a little below the knee, the sleeves reaching only to the elbow.
V. 7. *In the midst of the field.* The language expresses the minute particularity of the scene, as presented to him in his dream. It is not merely the general conception, "in the field;" they were "in the midst of it," as it stretched away, far and wide, on every side of them.

⁹ And he dreamed yet another dream, and he related it to his brothers. And he said: Behold, I have dreamed a dream yet again; and behold, the sun, and the moon, and eleven stars, bowed down to me.
¹⁰ And he related it to his father, and to his brothers. And his father chided him, and said to him: What is this dream that thou hast dreamed? Shall we indeed come, I, and thy mother, and thy brothers, to bow ourselves down to thee to the earth?
¹¹ And his brothers envied him; but his father kept the saying.
¹² And his brothers went to feed their father's flock in
¹³ Shechem. And Israel said to Joseph: Are not thy brothers feeding the flock in Shechem? Come, and I will send thee to them. And he said to him: Here am I.
¹⁴ And he said to him: Go, I pray, see whether it is well with thy brothers, and well with the flocks; and bring me word again. And he sent him from the valley of Hebron; and he came to Shechem.
¹⁵ And a man found him, and behold, he was wandering in the field. And the man asked him, saying: What seekest
¹⁶ thou? And he said: I seek my brothers. Tell me, I
¹⁷ pray, where they feed their flocks. And the man said: They have removed from hence; for I heard them say:

VV. 9-11. His second dream he relates, first to his brothers, and then to his father and his brothers. The former affects to chide him for the extravagance of the obvious import of his dream, but, with the natural presentiment of parental partiality, treasures it up in his memory (v. 11).
V. 10. *Thy mother.* Rachel is doubtless meant. As the whole matter belongs to the sphere of the ideal, this reference to the mother, "deceased, but neither forgotten nor lost,"* is not out of place.
V. 12. *In Shechem.* Compare ch. 12 : 6, 7, and note, and ch. 33 : 19, and note.†
V. 14. *Valley of Hebron;* where Jacob was dwelling. Compare ch. 35 : 27.

* *Delitzsch,* on the passage, p. 529.
† "A few hours north of Bethel, a valley suddenly opens upon the traveler among the hills, which, though not so extensive as Esdraelon or Sharon, is yet unsurpassed, in point of beauty and fertility, by any other region in the holy land. . . . It runs very nearly north and south, and may be ten or twelve miles in length, and a mile and a half in breadth. . . . Toward the upper part of the plain, the mountains which skirt its western side fall apart, leaving a somewhat narrow defile between them, where stands Nablus, the ancient Shechem or Sychar. A more lovely spot than that which greets the eye here it would be difficult to find in any land. Streams, which gush from perennial fountains, impart a bright and constant freshness to the vegetation."—*Dr. Hackett's Illustrations of Scripture,* 8th ed., p. 193.

Let us go to Dothan. And Joseph went after his brothers, and found them in Dothan. ¹⁸ And they saw him afar off; and before he came near ¹⁹ them, they plotted against him to slay him. And they ²⁰ said one to another: Behold, this dreamer comes. Now therefore, come, and let us slay him, and cast him into one of the pits; and we will say: An evil beast devoured him. And we shall see what will become of his dreams.

²¹ And Reuben heard it, and he delivered him out of their ²² hand; and he said: Let us not kill him. And Reuben said to them: Do not shed blood; cast him into this pit that is in the wilderness, and do not lay a hand upon him; that he might deliver him out of their hand, to return him to his father.

²³ And it came to pass, when Joseph came to his brothers, that they stripped Joseph of his garment, the full length ²⁴ garment, that was on him; and they took him, and cast him into the pit. And the pit was empty; there was no water in it.

²⁵ And they sat down to eat bread. And they lifted up their eyes and saw, and behold, a caravan of Ishmaelites coming from Gilead, and their camels bearing tragacanth, and balsam, and ladanum, going to carry it down to Egypt.

V. 17. *Dothan;* meaning, two cisterns. The site has recently been found, still bearing its ancient name, about twelve miles north of Shechem. At the base of the hill Dothan is a natural fountain, and in the vicinity are remains of large cisterns. It is among the richest pasture-grounds in the country.*

VV. 21, 22. Reuben, as the elder brother, and hence bearing the chief responsibility, endeavors to save him; dreading to encounter his father's grief and displeasure (v. 30) if he suffered Joseph to fall by their hands. To them he proposes, that they should leave him to perish in the pit, instead of imbruing their hands in his blood.

V. 25. *From Gilead—to Egypt.* Dothan was on the great caravan route from Damascus to Egypt, which would naturally be taken by traveling merchants from northern Gilead.

The substances here mentioned were among the most celebrated products of the country. Compare ch. 43 : 11.

Ladanum; a precious gum, used as a medical stimulant, and as a perfume.†

* " Here is found at the present day 'the best pasturage in all that region;' and thus, though the narrative is silent as to the reason why the sons of Jacob went from Shechem to Dothan, we see that it is the very place which herdsmen, such as they were, would naturally seek after having exhausted the supplies of their previous pasture-ground."—*Smith's Bible Dictionary,* art. Dothan, addition to the American edition.

† See *Smith's Bible Dictionary,* art. Myrrh, No. 2, *Lot.*

²⁶ ²⁷ And Judah said to his brothers: What profit is it that we slay our brother, and cover his blood? Come, and let us sell him to the Ishmaelites, and let not our hand be upon him; for he is our brother, our flesh. And his brothers hearkened to it.

²⁸ And Midianites, merchants, passed by; and they drew and raised up Joseph out of the pit; and they sold Joseph to the Ishmaelites for twenty pieces of silver; and they brought Joseph into Egypt.

²⁹ ³⁰ And Reuben returned to the pit; and behold, Joseph was not in the pit; and he rent his clothes. And he returned to his brothers, and said: The child is not; and I, whither shall I go?

³¹ ³² And they took Joseph's garment, and they killed a buck of the goats, and dipped the garment in the blood. And they sent the full length garment, and brought it to their father. And they said: This have we found; discern now,

---

VV. 26, 27. Judah, apparently not aware of Reuben's purpose, or perhaps willing to have Joseph removed out of the way, proposes to spare his life, and sell him to the Ishmaelites. A chance was thus left, if this was what he sought, for his restoration to his father.

V. 28. The Midianites and Ishmaelites were both descendants of Abraham, one by Hagar, and the other by Keturah (ch. 25 : 2, 4). Compare the remarks on ch. 25 : 2-4, first and fifth paragraphs.

There is hardly room for doubt, that by the subject of the second and third paragraphs ("they drew,"—"they sold") are meant the brothers of Joseph. Compare Judah's proposal, v. 27, and Joseph's statement, ch. 45 : 5, " ye sold me hither."

It has been suggested, that the "Midianites," the subject of the first clause, are meant by the pronoun "they" in the second and third clauses; that their attention was attracted, or directed, to the pit where Joseph lay, and that they drew him out and sold him to their companions the Ishmaelites. It is claimed that this accords better with Joseph's statement (ch. 40 : 15), "I was verily stolen from the land of the Hebrews," and equally well with the statement (ch. 45 : 5), "ye sold me hither," inasmuch as they were parties to the crime, being cognizant of it and conniving at it.

The only thing that favors this construction of the sentence* is the language in ch. 40 : 15; and this is certainly applicable, in a free use of language, to the manner in which Joseph's brothers disposed of him, since neither they, nor those to whom they sold him, had any right to his person.†

Twenty pieces of silver. Compare Lev. 27 : 5.

VV. 29, 34. Sudden and overwhelming grief, as well as other violent and painful emotions, were expressed by rending the garments. Compare ch. 44 : 13; Num. 14 : 6; Josh. 7 : 6; Judges 11 : 35; 2 Sam. 13 : 19; Ezra 9 : 3.

* The attentive reader must have observed, that the change of subject, as well as object, in successive clauses, without any indication of it, is very common in the structure of Hebrew sentences.

† In that passage, he aims only to show that he is guiltless of any offense. Hence he affirms, that he was not in slavery on account of crime; that he was stolen from his home, that is, was taken away wrongfully and without just cause.

33 whether it is thy son's garment, or not. And he knew it; and he said: It is my son's garment; an evil beast has devoured him; Joseph is surely torn in pieces.
34 And Jacob rent his garments, and put sackcloth on his
35 loins, and mourned for his son many days. And all his sons, and all his daughters, rose up to console him. And he refused to be consoled; and he said: I will go down to my son mourning, to the underworld. And his father wept for him.
36 And the Midianites sold him into Egypt, to Potiphar, an officer of Pharaoh, captain of the life-guard.

1 And it came to pass at that time, that Judah went down from his brothers, and turned aside to a man, an Adullamite, whose name was Hirah.

V. 1. *Or*, stretched his tent near by an Adullamite

Sackcloth was a coarse fabric of goat's hair, used for making sacks, the same word in Hebrew meaning both. It was of a dark and sombre color, and was worn as an expression of mourning (2 Sam. 3 : 31), and of self-humiliation (1 Kings 20 : 31, 21 : 27), sometimes next the skin (2 Kings 6 : 30; Job 16 : 15).
V. 35. *All his daughters.* By these are meant his one daughter (Dinah), and his daughters-in-law.
I will go down to my son. Compare the remarks on ch. 25 : 8, third and fourth paragraphs.*
The underworld. By this term is meant (of course only in figurative conception) the abode of the departed, the world of spirits. It is conceived of as *beneath* (Isaiah 14 : 9), as *under the earth* (Rev. 5 : 3, 13, Philip. 2 : 10), as reached by *digging into it* (Amos 9 : 2); men are said to *go down* into it (Num. 16 : 33); its *depth below* is contrasted with the height of heaven above (Job 11 : 8). Such expressions are intended to accommodate what is said to common apprehension, and not to teach us anything respecting the *locali*y of the abode of departed spirits.
V. 36. *The Midianites sold him.* Compare the remarks on ch. 39 : 1.
Pharaoh. See the note on ch. 12 : 15.
Ch. 38. Judah's marriage with the daughter of a Canaanite. His unlawful connection with Tamar.
The incidents of this strange story are instructive in many points of view. They show the character and the moral influence of heathenism, with which Judah, voluntarily and in disregard of the divine will, brought himself in connection.
V. 1. *Turned aside to*, etc.; that is, accepted his hospitality, and became his guest. The phrase, in this sense, originated in the custom of turning off from the beaten road to a dwelling near it, to obtain lodging and food. Compare the remark on ch. 19 : 5.
Some scholars translate as in the margin;† but the rendering given in the text is more probably the true one.
Adullamite. Adullam was one of the many small principalities in Canaan (Josh. 12 : 15), situated in the low country of Judah (Josh. 15 : 20, 33, 35).‡

---

* "To follow him thither, there to find him again, is the only consolation of the aged father." —*Delitzsch, Commentar über die Genesis*, 3te Ausg., p. 531.
† *Delitzsch, Keil, Lange.*
‡ On the site of the *cave of Adullam* (1 Sam. 22 : 1; 2 Sam. 23 : 13; 1 Chron. 11 : 15), see Dr. Hackett's addition to the art. Adullam, in *Smith's Bible Dictionary*, American edition.

2 And Judah saw there a daughter of a Canaanite, whose name was Shuah; and he took her, and went in to her.
3 And she conceived, and bore a son; and he called his name Er.
4 And she conceived again, and bore a son; and she called his name Onan.
5 And she conceived yet again, and bore a son; and she called his name Shelah. And he was at Chezib when she bore him.
6 And Judah took a wife for Er his first-born, and her
7 name was Tamar. And Er, Judah's first-born, was wicked in the sight of Jehovah; and Jehovah slew him.
8 And Judah said to Onan: Go in to thy brother's wife, and perform the duty of a husband's brother to her, and raise up seed to thy brother.
9 And Onan knew that the seed would not be his. And it came to pass, when he went in to his brother's wife, that he wasted it on the ground, in order not to give seed
10 to his brother. And that which he did was evil in the sight of Jehovah; and he slew him also.
11 And Judah said to Tamar his daughter-in-law: Abide a widow in thy father's house, till Shelah my son shall grow up. For he said: Lest he also die, as his brothers. And Tamar went, and abode in her father's house.

V. 2. The occurrence mentioned in this verse seems to have determined Judah to fix his abode there for a time.
Took her, as a wife; the word meaning, to take in marriage.
V. 5. *Chezib;* the same as Achzib, in the low country of Judah (Josh. 15 : 33, 44). *Shelah's* posterity, "the family of the Shelanites," are mentioned among "the sons of Judah after their families," in Num. 26 : 20. The fact incidentally mentioned in the last clause of this verse fixes the birthplace of their ancestor.
V. 8. For the usage here referred to see Deut. 25 : 5, 6. This passage shows that it was much older than the date of the Mosaic law, which only regulated its observance, as in the case of many other of the previously existing institutions of civil society. Compare the Savior's remark, Matt. 19 : 8, Mark 10 : 5. Its object was to prevent the extinction of the name of any member of the family. Compare the similar instance of the desire for the perpetuation of one's name and memory, referred to in the notes on ch. 16, introductory remarks, second paragraph.
Perform the duty of a husband's brother to her. So the import of the Hebrew word is correctly expressed, in the common English version, in Deut. 25 : 5.
V. 9. *Would not be his;* so that he would alienate from himself both the name and the patrimony, in favor of his deceased elder brother.
V. 11. *A widow in thy father's house.* Compare Lev. 22 : 13. It is there implied, that it was customary for a childless widow to return to her father's house.

GENESIS. Chap. XXXVIII.

¹² And after many days, the daughter of Shuah, Judah's wife, died. And Judah consoled himself; and he went up to his sheep-shearers, he and Hirah his friend the Adullamite, to Timnah. ¹³ And it was told Tamar, saying: Behold, thy father-in-¹⁴ law goes up to Timnah, to shear his sheep. And she put off from her the garments of her widowhood, and covered herself with a vail, and wrapped herself, and sat at the entrance to two fountains, which is by the way to Timnah. For she saw that Shelah was grown up, and she was not given to him for a wife.

V. 14. *Or*, at the entrance of Enayim

V. 12. *Consoled himself;* ceased to mourn for her.
Went up—to Timnah (as the name should be written); the place spoken of in Josh. 15 : 57, as "in the mountains" (v. 48), namely of Judah (v. 20).
V. 14. *Wrapped herself;* so as to disguise her form, her face being covered by the vail.
Entrance to two fountains. A fountain, by the way-side, was the place where she would be most likely to attract the attention of one passing by. She therefore sat at the entrance to the two fountains near the beaten road (v. 21), so that one could not turn aside to them without observing her.
The Hebrew word meaning *two fountains* (enayim) is commonly understood to be here the name of a town (Enayim), so called from the fountains to which it owed its origin. See the marginal rendering. But to this rendering there are the following objections. First, the entrance to a town was too public and frequented a place for her object. Secondly, a town would not be identified by speaking of it (as in v. 21) as being "by the way;" but it would be natural to speak of the fountains as being "by the way," if the public road passed by them. Thirdly, the expression, "turned aside to her by the way" (v. 16), shows that she was sitting by the road-side, and not at the entrance to a town. Fourthly, the narrator says (v. 21), that Hirah made inquiry of "the men of her place" (not "of that place," as in the common English version); by which the narrator means the place where she resided, being not far from the two fountains. When Hirah himself speaks (v. 22), he simply says, "the place," not knowing anything of her or her residence.* It does not follow, therefore, that by "men of the place" are meant people of the town at the gate of which she sat.
It is not improbable that the fountains were at a little distance outside (ch. 24 : 11) of the town named from them; and that Tamar, perhaps residing there, sat down by the road-side at the entrance to them, in order to attract the notice of Judah as he passed by.
Enayim (margin); probably the same as *Enam* (both forms having the same meaning) mentioned in Josh. 15 : 34.†

---

* The evidence to the minute truthfulness of the narrative, furnished by such slight but singularly apt coincidences, should not be overlooked. Several occur in this brief and striking narrative. In v. 1, it is said, he "went down;" and we learn elsewhere (see the note on the verse) that Adullam was in the low country. While he was in that region, it is said (v. 5), "he was at Chezib" when his third son was born; and we learn elsewhere (see the note on the verse) that this place was also in the low country. While he was still there, it is said (v. 12), he "went up to Timnah;" and this place (as we learn elsewhere, see the note on the verse), was in the mountain district.
No book is so rich as the Bible in these casual (so to speak) and undesigned coincidences, which are the surest attestation of truthfulness, and can be accounted for on no other supposition.

† Compare the art. Enajim (properly, Enayim), added by Dr. Hackett to *Smith's Bible Dictionary*, American edition.

¹⁵ And Judah saw her, and he thought her to be a harlot; because she covered her face.
¹⁶ And he turned aside to her by the way, and said: Come, I pray, let me come in to thee. For he knew not that she was his daughter-in-law. And she said: What wilt thou give me, that thou mayest come in to me?
¹⁷ And he said: I will send a kid of the goats, from the flock. And she said: Wilt thou give a pledge, till thou
¹⁸ send it? And he said: What is the pledge that I shall give thee? And she said: Thy signet-ring, and thy cord, and thy staff that is in thy hand. And he gave them to her; and he went in to her, and she conceived by him.
¹⁹ And she arose, and went away; and she put off her vail from her, and put on the garments of her widowhood.
²⁰ And Judah sent the kid of the goats by the hand of his friend the Adullamite, to receive the pledge from the hand
²¹ of the woman; and he found her not. And he asked the men of her place, saying: Where is the harlot, she at the two fountains, by the way? And they said: There was no harlot here.
²² And he returned to Judah, and said: I did not find her; and also the men of the place said: There was no harlot here.
²³ And Judah said: Let her take them for herself, lest we be scorned. Behold I sent this kid, and thou didst not find her.
²⁴ And it came to pass, about three months after, that it was told Judah, saying: Tamar, thy daughter-in-law, has committed harlotry; and also, behold, she is with child

---

V. 21. *Or*, she at Enayim

V. 18. *Cord*, by which the signet-ring was attached to the neck.
VV. 21, 22. *Her place*. See the remarks on v. 14, third paragraph, under the fourth objection.
Enayim (margin); see the remarks on v. 14, fifth paragraph.
The word rendered *harlot*, in these two verses, and for which we have no other intelligible expression, means *consecrated*; namely, to the goddess of licentiousness, to whose temple and worship her gains were devoted. The name, and the custom on which it was founded, only partially reveal the fearful corruption of religion and morals wherever idolatry prevailed.

by harlotry. And Judah said: Bring her out, and let her be burnt.

25 She was brought out; and she sent to her father-in-law, saying: By the man, whose these are, am I with child. And she said: Discern, I pray, whose are these, the signet-ring, and the cord, and the staff.

26 And Judah knew them; and he said: She is more in the right than I; because I gave her not to Shelah my son. And he knew her again no more.

27 And it came to pass at the time of her labor, that,
28 behold, there were twins in her womb. And it came to pass, when she was in labor, that one put out a hand; and the midwife took and bound on his hand a scarlet
29 thread, saying: This came out first. And it came to pass, as he drew back his hand, that, behold, his brother came out. And she said: How hast thou broken forth? On thee be a breach! And his name was called Pharez.
30 And afterward came out his brother, on whose hand was the scarlet thread. And his name was called Zarah.

V. 26. *Or, for therefore I gave her not*

V. 24. *Let her be burnt.* On the authority of the head of the family and household, compare ch. 31 : 32.
Tamar was regarded as betrothed to Shelah (vv. 11, 14), and the penalty of her crime was death. But Judah's sentence was more severe than that of the Mosaic law, by which only incest (Lev. 20 : 14), and violation of chastity by a priest's daughter, a profanation of the sacred order (Lev. 21 : 9), were punishable by burning with fire.
V. 25. Not till she was brought out to die this horrible death did she expose the author of her ignominy, and then only to himself. Though highly culpable, in the eye of the divine law, for the course she adopted, she seems to have intended merely to test her own rights, denied her by the timid policy of Judah. In regard to these rights, Judah himself acknowledged that her claim was just, and that he was the offender.
Allowance must of course be made, in her case, for the loose sentiments and practices of the age. It has been justly said * that her conduct, culpable as it was, was marked by shrewdness, tenderness, and magnanimity.
V. 26. *She is more in the right than I.* That is, her cause is more just than mine; I am the offender. He admits that in withholding Shelah, her rightful husband (v. 11), he had been guilty of a wrong, and that her claim, which he had denied, was just.
For therefore (margin); namely, that it might come to this, expressing, not the purpose, but the necessary result of his conduct.
V. 28. *Bound on his hand a scarlet thread;* as the only means of determining, in such a case, which should be entitled to the rights of primogeniture.
VV. 29, 30. *On thee be a breach!* That is, bear this name, and the wrong implied in it. *Pharez;* meaning, breach. *Zarah;* a coming forth, said especially of the rising sun, and indicating that the one so called was foremost, and should be recognized as leader.

---

* *Delitzsch, Commentar über die Genesis,* 3te Ausg., p. 538.

¹ And Joseph was brought down to Egypt. And Potiphar, an officer of Pharaoh, captain of the life-guard, an Egyptian, bought him at the hand of the Ishmaelites, who brought him down thither.

² And Jehovah was with Joseph, and he was a prosperous man; and he was in the house of his master, the Egyptian.

³ And his master saw that Jehovah was with him; and all that he did Jehovah made to prosper in his hand.

⁴ And Joseph found favor in his sight, and served him. And he made him overseer over his house, and all that he had he gave into his hand.

⁵ And it came to pass from the time that he made him overseer in his house, and over all that he had, that Jehovah blessed the house of the Egyptian on account of Joseph; and the blessing of Jehovah was upon all that he had, in the house and in the field. ⁶ And he left all that he had in Joseph's hand; and he knew not aught with

---

The omen was not prophetic, however; for Pharez took the lead in the family of Judah, and through him its glory and influence were perpetuated.*

Through Pharez, the offspring of Judah by Tamar, she is included in the genealogy of our Lord (Matt. 1 : 3). It is not strange that this, and other like cases, should be ground of offense. There were Pharisees in the days of our Lord, who scoffed at his permitting the humble approach of sinners, whose burdens they themselves would not lift with their finger. And there are Pharisees still, who mock at his origin from such as he came to seek and save, of whom no outcast is so vile as not to be assured of his sympathy and help.†

But such is not the wisdom of God. He chose the foolish things of the world to put to shame the wise; and weak things of the world to put to shame the strong; and base things of the world, and things which are despised; that no flesh should glory before God.‡

Ch. 39. Joseph is brought down to Egypt, and sold as a slave. He is falsely accused to his master, and imprisoned.

V. 1. *Pharaoh.* See the note on ch. 12 : 15. On the Pharaoh of this and the following chapters, see the remarks at the close of ch. 41.

Bought him—of the Ishmaelites. The Ishmaelites seem to have formed the main body of the caravan, and hence it was named from them in ch. 37 : 25, 28. For the same reason the caravan is so named here, though Midianites, who joined it and were a part of it, were the immediate authors of the sale. See ch. 37 : 36.

V. 3. *Saw that Jehovah was with him;* in its results. It does not necessarily follow, that he recognized Jehovah as the author of them.

V. 6. *Knew not aught with him;* that is, in common with him. He left all in his care, taking no share with him in the direction or knowledge of his own affairs.

---

* See the table of his numerous descendants, in their several branches, in *Smith's Bible Dictionary*, art. Pharez.

† Calvin well suggests, that he derived no nobility from his birth, and that his descent from such ancestors was part of that "emptying of himself" (Philipp. 2 : 7), when he assumed our nature.—*Calvin in librum Geneseos.*

‡ 1 Cor. 1 : 27–29.

GENESIS. CHAP. XXXIX.

him, save the bread that he ate. And Joseph was of beautiful form, and of beautiful countenance.

7 And it came to pass after these things, that his master's wife lifted her eyes toward Joseph; and she said: Lie with me.

8 And he refused. And he said to his master's wife: Behold my master knows not with me what is in the house, 9 and all that he has he has given into my hand. He is not greater in this house than I; and he has not withheld from me anything, except thee, because thou art his wife; and how can I do this great evil, and sin against God?

10 And it came to pass, as she spoke to Joseph day by day, that he hearkened not to her, to lie down by her 11 side to be with her. And it came to pass at this time, that he went into the house to do his business, and there was no one of the men of the house there in the house. 12 And she laid hold of him by his garment, saying: Lie with me; and he left his garment in her hand, and fled, and went forth out of the house.

13 And it came to pass, when she saw that he left his gar- 14 ment in her hand, and fled out of the house, that she called to the men of her house, and spoke to them, saying:

Save the bread that he ate; a proverbial expression, implying the least possible concern about his own affairs, or knowledge of them.

V. 7. Both ancient and modern writers agree in ascribing to Egyptian women, in general, the character here exhibited in this conduct of Potiphar's wife. This fact, in connection with the confidence Joseph had before inspired, strengthened by an ingenuous and truthlike assertion of his innocence, may account for the lenity shown him, which is otherwise unintelligible.

V. 8. *Knows not with me;* as in v. 6.

V. 9. *He is not greater in this house than I.* He has clothed me with his own authority over all in the house, making me equal to himself.

How can I do this great evil, and sin against God. A golden saying, which should be ever at hand, to resist temptation to any wrong act. It should be the first lesson of childhood. Let every one, when tempted to do wrong, pause and say: HOW CAN I DO THIS EVIL, AND SIN AGAINST GOD?

V. 10. *To be with her;* in the sense in which this phrase is used in 2 Sam. 13: 20.

V. 11. *At this time;* namely, the time when she was thus importuning him.

To do his business; not putting himself in the way of temptation or of danger, but attending to the duties which he owed to his master.

V. 14. *He has brought in a Hebrew.* This she intimates as an offense; though, with a reserve natural in such a case, she forbears to refer to the offender by name. The elevation over them of a foreigner and a Hebrew had prepared them to be favorable listeners to the tale of pretended outrage. Compare ch. 43: 32, 46: 34.

See, he brought in to us a Hebrew, to mock us. He came in to me to lie with me, and I cried with a loud voice. ¹⁵ And it came to pass, when he heard that I raised my voice and cried, that he left his garment by me, and went forth out of the house.

¹⁶ And she laid up his garment by her, until his master ¹⁷ came to his house. And she spoke to him according to these words, saying: The Hebrew servant, whom thou ¹⁸ hast brought in to us, came in to me to mock me. And it came to pass, when I raised my voice and cried, that he left his garment by me, and fled out of the house.

¹⁹ And it came to pass, when his master heard the words of his wife, which she spoke to him, saying: According to these words did thy servant to me, that his anger was ²⁰ kindled. And Joseph's master took him, and put him into the prison, the place where the king's prisoners were bound; and he was there in the prison.

²¹ And Jehovah was with Joseph; and he caused kindness to be shown him, and gave him favor in the eyes of the ²² keeper of the prison. And the keeper of the prison gave into Joseph's hand all the prisoners that were in the prison; and whatever they did there, he was the doer of ²³ it. The keeper of the prison looked not to anything in

---

To mock; to make light of, by rude and indecent treatment, such as improper liberties attempted with a modest woman.

Us; including with herself the other female members of the household, as though all were exposed to the like indignities.

The whole account shows that women were not condemned to the absolute seclusion required in some ancient countries.*

V. 19. *According to these words;* namely, as has been told.

V. 20. *Put him into the prison;* of which he had charge, as captain of the king's life-guard (v. 1), who were also his executioners. This being the place of confinement for "the king's prisoners" (next clause), it was therefore under his control.

Were bound; that is, restrained of their liberty by confinement within the prison walls, equivalent to being bound, a practice in which the expression originated.

V. 21. *Keeper of the prison;* an officer having immediate charge of the prison, and subordinate to the captain of the life-guard.

V. 22. *He was the doer of it.* Whatever was done there was done through him; namely, by his authority.

---

* "The Egyptian women enjoyed greater liberty, confidence, and consideration, than under the *hareem* of the Greeks and Persians."—*Sir Gardner Wilkinson*, note to Rawlinson's Herodotus, book ii., ch. 34. Compare *Manners and Customs of the Ancient Egyptians*, first series, vol. ii., p. 389.

his hand, because Jehovah was with him; and what he did Jehovah made to prosper.

1 And it came to pass, after these things, that the butler of the king of Egypt and the baker offended against their 2 lord, the king of Egypt. And Pharaoh was wroth against his two officers, against the chief of the butlers, and against 3 the chief of the bakers. And he put them in ward in the house of the captain of the life-guard, into the prison, the place where Joseph was bound.
4 And the captain of the guard appointed Joseph to be with them, and he served them. And they were for a time in ward.
5 And they dreamed a dream both of them, each his dream in one night, each according to the interpretation of his dream, the butler and the baker of the king of Egypt, who were bound in the prison.
6 And Joseph came in to them in the morning; and he 7 saw them, and behold, they were sad. And he asked Pharaoh's officers, who were with him in ward in his master's house, saying: Wherefore are your faces sad to-day?
8 And they said to him: We have dreamed a dream, and there is no interpreter of it. And Joseph said to them: Do not interpretations belong to God? Relate it to me, I pray.

Ch. 40. Joseph interprets the dreams of the chief butler and the chief baker of the king.

V. 2. *Was wroth.* The Hebrew word was used to express the anger of persons high in station and authority.

V. 3. *House of the captain of the life-guard;* connected, as was also the prison, with the quarters of the life-guard.

Was bound; used as in ch. 39 : 20, note, second paragraph.

V. 4. These high officers of state (for such they were, in accordance with Oriental usage; compare the case of Nehemiah, Neh. 2 : 1-9), were treated with the consideration due to their rank, while the issue of their arrest was pending. The captain of the life-guard himself assigned Joseph as their personal attendant.

V. 5. *According to the interpretation of his dream;* that is, corresponding to its import and significance. Each one's dream had its special application, and was conformed to it.

V. 8. We have no interpreter, as we might have were we at liberty, so as to have access to those skilled in such things.

Joseph suggests, in reply, that interpretations are God's special prerogative and his gift, and not the exclusive right of professional interpreters, such as they refer to.

⁹ And the chief of the butlers related his dream to Joseph. And he said to him: In my dream, behold, a vine was ¹⁰ before me. And in the vine were three branches. And it was budding, its blossom sprang up, its clusters yielded ¹¹ ripened grapes. And Pharaoh's cup was in my hand; and I took the grapes, and pressed them into Pharaoh's cup; and I gave the cup into Pharaoh's hand. ¹² And Joseph said to him: This is its interpretation. ¹³ The three branches are three days. Within three days will Pharaoh lift up thy head, and restore thee to thy place; and thou wilt give Pharaoh's cup into his hand, ¹⁴ after the former manner, when thou wast his butler. But remember me by thyself, when it shall be well with thee, and show kindness to me I pray, and make mention of me ¹⁵ to Pharaoh, and bring me out from this house. For I was verily stolen from the land of the Hebrews; and also here

---

V. 9. *A vine was before me.* The cultivation of the vine by the ancient Egyptians has been denied. But it is abundantly attested by the sculptures on the ancient monuments, where all its various processes are minutely represented.*

V. 10. *It was budding,* etc.; was in the act of budding (began to put forth buds), and forthwith its blossom sprang up (it blossomed), and its clusters became ripened grapes; all passing, almost at once, before his eyes.

V. 11. *Pressed them into Pharaoh's cup,* etc. This was a part of the dream, and necessary to its coherency; and we are not to infer from it the nature of the drink presented to Pharaoh, any more than we infer, from the preceding statement, that in Egypt the budding, flowering, and ripening of the grape, were nearly simultaneous.†

V. 13. *To lift up the head* of one, means to raise him from a state of humiliation and dishonor (2 Kings 25 : 27, 28; Psalm 3 : 3); as, on the contrary, to "hang down the head" (Lam. 2 : 10), or "bow down the head" (Isaiah 58 : 5) is a sign of humiliation and abasement.

V. 14. *By thyself;* when alone, and thoughts of the past and present should bring me to mind.

V. 15. *I was verily stolen.* See the remark on ch. 37 : 28, fourth paragraph and second foot-note.

Land of the Hebrews. Abraham's descendants had long been known in Canaan as *Hebrews*

---

* See *Wilkinson's Manners and Customs of the Ancient Egyptians,* first series, vol. ii., pp. 142-152. "Some have pretended to doubt that the vine was commonly cultivated, or even grown in Egypt; but the frequent notice of it, and of Egyptian wine, in the sculptures, and the authority of ancient writers, sufficiently answer these objections."—Page 152.

"In the neighborhood of Memphis, at Thebes, and the places between these two cities, as well as at Eileithyas, they cultivated the vine. . . . Most of the other vineyards were at Marea, and in places similarly situated near the edge of the desert, where the light soil was better suited to them; though grapes for the table were produced in all parts of the country. Wine was universally used by the rich throughout Egypt."—*Sir Gardner Wilkinson,* note to Rawlinson's *Herodotus,* book ii., ch. 77.

† The Egyptian kings, according to ancient writers and the sculptures on Egyptian monuments, were allowed the use of wine, but only in a moderate quantity prescribed by the sacred books (Diodorus Siculus, i., 70; Hecatæus, in Plutarch On Isis and Osiris, 6). But customs differed under the different dynasties, domestic and foreign.

I have done nothing, for which they should put me into the dungeon.

16 And the chief of the bakers saw that the interpretation was good. And he said to Joseph: As for me also, in my dream, behold, three baskets of white bread were on 17 my head. And in the uppermost basket were all kinds of food for Pharaoh, work of the baker; and the birds ate them out of the basket, off from my head.

18 And Joseph answered and said: This is its interpreta-
19 tion. The three baskets are three days. Within three days will Pharaoh lift up thy head from thee, and will hang thee on a tree; and the birds will eat thy flesh off from thee.

20 And it came to pass on the third day, Pharaoh's birthday, that he made a feast for all his servants. And he lifted up the head of the chief of the butlers, and of the 21 chief of the bakers, among his servants. And he restored the chief of the butlers to his butlership, and he gave the 22 cup into Pharaoh's hand; and the chief of the bakers he hanged, as Joseph interpreted to them.

23 And the chief of the butlers remembered not Joseph, and forgot him.

(ch. 14 : 13, note); and in speaking of them, the country where they had so long resided would naturally be called their land.

V. 16. *As for me also;* implying that his dream was similar, and of like import.

Three baskets of white bread were on my head. This menial service did not pertain to his high office. The dream shaped itself in accordance with the intended interpretation. See v. 5, and note.

White bread; of the finest and purest material, in distinction from that of a coarser quality.

On my head; as represented in sculptures on the ancient monuments.*

V. 19. *Will hang thee on a tree.* Compare Deut. 21 : 22; Josh. 10 : 26; 2 Sam. 4 : 12.†

V. 20. *Pharaoh's birthday.* The king's birthday was celebrated with great pomp and festivity.‡

He lifted up, etc. He lifted up the heads of both; but in different ways, as related in the two following verses.

---

* *Wilkinson* (as above), vol. ii., p. 151, plate 139, and p. 395, plate 277. "The men [of Egypt] carry burdens on their heads, the women carry them on their shoulders."—Herodotus, book ii., ch. 35.

† "Beheading (which, among the Jews, did not become one of the four legal death-penalties till after the Exile) was practiced in Egypt; and the hanging of the dead body was a customary aggravation of the death-penalty in all ancient nations."—*Delitzsch, Commentar über die Genesis,* 3te Ausg., p. 543.

‡ As is shown in the Priests' decree, inscribed on the Rosetta stone, lines 46 and 47 of the Greek copy.

1 And it came to pass, at the end of two full years, that Pharaoh dreamed; and behold, he was standing by the river.
2 And behold, there came up from the river seven heifers, fair-looking and fat in flesh; and they fed on the marsh-grass.
3 And behold seven other heifers came up after them from the river, ill-looking and thin in flesh; and they stood by the side of those heifers, on the bank of the river.
4 And the heifers that were ill-looking and thin in flesh devoured the seven heifers that were fair-looking and fat. And Pharaoh awoke.
5 And he slept, and dreamed a second time; and behold,
6 seven ears came up on one stalk, plump and good. And behold, seven ears, thin and blasted by the east wind,
7 sprang up after them. And the thin ears consumed the seven plump and full ears. And Pharaoh awoke; and behold, it was a dream.
8 And it came to pass, in the morning, that his spirit was troubled. And he sent and called for all the scribes of Egypt, and all its wise men. And Pharaoh related to

---

, V. 1. *Or,* two years of days

Ch. 41. Joseph interprets Pharaoh's dreams, and is made ruler over the land of Egypt. The seven years of plenty, and the seven years of famine.
V. 1 (margin). *Two years of days.* Compare ch. 29 : 14, and note.*
The river. The Nile of course is meant here. The word in the Hebrew text is an Egyptian word meaning river, and in the Pentateuch is used only of the Nile.
V. 2. *Heifers;* as the Hebrew word is properly rendered, in the common English version, in Num. 19 : 2, 5, 6, 9; Hos. 4 : 16. Young and vigorous animals are chosen, as representatives of their kind. Compare the remarks on v. 5, second and third paragraphs.
Marsh-grass; herbage growing in wet grounds, as on the margin of a river. Compare Job 8 : 11, "Will the marsh-grass grow without water?"
V. 5. *Seven ears;* namely of wheat, the noblest and most important of the vegetable products of Egypt.
On one stalk. A kind of wheat is still grown in Egypt, having several ears on one stalk. Seven on a single stalk was an indication of extraordinary fertility.
It seems intended, in these two dreams, to represent the most valuable and necessary of the products of the country, in one of the animal, in the other of the vegetable kingdom.
V. 8. *Scribes;* men skilled in the sacred sciences, and in expounding the sacred writings and usages, and in the interpretation of dreams. They were also skilled in magic arts (Ex. 7 : 11, 22, 8 : 7, 18, properly, "the scribes did so").

* "The word *days* . . . is possibly used to distinguish the ordinary year from a greater period, the year of days from the year of years."—*Smith's Bible Dictionary,* art. Joseph, eighth paragraph, foot-note.

them his dream. And there was no one that interpreted them to Pharaoh.

9 And the chief of the butlers spoke to Pharaoh, saying:
10 I remember my faults this day. Pharaoh was wroth against his servants; and he put me in ward in the house of the captain of the life-guard, me and the chief of the
11 bakers. And we dreamed a dream in one night, I and he; we dreamed, each according to the interpretation of
12 his dream. And there was with us a Hebrew young man, servant to the captain of the life-guard; and we related them to him, and he interpreted to us our dreams; accord-
13 ing to each one's dream did he interpret. And it came to pass, that as he interpreted to us, so it was; me he restored to my place, and him he hanged.
14 And Pharaoh sent and called Joseph, and they brought him hastily out of the dungeon. And he shaved himself, and changed his garments, and came in to Pharaoh.
15 And Pharaoh said to Joseph: I have dreamed a dream, and there is no one that interprets it. And I have heard it said of thee, that thou understandest a dream, to inter-
16 pret it. And Joseph answered Pharaoh, saying: It is not for me; God will give Pharaoh an answer of peace.
17 And Pharaoh said to Joseph: In my dream, behold, I
18 was standing on the bank of the river. And behold, there

V. 9. *My faults;* meaning his offense against the king (ch. 40 : 1), and with it his ungrateful forgetfulness of Joseph, to whom he owed the first intimation of returning royal favor.
V. 11. *According to,* etc. See the remark on ch. 40 : 5.
V. 12. *According to each one's dream;* in accordance with the terms of each dream.
V. 14. As an object now of the royal interest and attention, he is released in all haste from confinement, and then prepares himself for admission to the presence of the king.
Shaved himself; according to the custom of the Egyptians, who allowed the hair and beard to grow only when in mourning, as attested by ancient writers,* and the sculptures on Egyptian monuments.†
V. 16. *It is not for me.* Ascribe it not to me; it belongs to God alone.
VV. 17–24. The king's relation of his dreams is naturally more animated, and more pointed in some of its expressions, than the calm historical statement of the narrator in vv. 1–7. See, for example, vv. 19, 21, and 23.

* Herodotus, ii., 36.
† "Though foreigners, who were brought to Egypt as slaves, had beards on their arrival in the country, we find that so soon as they were employed in the service of this civilized people, they were obliged to conform to the cleanly habits of their masters; their beards and heads were shaved, and they adopted a close cap."—*Wilkinson, Manners and Customs of the Ancient Egyptians,* vol. iii., p. 358.

came up from the river seven heifers, fat in flesh, and fair-
19 formed; and they fed on the marsh-grass. And behold, seven other heifers came up after them, poor and very ill-formed and lean in flesh; I have not seen such as they in
20 all the land of Egypt for vileness. And the lean and ill-
21 looking heifers devoured the first seven fat heifers. And they went into them; and it could not be known that they went into them, and they were ill-looking as at the beginning. And I awoke.
22 And I saw in my dream, and behold, seven ears came
23 up on one stalk, full and good. And behold, seven ears, withered, thin, blasted by the east wind, sprang up after
24 them. And the thin ears consumed the seven good ears. And I told it to the scribes; and there was none that made it known to me.
25 And Joseph said to Pharaoh: The dream of Pharaoh, it is one. What God is about to do he has showed to Pharaoh.
26 The seven good heifers, they are seven years; and the seven good ears, they are seven years. The dream, it is
27 one. And the seven lean and ill-looking heifers that came up after them, they are seven years; and the seven ears, empty, blasted by the east wind, will be seven years of famine.
28 This is the thing which I have spoken to Pharaoh; what God is about to do, he has caused Pharaoh to see.
29 Behold, there are coming seven years of great plenty in all
30 the land of Egypt. And there will arise after them seven years of famine; and all the plenty will be forgotten in the
31 land of Egypt, and the famine will consume the land. And the plenty will not be known in the land, on account of that famine afterward; for it will be very grievous.
32 And as the dream was twice repeated to Pharaoh, it is

V. 24. *Made it known to me;* made me understand it, by unfolding its meaning.
V. 25. *Is one;* in design and import.
V. 28. *Which I have spoken to Pharaoh;* referring to what he has said in v. 25.
V. 32. The repetition of a dream was accounted an assurance of the certainty of what it portended, and of its speedy fulfillment.

because the thing is established by God, and God hastens to do it.

33 Now therefore, let Pharaoh look out a man discerning 34 and wise, and set him over the land of Egypt. Let Pharaoh cause that he appoint officers over the land; and let him take the fifth part of the land of Egypt in the 35 seven years of plenty. And let them gather all the food of these good years that are coming, and lay up grain under the hand of Pharaoh for food in the cities, and 36 keep it. And the food shall be for store for the land, for the seven years of famine which shall be in the land of Egypt; that the land perish not in the famine.

37 And the thing was good in the eyes of Pharaoh, and in 38 the eyes of all his servants. And Pharaoh said to his servants: Can we find such a one as this, a man in whom is the spirit of God?

39 And Pharaoh said to Joseph: Since God has made all this known to thee, there is no one so discerning and wise 40 as thou art. Thou shalt be over my house, and to thee shall all my people do homage; only as to the throne will I be greater than thou.

41 And Pharaoh said to Joseph: See, I have set thee over 42 all the land of Egypt. And Pharaoh took off his signet-ring from his hand, and put it on Joseph's hand, and

---

V. 34. *The fifth part of the land;* the fifth of its annual produce, to be taken as a tax for the government.

V. 35. *In the cities;* as centres of accumulation and distribution for the surrounding rural districts. Compare v. 48.

The expressions used in this and the following verse, and in v. 48, imply that all the grain produced was stored in the cities, "under the hand of Pharaoh," that is, under his control. This may have been done to prevent the exportation of grain from the country, during the years of plenty, in order to secure a sufficient supply for the years of famine. The appointment of a special regent "over the land of Egypt" (v. 33), and of his subordinate "officers over the land" (v. 34), for this special emergency, and Joseph's mission "through all the land of Egypt" (v. 46), imply the exercise of extraordinary functions conferred for a special purpose.

V. 37. *His servants.* Those are meant who are more particularly mentioned in ch. 50: 7.

V. 39. *Since God has made all this known to thee;* taken as an evidence of the spirit of wisdom and discernment with which God would continue to endow him.

V. 40. *To thee shall all my people do homage;* shall acknowledge thee as the representative of sovereign power.

Only as to the throne, etc. Only the occupancy of the throne, the regal state, shall distinguish between us. In authority and power, thou shalt be my representative and equal.

V. 42. *Put it* (the signet-ring) *on Joseph's hand;* the customary token, by which a monarch conferred his own authority on another. Compare Esther 3: 10, 11.

clothed him in vestures of fine linen, and put the chain of gold on his neck; and he made him ride in the second chariot which he had; and they cried before him: Bow the knee; and he set him over all the land of Egypt. [44] And Pharaoh said to Joseph: I am Pharaoh, and without thee shall no man lift his hand or his foot in all the land of Egypt. [45] And Pharaoh called Joseph's name Zaphnath-paaneah. And he gave him for a wife Asenath, daughter of Potipherah priest of On. And Joseph went out over the land of Egypt. [46] And Joseph was thirty years old when he stood before Pharaoh king of Egypt. And Joseph went out from the presence of Pharaoh, and passed through all the land of Egypt. [47] And in the seven years of plenty, the earth brought forth by handfulls. [48] And he gathered all the food of the seven years which were in the land of Egypt; and he put

---

Fine linen; worn by the highest class in the realm.

Put the chain of gold on his neck. This was a part of the ceremony of investiture in office, as represented in ancient Egyptian sculptures.*

The chain; with the definite article, as being one of the customary insignia of office.

V. 43. After being thus invested with the insignia of vice-regent, he is assigned the royal chariot next to that of the king, and all are required to bow the knee before him.

V. 44. *I am Pharaoh;* my will is law, and no one in my kingdom shall do aught without permission from thee.†

V. 45. Joseph receives from the king an Egyptian name (Zaphnath-paaneah,‡ meaning Preserver of life), expressive of the service he had rendered by pointing out the peril which threatened the country, and the means of averting it.

On; an ancient city of Egypt, about twenty miles northeast of Memphis. It is known in general history by its Greek name Heliopolis (meaning city of the sun), corresponding to its sacred Egyptian name HA-RA, meaning abode of the sun, that being the principal object of worship in the city.

The order of priests was the highest class in the realm. The king was always either of this or of the military class; and if of the latter, it was necessary that he should be initiated into the former.

V. 46. *Stood before Pharaoh;* as his servant and minister of state. Compare Deut 1 : 38; 1 Kings 10 : 8; Dan. 1 : 5.

V. 47. *By handfulls;* a proverbial expression implying abundance, filling the hand, in contrast with a meagre and stinted supply.

V. 48. *The seven years which were in the land.* The expression is peculiar. The obvious meaning is, the seven years of plenty, as indicated by the word " food."

* *Wilkinson, Manners and Customs of the Ancient Egyptians,* vol. ii. (second series), p. 293, and plate 80.

† The explanation,—I am Pharaoh, that I reserve to myself (*Knobel, Delitzsch, Keil*), is a singular misapprehension of the very obvious meaning of the expression.

‡ Compare the article in *Smith's Bible Dictionary.*

food in the cities; the food of the field, which was around
49 the city, he put within it. And Joseph laid up grain as
the sand of the sea, exceedingly abundant, until he left off
numbering; for it was without number.
50 And to Joseph were born two sons, before the year of
famine came, whom Asenath, daughter of Poti-pherah
51 priest of On, bore to him. And Joseph called the name
of the first-born Manasseh; for God has made me forget all
52 my trouble, and all my father's house. And the name of
the second he called Ephraim; for God has made me
fruitful in the land of my affliction.
53 And the seven years of plenty, that was in the land of
54 Egypt, were ended. And the seven years of famine began
to come, according as Joseph said. And the famine was
in all lands; but in all the land of Egypt there was bread.
55 And all the land of Egypt was famished; and the people
cried to Pharaoh for bread. And Pharaoh said to all the
Egyptians: Go to Joseph; what he says to you, do.
56 And the famine was over all the face of the earth. And
Joseph opened all the storehouses, and sold grain to the
Egyptians; and the famine was severe in the land of
57 Egypt. And all countries came into Egypt, to Joseph, to
buy grain; for the famine was severe in all the earth.

Cities. Compare the note on ch. 4:17. A city, so called, often answered to our village; a small settlement, where the inhabitants of the district congregated for mutual convenience and security. This accounts for the large number of cities said to have been in ancient Egypt, which is supposed by some to be exaggerated.

V. 49. *Left off numbering.* In sculptures on the ancient Egyptian monuments, scribes are represented entering in their written tablets the number of measures given and delivered.*

V. 50. *The year of famine;* namely, the commencement of the period of seven years' famine.

VV. 51, 52. *Manasseh;* meaning, who makes forget. *My father's house;* he means the longing for it, which has now given place to the cares and enjoyments of his own home. *Ephraim;* meaning, double fruitfulness.

VV. 55, 56. The transactions here referred to are more fully narrated in ch. 47:13-20.

Was famished; after consuming, from year to year, its portion of the yearly produce, and of the surplus deposited in the cities (vv. 35, 36, and note).

The Pharaoh of this and the following chapters seems to have been of the same race of kings as ruled in the time of Abraham. See the remarks on ch. 12:15. This accounts for the favor shown by the reigning monarch to foreigners in the persons of Joseph and his family; and for the absolute power of this prince, and his arbitrary use of it, in marked contrast with the government of the native kings, as regulated by the laws and traditional usages of the country.

* Wilkinson (as above), second series, vol. i., pp. 86 and 91.

¹ And Jacob saw that there was grain in Egypt; and Jacob said to his sons: Why do ye look one upon ² another? And he said: Behold, I have heard that there is grain in Egypt. Go down thither, and buy grain for us from thence; that we may live, and not die.
³ And Joseph's ten brothers went down to buy grain from ⁴ Egypt. And Benjamin, Joseph's brother, Jacob sent not with his brothers; for he said: Lest harm befall him.
⁵ And the sons of Israel came to buy grain among those that came; for the famine was in the land of Canaan.
⁶ And Joseph, he was the ruler over the land; and he it was that sold grain to all the people of the land. And Joseph's brothers came, and bowed down to him, with their faces to the earth.
⁷ And Joseph saw his brothers, and knew them; and he made himself strange to them, and spoke with them roughly. And he said to them: Whence are ye come? And they said: From the land of Canaan, to buy grain for food.

Ch. 42. Ten of Jacob's sons are sent by him to Egypt to buy food for the household.
The narrative now returns to the humble shepherds on the plains of Canaan. Twenty years have passed away.* The shepherd boy, who was sold into slavery, falsely accused and imprisoned, has been raised to a seat next the throne, and made ruler of the most powerful and enlightened people of the ancient world. All this wonderful change in his fortunes has been wrought by means perfectly simple and intelligible,—the exhibition of divinely given endowments, fitting him above all others for the duties of his exalted station.
The narrator deals with both phases of this wonderful story with simple earnestness, and freedom from all effort for effect, as of one whose only concern is to record the facts.
V. 5. *Israel.* See ch. 32:28.
Among those that came; many joining together, and forming a large caravan for mutual aid and protection.
V. 6. *He it was that sold;* through his subordinate officers, he having the direction of all. In this case, for his own special purpose, he requires the applicants for food to appear before himself.
V. 7. *Spoke with them roughly.* The evident design of Joseph, in his treatment of his brothers, was to bring them to a just sense of their guilt. For this purpose, he put them through a process that certainly ought to have been effectual, and probably was. At the same time, his tender regard for them is repeatedly shown, both in vain efforts to restrain the expression of it (v. 24; ch. 43:1), and in acts of forbearance and kindness (v. 19; ch. 43:16). It has been

* Joseph was thirty years old when he stood before Pharaoh (ch. 41:46), and the seven years of plenty are ended and the years of famine have commenced (ch. 41:53, 54). As Joseph was seventeen years of age when he was sold into Egypt (ch. 37:2), at least twenty years must have passed away; and not much more, if we suppose the years of plenty to have commenced soon after his elevation, which is the natural construction of the narrative.

⁸ And Joseph knew his brothers; and they knew not
⁹ him. And Joseph remembered the dreams which he dreamed of them. And he said to them: Ye are spies; to see the nakedness of the land are ye come.
¹⁰ And they said to him: Nay, my lord; for thy servants
¹¹ have come to buy grain for food. We are all sons of one man. We are true men; thy servants are not spies.
¹² And he said to them: Nay; for ye have come to see the nakedness of the land.
¹³ And they said: Thy servants are twelve; we are brothers, sons of one man in the land of Canaan; and behold, the youngest is this day with our father; and one is not.
¹⁴ And Joseph said to them: This is what I spoke to you,
¹⁵ saying: Ye are spies. By this ye shall be tested. By the life of Pharaoh, ye shall not go out hence, except
¹⁶ when your youngest brother comes hither. Send one of you, and let him fetch your brother, and be ye bound, that your words may be tested, whether there is truth with you; and if not, by the life of Pharaoh, ye are surely spies.

---

thought strange that he should have caused his father, and his own innocent brother, so much pain. But this was unavoidably incident to his main purpose, which was just and laudable.

V. 9. *Remembered*, etc. Their presence, and their prostration before him (v. 6), called his dreams to mind. No more than this seems to be intended.

Nakedness of the land; its destitute and exposed condition, or the exposed and undefended parts of it.*

V. 11. *All sons of one man;* and hence not likely to be engaged in a perilous service, exposing the whole family to destruction.

V. 13. *Thy servants are twelve;* there are twelve of us in all, two being absent, as accounted for in the following clause. These statements, as we learn from ch. 43: 7, were partly made in answer to the close questioning of Joseph.

VV. 14-17. Their statements, if accepted as true, seem to make their case very clear. But Joseph retorts, that these pretences only betray their character as spies; and demands that their statements be proved true, as the only refutation of the charge.

By the life of Pharaoh. A customary form of asseveration, suited to his assumed character as an Egyptian.†

---

* "The charge suits well with the highest officer of state under the Hyksos [ch. 12: 15, note, second paragraph]. For these, according to Manetho, were in constant dread of attacks from the then powerful Assyrians. . . . Those who came from Asia might well be treated as Assyrian spies, especially the sons of Jacob, who, from their Chaldæan origin, bore a resemblance to the eastern Semites."—*Knobel, die Genesis erklärt,* p. 321.

† "How truly has the narrator represented the constraint which Joseph puts upon himself, in dealing so harshly, and concealing their common faith in the One God under the oath by the life of Pharaoh!"—*Delitzsch, Kommentar über die Genesis,* p. 549.

¹⁷ And he put them all together in ward, three days.

¹⁸ And Joseph said to them, on the third day: This do ¹⁹ and live. I am one that fears God. If ye are true men, let one of your brothers be bound in your prison-house; and do ye go, carry grain for the famine of your houses. ²⁰ And bring your youngest brother to me, and your words shall be found true, and ye shall not die. And they did so.

²¹ And they said one to another: We are verily guilty concerning our brother, whose anguish of soul we saw, when he besought us, and would not hear; therefore is ²² this anguish come upon us. And Reuben answered them, saying: Did not I speak to you, saying: Do not sin against the child, and ye would not hear? And also his blood, behold, is required.

²³ And they knew not that Joseph heard; for the interpreter was between them.

²⁴ And he turned about from them, and wept. And he returned to them, and talked to them; and he took from them Simeon, and bound him before their eyes.

²⁵ And Joseph commanded that they should fill their vessels with grain; and to return their money into each one's sack, and to give them provision for the way. And thus he did to them.

VV. 18–20. The severity of his first demand (v. 16) is moderated by the more lenient requirement, that one should be retained as a hostage, to insure the return of the others.

And they did so ; a summary statement of what is afterward narrated in detail.

V. 21. The object of this severity is partially attained, in the awakened sense of guilt.

When he besought us. This trait in the tragic scene here comes incidentally to light; and the want of any allusion to it, in ch. 37 : 23–28, shows the absence of all study for effect in this simple narration of facts.

V. 22. *And also his blood;* inasmuch as they gave him up to those in whose hands they had reason to suppose he perished. *Is required.* See ch. 9 : 5, note, fourth paragraph.

V. 23. *The interpreter;* with the definite article, indicating one whose business it was to act in that capacity, and appointed for it.

Was between them; as the medium of communication, thus interposing between them and Joseph, and separating him from their cognizance.

V. 24. *Took from them Simeon.* The selection was purposely and appropriately made. Compare ch. 34 : 25, 26, and ch. 49 : 5–7.

V. 25. *He did to them;* namely, he who had charge of returning their money, and giving them provision for the way. Others seem to be meant in the first clause, "that they should fill," etc.

As a matter of delicacy, Joseph could not receive their money; but they could regard its restoration only as an omen of evil (vv. 28, 35).

26 And they lifted their grain upon their asses, and went from thence.

27 And one of them opened his sack to give provender to his ass at the lodging-place, and he saw his money; and 28 behold, it was in the mouth of his bag. And he said to his brothers: My money is returned; yea, and behold, it is in my bag. And their heart went out; and they turned trembling one to another, saying: What is this that God has done to us?

29 And they came to Jacob their father, to the land of Canaan. And they told him all the things that befell 30 them, saying: The man, the lord of the land, spoke 31 roughly with us, and took us for spies of the land. And we said to him: We are true men; we are not spies. 32 We are twelve brothers, sons of our father; one is not, and the youngest is this day with our father in the land of Canaan.

33 And the man, the lord of the land, said to us: By this I shall know that ye are true men; let one of your brothers remain with me, and take what the famine of 34 your houses requires, and go. And bring your youngest brother to me, and I shall know that ye are not spies, that ye are true men. Your brother I will deliver to you, and ye shall traffic in the land.

35 And it came to pass as they emptied their sacks, that, behold, each one's bundle of money was in his sack; and they saw their bundles of money, they and their father, and they were afraid.

V. 27. *The lodging-place;* as the common English version properly renders the Hebrew word in Josh. 4 : 3; Jer. 9 : 2; and similarly in Josh. 4 : 8; 2 Kings 19 : 23; Isaiah 10 : 29.

V. 28. *Yea, and behold, it is in my bag;* where it must have been placed purposely, and with some secret design, by the one charged with the duty of filling their sacks with grain. Hence the emphatic reference to this fact, "yea and," etc., and the alarm it excited.

Their heart went out. No heart was left them. This is the striking and forcible expression of the thought in the Hebrew, and it should be retained in the version.

That God has done to us. They recognize his hand in its dealing with the guilty.

V. 32. *Sons of our father;* of our common father, being all sons of one man, as more fully expressed in v. 13.

V. 35. For some reason, the money was not discovered on the way, except in one instance, when it was deposited in the mouth of a sack which there was occasion to open. Compare the remark on ch. 43 : 21.

36 And Jacob their father said to them: Me do ye bereave; Joseph is not, and Simeon is not, and Benjamin ye will take. On me are all these things.

37 And Reuben spoke to his father, saying: My two sons shalt thou slay, if I bring him not to thee. Deliver him into my hand, and I will return him to thee.

38 And he said: My son shall not go down with you. For his brother is dead, and he alone is left; and if harm befall him by the way in which ye go, ye will bring down my gray hairs in sorrow to the underworld.

1 And the famine was grievous in the land.

2 And it came to pass, when they had eaten up the grain which they brought from Egypt, that their father said to them: Return, buy us grain for a little food.

3 And Judah spoke to him, saying: The man solemnly protested to us, saying: Ye shall not see my face, unless **4** your brother be with you. If thou wilt send our brother with us, we will go down and buy thee grain for food. **5** But if thou wilt not send him, we will not go down. For the man said to us: Ye shall not see my face, unless your brother be with you.

6 And Israel said: Wherefore dealt ye so ill with me, to tell the man whether ye had yet a brother?

7 And they said: The man strictly questioned concerning us, and concerning our kindred, saying: Is your father yet alive? Have ye a brother? And we told him according to these words. Could we surely know that he would say: Bring your brother down?

V. 7. *Or*, according to these things

V. 36. *Me do ye bereave.* It is I that am bereft; the stroke falls on me.
On me are all these things. They fall on me alone; I must bear them all. His complaint is just so far as this, that he alone has a father's grief to bear. In this they have no part.
V. 38. *Underworld.* See the remarks on ch. 37 : 35, third paragraph.
Ch. 43. Jacob's sons are sent the second time to Egypt to buy grain.
V. 2. *Return.* See the remark on v. 13.
V. 7. Compare the remark on ch. 42 : 13.
According to these words; according to the words he used, word for word, in answer to his questions. *According to these things* (margin); namely, as these things are. We gave him true answers, in accordance with the facts.

⁸ And Judah said to Israel his father: Send the lad with me, and we will arise and go; and we shall live, and not ⁹ die, both we, and also thou, and also our little ones. I will be surety for him; of my hand shalt thou require him. If I do not bring him to thee, and set him before ¹⁰ thee, then will I be guilty to thee forever. For unless we had lingered, surely now we had returned this second time.

¹¹ And Israel their father said to them: If then it is so, do this; take of the boast of the land in your vessels, and carry down a present for the man, a little balsam, and a little honey, tragacanth and ladanum, pistacia-nuts and ¹² almonds. And take a second supply of money in your hand; and the money that was returned in the mouth of your bags ye shall carry back in your hand; perhaps it ¹³ was an error. And take your brother, and arise, return ¹⁴ to the man. And God Almighty grant you compassion before the man, that he may release to you your other brother, and Benjamin. And I, in case I am bereaved, I am bereaved!

¹⁵ And the men took that present; and double money they took in their hand, and Benjamin; and they rose up, and went down to Egypt; and they stood before Joseph.

¹⁶ And Joseph saw Benjamin with them; and he said to him who was over his house: Bring the men into the

---

V. 9. *Guilty to thee;* to thee the injured party, so that thou canst hold me guilty, and answerable for the wrong.
V. 11. *Of the boast of the land;* of its boasted products, those in which its people glory. These substances were much valued in Egypt, some being used in great quantities in embalming. *Ladanum,* etc. Compare the note on ch. 37 : 25.
V. 12. *A second supply of money;* called "other money," in v. 22.
V. 13. *Return to the man;* they having left him with the promise to return, of which the retention of Simeon was a pledge.*
V. 14. *And I,* etc. Compare Esther 4 : 16, properly, "in case I perish, I perish!" It is the language of hopeless resignation, of one who makes up his mind to bear whatever may be the issue.
V. 15. *Double money;* both the former purchase-money that was returned, and the second supply spoken of in v. 12.

* Not, as in the common English version, "go again;" in which the point of the expression is lost.

house; and slay, and make ready; for the men will eat with me at noon.

17 And the man did as Joseph said. And the man brought the men into the house of Joseph.

18 And the men were afraid, because they were brought into the house of Joseph. And they said: Because of the money that returned in our bags at the first are we brought in; that he may find occasion against us, and fall upon us, and take us for servants, and our asses.

19 And they came near to the man who was over the house of Joseph; and they spoke to him at the door of the house. 20 And they said: Beseech thee, my lord! We 21 verily came down at the first to buy grain for food. And it came to pass, when we came to the lodging-place, and opened our bags, that, behold, each one's money was in the mouth of his bag, our money in its full weight; and 22 we have brought it back in our hand. And other money have we brought down in our hands to buy grain for food. We know not who put our money in our bags.

23 And he said: Peace be to you; fear not. Your God, and the God of your father, gave you hidden treasure in your bags. Your money came to me. And he brought Simeon out to them.

24 And the man brought the men into the house of Joseph. And he gave water, that they might wash their feet; and he gave provender for their asses.

V. 16. *Slay.* The Egyptians made free use of animal food, as is shown by the testimony of ancient writers,* and by the sculptures on the Egyptian monuments.†

V. 18. *That returned;* how, or by what means, they knew not, and hence this indefinite form of expression. *Find occasion against us;* as he seemed bent on doing at the former interview.

V. 20. *We verily,* etc. It was no pretense to cover a criminal purpose and object.

V. 21. *When we came,* etc. They make a general statement of the case, without entering into the minute details, which had no bearing on it. These the narrator has stated in ch. 42 : 35. What concerned *them* was the discovery of their money; when, or where, was of no moment, and the first instance is made the occasion for mentioning all.

V. 23. His kindly greeting, and quieting assurances, are a part of the gracious reception which Joseph purposed to give them, when he saw that Benjamin was with them (v. 16). His yearning toward his brother, and desire to manifest his regard for him, explain the temporary change in his treatment of them.

V. 24. *Might wash their feet.* Compare the remark on ch. 18 : 4.

* Herodotus, ii., 37; Diodorus Siculus, i., 70.
† *Wilkinson, Manners and Customs of the Ancient Egyptians,* vol. ii., pp. 375, 383, 388, 393, 401.

²⁵ And they made ready the present against the coming of Joseph at noon; for they heard that they should eat bread there.

²⁶ And Joseph came into the house; and they brought him the present which was in their hand, into the house; and they bowed down to him to the earth.

²⁷ And he asked them of their welfare, and said: Is your father well, the old man of whom ye spoke? Is he yet ²⁸ alive? And they answered: Thy servant our father is well; he is yet alive. And they bent the head, and bowed down.

²⁹ And he lifted up his eyes, and saw Benjamin his brother, the son of his mother; and he said: Is this your younger brother, of whom ye spoke to me? And he said: God be gracious to thee, my son.

³⁰ And Joseph made haste, for his bowels yearned toward his brother, and he sought where to weep; and he entered ³¹ into the inner chamber, and wept there. And he washed his face, and went forth. And he refrained himself, and said: Set on food.

³² And they set on for him by himself, and for them by themselves, and for the Egyptians, who ate with him, by themselves; because the Egyptians could not eat food with the Hebrews, for that is an abomination to Egyptians.

³³ And they sat before him, the first-born according to his birthright, and the younger according to his minority.

V. 28. *Bent the head, and bowed down;* inclined the head, and bowed down to the ground,— the Oriental form of prostration before a superior magistrate, as often represented in the sculptures on Egyptian monuments. The bending of the head was in acknowledgment of his courteous and kindly inquiries after the welfare of their father.

V. 32. They considered foreigners unclean, as not observing the strict rites prescribed to themselves, and because they killed and ate animals held sacred by the Egyptians.*

V. 33. *Sat before him.* That the custom of *sitting* at meals prevailed among the ancient Egyptians is shown by the sculptures on the monuments.†

Wondering, that their respective ages should be exactly known, where all of them were strangers.‡

* Herodotus, ii., 41. Compare, on the exclusiveness of the ancient Egyptians, Diodorus Siculus, i. 67.

† See, for example, the group represented in *Wilkinson* (as above), vol. ii., p. 393.

‡ This "attention to precedence was characteristic of Egyptian customs," as remarked in *Smith's Bible Dictionary* (art. Egypt, *domestic life*); but that it was the cause of their surprise, as is there suggested, seems less probable than the explanation in the text.

³⁴ And the men looked wondering one at another. And he took portions from before him for them; and Benjamin's portion was five times more than any of theirs. And they drank, and were merry with him.

¹ And he commanded him who was over his house, saying: Fill the men's bags with food, as much as they can bear, and put each one's money in the mouth of his bag.
² And my cup, the silver cup, thou shalt put in the mouth of the bag belonging to the youngest, and the money for his grain. And he did according to the word of Joseph, which he had spoken.
³ The morning dawned, and the men were sent away, they and their asses.
⁴ They were gone out of the city, were not far away, when Joseph said to him who was over his house: Arise, follow after the men, and overtake them, and say to them:
⁵ Wherefore have ye requited evil for good? Is not this that in which my lord drinks? And he verily divines therewith. Ye have done evil in that ye have done.
⁶ And he overtook them, and spoke to them these words.
⁷ And they said to him: Wherefore does my lord speak according to these words? Far be it from thy servants to
⁸ do such a thing. Behold, the money, which we found in the mouths of our bags, we brought back to thee from the

---

Chs. 44, 45. Joseph's final trial of his brothers, and his disclosure of himself to them. He sends for his father's family.

VV. 4, 5. The crime with which they are charged is aggravated by several circumstances. First, it is returning evil for good. Secondly, the stolen cup belongs to the lord of the land, and their offense is against the highest officer of the realm. Thirdly, the cup is for his own private use, and the theft is an affront to his person. Fourthly, it is a sacred vessel, and kept for a sacred use, and the theft is a violation of its sanctity. All these grave offenses are combined in the alleged theft of the cup.

Divines. Compare ch. 30 : 27, note, third paragraph. It is not necessary to suppose, either here or in v. 15, that there is reference to the actual use of divination.

V. 7. *According to these words;* according to their tenor and import, meaning the charge contained in them. It would be less delicately respectful to say: Wherefore does my lord speak these words?

V. 8. Here again (compare the note on ch. 42 : 14) they make a very clear case for themselves; and their question, "and how should we steal from thy lord's house," would have been unanswerable, but for the advantage covertly taken of them. An important end is gained by this arbitrary proceeding, namely, that the sympathies of the reader are now with them; though the justness of their own self-condemnation (ch. 42 : 21) can not be denied. Compare ch. 45 : 5–8, and note.

land of Canaan; and how should we steal from thy lord's
9 house silver or gold? With whomsoever of thy servants it shall be found, let him die; and we also will be servants to my lord.

10 And he said: Yea now, according to your words, so be it. With whomsoever it shall be found, he shall be my servant; and ye shall be blameless.

11 And they made haste, and took down each one his bag
12 to the earth; and they opened each one his bag. And he searched; he began at the eldest, and ended at the youngest; and the cup was found in Benjamin's bag.

13 And they rent their garments; and they loaded each one his ass, and returned to the city.

14 And Judah came, and his brothers, to the house of Joseph; for he was yet there; and they fell before him to the earth.

15 And Joseph said to them: What is this deed that ye have done? Did ye not know, that such a man as I can surely divine?

16 And Judah said: What shall we say to my lord? What shall we speak? And how shall we clear ourselves? God has found out the iniquity of thy servants. Behold, we are servants to my lord, both we, and he in whose hand the cup was found.

17 And he said: Far be it from me to do this. The man in whose hand the cup was found, he shall be my servant; and do ye go up in peace to your father.

18 And Judah came near to him and said: Beseech thee, my lord! Let thy servant, I pray, speak a word in the ears of my lord; and let not thine anger burn against thy servant; for thou art even as Pharaoh.

19 My lord asked his servants, saying: Have ye a father,
20 or a brother? And we said to my lord: We have a

V. 14. *Fell before him to the earth.* This was not the reverential bowing down before a superior and a magistrate. They cast themselves on the ground, as criminals before their judge.
V. 15. *Can surely divine.* Compare the remarks on vv. 4, 5, second paragraph.
V. 18. *Thou art even as Pharaoh.* For this reason he craves indulgence for his presumption in addressing one so exalted in station and power.

father, an old man, and a child of old age, a little one; and his brother is dead, and he alone is left of his mother, and his father loves him.

21,22 And thou saidst to thy servants: Bring him down to me, that I may set my eyes upon him. And we said to my lord: The lad can not leave his father; for if he leaves his father, he will die.

23,24 And thou saidst to thy servants: If your youngest brother comes not down with you, ye shall see my face no more. And it came to pass, when we went up to thy servant my father, that we told him the words of my lord.

25,26 And our father said: Return, buy us grain for a little food. And we said: We can not go down. If our youngest brother be with us, then will we go down; for we can not see the face of the man, if our youngest brother is not with us.

27,28,29 And thy servant my father said to us: Ye know that my wife bore me two. And one went out from me; and I said: Surely he is torn in pieces; and I saw him not since. And if ye take this also from my presence, and harm befall him, ye will bring down my gray hairs in sorrow to the underworld.

30,31 Now therefore, when I come to thy servant my father, and the lad is not with us, seeing that his soul is bound to his soul, it will come to pass, when he sees that the lad is not, that he will die; and thy servants will bring down the gray hairs of thy servant our father in sorrow to the underworld.

V. 27. *Bore me two.* See ch. 30 : 22–24, and ch. 35 : 16–18.

The expression, "my wife," as though he had no other, indicates the tenderness of the relation while she lived, and the fondness with which her memory was cherished. Compare ch. 29 : 18–20, and chs. 35 : 20, 48 : 7.

VV. 28, 29. Compare the parallel expressions, "went out from me" (v. 28), and "from my presence" (v. 29). One went from the paternal home, and was seen no more; and how can he permit the other to go from his presence and guardianship!

Underworld. See the remarks on ch. 37 : 35, third paragraph.

V. 30. *His soul is bound to his soul.* So the same phrase is used in 1 Sam. 18 : 1; in the common English version, "The soul of Jonathan was knit with" (properly, was bound to) "the soul of David."

V. 31. *Is not.* Compare this expression in ch. 5 : 24, and in chs. 37 : 30, 42 : 36.

GENESIS. Chap. XLV.

³² For thy servant by his surety obtained the lad from my father, saying: If I bring him not to thee, then will I be guilty to my father forever. ³³ Now therefore, I pray, let thy servant remain instead of the lad a servant to my lord, and let the lad go up with ³⁴ his brothers. For how shall I go up to my father, and the lad not with me? Lest I see the evil that will come on my father.

¹ AND Joseph was not able to refrain himself before all that stood by him; and he cried: Cause every man to go out from me. And no one was standing with him, when ² Joseph made himself known to his brothers. And he wept aloud; and the Egyptians heard, and the house of Pharaoh heard.
³ And Joseph said to his brothers: I am Joseph; is my father yet alive? And his brothers could not answer him; for they were confounded before him.
⁴ And Joseph said to his brothers: Come near to me, I pray. And they came near. And he said: I am Joseph ⁵ your brother, whom ye sold into Egypt. Now therefore be not grieved, and be not angry with yourselves, that ye sold me hither; for God sent me before you to preserve ⁶ life. For these two years has the famine been in the land; and there are yet five years in which there will be ⁷ no plowing or harvesting. And God sent me before you to make for you a remnant in the earth, and to save you alive, for a great deliverance.

V. 32. *By his surety*, etc. The idea of *obtaining* is the prominent one here. I prevailed on his father to let him go, by becoming surety for his safe return. See ch. 43 : 9.

V. 34. *Lest I see*, depends on the assertion implied in the preceding question; I can not go up, and the lad not with me, lest I see, etc. The construction is not rhetorically correct, but is none the less elegant and effective.

Ch. 45 : 1. *That stood by him ;* the subordinate officers in attendance on his person.

VV. 5-8. The sentiment of these verses shows that his severity toward his brothers had not been dictated by resentment, and that the wrong he had suffered at their hands was fully forgiven. While he does not justify their conduct, or seek to lessen its guilt in their own eyes, he turns their thoughts to the higher aims of Providence, which overruled their evil intent for good.

V. 7. *For a great deliverance ;* great in the magnitude of the threatened danger, and in the wonderful means by which it was averted.

⁸ Now therefore, it was not ye that sent me hither, but God; and he has made me a father to Pharaoh, and lord of all his house, and ruler over all the land of Egypt.
⁹ . Make haste, and go up to my father, and say to him: Thus says thy son Joseph: God has made me lord of all ¹⁰ Egypt; come down to me, tarry not. And thou shalt dwell in the land of Goshen, and thou shalt be near to me, thou, and thy sons, and thy sons' sons, and thy flocks, ¹¹ and thy herds, and all that thou hast. And I will nourish thee there; for there are yet five years of famine; lest thou be impoverished, thou, and thy house, and all that thou hast.
¹² And behold, your eyes see, and the eyes of my brother ¹³ Benjamin, that it is my mouth that speaks to you. And ye shall tell my father of all my glory in Egypt, and of all that ye have seen; and ye shall haste and bring down my father hither.
¹⁴ And he fell on the neck of Benjamin his brother, and ¹⁵ wept; and Benjamin wept on his neck. And he kissed all his brothers, and wept on them; and after that his brothers talked with him.
¹⁶ And the rumor was heard in the house of Pharaoh, saying: The brothers of Joseph have come; and it was good in the sight of Pharaoh, and in the sight of his servants.
¹⁷ And Pharaoh said to Joseph: Say to thy brothers:

V. 8. *A father to Pharaoh*, as being his most trusted counselor and guide; an Oriental designation of the highest minister of state.

V. 10. *Land of Goshen;* the original seat of the Hebrews, on their first settlement in the country.* It was a border land of Egypt on the north, lying between the delta of the Nile † and the western border of Palestine.‡ Compare ch. 46 : 28, 29. From the place where the march of the Hebrews commenced, when they went out of Egypt, their nearest way was through the "land of the Philistines" (Ex. 13 : 17, 18), and the distance to the Red Sea (its ancient western shore) was a journey of three days (Ex. 12 : 37, 13 : 20, 14 : 2; Num. 33 : 5-8).

* It is not necessary to suppose, nor is it at all probable, that the Hebrews did not subsequently spread beyond its limits, as a subject people under the control of their masters.

† On its eastern branch was a royal residence of the Shepherd kings for a portion of the year (note to ch. 12 : 15, second paragraph); compare the language of Joseph in this verse, "thou shalt be near to me."

‡ See the discussion of the subject in *Smith's Bible Dictionary*, art. Goshen, and in *Herzog's Real-Encyclopädie*, art. Gosen.

This do ye; load your beasts, and go, get to the land of
18 Canaan; and take your father and your households, and
come to me; and I will give you the best of the land
19 of Egypt, and ye shall eat of the fat of the land. Now
therefore thou art commanded; this do ye, take for you
wagons out of the land of Egypt, for your little ones, and
20 for your wives, and bring your father, and come. And let
not your eye look regretfully on your goods; for the best
of all the land of Egypt, it is yours.
21 And the sons of Israel did so. And Joseph gave them
wagons, according to the command of Pharaoh, and gave
22 them provisions for the way. To each of them all he
gave changes of raiment; and to Benjamin he gave three
hundred pieces of silver, and five changes of raiment.
23 And to his father he sent after this manner; ten asses
bearing the good things of Egypt, and ten she-asses bearing grain, and bread, and food, for his father by the way.
24 And he sent his brothers away, and they went. And
he said to them: Do not fall out by the way.
25 And they went up from Egypt, and came to the land of
26 Canaan, to Jacob their father. And they told him, saying:
Joseph is yet alive; yea, and he is ruler over all the land

V. 18. *The best of the land.* No less than this would express his sense of obligation to the family of one who had saved the whole land. But while free to avail themselves of the royal grant, they chose that part of the land which was best adapted to their own wants. Compare chs. 46 : 31-34, 47 : 3-6.

V. 19. *Thou art commanded.* The command, addressed to Joseph, is intended for his brothers, as is shown by the plural forms, "this do ye," etc., including them with him.

Wagons. Wheel-carriages were in common use in Egypt,* but were not so well adapted to the more uneven surface of Palestine, where beasts of burden were used for transportation.

V. 23. *Food,* in general, and comprehending what is not included in the term bread.

V. 24. *Do not fall out by the way.* The violence of temper manifested on other occasions, and the conflict of interests likely to arise, in view of their past and future relations to Joseph, justify the caution here given them.† Some translate : *Be not afraid by the way.* But there is little significance in this admonition, or occasion for it, under the circumstances.

* As represented, from ancient sculptures, in *Wilkinson's Manners and Customs of the Ancient Egyptians,* vol. iii., p. 179. "They were commonly used in Egypt for traveling; and Strabo performed the journey from Syene to the spot where he crossed the river to visit Philæ, in one of these carriages" (p. 180).

† "Joseph is* concerned lest, on their homeward journey, discussions should arise respecting the sale of him, with mutual reproaches, and strife, and altercation, to which Reuben had already (ch. 42 : 22) led the way."—*Knobel, die Genesis erklärt,* p. 335.

"There was ground to fear that each, in clearing himself, would seek to transfer the blame to others, and thus contention would arise."—*Calvin in librum Geneseos.*

of Egypt. And Jacob's heart was cold, for he believed them not.

²⁷ And they told him all the words of Joseph which he spoke to them, and he saw the wagons which Joseph sent to carry him; and the spirit of Jacob their father revived. ²⁸ And Israel said: Enough! Joseph my son is yet alive; I will go, and see him before I die.

¹ AND Israel removed, and all that he had, and came to Beer-sheba; and he offered sacrifices to the God of his father Isaac. ² And God spoke to Israel in visions of the night, and ³ said: Jacob! Jacob! And he said: Here am I. And he said: I am God, thy father's God. Fear not to go down to Egypt; for I will there make thee a great nation. ⁴ I will go down with thee to Egypt; and I will also surely bring thee up; and Joseph shall put his hand upon thine eyes. ⁵ And Jacob rose up from Beer-sheba; and the sons of Israel bore Jacob their father, and their little ones, and their wives, in the wagons which Pharaoh sent to bear ⁶ them. And they took their cattle, and their goods, which they had gathered in the land of Canaan, and came to ⁷ Egypt, Jacob, and all his seed with him. His sons, and his sons' sons with him, his daughters, and his sons'

V. 26. *Was cold.* Instead of being warmed and animated by the intelligence, he remained unmoved, for it seemed to him incredible.

Chs. 46 : 1—47 : 12. Jacob goes down with his family to Egypt. He is presented to Pharaoh; and a possession is given him in the land of Egypt.

V. 1. *Removed;* from the valley of Hebron (ch. 37 : 14).

Beer-sheba. See ch. 21 : 14, note, third paragraph; and v. 31, note, second paragraph. Here Abraham planted a grove, and under its shade "called on the name of Jehovah, the eternal God" (ch. 21 : 33); and here Isaac "built an altar, and called on the name of Jehovah" (ch. 26 : 25). On this spot, so hallowed in the remembrances of the past, Jacob pauses in his journey, and "offers sacrifices to the God of his father Isaac."

Of his father Isaac. Compare the similar expression of filial feeling in ch. 31 : 53.

VV. 2-4. Jacob is now making the most momentous and perilous change recorded in his history; leaving the familiar land of his sojournings with its promised blessings, for a strange land and an unknown future. Hence the divine assurances here given him. Compare the similar record in the case of Abraham, ch. 15 : 1, and note.

In visions of the night. See the remarks on ch. 15 : 1, second paragraph.

Shall put his hand upon thine eyes; the last office of filial love. That he should receive it from the beloved Joseph, the lost and found, is the crowning blessing reserved for the aged patriarch.

daughters, and all his seed, he brought with him to Egypt.

8 And these are the names of the sons of Israel, who came to Egypt, Jacob and his sons. The first-born of Jacob, Reuben.

9 And the sons of Reuben; Hanoch, and Phallu, and Hezron, and Carmi.

10 And the sons of Simeon; Jemuel, and Jamin, and Ohad, and Jachin, and Zohar, and Shaul son of the Canaanitish woman.

11 And the sons of Levi; Gershon, Kohath, and Merari.

12 And the sons of Judah; Er, and Onan, and Shelah, and Pharez, and Zarah. And Er and Onan died in the land of Canaan. And the sons of Pharez were Hezron and Hamul.

13 And the sons of Issachar; Tola, and Phuvah, and Job, and Shimron.

14 And the sons of Zebulun; Sered, and Elon, and Jahleel.

15 These are the sons of Leah, whom she bore to Jacob in Padan-aram, and Dinah his daughter. All the souls of his sons and his daughters were thirty-three.

V. 8. *Who came to Egypt.* This phrase, here and in v. 26, is to be understood in the same manner as the similar statement in ch. 35 : 26; compare the note on vv. 23-26 of that chapter.

The object here is to give the family of Jacob, as constituted on their first settlement in Egypt; showing from what beginning sprang the numerous race that afterward spread abroad in the land, and were finally brought out from it in such numbers (Ex. 12 : 37). Hence Joseph (v. 19), and all of Benjamin's ten sons (v. 21), and Judah's two grandsons (v. 12), are included in the summary in v. 26; and Joseph's two sons, " born to him in Egypt," are included among the seventy "who came to Egypt" (v. 27). All these expressions are to be understood in accordance with the evident intention of the writer, as above stated. Virtually, indeed, all came into Egypt, since all were of foreign parentage, and originated in Canaan the birthplace of the family.*

V. 12. *The sons of Pharez were Hezron and Hamul.* It is only said that they were his sons, not that they were born in Canaan. For reasons stated in the note on v. 8, they are included in the summary in v. 26.

V. 15. *All the souls of his sons.* His sons by Leah are meant, her sons (see the first clause) being the subject of this verse.

In the summing up, in this verse, Jacob is included (see v. 8, *Jacob and his sons*), though not

---

* That in the interval of about twenty-two years, between the occurrences related in ch. 37 and those related here, Judah should have married and had sons and grandsons born to him (v. 12), though quite improbable, is certainly possible ; and the interval of time can be somewhat extended on more than one possible supposition. But the reader, whose sympathies have been deeply moved by the touching allusions to Benjamin in the preceding narrative, would be amazed to find that the "little one," "the lad who can not leave his father" (ch. 44 : 20, 22), is a married man with ten children ! The supposition shocks all sense of probability; and it is not required by the sacred writer's statement.

¹⁶ And the sons of Gad; Ziphion and Haggi, Shuni and Ezbon, Eri, and Arodi, and Areli.

¹⁷ And the sons of Asher; Jimnah, and Ishuah, and Isui, and Beriah, and Serah their sister. And the sons of Beriah; Heber and Malchiel.

¹⁸ These are the sons of Zilpah, whom Laban gave to Leah his daughter; and these she bore to Jacob, sixteen souls.

¹⁹ The sons of Rachel, Jacob's wife; Joseph, and Benjamin.

²⁰ And to Joseph were born, in the land of Egypt, Manasseh and Ephraim, whom Asenath, daughter of Poti-pherah priest of On, bore to him.

²¹ And the sons of Benjamin were Belah, and Becher, and Ashbel, Gera and Naaman, Ehi and Rosh, Muppim, and Huppim, and Ard.

²² These are the sons of Rachel, who were born to Jacob. All the souls were fourteen.

²³ And the sons of Dan; Hushim.

²⁴ And the sons of Naphtali; Jahzeel, and Guni, and Jezer, and Shillem.

²⁵ These are the sons of Bilhah, whom Laban gave to Rachel his daughter, and she bore these to Jacob. All the souls were seven.

²⁶ All the souls belonging to Jacob, that came to Egypt,

V. 26. *Or,* All the souls besides Jacob

---

in v. 26. He might properly be included in the number of the family of which he was the head; and counting him under the heading, "his sons and his daughters," is a mere matter of form.*
Such peculiarities are to be carefully noted in a document of this kind.

The daughter, Dinah, is here expressly mentioned, and is included in the enumeration of Leah's offspring in this verse (as is Serah, v. 17, among those of Zilpah), and in the final summary in v. 27; though she is omitted in the general summary in v. 26.

These are trifling variations from uniformity of method; and they show that it was not strictly regarded, in a matter of indifference.

V. 22. *Were fourteen;* including, as Rachel's progeny, the two sons of Joseph (v. 20), though they are not included in the summary in v. 26, being there reserved for the following statement in v. 27.

V. 23. *Sons.* See the remark on ch. 36 : 25.

* "Jacob, in v. 15, is counted among the sons of Leah (among these, because with them his posterity began), instead of being added to them."—*Delitzsch, Commentar über die Genesis,* p. 563.

that came out of his loins, besides the wives of Jacob's sons,
²⁷ all the souls were sixty-six. And the sons of Joseph, who were born to him in Egypt, were two souls. All the souls of the house of Jacob, that came to Egypt, were seventy.
²⁸ And Judah he sent before him to Joseph, to show the way before him to Goshen; and they came to the land of
²⁹ Goshen. And Joseph harnessed his chariot, and went up to meet Israel his father, to Goshen; and he appeared before him, and he fell on his neck, and wept on his neck continually.
³⁰ And Israel said to Joseph: Now let me die, since I have seen thy face, that thou art yet alive.
³¹ And Joseph said to his brothers, and to his father's house: I will go up, and tell Pharaoh, and say to him: My brothers, and my father's house, who were in the land
³² of Canaan, are come to me. And the men are shepherds; for they are herdsmen, and have brought their flocks, and their herds, and all that they have.
³³ And it shall be, when Pharaoh shall call you, and shall
³⁴ say: What is your occupation? that ye shall say: Thy servants have been herdsmen from our youth even till now, both we and our fathers; in order that ye may dwell in the land of Goshen. For every shepherd is the abomination of Egyptians.

V. 28. He sent Judah forward in advance to Joseph, to learn from him how to direct their course to the place intended for them.

V. 29. *Appeared before him.* The expression indicates the imposing equipage and attendance required by his position as the highest officer of the realm. Compare ch. 41 : 43.

V. 34. *Every shepherd is the abomination of Egyptians.* This prejudice is strikingly illustrated in the sculptures on the ancient Egyptian monuments.* But it seems not to have been shared by the reigning family (see v. 32, and ch. 47 : 5, 6); as Joseph would naturally have sought to avoid this frank disclosure of their occupation, if it had been offensive.

The two facts, apparently inconsistent, are reconciled on the supposition referred to in the note to ch. 12 : 15, second paragraph, and in the closing remarks on ch. 41; the oppressive domination of the foreign race of Shepherd kings having made the name and occupation of the shepherd odious to native Egyptians.† The prejudice may be accounted for on other grounds; but not the apparent absence of it in the reigning family.

* "The artists, both of Upper and Lower Egypt, delighted on all occasions in representing them as dirty and unshaven; and at Beni Hassan and the tombs near the Pyramids of Geezeh, we find them caricatured as a deformed and unseemly race."— *Wilkinson, Manners and Customs of the Ancient Egyptians,* vol. ii., p. 16.

† The date of their occupation of Egypt, or of a part of it, is still a subject of discussion; but the weight of evidence seems to be in favor of the supposition here referred to.

1 And Joseph came and told Pharaoh, and said: My father and my brothers, and their flocks, and their herds, and all that they have, are come from the land of Canaan; and behold, they are in the land of Goshen.
2 And of the whole number of his brothers he took five
3 men, and presented them before Pharaoh. And Pharaoh said to his brothers: What is your occupation? And they said to Pharaoh: Thy servants are shepherds, both we and our fathers.
4 And they said to Pharaoh: We have come to sojourn in the land; for there is no pasturage for the flocks which belong to thy servants; for the famine is grievous in the land of Canaan. Now therefore, we pray thee, let thy servants dwell in the land of Goshen.
5 And Pharaoh spoke to Joseph, saying: Thy father and
6 thy brothers are come to thee. The land of Egypt is before thee. Cause thy father and thy brothers to dwell in the best of the land. They shall dwell in the land of Goshen; and if thou knowest that there are capable men among them, make them master-herdsmen over what I have.
7 And Joseph brought in Jacob his father, and placed him before Pharaoh; and Jacob blessed Pharaoh.
8 And Pharaoh said to Jacob: How many are the days of the years of thy life?
9 And Jacob said to Pharaoh: The days of the years of my sojournings are a hundred and thirty years. Few and evil have been the days of the years of my life; and they have not attained to the days of the years of the life of my fathers, in the days of their sojournings.

Ch. 47 : 2. *Five men;* the most presentable, we may presume, of the whole number.
V. 6. *In the best of the land.* See the note on ch. 45 : 18.
They shall dwell in the land of Goshen; as requested by them (v. 4), in accordance with Joseph's instructions in ch. 46 : 33, 34.
VV. 7 and 10. *Blessed.* See the remark on ch. 27 : 23, and the references in the foot-note.
V. 8. Observing his great age, Pharaoh puts the question in a form which indicates how many he conceived must be the days, of the years, of his life.
V. 9. *Sojournings.* Compare the remark on ch. 17 : 8.
Have not attained, etc. Compare chs. 25 : 7, and 35 : 28.

¹⁰ And Jacob blessed Pharaoh, and went out from before Pharaoh.
¹¹ And Joseph appointed his father and his brothers a dwelling-place, and he gave them a possession in the land of Egypt, in the best of the land, in the land of Rameses, ¹² as Pharaoh commanded. And Joseph nourished his father, and his brothers, and all his father's house, with bread, according to their little ones.
¹³ And there was no bread in all the land; for the famine was very grievous, and the land of Egypt, and the land of Canaan fainted by reason of the famine.
¹⁴ And Joseph gathered up all the money that was found in the land of Egypt, and in the land of Canaan, for the grain which they bought. And Joseph brought the money into the house of Pharaoh.
¹⁵ And the money was spent from the land of Egypt, and from the land of Canaan; and all the Egyptians came to Joseph, saying: Give us bread; for wherefore should we die in thy presence? For there is no more money.
¹⁶ And Joseph said: Give your cattle, and I will give it you for your cattle, if there is no more money.
¹⁷ And they brought their cattle to Joseph. And Joseph gave them bread for the horses, and for the flocks, and for the herds, and for the asses; and he provided them with bread for all their cattle in that year.
¹⁸ And that year was ended. And they came to him in the second year, and said to him: We will not hide it from my lord, that since the money and the beasts are all my lord's, there is nothing left in the sight of my lord, ¹⁹ except our bodies and our lands. Wherefore should we

V. 11. *Land of Rameses;** the same as the land of Goshen, or a district of it. The city Rameses was built subsequently by the Hebrews (Ex. 1 : 11), and was distant from the Red Sea about three days' journey. See the references in the note on ch. 45 : 10.
V. 12. *According to their little ones;* according to the number of children, of all ages, remaining in the paternal home.
VV. 13–26. Conditions on which Joseph supplies the people of the land with food. Compare ch. 41 : 47–49.
VV. 18, 19. *There is nothing left in the sight of my lord,* etc. My lord can find nothing more, to require in payment for bread, except our bodies and our lands.

* See the article in *Smith's Bible Dictionary*.

die before thine eyes, both we and our land? Buy us and our land for bread, and we and our land will be servants to Pharaoh; and give us seed, that we may live and not die, and that the land be not waste.

20 And Joseph bought all the land of Egypt for Pharaoh. For the Egyptians sold every man his field, because the famine was too strong for them. And the land became Pharaoh's.

21 And the people, he transferred them to the cities, from one end of the territory of Egypt even to the other end 22 thereof. Only the land of the priests he bought not; for the priests had a portion from Pharaoh, and they ate their portion which Pharaoh gave them. Therefore they sold not their land.

23 And Joseph said to the people: Behold, I have bought

Die—both we and our land; literally, in reference to the former, and in a figurative sense (literally expressed in the last clause of the verse, "that the land be not waste") in reference to the latter.

We and our land will be servants to Pharaoh; both to be regarded as property of the crown, the land doing service by rendering its products to the royal treasury.

V. 20. See the remarks on vv. 23-26.

V. 21. *To the cities* (ch. 41 : 48, note, second paragraph). This seems to have been done for the more convenient distribution of the stores of grain there accumulated; see ch. 41 : 35, and note.

The form of the expression does not admit the interpretation some have given it; namely, that Joseph, for a government purpose, shifted the population of the country from one extremity of it to the other, transferring the people of each city to some other one.*

V. 22. The priests were not obliged to sell their lands; for they had a daily allowance of food sufficient for their wants.

To the same effect it is said, by the earliest of the ancient writers on Egypt:† "They neither consume anything of their own, nor are they at any expense; but bread of the sacred grain is baked for them, and each has an abundant supply of the flesh of oxen and of geese, every day."

VV. 23-26. An ancient writer,‡ who traveled in Egypt, states that all the lands were taken by the kings for revenue (v. 26 §), except those belonging to the priests (compare v. 22), and the soldiery.∥

We can not form a satisfactory judgment of Joseph's conduct in this matter (vv. 13-26)

* It has been thought, but with little probability, that this was the origin of the division of the country into Nomes (districts, or cantons). This division seems to have been of earlier date, and was of much wider extent, than what is here narrated.

† Herodotus, ii., 37.

‡ Diodorus Siculus, i., 73.

§ "The evidence of the monuments, though not very explicit, seems to show that this law was ever afterward in force under the Pharaohs. The earliest records afford no information as to the tenure of land; but about Joseph's time we find frequent mention of villages with their lands, the two being described under one designation, as held by the great officers of the crown, apparently by the royal gift."—*R. S. Poole,* in *Smith's Bible Dictionary,* art. Egypt (*cultivation and agriculture,* second paragraph).

∥ The latter exemption belongs to a period later than the date of the sacred writer's statement, which was made more than fifteen hundred years earlier than the one here referred to.

you this day, and your land, for Pharaoh. Behold, there
24 is seed for you, and ye shall sow the land. And it shall
be that of the increase ye shall give a fifth to Pharaoh;
and four parts shall be your own, for seed of the field,
and for your food, and for those who are in your houses,
and for food for your little ones.
25 And they said: Thou hast saved us alive. Let us find
favor in the sight of my lord, and we will be servants to
Pharaoh.
26 And Joseph made it a statute over the land of Egypt
to this day, that every fifth is Pharaoh's; except that the
land of the priests alone became not Pharaoh's.
27 And Israel dwelt in the land of Egypt, in the land of
Goshen; and they had possessions therein, and were fruitful, and multiplied exceedingly.
28 And Jacob lived in the land of Egypt seventeen years.
And the days of Jacob, the years of his life, were a hundred and forty-seven years.
29 And the days of Israel drew near to death. And he
called to his son, to Joseph, and said to him: If now I
have found favor in thy sight, put, I pray, thy hand under
my thigh, and deal with me kindly and truly. Do not, I

without a more full knowledge of all the facts of the case.* That he should act in the interest of the government, would of course be expected and required of him. It is to be observed, however, that the claim acquired for the government was used with moderation, a fifth part of the produce from its own lands being required for its use.† The government, moreover, was thus enabled to abolish some of the unequal and oppressive distinctions in regard to landed property.‡

VV. 27–31. Jacob, in anticipation of his approaching death, provides that his remains shall be conveyed for burial to the land of Canaan.

V. 29. *Put thy hand under my thigh.* See the remarks on ch. 24 : 2, 3, third paragraph.

* "If, as we may reasonably suppose, the people were warned of the famine and made no preparation for it, the government had a clear claim upon its subjects for having taken precautions which they neglected. In any case, it may have been desirable to make a new allotment of land, and to reduce an unequal system of taxation to a simple claim to a fifth of the produce."—*Smith's Bible Dictionary*, art. Joseph, eighteenth paragraph.

† Long after this it was observed by an ancient writer and traveler in Egypt (Diodorus Siculus, i., 73), that the kings were enabled, by the abundant revenues derived from the crown lands, to defray the expenses of wars and of their own regal state, and to reward those who distinguished themselves in the public service, without overwhelming the common people with taxes.

‡ "Joseph certainly had in view no less the good of the country than the interest of the king; inasmuch as he converted the disproportionate division of the landed property into an equable leasing of it in small portions, for an annual rent."—*Delitzsch, Commentar über die Genesis*, 3te Ausg., p. 571.

³⁰ pray, bury me in Egypt. But I will lie with my fathers, and thou shalt carry me out of Egypt, and bury me in their burying-place. And he said: I will do according to ³¹ thy word. And he said: Swear to me. And he swore to him. And Israel bowed himself on the head of the bed.

¹ AND it came to pass after these things, that they said to Joseph: Behold, thy father is sick; and he took with him his two sons, Manasseh and Ephraim.
² And they told it to Jacob, and said: Behold, thy son Joseph is come to thee. And Israel strengthened himself, and sat upon the bed.
³ And Jacob said to Joseph: God Almighty appeared to ⁴ me at Luz in the land of Canaan, and blessed me. And he said to me: Behold, I will make thee fruitful, and will multiply thee, and will make thee an assemblage of peoples, and will give this land to thy seed after thee for an everlasting possession.
⁵ Now therefore, thy two sons, that were born to thee in the land of Egypt before I came to thee to Egypt, they are mine; Ephraim and Manasseh shall be to me as Reu- ⁶ ben and Simeon. And thy offspring, which thou begettest after them, shall be thine; after the name of their brothers

---

V. 30. *Thou shalt carry me out of Egypt*, etc. He here requires this of Joseph, in whom he most confided, and who could most easily carry his wishes into effect. See ch 50 : 4-9. But he also required it of all his sons (ch. 49 : 29-31).
V. 31. *Bowed himself on the head of the bed;* in worship, being too feeble to rise from the bed on which he reclined.
Ch. 48. Jacob adopts as his own the two sons of Joseph, Manasseh and Ephraim, and blesses them.
V. 1. *Took with him.* It is implied, as being a matter of course, that he hastened to the bedside of his suffering parent, and it is only said that he took with him his two sons.
V. 2. *Strengthened himself;* collected all his remaining strength for the last private meeting with his son.
V. 3. *Luz.* Compare the remarks on ch. 28 : 19.
V. 4. *Said to me,* etc. Compare ch. 35 : 6 and 11.
V. 5. *Now therefore,* etc.; in virtue of this promise, and to give it the fullest effect. By adopting Joseph's two sons as his own, he constituted two heads of tribes in place of one, among his own sons.
Born—before I came to thee to Egypt; as were the other heads of tribes among Jacob's own sons.
As Reuben and Simeon; in place of my own first and second born. Compare ch. 49 : 4, 7.
V. 6. *Called after the name of their brothers;* bearing the name of their brothers, Manasseh and Ephraim, not being themselves heads of tribes with their own separate inheritance.

⁷ shall they be called in their inheritance. And as for me, when I came from Padan, Rachel died by me in the land of Canaan on the way, when there was yet a length of way to come to Ephrath; and I buried her there on the way to Ephrath. That is Bethlehem.
⁸ And Israel saw Joseph's sons; and he said: Who are
⁹ these? And Joseph said to his father: They are my sons, whom God has given me here. And he said: Bring them to me, I pray, that I may bless them.
¹⁰ And the eyes of Israel were dim with age; he could not see. And he brought them near to him; and he kissed them, and embraced them.
¹¹ And Israel said to Joseph: I did not think to see thy face; and behold, God has made me see also thy seed.
¹² And Joseph brought them out from between his knees;
¹³ and he bowed himself before him to the earth. And Joseph took them both, Ephraim in his right hand toward Israel's left, and Manasseh in his left hand toward Israel's right, and brought them near to him.
¹⁴ And Israel stretched out his right hand, and laid it on the head of Ephraim, and he was the younger, and his left hand on the head of Manasseh; he guided his hands
¹⁵ knowingly, for Manasseh was the first-born. And he blessed Joseph, and said: The God before whom my fathers walked, Abraham and Isaac, the God who fed me all my

V. 7. *As for me.* This connects with the first clause of v. 6, the words, "thy offspring," intimating the hope of future progeny; but "as for me," mine ceased with the untimely end of the mother of my first-born in giving birth to her second son. In honor of her memory, to whom further progeny was denied, he adopts the offspring of her elder-born as his own.
Rachel died, etc. See ch. 35 : 16-19.
V. 10. *Could not see.* Could not see clearly, so as to distinguish features of the countenance, though he could perceive the forms of persons present (v. 8).
V. 12. *From between his knees;* of Jacob is meant, who had taken them between his knees and to his bosom, as he embraced and kissed them (v. 10).
In order to present them properly for the promised blessing (v. 9), Joseph takes them from his father's embrace, and first reverently bowing down before him, presents himself and his sons to receive the blessing (vv. 15, 16).
V. 14. *Knowingly.* It was not done accidentally or by mistake. He had a purpose in it; and fully knowing what he did, he placed his right hand on the head of the younger, and his left on the head of the elder. Compare v. 19.
For Manasseh was the first-born; showing that he had a purpose in thus crossing his hands, in order to avoid laying his right hand on the head of the first-born.
V. 15. *Blessed Joseph;* in his offspring. See v. 16. *Fed me;* as a shepherd does his flock, implying every other provision for his welfare.

¹⁶ life long to this day, the Angel who redeemed me from all evil, bless the lads; and let my name be named on them, and the name of my fathers Abraham and Isaac; and let them increase to a multitude in the midst of the land. ¹⁷ And Joseph saw that his father laid his right hand on the head of Ephraim, and it was wrong in his sight; and he took hold of his father's hand, to remove it from the ¹⁸ head of Ephraim to the head of Manasseh. And Joseph said to his father: Not so my father, for this is the first- ¹⁹ born; lay thy right hand on his head. And his father refused, and said: I know it, my son, I know it. He also shall become a people, and he also shall be great; but yet his younger brother shall be greater than he, and his seed shall become the fullness of the nations. ²⁰ And he blessed them on that day, saying: By thee shall Israel bless, saying: God make thee as Ephraim and as Manasseh. And he put Ephraim before Manasseh. ²¹ And Israel said to Joseph: Behold, I die; and God will be with you, and will return you to the land of your ²² fathers. And I, I give thee one tract above thy brothers, which I take out of the hand of the Amorite with my sword and with my bow.

V. 16. *The Angel.* See Ex. 3 : 2, and compare v. 4 (properly, "Jehovah saw"), and vv. 6, 7 (properly, "Jehovah said"), 11, 13, 14, 15.*
The land; namely, of Abraham and Isaac (see the preceding clause), and of their posterity.
V. 19. *Greater than he;* as shown in the history of the nation, from the times of the Judges onward.
The fullness of the nations. Such he became, when the tribe of Ephraim was the head of the northern kingdom of the ten tribes, representing them all (" the fullness of the nations") in itself. See the numerous allusions to Ephraim, as not only representing, but mainly constituting, the kingdom of the ten tribes.†
Nations; used as in ch. 35 : 11. The word *peoples* is more commonly used of the several tribes descended from Jacob.
V. 20. *By thee shall Israel bless.* Compare an example of the mode of blessing here referred to, in another and similar case, in Ruth 4 : 11, 12.
V. 22. *And I;* that is, on my part, when you shall have been thus divinely restored (v. 21) to the land of your fathers.
I give thee; a prophetic gift to Joseph's descendants.‡ So the words, "which I take," are a

---

* Compare *Smith's Bible Dictionary*, art. Angels, (I).
† For example: Isaiah 7 : 2, 8, 9, 17; 9 : 9; 11 : 13; Ezek. 37 : 16, 19; Hos. 6 : 4, 10; 7 : 1, 11; 8 : 8 and 9.
‡ " As a man of God, the Patriarch speaks in God's name, and hence ascribes to himself the conquest and the grant, which will proceed from God."—*Knobel, die Genesis erklärt,* 2te Anfl., p. 351. Compare ch. 49 : 7, " I will divide them," etc., and the note, second paragraph.

¹ And Jacob called to his sons and said: Gather yourselves together, that I may tell you what will befall you in after days.
² Assemble yourselves and hear, sons of Jacob, and hearken to Israel your father.
³ Reuben, my first-born thou,
My might, and firstling of my strength,
Excellency of dignity, and excellency of power.
⁴ Boiling over like water, thou shalt not excel.
Because thou wentest up to thy father's bed;
Then thou didst defile it.
He went up to my couch!

prophetic anticipation of their forcible occupation of the tract, in his name and by virtue of the gift here made to them.*

The "tract" here spoken of was Shechem, where Jacob purchased "a part of the field," namely, of the open field outside of the inclosed city (ch. 33 : 19, and note). From Josh 24 : 32 we learn that the sons of Joseph came into possession of this tract, as their inheritance. Some translate, "which I took;" and they suppose that the treacherous and vindictive act of Simeon and Levi in the slaughter of the Shechemites, and the plunder of the place, (ch. 34 : 25-29,) are here referred to. But that was in no sense the act of Jacob. It was disapproved by him at the time (ch. 34 : 30), and is sternly rebuked, and its punishment prophetically declared, in his final charge to his sons, ch. 49 : 5-7. That he should, notwithstanding all this, claim the act as his own, and by virtue of it bestow the place as a gift on his son, is incredible.†

The Amorite. See Num. 13 : 29, "The Hittites, and the Jebusites, and the Amorites, dwell in the mountains," namely, the mountainous region of Judah and Ephraim; compare Josh. 5 : 1, 10 : 5, 6, 11 : 3.‡

Ch. 49. Jacob's final prophetic charge to his twelve sons. His death.

V. 1. *Will befall you;* namely, in your posterity, in whom you will be represented in after years.

V. 3. *Firstling of my strength;* first-fruits of the strength of my manhood's prime.

Excellency of dignity, and excellency of power; namely, as first-born, and as such entitled to pre-eminence in rank and authority.

This is said, not of Reuben himself, as though these were personal traits belonging to him, but of the first-born, as prerogatives of that relation, forfeited by Reuben's crime.

V. 4. *Boiling over like water;* in the violence of passion, breaking through all restraints, like swelling and boiling floods that no barriers can confine. Or the allusion may be to water boiling over with heat, emblematic of the heat and violence of unrestrained passion.

Shalt not excel; shalt not be allowed the pre-eminence belonging to thy birth.

He went up to my couch! See ch. 35 : 22. This ejaculation, apart to himself, is characteristic of the depth of emotion with which the Patriarch recalls the unnatural crime.

---

* " As 'I give' is prophetically said, in reference to the future viewed as already present, so 'I take' must be understood as prophetic, meaning that Jacob, not in his own person but in his posterity, wrests the land from the Amorites."—*Keil, Biblischer Commentar*, vol. i., 2te Aufl., p. 292.

† "As in ch. 34 : 30 he utters bitter complaints of the act of Simeon and Levi, so here [ch. 49 : 5-7] dying he disclaims all participation in it."—*Delitzsch, Commentar über die Genesis*, 3te Ausg., p. 584 (note on ch. 49 : 5-7).

‡ See the article Amorite, in *Smith's Bible Dictionary.*

5 Simeon and Levi are brethren;
Instruments of violence are their devices.
6 My soul come not into their council;
To their assembly be not my honor united!
For in their anger they slew a man,
And in their self-will they undermined a wall.
7 Cursed be their anger, for it was fierce;
And their wrath, for it was cruel.
I will divide them in Jacob,
And scatter them in Israel.
8 Thee, Judah, thee will thy brethren praise;
Thy hand will be on the neck of thine enemies;
Thy father's sons will bow down to thee.

V. 5. *Or*, are their swords   V. 6 (4th line). *Or*, they houghed an ox

V. 5. *Are brethren;* not only brothers by natural birth, but brethren in spirit and purpose.
Instruments of violence are their devices. Their devices (ch. 34 : 15, 16, 25) are instruments (means) of violence. The same metaphorical use of this word occurs in Isaiah 32 : 7, where by the "instruments" of the deceiver are meant his "wicked devices."
Are their swords (margin) is regarded by many as the true rendering. The force of the accusation is, that their swords are instruments of violence and wrong, and not merely of defense.

V. 6. *They slew a man;* they did not shrink from taking the life of man; human life had no sacredness for them. The point made here, is their disregard of human life. Whether few or many were slain is not taken into account.
Undermined a wall; secretly and treacherously destroyed the defenses of a peaceful city, when off its guard. This explanation is not necessarily inconsistent with what is said in ch. 34 : 25 ("came upon the city boldly"), as the statement there made is very brief, and does not enter into the particulars of the treacherous assault. But the phrase may be a proverbial saying, referring to the underhand and treacherous device (ch. 34 : 15, 16, 25) by which they took advantage of their victims.
Houghed an ox (margin) is supposed to be the true, though it is not the most ancient, rendering. It is understood to mean that they, in the wantonness of revenge, maimed the cattle which they could not take away for their own use (compare Josh. 11 : 6, 9; 2 Sam. 8 : 4; 1 Chron. 18 : 4). This is not strictly at variance with the statement in ch. 34 : 27-29, though no intimation of such an act is there given. But it is quite as probable that the phrase is here used proverbially, meaning to take advantage of another by covertly disabling him, referring to the treacherous device of which Simeon and Levi availed themselves.

V. 6. *My soul come not*, etc. An expression of abhorrence, in the form of earnest deprecation.

V. 7. *I will divide*, etc. See Josh. 19 : 1-9, and 21 : 1-42. According to the former of these passages, the tribe of Simeon received no separate inheritance, but certain cities were assigned them within the bounds of Judah. According to the latter passage, the several families of Levi were scattered through cities of all the other tribes.
I will divide them. He personates the divine will, in declaring it; the announcement of the divine purpose being equivalent to its execution, since that will certainly follow.

V. 8. *Judah;* meaning, praised (see note on ch. 29 : 33-35). The subject, not being expressed in the word itself, and only implied in the connection in ch. 29 : 35, is here changed to accord with the object of the speaker.*

* "This *nomen* [name] the Patriarch in his blessing seizes upon as an *omen*, and explains it as a premonition of Judah's future."—*Delitzsch, Commentar über die Genesis*, 3te Ausg., p. 585.

⁹ Judah is a lion's whelp.
From the prey, my son, thou art gone up.
He bowed himself, he lay down, as a lion,
And as a lioness; who shall rouse him!
¹⁰ The sceptre will not depart from Judah,
Nor the ruler's staff from between his feet,
Until Shiloh come ;
And to him belongs the obedience of the peoples.
¹¹ Binding his foal to the vine,
And his ass's colt to the choice vine ;
He laves his clothes in wine,
And his raiment in the blood of grapes.

V. 9. *A lion's whelp.* Such he appears now, in his yet undeveloped strength. But to the prophetic glance he next appears as the full-grown lion, or as the still more dreaded lioness guarding her young.

From the prey, etc. In the mixed metaphor that follows is a vivid picture of this dread of the shepherd, familiar to the shepherd life of Palestine in Jacob's time.* Compare ch. 37 : 33.

From the plains, where he seeks his food, he has gone up to his mountain den.† Gorged with his prey, he has stretched himself down for rest. Who so bold, as will venture to rouse him! The shepherd, whose fold he has robbed, dares not follow him to his lair.

V. 10. *Shall not depart from Judah.* Shall not pass from him to another, is the meaning. So general an expression should be taken in its obvious general import; namely, that Judah should retain the supremacy among the tribes of Israel, and should yield it to no other. This is verified in its history. For notwithstanding the revolt of the ten tribes, and the seventy years of captivity, it (and it alone) maintained its nationality to the coming of the Messiah, at which time it still had its own national institutions and laws. At the captivity, the nationality of the rival kingdom of the revolted tribes ceased, and was known no more ; that of Judah continued to the coming of the Messiah, and soon after ceased forever.

Ruler's staff—between his feet; as often represented in ancient sculptures.

Shiloh; meaning, Peaceful, or Maker of peace. Compare Prince of peace, in Isaiah 9 : 6.
That this refers to the Messiah, was held by the oldest Jewish interpreters, and there is no sufficient ground for dissenting from their opinion.‡

To him; referring either to the nearest subject, Shiloh, the most obvious grammatical reference, or to Judah the leading subject of the sentence. In the former case, the word *peoples* is to be taken in its widest sense. In the latter, it has its more usual meaning, namely the tribes of Israel; and the reference is to the most brilliant period of Judah's supremacy, when all were united under the sway of David and Solomon.

VV. 11, 12. A poetic image of affluence and ease.

Binding his foal to the vine; as one whose life is passed in the rich luxuriance of the vineyard; who, when he dismounts, ties his beast to the vine-stock, among the choicest vines.

Laves his clothes in wine; either a poetic hyperbole,§ implying that wine is as abundant as water; or a reference to the actual bathing of the garments, in treading the wine-press. Compare Isaiah 63 : 2.

The blood of grapes; poetically for wine, as in Deut. 32 : 14.

* As it continued to be long afterward. Compare Judges 14 : 5; 1 Sam. 17 : 34 ; 2 Sam. 23 : 20; 1 Kings 13 : 24; 20 : 36; 2 Kings 17 : 25.
† Compare Cant. 4 : 8.
‡ The discussion of the subject may be found in the philological notes.
§ Compare a similar one in Job 29 : 6;
When my steps were bathed in milk,
And the rock poured out by me streams of oil.

GENESIS.

¹² Dark are the eyes with wine,
And white the teeth with milk.
¹³ Zebulon will dwell by the sea-coasts,
And he will be a coast for ships;
And his flank will be upon Zidon.
¹⁴ Issachar is a bony ass,
Crouching down among the folds.
¹⁵ And he saw that rest was good,
And that the land was pleasant;
And he bowed his shoulder to bear,
And became a tributary servant.
¹⁶ Dan will judge his people,
As one of the tribes of Israel.
¹⁷ Dan shall be a serpent by the way,

Dark are the eyes, etc. Darkly flashing, is meant, the first effect of a moderate draught of wine. *Wine and milk.* Compare Cant. 5 : 1; Isaiah 55 : 1.
V. 13. *Zebulon.* See Josh. 19 : 10-16, and compare Deut. 33 : 19.
Will dwell; an allusion to the name Zebulon, which (from another Hebrew word) means *dwelling.* Ch. 30 : 17-21, note, third paragraph.
By the sea-coasts. According to Josephus,* their territory extended from the sea of Galilee to the Mediterranean.†
Upon Zidon; that is, Phœnicia, the name standing as the representative of the whole country. Compare Josh. 13 : 6; Judges 18 : 7.
It will be observed that Zebulon is not mentioned in his proper place, which, in the order of birth of Jacob's sons, would be after Issachar (ch. 30 : 17-20). In this order they are mentioned also in the blessing of Moses, Deut. 33 : 18.
VV. 14, 15. *A bony ass;* one of powerful frame, and capable of great endurance.‡ The tribe was famed for its vigorous participation in the early wars for the possession of Palestine. See Judges 5 : 15. What is said here refers to the subsequent history of the tribe, enjoying, in luxurious ease, the abundance of its fertile fields and rich pasturage.
Became a tributary servant; rendering service, by payment of tribute; preferring to purchase safety and ease, rather than assert his rightful independence. In this condition of a *hireling* there may be a reference to the meaning (reward, hire) of the name Issachar (ch. 30 : 17-21, note, second paragraph).
VV. 16, 17. *Will judge;* alluding to the meaning of the name Dan (ch. 30 : 6, note, second paragraph). There is probably reference here to the most noted of the Judges of Israel, furnished by the tribe of Dan (Judges chs. 13-16).
His people. By this is meant the people of the twelve tribes, as in Deut. 33 : 7.
As one of the tribes of Israel. Being the first here mentioned of the sons by the maid-servants (Bilhah and Zilpah, ch. 30 : 4-6, 9-13), it is expressly said that he shall rank, notwithstanding his birth, as one of the tribes of the chosen people, and entitled to its highest honors. This was the more pertinent here, as Ishmael, son of the handmaid, was excluded from the inheritance of the promised seed (ch. 21 : 10-12).
Shall be. He here uses the more authoritative form, sometimes employed in prophetic declarations of the future.

---

* Antiquities, v., 1, 22; Jewish War, iii., 3, 1.
† Compare, in the blessing of Moses, Deut. 33 : 18, 19, "they shall suck the abundance of the seas."
‡ "The 'strong-boned he-ass,' the large animal used for burdens and field work, not the lighter and swifter she-ass for riding."—*Smith's Bible Dictionary*, art. Issachar, fifth paragraph.

A horned viper by the path;
That bites the horse's heels,
And his rider falls backward.
18 I wait for thy salvation, Jehovah!
19 Gad, a troop will press upon him;
But he will press upon the heel.
20 Out of Asher is fatness, his bread!
And he will yield dainties of a king.
21 Naphtali is a hind let loose;
One that utters brilliant words.
22 Joseph is a fruitful bough,

Horned viper; a venomous serpent, found in western Asia, Arabia, and northern Africa. It buries itself in the hot sand, which it resembles in color so as to be hardly distinguishable, and attacks animals passing by, springing two or three feet, and holding firmly to its victim.

It is the image of an insidious and deadly foe; and the application is not difficult to trace in the history of the tribe.

V. 18. *I wait,* etc. Anticipating the struggles of his posterity for the possession of the promised land, the Patriarch breathes this prayer for divine help on their behalf.*

V. 19. *A troop;* alluding to the name Gad, nearly related in form to the Hebrew word for "troop." Compare the note on ch. 30 : 11.

Upon the heel; of the flying foe, is meant. He will put his enemy to flight, and will closely press him in pursuit.

For the fortunes of this tribe, compare Joshua 13 : 24–28; Judges 10 : 8, 17, 18, and 11 : 4–33; 1 Chron. 5 : 18–22. Compare Deut. 33 : 20, 21, and 1 Chron. 12 : 8–15.

V. 20. *Out of Asher* (put here for his territory) *is fatness,* the richest fruits of the soil : of such is his food, dainties fit for the royal table. Compare Deut. 33 : 24, properly : "Let him be the accepted among his brethren, and dip his foot in oil." See Job 29 : 6.

For the territory assigned to the tribe of Asher (meaning happy, ch. 30 : 13, note), see Josh. 19 : 24–31. It was among the richest portions of Palestine.

V. 21. *Hind,* the female deer; or possibly the wild she-goat of the mountains, these two animals not being accurately distinguished in Hebrew.

A hind let loose; bounding away unrestrained, and roaming at will. Compare Hab. 3 : 19, "He will make my feet like hinds'." It is an expressive image of the gallant and freedom-loving mountaineer.† Fleetness of foot is mentioned as the trait of a warrior (2 Sam. 2 : 18), "light of foot as the wild roe."

Utters brilliant words.‡ Both characterizations of the tribe were illustrated in the gallant bearing of Barak of Kedesh-Naphtali (Judges 4 : 6) and his ten thousand followers, and the commemorative song of triumph in which he took part (Judges 5 : 1).

V. 22. The comparison is with a luxuriant vine, planted by a perennial spring. Of this

---

* "He connects this utterance immediately with the tribe of Dan, which had many conflicts with the Amorites and Philistines, for whom they were no match, but were obliged to make up their lack of strength by cunning, showing clearly how much Israel must rely on higher aid."— *Knobel, die Genesis erklärt,* 2te Aufl., p. 370.

† Their home was in the "Mount of Naphtali" in the north, corresponding to the "Mount of Ephraim" in central, and the "Mount of Judah" in southern Palestine (Josh. 20 : 7).

‡ "The history of the tribe is indeed too little known to enable us to show how Naphtali has specially distinguished himself by 'brilliant words,' which seems to intimate that he was to be peculiarly the poet (or orator) tribe of Israel; but it may at least remind one of the fact, that the song of Deborah (Judges, ch. 5) is introduced as the song of Deborah and of Barak the Naphtalite."—*Delitzsch, Commentar über die Genesis,* 3te Ausg., p. 599.

"It scarcely admits any other reference than to poetic gifts."—*Tuch, über die Genesis,* p. 565.

A fruitful bough by a spring,
The branches running over the wall.
23 And archers sorely grieved him,
And shot at, and persecuted him.
24 And his bow abode in strength;
And strong were the arms of his hands,
From the hands of the Mighty One of Jacob,
From thence, the Shepherd, the Stone of Israel;
25 From the God of thy father,—and he will help thee,
And from the Almighty,—and he will bless thee,
With blessings of the heavens above,
Blessings of the abyss that lies under,
Blessings of the breasts and of the womb.
26 The blessings of thy father prevail,
Above the blessings of the eternal mountains,
The delight of the everlasting hills.
They shall be for the head of Joseph,
And for the crown of him that was separated from his brethren.

Joseph is "a fruitful bough," its "branches running over the wall," spreading beyond the limits of the inclosure. The allusion is to the exuberant fruitfulness of the house of Joseph (compare the name *Ephraim*, ch. 41 : 51, 52, and note), and its wide extension in his posterity.

VV. 23, 24. The image changes; the mind of the Patriarch reverting to former days and the earlier fortunes of Joseph. He is here the object of hatred and violence, under the image of a champion beset by deadly foes, and sustained in the unequal contest by divine support.*

From thence, the Shepherd, the Stone of Israel. This is an emphatic repetition of the thought in the preceding line; the "Mighty One of Jacob" represented here as the "Shepherd, the Stone of Israel;" the Shepherd, as being his overseer, director, and guardian; the Stone, as an image of firmness and strength. Compare "Rock of Israel," in 2 Sam. 23 : 3, and Isaiah 30 : 29 (properly, "the Rock of Israel").

V. 25. *The abyss that lies under;* the "waters beneath the earth" (Deut. 5 : 8), supposed to be the source of the springs that water its surface. Compare Deut. 8 : 7, properly, "and of depths (abysses) issuing forth in valley and in mountain."

V. 26. *Prevail above* (have a power and efficacy that exceeds) *the blessings of the eternal mountains,* in value and in perpetuity.

Blessings of the eternal mountains—delight of the everlasting hills. Compare, in Isaiah 35 : 2, "the glory of Lebanon," "the excellency of Carmel and Sharon."

That was separated from his brethren. This may mean, that was violently severed from them by their own vindictive and cruel act; or that, in the providence of God, was separated from his kindred, by being raised to official rank and power far above them all.

The former seems the more probable meaning. All this wealth of blessing is in reserve for

---

* Against this view it has been urged, by Knobel, Delitzsch, Keil, Lange, and others, that this image is unsuited to the case of Joseph; and they interpret these verses as referring to the subsequent fortunes of Joseph's posterity. But the image seems to be appropriate, as explained in the text, and strikingly illustrative. A good man, unjustly persecuted and oppressed, and through divine aid made to triumph over his enemies, may properly be represented as a champion aggressively assailed, and sustained against the assault.

²⁷ Benjamin will raven as a wolf;
In the morning he will devour the prey,
And at evening he will divide the spoil.

²⁸ All these are the twelve tribes of Israel. And this is what their father spoke to them, and blessed them : each according to his blessing he blessed them.
²⁹ And he commanded them, and said to them : I am to be gathered to my people. Bury me with my fathers, in ³⁰ the cave that is in the field of Ephron the Hittite ; in the cave that is in the field of Machpelah, which is before Mamre in the land of Canaan, which Abraham bought with the field of Ephron the Hittite, for a possession of a ³¹ burying-place ; there they buried Abraham and Sarah his wife ; there they buried Isaac and Rebekah his wife, and ³² there I buried Leah ; the possession of a field, and the cave that is therein, from the sons of Heth.
³³ And Jacob made an end of commanding his sons ; and he gathered up his feet into the bed, and he expired, and was gathered to his people.

---

him who was treacherously and cruelly severed from home and kindred, and sold into the hand of strangers. There is comparatively little force in the other view.

There is here a fullness of paternal feeling, a richness and prodigality of blessing, such as would naturally be poured forth on the lost and recovered child of the object of early love, and child of old age. These natural affections, under divine guidance, often become, as here, the fittest instruments for the expression of the divine will.

V. 27. The tribe was distinguished for military spirit and prowess. See Judges 20 : 15, 16 ; 2 Chron. 11 : 8. The verse describes the fierce military spirit, sometimes amounting to ferocity, displayed in the history of the tribe. See, for example, Judges, ch. 20, vv. 12 and following, and compare 2 Sam. 2 : 15, 16.

Morning—evening. His time is spent in war and plunder; the morning in devouring the prey (routing and destroying the enemy), the evening in dividing the spoils. Or the language may express the vigor and rapidity of his conquests. The morning and the evening witness his victory and the division of the spoils.

VV. 28–33. Jacob's charge respecting his burial ; his death.
V. 28. *According to his blessing ;* such as he was entitled to, and received.
V. 29. *I am to be gathered to my people.* See v. 33, and ch. 25 : 8, note, second paragraph.
V. 30. See ch. 23 : 17, 18. *Cave,* etc. ; ch. 23 : 7–9, note, third paragraph.
Possession of a burying-place ; ch. 23 : 3, 4, note, end of second paragraph.
V. 31. *There they buried Abraham* (ch. 25 : 9, 10) ; *and Sarah* (ch. 23 : 19). *They buried Isaac* (ch. 35 : 29). *Rebekah—Leah.* There is no statement given elsewhere respecting their burial.
V. 32. *The possession of a field,* etc. These words are connected, in grammatical construction, with the last two clauses in v. 30, thus : " which Abraham bought with the field of Ephron the Hittite, for a possession of a burying-place——the possession of a field, and the cave that is therein, from the sons of Heth."
V. 33. *Gathered to his people.* See ch. 25 : 8, and note, second paragraph.

1 And Joseph fell upon his father's face; and he wept upon him, and kissed him.

2 And Joseph commanded his servants, the physicians, to embalm his father; and the physicians embalmed Israel.

3 And forty days were completed for him; for so are completed the days of embalming. And the Egyptians wept for him seventy days.

4 And the days of mourning for him were past. And Joseph spoke to the house of Pharaoh, saying: If now I have found favor in your eyes, speak, I pray, in the ears

5 of Pharaoh, saying: My father made me swear, saying: Behold I die; in my grave which I have dug for me in the land of Canaan, there shalt thou bury me. Now therefore let me go up, I pray, and bury my father, and return.

6 And Pharaoh said: Go up, and bury thy father, according as he made thee swear.

7 And Joseph went up to bury his father; and there went up with him all the servants of Pharaoh, the elders

8 of his house, and all the elders of the land of Egypt, and

Ch. 50. Burial of Jacob. Joseph's death.

VV. 2, 3. The art of embalming was a very ancient one in Egypt, some mummy-cases bearing the date of the oldest kings.

It is here said that the process of embalming occupied forty days. An ancient writer,[*] familiar with Egyptian customs, says that it required "more than thirty" (in some manuscripts of his work, forty) "days." According to another ancient writer[†] it lasted seventy days. But this probably included the whole time from death to the interment of the body.[‡] This account, moreover is many centuries earlier than the age of the oldest of these two writers.

V. 4. *Spoke to the house of Pharaoh.* Egyptian custom required that the hair and beard, for the sake of cleanliness, should be closely shaven, except in seasons of mourning;[§] and to appear unshaven in the presence of the monarch was an affront.

It is also pertinent to remark, that he could prefer a petition on his own behalf more delicately, and with more propriety, through others.

V. 7. *Elders of his house—elders of the land of Egypt.* By the former are meant officers of his household, who had the oversight of its several departments; and by the latter officers of

---

[*] Diodorus Siculus, i., 91.
[†] Herodotus, ii., 86.
[‡] "A careful examination of the passage shows that it fixes the whole period, during which the body was in process of embalmment, at seventy days. As this period began with the death and ended with the interment, and as the mourning had the same commencement and termination, it follows that the statement of Herodotus, and that of the sacred writer who says that the mourning lasted seventy days, are in perfect agreement."—*Hengstenberg, die Bücher Mose's und Egypten,* p. 70.
[§] See ch. 41 : 14, and note, second paragraph.

all the house of Joseph, and his brothers, and his father's house; only their little ones, and their flocks and their
9 herds, they left in the land of Goshen. And there went up with him both chariots and horsemen. And the company was very great.
10 And they came to the threshing-floor of Atad, which is beyond the Jordan; and there they mourned with a great and very grievous lamentation; and he made a mourning for his father seven days.
11 And the inhabitants of the land, the Canaanites, saw the mourning in the threshing-floor of Atad, and they said: A grievous mourning this, of the Egyptians! Therefore its name was called Abel-mizraim, which is beyond the Jordan.
12 And his sons did to him thus, according as he com-
13 manded them. And his sons carried him to the land of Canaan; and they buried him in the cave of the field of Machpelah, which Abraham bought with the field, for a possession * of a burying-place, from Ephron the Hittite, before Mamre.
14 And Joseph returned to Egypt, he, and his brothers, and all who went up with him to bury his father, when he had buried his father.

---

state, who had direction of the affairs of the realm. As these were men of age and experience, they are called *Elders*, a title of official dignity and rank.

V. 9. *Chariots and horsemen;* for both of which Egypt was celebrated, as shown in the sacred records, and on the monuments of ancient Egypt.

Funeral processions, conducted with great pomp, were a custom of the Egyptians from very early times.*

VV. 10, 11. *Atad;* properly meaning thorn-bush, from which the place took its name.

Beyond the Jordan; that is, on the other side of it, which side is meant depending on the writer's point of view.

The position of the place, afterward called Abel-mizraim, is not satisfactorily ascertained, but it was probably on the west side of the Jordan.† *Abel-mizraim;* meaning, mourning of the Egyptians.

There is nothing improbable, as has been alleged, in this account of the honors thus paid to Joseph. To judge rightly of the credibility of a transaction, the whole of it must be taken into account. It can not certainly be deemed improbable that one should be so honored, whose superhuman foresight, and administrative ability, had saved the nation from destruction by famine, and who-e sagacious management had secured signal advantages to the government itself (ch. 47 : 14-26).

* *Wilkinson, Manners and Customs of the Ancient Egyptians,* plates 83, 84.

† Compare Dr. Hackett's note to the article Abel-mizraim, in *Smith's Bible Dictionary,* American edition.

¹⁵ And Joseph's brothers saw that their father was dead, and they said: If Joseph should purpose evil against us, and should surely requite to us all the evil which we did ¹⁶ to him! And they sent a charge to Joseph, saying: Thy ¹⁷ father commanded before he died, saying: Thus shall ye say to Joseph: O forgive, I pray, the trespass of thy brothers and their sin, that they did evil to thee. Now therefore, forgive, we pray, the trespass of the servants of thy father's God. And Joseph wept, when they spoke to him.
¹⁸ And his brothers also went and fell down before him; and they said: Behold, we are thy servants.
¹⁹ And Joseph said to them: Fear not; for am I in the ²⁰ place of God? And as for you, ye intended evil against me; God intended it for good, in order to do as at this ²¹ day, to preserve much people alive. Now therefore, fear not. I will nourish you and your little ones. And he consoled them, and spoke to their heart.
²² And Joseph dwelt in Egypt, he and his father's house.
²³ And Joseph lived a hundred and ten years. And Joseph saw Ephraim's sons of the third generation. The sons also of Machir, son of Manasseh, were born upon Joseph's knees.

VV. 15–21. These verses furnish conclusive proof, if any were needed, of the truth of the suggestion (notes to chs. 42 : 7, and 45 : 5–8), that there was nothing vindictive or resentful in Joseph's severity toward his brothers. Their dread of his just resentment, no longer restrained by their father's presence, only moves him to tears, and assurances of protection and support. But it is not the weak tenderness that overlooks or palliates wrong. He is just to the claims of conscience, and to the higher good of the offender himself; and does not allow him to forget that he intended evil, while consoling him with the assurance that God intended good.

Servants of thy father's God; pleading that sacred relation, as a shield from his displeasure.

V. 23. *Sons of the third generation;* probably meaning Ephraim's sons who were of (belonged to) the third generation, namely, Joseph's great grandsons. Some,* with less probability, understand by it sons of (that is, offspring of) the third generation, namely, Joseph's great great-grandsons. The expression can hardly mean at the same time Ephraim's sons and sons of the third generation.

Machir; ancestor of the Machirites, Num. 26 : 29, 32 : 39; Judges 5 : 14.

Were born upon Joseph's knees. This is a proverbial expression, meaning that he lived to receive them on his knees, when they were born.†

* *Keil,* on the passage.

† According to a form of expression quite common in Hebrew, equivalent to, "were born" (and laid upon) "Joseph's knees." The expression is obviously used for a different purpose in ch. 30 : 3. See the remark on it, and the reference (in the foot-note) to Job 3 : 12, and the writer's note on the passage (*Book of Job, Part Second, explanatory notes*).

24 And Joseph said to his brothers: I die; and God will surely visit you, and will bring you up from this land to the land which he swore to Abraham, to Isaac, and to
25 Jacob. And Joseph made the sons of Israel swear, saying: God will surely visit you, and ye shall carry up my bones from hence.
26 And Joseph died, a hundred and ten years old. And they embalmed him, and put him in a coffin in Egypt.

V. 24. *Will visit.* See ch. 21 : 1, and note.
V. 26. *Embalmed.* See the note on vv. 2, 3. *Coffin;* the case in which the embalmed body was preserved.

Here ends the fourth and last division of the book (chs. 12–50), containing the history of the Patriarchs. The groundwork is now fully laid for the history of the people of Israel, and for all the historical allusions necessary for the illustration of their history, and of the purpose of God in selecting and setting them apart as his chosen people.

www.ingramcontent.com/pod-product-compliance
Lightning Source LLC
Chambersburg PA
CBHW021836230426
43669CB00008B/991